POSITION AND CONDITION

An Exposition of the Book of Ephesians

David R. Anderson, Ph.D.

GRACE THEOLOGY PRESS

Position and Condition: An Exposition of the Book of Ephesians

Published by Grace Theology Press

The website addresses recommended throughout this book are offered as a resource to you. These websites are not intended in any way to be or imply an endorsement on the part of the author or publisher, nor do we vouch for their content.

Unless otherwise noted, all Scripture quotations are taken from the New King James Version®. Copyright © 1982 by Thomas Nelson, Inc. Used by permission. All rights reserved. Scripture quotations marked ESV are taken from The Holy Bible, English Standard Version® (ESV®), copyright © 2001 by Crossway, a publishing ministry of Good News Publishers. Used by permission. All rights reserved; KJV are taken from the King James Version of the Bible. (Public Domain); NASB are taken from the New American Standard Bible®, Copyright © 1960, 1995 by The Lockman Foundation. Used by permission. (www.Lockman. org); NIV are taken from the Holy Bible, New International Version®, NIV®. Copyright © 1973, 1984 by Biblica, Inc.™ Used by permission of Zondervan. All rights reserved worldwide. www.zondervan.com; and NRSV are taken from the New Revised Standard Version Bible, copyright 1989, Division of Christian Education of the National Council of the Churches of Christ in the United States of America. Used by permission. All rights reserved. The author has added italic and bold treatment to words in Scripture quotations for emphasis.

ISBN-10: 0998138525
ISBN-13: 9780998138527
eISBN-10: 0998138533
eISBN-13: 9780998138534

© 2017 David R. Anderson

Printed in the United States of America

First Edition 2017

DEDICATION

I would like to dedicate this book to Mark and Cindy Albers for their kindness in offering me a place of beauty and solitude to write and for their ongoing support of Grace School of Theology.

CONTENTS

Acknowledgements vii

Preface ix

1. The Purpose Driven Church
   But It's Not About You (Ephesians 1:1-14) 1

2. A Head Start Is Not Enough (Ephesians 1:15-23) 24

3. God's Poetry (Ephesians 2:1-10) 40

4. Dream On (Ephesians 2:11-22) 60

5. Free Grace (Ephesians 3:1-13) 76

6. Fill 'Er Up, Please (Ephesians 3:14-21) 87

7. Us-Us (Ephesians 4:1-6) 109

8. Captured By Grace (Ephesians 4:7-10) 128

9. Gifted And Talented (Ephesians 4:11) 143

10. Winds Of Doctrine
    Part 1 – Freed to Grow Mature (Ephesians 4:12-16) 160

11. Winds Of Doctrine
    Part 2 – Freed to Fly (Ephesians 4:17-24) 176

12. Winds Of Doctrine
    Part 3 – Freed for Interdependence (Ephesians 4:25-29) 196

13. Winds Of Doctrine
    Part 4 – Freed to Change Clothes (Ephesians 4:30-32) 214

14. Winds Of Doctrine
    Part 5 – Freed to Imitate Christ (Ephesians 5:1-6).................. 235

15. Winds Of Doctrine
    Part 6 – Freed to Walk in the Light (Ephesians 5:7-14)............ 252

16. Redeeming The Time (Ephesians 5:15-16) 265

17. God's Pain Killer (Ephesians 5:17-21)..................................... 285

18. God's Role Call To Wives (Ephesians 5:22-24, 33b)................. 299

19. God's Role Call To Husbands (Ephesians 5:25-33a) 313

20. Where Have All The Fathers Gone? (Ephesians 6:1-4)............ 328

21. Who's The Boss? (Ephesians 6:5-9) 343

22. Operation Overlord (Ephesians 6:10-13).................................. 360

23. Armed And Dangerous
    Part 1 (Ephesians 6:14-17).. 373

24. Armed And Dangerous
    Part 2 – The Helmet of Salvation (Ephesians 6:17) 384

25. Armed And Dangerous
    Part 3 – The Shield of Faith 406

26. Armed And Dangerous
    Part 4 – Stealth Christians 417

27. Armed And Dangerous
    Part 5 – "Truth or Consequences".. 433

28. Armed And Dangerous
    Part 6 – Critical Mass (Ephesians 6:18-20) 448

29. God Bless (Ephesians 6:23-24)... 464

ACKNOWLEDGEMENTS

Most books are a collaborative effort. This one is no different. Though I did the writing, I am dependent on many others to bring this work to print. I want to thank my editors—Ken Wilson, especially, and Merritt Johnston with her team in the Philippines. My gratitude also goes out to Fred Chay for his inspiration to finish this work and get it to Grace Theology Press for publication. Finally, I wish to thank Grace School of Theology for allowing me the time to write. All of you are part of my Dream Team!

PREFACE

Through my years of teaching both in church and at a seminary level, I have seen more confusion on the difference between our Position in Christ and our Condition on earth than any other doctrine. Without thinking in categories and keeping these categories distinct, both the Bible and the Christian life wind up like tangled underbrush. It is incredibly important that we understand Luther's famous statement: *simul iustus et peccator* (simultaneously justified and a sinner). This paradoxical statement makes sense when we realize he is making a statement about both our Position and our Condition. In our Position in Christ in heavenly places (Eph 1:3ff), we are completely justified before God—declared righteous. And nothing in our Condition on earth can change our Position in heaven. But even though we are completely "accepted in the Beloved" (Eph 1:6) in heaven with His perfect righteousness credited to our account, our Condition on earth can be quite riddled with sin. The contrast between our Position and our Condition can become depressing . . . if we keep focusing on our miserable Condition. But when we learn to focus on our Position in Christ with all of its attendant circumstances, our Condition will actually improve. Why? Because "as a man thinks in his heart, so is he" (Prov 23:7). We become what we think about. As we think about (dwell) on who we are in Christ (our Position), our Condition will slowly but surely conform to our Position.

The first three chapters of Ephesians is about our Position in

Christ; the last three are about our Condition on earth. But the two are not disconnected. In the last three chapters we are called to walk (our Condition) worthy of our calling (our Position)—Ephesians 4:1. The last three chapters begin with "therefore." In other words, based on all Paul has just taught them about their current Position in heaven, a certain type of behavior (Condition) should ensue. This order (Position before Condition) is crucial. It's when we think our Position is dependent on our Condition that the fog sets in. Nothing in our Condition can affect/change our Position. This works in two ways: 1) No matter how good an unbeliever is (Condition), it will not open the gates of heaven for him (Position); 2) No matter how bad a believer might be (Condition), it will not close the gates of heaven for him. Can you handle that statement? If not, there is much to learn about God's grace and His ways of dealing with mankind. To learn more, read on.

1

THE PURPOSE DRIVEN CHURCH
BUT
IT'S NOT ABOUT YOU

Ephesians 1:1-14

INTRODUCTION

Rick Warren is an American pastor who became rich through the sales of one book, *A Purpose Driven Life*.[1] True, it became the best selling book in the history of the English language, excepting the Bible. For a while it sold over a million copies per month, and before its primary run ended, it had sold over a hundred million copies. He came here to The Woodlands, TX, back in 2005 and was still asking the question "Why?" He claims that he didn't put anything new in the book not said by others before him. He sprinkled it with Bible verses and biblical principles, yet the secular world was buying

---

1   Rick Warren, *A Purpose Driven Life* (Grand Rapids, MI: Zondervan, 2002).

1

it like crazy. He said about a month before his visit here the leader of Rwanda, Africa, had invited him to come to Africa to help them establish a purpose driven nation. Wow, a purpose driven nation; a government was asking for that.

And we all have to ask "Why?" Why now, at this particular juncture of human history are so many people, Christians and non-Christians alike, looking for purpose? As I have pondered this question my mind has taken me back to the beginning of the modern world, which most pundits put at around AD 1750. That's when *The Age of Reason* began. Reason rose to near deity status. Reason could solve anything. Man's mind became the supreme power on our earth—nothing higher. Reason went up to the top floor above faith, and, in fact, within a hundred years or even less had driven faith completely out of the house. Through our science and technology we could achieve a humanitarian utopia and, for those who still believed in Christ, the millennial kingdom (an approach known as postmillennialism).

WWI was our first hint: maybe advanced technology is not making our society better and better. If WWI rattled the cage of the modern world with its faith in human reason and the ability of our minds to make a better world, WWII dismantled the cage completely. Adolf Hitler used the science of eugenics to help justify his "final solution."[2] And Albert Einstein said the greatest mistake of his life was allowing Leo Szilard to persuade him to write a letter to President Roosevelt that would ultimately lead to the Manhattan Project.[3] Little Boy and Fat Man ended the modern era.[4] The intentional attempt to destroy an entire race (the Jews) with the use of modern science,

---

2 Nazi Eugenics, https://en.wikipedia.org/wiki/Nazi_eugenics/, accessed September 1, 2016.

3 Albert Einstein, https://en.wikipedia.org/wiki/Albert_Einstein/, accessed September 1, 2016.

4 The names given to the two bombs dropped on Japan.

and the nuclear age with its potential for self-annihilation, suggested to the baby-boomers that something was wrong with reason. Our reason is flawed; it's spoiled cheese no matter how you slice it. Science and reason will not bring answers to the problems of the human race.

Thus began our *Postmodern Era*. The signs of this era tell us that things do not make sense; things are not logical; much of life is nonsense; words have lost their meaning. The latter is known as deconstructionism, that is, we deconstruct the meaning of words until they have no meaning. At the very best, what words mean to you may not be what they mean to me. Every man just does what is right in his own eyes. But who said there was a right and wrong to begin with?

The depressing approach of postmodernity was short-lived, about two generations. The Gen-Xers and the millennials drifted back to the same questions that have plagued mankind from the beginning: who am I, why am I here, and where am I going? All three of those questions scream PURPOSE. Into the vacuum of no answers came Rick Warren's book. And what a wonderful book it is. But long before Warren wrote about purpose, another book addressed the subject of purpose. We might say the whole Bible does this, but more specifically there is one book of the Bible that zeros in on the subject.

The Book of Ephesians opens with this thought—**God has a purpose for your life, but it's not about you.** This letter talks about the Creation and the Conduct of the Church. The church was a mystery unforeseen in the Old Testament. Yet God says, "I have created this Body, this entity for a very special purpose." I'd like to call the Book of Ephesians the Purpose Driven Church because I think that's what it's about. It's about God's special purpose for believers in the Body of Christ. Here is an outline we can use as we move through the book:

EPHESIANS
"The Purpose Driven Church"

SALUTATION   1:1-2

INTRODUCTION—"Spiritual Blessings in the Heavenlies"   1:3-14

    A. Selected by the Father   3-6

    B. Saved by the Son   7-12

    C. Sealed by the Spirit   13-14

BODY   2:1-6:9

   I. Creation of the Church (Its Position)   2:1-3:21

  II. Conduct of the Church (Its Condition)   4:1-6:9

CONCLUSION—"Spiritual Battles in the Heavenlies"   6:10-20

FAREWELL   6:21-24

Since this study in no way pretends to be a scholarly work, we are not going to dwell on the first two verses. They are important for identifying the author and the destination. Both have been questioned by modern scholarship, but these are not discussions on which we are going to dwell. We will accept Pauline authorship and Ephesus as the primary destination even if the letter was circulated "around the horn" in western Turkey. It is interesting to visit the extensive remains of Ephesus today in that it was a port city during the time of Paul, whereas today it is five miles from the Aegean Sea.

There is, however, one more phrase we want to look at more closely. Often in the salutation of a book the author drops a hint as to what he wants to cover. Here Paul mentions the saints who are in Ephesus and the faithful "in Christ Jesus." We see these as the same people, not the "faithful" as a subset of the "saints." It is this phrase "in Christ Jesus" that catches our attention. Only Paul uses this phrase in his salutations. He does it four times (1 Cor 1:2; Eph 1:2; Phil 1:1; Col 1:2). Only 1 Corinthians was written before AD 60. Ephesians,

Philippians, Colossians, and Philemon are known as the *Prison Epistles* since Paul wrote them during his imprisonment in Rome (AD 61-62).[5]

Paul uses this phrase ("in Christ") 51x in his epistles. All the rest of the NT uses it only 3x (1 Pet 3:16; 5:14; Jude 1, although here the order is reversed: in Jesus Christ). Of Paul's 51 uses, about half (24x) occur in Ephesians (12x), Philippians (8x), and Colossians (4x). And if we include similar phrases such as "in Him," "in whom," and "in the Beloved," we add another seven uses just in Paul's introduction to Ephesians (1:3-14). As Sherlock Holmes would say, "We just may be on to something, Dr. Watson."

Yes, Ephesians is about the Creation and Conduct of the Church, but we could also say it is about our **Position** in Christ and our **Condition** on earth. When we see "in Christ" or its equivalent, we know Paul is talking about our **Position**. When we see the word "walk" (4:1, 17; 5:2, 8, 15), we know he is discussing our **Condition**. The first three chapters focus on our **Position**; the last three chapters focus on our **Condition**. There is a reason for that order: **Position** before **Condition**. Paul realizes that **NOTHING IN MY CONDITION CAN EVER AFFECT MY POSITION.** Therefore, he wants us to know as much as possible about our marvelous **Position** in Christ. He knows if we focus on our **Position**, our **Condition** will improve. However, he also knows **AS WE FOCUS ON OUR CONDITION, OUR CONDITION GETS WORSE.**

These twin truths of **Position** and **Condition** were captured by Martin Luther when he made his famous statement: *simul iustus et peccator*. He was saying that at the same time (*simul*) he was just/justified (*iustus*) and (*et*) a sinner (*peccator*). How could that seemingly contradictory claim be true? Paul could explain it. In heavenly places seated at the right hand of the Father **in Christ** (our **Position**), we

---

5   Rome is the consensus of scholarship. See Harold W. Hoehner, Ephesians (Grand Rapids, MI: Baker Academic, 2002), 92-96, for a thorough discussion.

are perfectly just or justified. This occurred by faith at a moment in time (Rom 4:3). All sins (past, present, and future) forgiven. The perfect righteousness of Christ—credited to our account. Justified—*fait accompli*. But in our **Condition** on earth we still wrestle with temptations in the world and our Sin Nature inherited from Adam. Paul wants to teach us how our **Condition** on earth can improve as we switch our focus from our **Condition** to our **Position**. Spoken theologically, he wants to show us how our progressive sanctification is linked to our justification.

So let's jump into Paul's introduction to his letter. We call this "Our Spiritual Blessings in the Heavenlies." In his conclusion to the letter Paul informs us as to "Our Spiritual Battles in the Heavenlies." But we are not ready for the battles until we understand the blessings. Or, as Watchman Nee put it in his little book: *SIT, WALK, STAND*,[6] we must rest in the heavenly blessings we have been given (SIT—1:3-3:21) and then conduct our lives in accordance with the truth of these blessings (WALK—4:1-6:9). Then we are ready to face the demonic foes that fight against us (STAND—6:10-20).

The introduction falls neatly into three parts organized around the Trinity: the Father (1:3-6); the Son (1:7-12); and the Spirit (1:13-14): Selected by the Father; Saved by the Son; Sealed by the Spirit.

I. SELECTED BY THE FATHER 1:3-6

> [3] Blessed *be* the God and Father of our Lord Jesus Christ, who has blessed us with every spiritual blessing in the heavenly *places* in Christ, [4] just as He chose us in Him before the foundation of the world, that we should be holy and without blame before Him in love, [5] having predestined us

---

6 Watchman Nee, *Sit, Walk, Stand* (Fort Washington, PA: Christian Literature Crusade, 1974).

to adoption as sons by Jesus Christ to Himself, according to the good pleasure of His will, [6] to the praise of the glory of His grace, by which He made us accepted in the Beloved.

As we dive into the deep end of Paul's theology, let me state my very limited goals. To the disappointment of some, I do not intend to delve into the meaning of each and every word or doctrine in Ephesians, and especially in this introduction. Just the introduction deserves a book in itself if we are going to explicate the details. A former professor of mine, the late Harold Hoehner, wrote what I believe to be the definitive commentary on Ephesians.[7] He worked on it for fifteen years, if I remember correctly. He had a study carrel with research books and articles spread all around, and he would disappear in there whenever his schedule permitted. He left no stone unturned. But as his work surpassed 1,000 pages, he could not find a publishing company that wanted to print such a massive work. He finally got one. The book is 1,100 pages. I refer you to it for the details. It is a scholarly book written for pastors, seminary students, and other scholars. I have a different audience in mind. I am writing for people in the pew, especially those who have struggled with their own lack of holiness while claiming Sunday after Sunday to be part of God's forever family. Many of these struggle with assurance of their salvation or any hope of getting a grip on their Sin Nature. My hope is that the truths of **Position** and **Condition** will be some measure of help to them.

Paul jumps right into positional truth when he says, "**. . . we are blessed with every spiritual blessing in heavenly places in Christ.**" He goes on in his introduction to point out many of these blessings. But the one that jumps out in v. 4 is that the Father chose us before the foundation of the world. Of course, this is the doctrine of election, obviously a biblical doctrine. However, it has been the source of

---

7   Harold Hoehner, *Ephesians* (Grand Rapids, MI: Baker Academic, 2002).

much debate in Christian circles for centuries. If we were elected by God before he even made us, then what choice do we have in the matter?

That very question caught the eye of Augustine (d. 430) as he shifted his allegiance from Manichaeism to Christianity. The Manicheans also taught election. But to prove you were one of the elect instead of an auditor, one needed to enter a life of asceticism (denial of the flesh) and monkish meditation. The concept of election before the foundation of the world in Christianity did appeal to the Manichaean training Augustine had received during his nine years of attempting to become one of the elect in Manichaeism. You see, there were three primary philosophies that influenced Augustine's Christianity: Manichaeism, Neo-Platonism, and Stoicism. All three were pagan philosophies, and all three were deterministic.[8]

What do we mean by deterministic? Pure determinism eliminates human choice. Everything from the beginning of time has been and will be determined by fate. A thoroughgoing dependence on fate is at the core of each of these pagan philosophies. An election before creation fit right into a fatalistic understanding of the universe. And Augustine was the first church father to go against the *Regula Fide* (the Rule of Faith) of the fathers before him.[9] All of the church fathers before Augustine, without exception, believed in free will, or human choice. Augustine was the first to remove it through his deterministic system. And with this introduction of Greek philosophy into Christianity, some Eastern Orthodox scholars believe the

---

8   David R. Anderson, *Free Grace Soteriology* (The Woodlands, TX: Grace Theology Press, 2012), 343-70.

9   Kenneth M. Wilson, "Augustine's Conversion from Traditional Free Choice to 'Non-Free Free will': A Comprehensive Methodology," unpublished Doctor's Dissertation (University of Oxford, Harris Manchester College, Trinity Term, 2012), 1-46.

schism between eastern and western Christianity began.[10] The east rejected Augustine, even as a church father. The west, in time, embraced him.

But how are we going to get out of fatalistic determinism if God's choice was made before the foundation of the world? Obviously, we had nothing to do with the process if we did not exist. Obviously. But expressions like "before the foundation of the world" are simply accommodations for people like us who are caught in linear time. We exist on a time line. It moves inexorably forward into the future. We do not have the luxury of going back in time. But God knows of no such boundaries. He existed before time and outside of time. God is omnitemporal.

If we assume the scientific definition of time (cause and effect), then most would say time began with the creation of the universe. But we know, using the definition above, that time existed before time. In other words, there was cause and effect before the creation of the universe. The angels were around to watch the creation of the universe (Job 38:4-7). If God created the angels, then there was cause and effect before the creation of the universe. Ergo, time.

Nevertheless, the Father did not create the Son, nor the Son the Spirit. Each member of the Trinity is eternal, meaning each existed before time and will exist after time, if, as some suggest, time as we know it ceases to exist. Meanwhile, our God is not bound by time. He existed in eternity past and exists in eternity future. 1 Peter 1:2 says we were elected according to his foreknowledge, but it just as well might have said we were elected according to his postknowledge. Fore- and post- are accommodations for people stuck in linear time. But God, being omnipresent, exists everywhere at the same time. He exists in eternity future. He really doesn't need foreknowledge

---

10 Michael Azkoul, *The Influence of Augustine of Hippo on the Orthodox Church,* Texts and Studies in Religion 56 (Lewiston, NY: Mellen, 1990), ii-iii.

or postknowledge. **He just knows**. He has always known those who would be his elect. He chose them.

Does that mean they did not choose him, meaning they had no choice in the matter? I sometimes like to ask married students if they chose their spouses, or did their spouses chose them. If it is a married man I am talking to, and they hesitate, I say, "Well, did you date awhile before marriage? Did you ever take her out to a meal or show or concert?" Of course, the answer will be in the affirmative. Then I ask, "Well, why didn't you just hit her over the head with a club and drag her off to your cave? Would have saved a lot of time and money. Cut to the chase, you know." If they are still squirming, I'll ask them, "Well, did you ask her to marry you?" Yes. "Why? Why not just grab her and whisk her away on your white stallion?" By this time they know where I am going. "Did you give her a choice when you asked her to marry you? Could she have said no?" Most of them will say, "I gave her a choice because I wanted to know if she loved me. I wanted her to want me as much as I wanted her." Exactly. Do you think our God, who is the very essence of love, wants to be loved voluntarily any less than we?

And our text has a little something to say about that, doesn't it? "He chose us before the foundation of the world . . . in love." If nothing else, the Bible is a love story. In fact, I would suggest that one of the great questions of the universe opened by Satan with his rebellion was whether our God is worthy of being loved. I think he created the human race, in part, to answer that question. If we remove human choice from the equation, God will never know if we love him. If we remove human choice from the equation, that critical question remains unanswered. That is precisely what a deterministic system does. It pulls love right out of the Bible. The late Dave Hunt tried to address this question in his book *What Love is This?*, which exposed the soft underbelly of any purely deterministic system.[11] Force is not love. If we are dragged kicking and screaming into the kingdom of

---

11 Dave Hunt, *What Love is This?*

God, as some theologians teach,[12] where's the love. That's the same as hitting your spouse to be over the head and dragging her off to your man-cave. As C. S. Lewis claimed in *The Screwtape Letters*, "God never forces himself on anyone . . . He cannot ravish. He can only woo."[13]

I remember a preacher of yesteryear named William Dean describing how he wasn't gifted athletically. When he was growing up in school he was always the last one picked. One day it was another gym class, and they were going to play that game where you throw the volleyball and knock someone out on the other side. He was normally the last one chosen, but they had a visitor in the gym class that day, and in honor of his visit, the gym teacher allowed him to be one of the captains. The teacher said to the guest, "We'll give you first choice." He looked over all the boys and saw the big tough ones and those who looked really fast and coordinated. Then he pointed his finger at William Dean and said, "I want that one."

Well, everyone was shocked. William had trouble stepping out to join his side, but he did so and lined up. They went on to play the game. William didn't do very well. When it was all over, the gym teacher asked, "Why on earth did you pick that kid first? He's the worst player in the class." The visitor said, "Well, you don't understand. That boy is my little brother, and I love him."

Yeah, you may not be good at a lot of things and not that gifted, but he loves you. He didn't force you in; he loved you in; he wooed you in. He dated you. He persuaded you about how great he was and then you chose him. That's the way love works, isn't it? He chose you, and you chose him. He may have chosen you before time, after time, or during time. It doesn't matter because God is everywhere at the same time throughout time. He still gave you a choice,

---

12 R. C. Sproul, *Chosen by God* (Carol Stream, IL: Tyndale Houste Publishers, 1986), 52-55.

13 C. S. Lewis, *The Screwtape Letters*, in *The Best of C. S, Lewis* (Washington, D.C.: Canon Press, 1974).

because he loved you and he longed to be loved by you. Go against that and you go against the Greatest Commandment: Love the Lord your God. . . . No coincidence that the greatest commandment is about love.

Next we come to that word that has confounded so many through the centuries: predestination. Again, it sounds so deterministic. In fact, when Augustine brought his pagan religions with him into Christianity, predestination was a perfect match, at least his understanding of predestination. Although many scholars deny it, since its implications are so odious, Augustine actually taught DOUBLE predestination. That simply means, in his view, God determined before creation that Group A of his creatures would spend eternity in heaven, while Group B would spend eternity in hell. Group A predestined for heaven; Group B predestined for hell. Double predestination. And, unfortunately, Group B comprises the huge majority of mankind in the view of people that believe such things. Only the elite are elect, that is, elected to go to heaven.

We have documented in another work that Augustine's influence on Western Christianity has been so enormous that double predestination has been taught non-stop since around AD 800.[14] After the Reformation, the line went from John Calvin to Theodore Beza to William Perkins to the Westminster Confession to the English Puritans to America. Now it is going full circle. I was writing in northwestern Germany a couple of summers ago and my host, who owned a retreat center that was booked up two years in advance, asked me, "Why are you Americans bringing this Calvinism over to our country? We don't like it." I had to smile because church history confirms that it sprang up in Europe before the Puritans began to settle in America.

What's even more fascinating in this most controversial of discussions is that in the Bible the word "predestinated" never refers to the ultimate destination of a human soul. The word only occurs

---

14 Anderson, op. cit.

four times: twice right here in the introduction to Ephesians and twice in Romans 8. In none of these cases is a destination mentioned in the sense of a place of residence. Romans 8:29 says, "For whom He foreknew, He also **predestined** *to be* conformed to the image of His Son, that He might be the firstborn among many brethren." We are predestined to be conformed to the image of His Son. And here in Ephesians 1:5 it says we are predestined to the adoption as sons. There is nothing about heaven or hell, the New Jerusalem or the Lake of Fire. What we have in the normal understanding of predestination today is Augustine's distorted view imported from Manichaeism, Stoicism, and Neo-Platonism. It is not a biblical view. It is a deterministic view that eliminates all human choice and makes God into a . . . well, I'll leave the description up to you.

But will you notice with me the purpose of this process of adoption as sons? That's right. I used the word PURPOSE. This is the Purpose Driven Church. And the purpose of God's process has nothing to do with you or with me. The word "to" beginning v. 6 actually speaks of "goal" or "purpose" in the original (*eis*). The suggestion here is that human history is not anthropocentric (everything revolving around man) or even Christocentric (everything revolving around Christ). No, it is theocentric (everything revolving around God). For all these things are with a view to the praise of the glory of his grace. The glory of anything is the open, public manifestation thereof. So the glory of God would be the open, public manifestation of his attributes. And the glory of his grace would be the open public manifestation of the very meaning and essence of grace itself. For example, the cross. That would have to be the greatest open, public manifestation of his grace the universe has ever or will ever see. But it is God's grace displayed in the sacrifice of his son.

This phrase, "to the praise of his glory," occurs at the end of each section of the introduction. What the Father did is to the praise of his glory; what the Son did is to the praise of his glory (v. 12); and what the Spirit did is to the praise of his glory (v. 14). Are you getting the picture? There is purpose for our existence. It's all about God. And when we begin to grab hold of that purpose for living, all of a sudden we have a transcendent cause to live for: seek first his kingdom and his righteousness (Matt 6:33). It is a cause that is transcendent, meaning is rises above the setbacks and suffering of this time we spend in these mortal bodies. It gives us something to wake up for in the morning, something to dream about when we go to bed at night, something to sustain us through the hours of the day.

Here in 1:6 Paul speaks of the praise of the glory of his grace, and then he gives us one of the most beautiful pictures of grace in the entire Bible. It says in the NKJ that "he made us accepted in the beloved." From that English we cannot see the word in Greek for "made accepted." It is actually a verb form of the noun for grace. Grace is *charis*. This verb is *charitoō*. Can you see the similarity between the noun and the verb. It's all to the praise of his grace, and the best example is how he "graced" us in the beloved (his son).

I heard an example of this from Ray Steadman years ago that I wondered about at the time. It sounds so far out that perhaps it was just a preacher's story for effect. But no, my own sister became a shepherdess decades later. I asked her about what I heard and she confirmed that what I heard is one of two ways of saving the life of a lamb with no mother ewe. So here goes. A wicked winter storm covered Montana some years ago. It killed a lot of lambs and a lot of ewes. There were ewes whose lambs had died and lambs whose mother ewes had died. If that weren't bad enough, the ewes whose lambs had died would not allow the lambs whose mother ewes had died to nurse. So a bunch more lambs were in danger of dying. But these grizzled sheep ranchers knew how to fool Mother Nature. They had discovered if they skinned a dead lamb and sewed its coat onto a lamb whose mother ewe had died, the ewe whose lamb had died would let the lamb covered by the coat of its dead offspring nurse. She had accepted the living lamb **in the Beloved.** It's not that we are holy enough or blameless enough or righteous enough. The righteousness of the Son is sewn onto us (imputed righteousness). We come in the coat of the Lamb of God who took away the sins of the world, yours and mine. And we are accepted in the Beloved.

14

To what purpose? To the praise of the glory of his grace. Trophies of his grace. I have always viewed myself as a crumpled up coke can on the side of the road. One day Jesus was just walking by and tapped the Father on the shoulder and said, "Hmmm . . . I don't know. Looks like a piece of trash ready for the heap." But the Father says, "Well, let's see. Perhaps we can make something out of that." He reached down and selected the can and began twisting and twisting. Slowly he tries to twist it into something he can put on his mantle—a trophy of his grace.

Blessings in our **Position** in Christ in heavenly places—from the Father (3-6). What about the Son? The second part of Paul's introduction focuses on blessings from the Son. If we were Selected by the Father, we were Saved by the Son.

II. SAVED BY THE SON   7-12

> [7] In Him we have redemption through His blood, the forgiveness of sins, according to the riches of His grace [8] which He made to abound toward us in all wisdom and prudence, [9] having made known to us the mystery of His will, according to His good pleasure which He purposed in Himself, [10] that in the dispensation of the fullness of the times He might gather together in one all things in Christ, both which are in heaven and which are on earth—in Him. [11] In Him also we have obtained an inheritance, being predestined according to the purpose of Him who works all things according to the counsel of His will, [12] that we who first trusted in Christ should be to the praise of His glory.

In Christ we have redemption through his blood. There are three different Hebrew words and three different Greek words that express the idea of redemption. The common denominator in all these words is the idea of buying one's freedom. Generally, it meant to buy off the slave block. Someone else paid a price for the freedom the slave was incapable of paying.

I remember during my last year of high school I thought I would keep the Ten Commandments for thirty days just to prove to myself I could do it. In my non-Christian, non-illuminated understanding of them I thought it would be a piece of cake. Right in the middle of the test I failed miserably. That's when I realized I was a slave of sin, a sinaholic badly in need of a Savior. Is there a point in your life when you realized you could not keep from sinning? Until you come to that point you won't realize your need for a Savior.

But Jesus paid the price we could not pay. He went to hell on our behalf. He took the penalty we deserved. People ask, but how can the death of one man pay for the sins of billions of men and women? Good question. One man could not do that. But the God-man could. Because the Second Person of the Godhead humbled himself to become a man without yielding any of his divine attributes, as the God-man he could make an infinite sacrifice. He could pay for the sins of the whole world. People say, well what about the fallen angels? Did his death cover their sins? No. To pay for the sins of the fallen angels the Second Member of the Godhead would have to become an angel, a God-angel, and die in place of the fallen angels.

And what about aliens? If they exist, are they redeemed? Well, that is a big "if," isn't it? The only aliens I am convinced are anywhere on this planet are the fallen angels, unless you think of believers as aliens in the world. But if there is other intelligent life in the universe on our level or above, they must not have fallen, for Christ would have to become one of them to pay for their sins. He died once and for all for the sins of mankind. That's it. He shed his blood that we might be freed from the slave block of sin. Of course, blood is a figure of speech for his life, the ultimate sacrifice. Aren't you glad Christ looked down at you and me from his perch outside of time and said to his Father, "It's worth it, Dad. Let's go."

Imagine going down to Foley's to buy a mattress, and you find one that's not too hard, not too soft, just right. But then you look at the price tag and you say, "Oh, my gosh, it's too expensive. I can't afford it. It's too much." So you look around the store and find another one you like, but when you look at the sticker you say, "Oh, my gosh.

16

This is overpriced. I can afford it, but it's just overpriced." So you keep looking around the store and never can settle on one you like, can afford, and is fairly priced. Aren't you glad when it came time to pay the price for you, the death of his only begotten son, that God didn't say, "Oh, that's too much; I don't want to pay that price"? Aren't you glad he didn't say, "They're not worth it. They're overpriced"? Or aren't you glad he didn't say, "I don't like them. I won't pay any price"?

So Jesus paid the price to redeem us from slavery. Because the price has been paid, we have forgiveness of sins. It is very important to understand the difference between **Position** and **Condition** when it comes to the subject of forgiveness. People often ask, "If I was forgiven of all of my sins at the cross, including the sins I will commit in the future, then why does 1 John 1:9 say I need to confess my sins for forgiveness?" Great question. And, again, without a clear understanding of **Position** and **Condition** we will forever be confused. For approximately 1500 years the church did not get it. That's why confession to a priest and penance was required for forgiveness of one's sins committed between the last confession and the current one. The concept of future sins being forgiven in heaven was not part of their forgiveness paradigm. Forgiveness was only as good as your last confession.

We need to understand forgiveness in our **Position** and forgiveness in our **Condition**. Our **Position** is in the heavenly places. In a way we will never understand, at the moment of justification Christ exchanged our sins for his righteousness. I was listening to Tim Tebow share his story and the gospel to a group of four thousand fathers and their sons in Houston a few years ago. I loved the way he put it: "Christ comes up to you and offers you a deal. He says, 'I'll exchange my righteousness for your sins and it's free for you. Is it a deal?'" After a moment Tim said, "What are you waiting for, a better deal?"

There is no better deal, is there? My sins for his righteousness. Sort of an IQ test. Now this righteousness we get is his righteousness, the perfect righteousness of the Son of God. It is credited (imputed) to our account in heaven. But the sins that are forgiven include all the sins we ever have or will commit. This is the very basis for eternal security. And it is why the church with its sacraments could not offer eternal security. They had no understanding of positional forgiveness, and hence no way to take care of future sins. Forgiveness in our **Position** takes care of all sins regardless of time. After all, how many of your sins had not been committed when Christ died? All of them, right? You weren't even alive. Obviously, then, Christ's death is fully capable of providing forgiveness for future sins. Otherwise, none of your sins, or mine, would be forgiven.

So what is forgiveness in our **Condition**? Forgiveness in our **Position** gives us an eternal relationship with God. But forgiveness in our **Condition** gives us temporal fellowship with God. Don't forget that 1 John 1:9 comes in a book about fellowship, not relationship. At least that is what it claims in 1 John 1:3-4.

Think of it this way. Most of the sin in my life is sin of which I am not aware. That's just another way of saying I have a long way to go before I am conformed to the image of Christ. All that sin has been forgiven in heavenly places in my **Position**. And as far as fellowship (enjoying the relationship with God) is concerned, what I don't know about doesn't hurt me, that is, it doesn't hurt my fellowship with God. After all, the blood of Jesus Christ keeps on cleansing me from all sin (1 Jn 1:7). But as soon as I become aware of one of my sins, then it becomes a personal issue between me and God. If I do not deal with this sin I now know about, fellowship with God will be lost and a growing breach between him and me will develop.

It's the same between a husband and wife. At the altar we more or less gave each other forgiveness in our **Position**. When I took her as my wife, she had a new **Position**. I took her for better or for worse. That's advanced forgiveness, future forgiveness. I know intuitively some things will go wrong between her and me. Most of it will be my fault, but some of it hers. Nevertheless, I resolve to keep her in her new **Position** as my wife until death. She does the same with me—for better or for worse. But if I do things to hurt my wife, a breach in our fellowship with each other will grow until I seek her forgiveness. Wait a minute. I thought we had advanced forgiveness at the altar. Yes, that was forgiveness in our **Position**. But that is not forgiveness in our **Condition**. At the altar we got a new relationship: husband/wife. But if I want to have fellowship with my wife (enjoying the relationship), I need to seek her forgiveness for any personal wrongs.

This distinction between forgiveness in our **Position** and forgiveness in our **Condition** is crucial. And don't forget the order. The basis for **Fellowship** forgiveness is **Relationship** forgiveness. Because my wife gave me **Relationship** forgiveness when she took me for better or for worse, I can be assured she will give me **Fellowship** forgiveness when I ask for it. So the forgiveness of Ephesians 1:7 not only is the basis for eternal security, it is also the basis for fellowship with God in our **Condition** on earth even though we are still sinful: *simul iustus et peccator*—at the same time justified and a sinner.

Again, since this is not a scholarly commentary trying to explain every word, we are going straight to the third member of the Godhead, the Holy Spirit. We were Selected by the Father, Saved by the Son, and now we are Sealed by the Spirit. But before we get there, let's not forget how the section on the Son ended in v. 12: ". . . to the praise of his glory." It's not about you, and it's not about me; it's about him.

III. SEALED BY THE SPIRIT   1:13-14

> [13] In Him you also *trusted*, after you heard the word of truth, the gospel of your salvation; in whom also, having believed, you were sealed with the Holy Spirit of promise, [14] who is the guarantee of our inheritance until the redemption of the purchased possession, to the praise of His glory.

Here it says, "In Him," still going back to Christ. Do you see how many times it says, "In Him," "in the Beloved," "in Christ"? It is our

Position "in Him" Paul is emphasizing. And immediately after we believed we were sealed by the Holy Spirit. What does this mean? Sealing actually had three primary uses in Paul's culture:

A. To Authenticate

In 2 Corinthians 1:22 it says God has sealed us and given us the Holy Spirit in our hearts as a guarantee. Paul's converts were actually the authentication of his apostleship. They proved his genuineness, his authenticity.

B. For Protection

In Revelation 7:3-8 the word "sealed" is used 15 times. It was a seal of protection for the 144,000 (12,000 from each tribe of Israel) witnesses during the Tribulation period. Many believe the judgment of the sheep and goats is based, in part at least, on the Gentile treatment of these 144,000. It also makes us wonder about the Lost Ten Tribes of Israel, assimilated after the Assyrian invasion (722 BC). Not lost to God, apparently.

If a crate of goods in ancient times was sent from Caesarea by the Sea to Athens, it would be sealed with a wax seal to make sure no one tampered with the goods inside the crate.

C. For Ownership

We are God's "purchased possession." As in 2 Corinthians 1:22 God gives us the Holy Spirit as a "guarantee" (*arrabōn*). An *arrabōn* was a down payment. It was a way of saying, "I've paid for this, and to prove I am coming back to get what I have purchased, here is a down payment."

Now I belong to Jesus;
Jesus belongs to me.
Not for the days of time alone,
But for eternity.

Eternity. When I was a youth pastor, I would take our high schoolers out to Camp El Har in Dallas. One of the youth sponsors on our trip had a little girl about six years old. One day the little girl was sitting in the dirt talking to herself. I listened more carefully and realized she was talking to someone else because she kept saying My Darling this and My Darling that, but I couldn't see anyone. So I got a little closer and saw that she had drawn a circle in the dirt with about a one-foot radius. Inside this circle she had adopted a pet roach. The name of the pet roach was, of course, My Darling. She sat there crouched around the circle and of course the roach was always trying to escape. It would get right to the circle line and almost cross over when the little girl would say, "Oh no, My Darling," and push it back into the circle. Then it would head off in another direction. The little girl didn't seem to tire of this game. You see, she had a personal relationship with a roach, and I'm saying, "Only a child."

Well, the lunch bell went off, and My Darling crossed the line when the little girl looked toward the dining hall. She turned back, saw the roach, said, "Sorry, My Darling," and with one foot she squashed her pet roach. Splat! End of personal relationship. Aren't you glad that when you crossed the line even after finding a personal relationship with Christ, God doesn't go, "Sorry, My Darling," splat! Sealed unto the day of redemption. Not for the days of time alone, but for eternity.

And guess what? It's not about you ... it's not about me ... it's about God. Once again we read, "To the praise of his glory." Sounds kind of self-centered, doesn't it? Perhaps. Until we remember what glory means: the open public manifestation of the attributes of ... Fill in the blank. If it is God, then what's self-centered about wanting to display his incredible character qualities for all eternity: truth, justice, love, mercy, omnipotence, righteousness, ... and on we go. Our great purpose is to glorify God, that is, we become open displays of his character qualities. That's what we are predestined for: to be conformed to the image of his son, from character quality to character quality (Rom 8:29; 2 Cor 3:18).

CONCLUSION

We were Selected, Saved, and Sealed for His glory.

1. Our salvation is about him.

Wait a minute. Surely my salvation is about me; after all he saved ME. Yes, we are the objects of his salvation plan, but the purpose of the plan is about him—his glory. An American food company came out with the perfect cake mix. No additives, no sugar, no flavoring. All you had to do was mix the water with the powder. To their surprise the perfect cake mix didn't sell well. So they did a survey and asked, "How could you not buy our perfect cake mix? Look at all the work we've taken out of it." At the end of their survey they altered their formula and their advertising. Now, all you had to do was add one egg. It sold like wildfire. What is it about us that wants to take that which is already perfect and add something to it? Why, in this very Book of Ephesians, God says, "For by grace you have been saved through faith and that not of yourselves. It is the gift of God, not of works, lest anyone should boast." When it is all said and done and when these trophies of grace are displayed in heaven, there will be no boasting because it is not about us; it is all about him. Our salvation is all about him. So is our significance.

2. Our significance is about him.

G. R. Tweed looked across the Pacific waters at the American ship on the horizon. Brushing the jungle sweat from his eyes, the young naval officer swallowed deeply and made his decision. This could be his only chance for escape. Tweed had been hiding on Guam for nearly three years. When the Japanese occupied the island in 1941, he ducked into the thick tropical brush. Survival hadn't been easy, but he preferred the swamp to a POW camp.

Late in the day of July 10, 1944, he spotted the friendly vessel. He scurried up a hill and positioned himself on a cliff. Reaching into this pack, he pulled out a small mirror. At 6:20 PM he began sending signals. Holding the edge of the mirror in his fingers, he tilted it back and forth bouncing the sunrays in the direction of the boat. Three shorts flashes, three long flashes, three short flashes: SOS.

The signal caught the eye of a sailor on board the USS McCall. A rescue party boarded a motorized dinghy and slipped into the cove past the coastal guns. Tweed was rescued. He was glad to have that mirror, glad he knew how to use it, and glad that the mirror cooperated. Suppose it hadn't. Suppose the mirror had resisted and pushed its own agenda. Rather than reflect a message from the sun, suppose it had opted to send one of its own. After all, three years of isolation would leave one starved for attention. Rather than sending an SOS, the mirror could have sent a LAM—Look At Me. The mirror wasn't worth much on its own. It found significance and meaning in the hands of Tweed. And it led to his salvation.

Good thing Tweed's mirror didn't have a mind of its own. But God's mirrors do. We are God's mirrors. Our job description can be reduced to three words: REFLECT GOD'S CHARACTER. We learn to do that as we pass on messages from the Son. You see, the difference between Tweed's mirror and God's mirrors (us) is that we have minds of our own. We can choose to display our glory or his glory. As long as we think this life is all about us, life loses its lasting meaning. We never find our purpose for being. I think the *Purpose Driven Life* has become so popular because all of a sudden people are saying, "There is a purpose out there, and it's not about us. It just might be connected to the Son. We are here to reflect his glory." That is how we find our *raison d'etre*, our reason for being.

2

A HEAD START IS NOT ENOUGH

Ephesians 1:15-23

INTRODUCTION

It's hard to know what is on the inside. It's so much easier to observe what is on the outside. Joe Wagner was a judge at a state fair. The fair was for people who had prize bulls and lambs. One little girl just happened to own a champion lamb, a grand champion lamb, and it was being auctioned off to the highest bidder. As the bids began the price reached five dollars a pound, and the little girl was elated. Then suddenly the bidding jumped up to ten dollars a pound, and the reality of parting with her prized lamb ripped the little girl's heart. Tears began to come down her cheeks. When the bidding got to fifteen dollars a pound, she grabbed the lamb by the neck and held on tight. Finally one man stepped forward and just outbid everybody. He paid four thousand dollars for the lamb, and then he dedicated it back to the little girl, its owner. The crowd cheered and applauded.

Some years later Wagner was judging again, only this time it was an essay contest. He came across a girl who had told about the time her grand champion lamb had been auctioned. She said that the price began to get so high in the bidding that she started to cry from happiness. And the man who bought the lamb for so much more than she ever dreamed she would get returned the lamb to her. "When I got home," she concluded her story, "my daddy barbequed the lamb, and it was really delicious."

Kind of hard to tell what's on the inside, is it not? Our concern in this next lesson in Ephesians is not so much what is in our heads as what is in our hearts. I'm concerned about the wide gap about what Christians claim to believe and how they actually behave. You can try to explain that gap in a lot of ways. The easiest way is just to say they are not really Christians. They name the name of Christ and confess to be Christians, but they are not genuinely born again. They are professors but not possessors. And that is the route most people probably take. It is a good route for the self-righteous that are apparently oblivious to sin in their own lives. But there are too many cases in which a servant of God has been faithful for decades only to find him/herself in the ditch of despair or depravity. And there are too many new believers who run well for a season only to go into hibernation during the winter of their discontent. What about the gap in their lives between what they believe and how they behave? I think Ephesians 1:15-23 gives us some insight.

We are calling Ephesians the Purpose Driven Church. In 1:3-14 we made the bold claim through looking at our Selection by the Father, Salvation through the Son, and Sealing by the Spirit that this great purpose is not man-centered, or even Christ-centered. It is God-centered (theocentric). Of course, Christ is God, but he is just one member of the Trinity. When we say God-centered, we are saying glory goes to all three members of the Trinity—God. The universe was created for God's glory (Job 38:4-7), and man was created for God's glory. How so? This takes us outside Ephesians for the moment, but getting a broad brush on the purpose for human history might be helpful at this point.

We propose that Satan's rebellion opened two attributes of God into question: his sovereignty and his love. Who has the right to rule the universe (sovereignty)? Is it God or Satan? And who is worthy of being loved? Is it God or Satan? Love Satan? How ridiculous. Only devil worshippers love Satan. Really? In 1 John 2:14 it says the young men have overcome the wicked one, an obvious reference to the devil. Immediately thereafter it goes on to say (1 Jn 2:15ff) not to love the world nor the things in the world: the lust of the flesh, the lust of the eyes, and the pride of life. It even says if we love these things, the love of the Father is not in us. Apparently, to love this world is to love the god of this world. We are going to love something. If the love of the Father is not in us, then what or whom do we love?

We suggest humankind was created to answer these two questions: sovereignty and love. That is why dominion (kingdom) and love are such prominent themes in the Bible. The Bible starts with human dominion over the earth (Gen 1:26-28) and winds up with human dominion over the earth (Rev 20:4, 6—millennium) and (Rev 22:5— the saints reign with him forever). And if it is anything, the Bible is a love story (what's the most famous verse in the Bible and what's the greatest commandment in the Bible?). "For God so loved the world..." (Jn 3:16).

So God made a creature a little lower than the angels (Ps 8). Man has less intelligence, less power, less mobility, greater dependency (nutrition, oxygen, gravity) than the angels. He also has less revelation than the angels, who lived with God in the third heaven. But God contends with the devil (Satan) that even with these limitations humans will choose God over Satan. And part of choosing is obeying. When we obey God, we are answering both questions: sovereignty and love. We obey the Lord of our lives, the Sovereign One. And obedience is God's love language (Jn 14:21). Through obedience we demonstrate to God what is in our hearts (Deut 8:2).

That brings us back to Ephesians. The gap between what we believe and how we behave is caused by what is or is not in our hearts. Ephesians 1:15-23 tells us that very thing. Paul has revealed God's great purpose for our lives in Ephesians 1:3-14. But Purpose does not equal Persistence. If these Ephesian believers are going to become a Purpose Driven Church, the truths of Ephesians 1:3-14 must get from their heads into their hearts. And that is exactly what Paul prays for in Ephesians 1:15-23. This section of the letter is what I am calling a Parenthetical Prayer. Paul calls "Time Out" from diving in the deep end of theology. He is saying, "This is tough stuff. Your heads are probably hurting from all the mind-benders I have alluded to in just a few verses. Let's take a moment to pray. And my prayer is that these wonderful Principles of Position[15] would get from your minds to your hearts. A head start is not enough."

Seminaries are a great place to build your faith; they are also a great place to lose your faith. I had been a Christian all of four years when I went to seminary. It was a wonderful time of growth for me. But my world was rocked more than once by finding out that some students beat their wives, professors were discharged for sexual sin, and students stole books from the library. Imagine that—wanting spiritual knowledge so badly they would steal books from the seminary library. Clearly, the failure here was not head knowledge. The head knowledge did not get into the heart.

Yes, sadly perhaps, but most of us do what we **feel** like doing. Feeling is a heart issue, not a head issue. I did not go to seminary to become a pastor. My wife and I intended to go to the mission field. When I found myself in the position of a pastor, people began coming for counseling. I didn't even know how to preach, let alone counsel. So I checked out the known Christian counselors in Houston. In 1972 there were no known Christian psychologists in evangelical circles, but there were three Christian psychiatrists. So I began sending people in need of marital counseling to these psychiatrists. Everyone I sent got a divorce. I said to myself, "I can do that well," so I began counseling. Having no training at all, I asked for a set of notes from the only course taught at the time from the seminary I attended. Little did I know they were Rogerian (I had no idea who Carl Rogers was). The idea was to help the counselee to help himself. This humanistic approach assumed the power was within the counselee to solve his

---

15 Miles Stanford, *The Green Letters* (Grand Rapids, MI: Zondervan Publishing House, 1975).

own problems. So the counselor was to lead the counselee into a "light bulb" experience in which the counselee sees within himself the answer to his problems. It was very non-directive. Just repeat back to the counselee everything he/she says in different words. Never tell them what to do. The key also was to ask them how they "feel" about things. The idea was to unlock their emotions.

Well, at least that approach was an attempt to get beyond the head to the heart: "How do you **feel** about ...?" But it wasn't working for me. The people did not get any better. So I read a book on psychoanalysis. Oh boy, now we are really desperate—a theology student trying to practice Freudian techniques. Yowwwser. That lasted about three months. Then I ran into Jay Adam and his book *Competent to Counsel*. That's me, all right—competent to counsel. Not. His approach seemed to be to identify the counselee's sin and say, "Go and sin no more." Very directive. Fit my personality. And we did help some people, but not many. The people didn't need me to tell them to stop sinning. The Bible does that. And then there were the people that obviously needed medical treatment. Telling them to go and sin no more wasn't exactly the answer.

Finally, I got ahold of Larry Crabb's book *Effective Biblical Counseling*.[16] Now we were getting somewhere. I memorized the charts at the back of the book that showed women they would never find lasting security through a man and that men would never find eternal significance through their work (unless it was unto the Lord). So I would walk a hurting wife through the chart, show her that her basic assumption as to where she would find security had to change, and she would agree with me and just sit there nodding her head. Then she would start crying and say, "But I want my husband to love me."

Ground zero. I knew I was missing something, but couldn't figure it out. So I went to Colorado and met with Larry Crabb. I described

---

16 Larry Crabb, *Effective Biblical Counseling* (Grand Rapids, MI: Zondervan Publishing House, 1977).

my dilemma. He sat there patiently nodding his head. The he said, "You got it all right, except one thing." "Yes? "You are not peeling the onion." "Peeling the onion? That's not in your book." "You are trying to go from the head to the will, from the mind to behavior." But I thought we are to be changed through a renewing of our minds (Rom 12:2). He said, "Yes, but it just starts in the mind. You have to get to the heart. You can't go from the mind to the will (behavior change). You have to go through the heart. So peeling the onion means to peel back the layers of emotion the counselee has used to capture the will. They will only do what they feel like doing. When there is so much hurt and pain in their hearts, their will is incapable of doing what the mind says is the right thing to do. Learn to peel the onion."

Ah, that was the light bulb for me. I don't know that I ever became competent to counsel. I was so glad to see a relatively large number of Christians with masters degrees in counseling move into the Houston area. Most pastors are ill-equipped and don't have the time to give people the help they need. But the reason I go into this protracted trail of my counseling experience is to point out the importance of the **heart**. In Ephesians 1:18 Paul prays that the eyes of the **heart** might be opened in each of his readers:

> [15] Therefore I also, after I heard of your faith in the Lord Jesus and your love for all the saints, [16] do not cease to give thanks for you, making mention of you in my prayers: [17] that the God of our Lord Jesus Christ, the Father of glory, may give to you the spirit of wisdom and revelation in the knowledge of Him, [18] the eyes of your UNDERSTANDING being enlightened . . ."

You will notice I have capitalized the word "understanding." That is from the NKJ. Most of you probably use another version. All the ones I checked have the word "heart" instead of "understanding," and well they should. The Greek word here is *kardia*. Just change the "k" to a "c" and pronounce it. Can you tell what English words we get from this Greek word? Cardiology, cardiologist, cardiac arrest. What is a cardiac arrest? A heart attack. The word *kardia* means "heart." That one word is the key to my entire thesis in this lesson.

Paul is peeling the onion. He wants the heart opened up. He wants to do some by-pass surgery. His patients have some clogged arteries. Specifically, he wants their hearts opened up to three things: Our Hope, Our Heritage, and Our Help. As we look at these three areas for enlightenment in our hearts, we will see that each petition is tied to one of the sections in the introduction: Selection by the Father (3-6)/ Hope of His calling; Saved by the Son (7-12)/Inheritance among the saints; Sealed by the Spirit (13-14)/His mighty power available to us through the Holy Spirit.

I. OUR HOPE   1:18B

. . . that you may know what is the hope of His calling . . .

Now, I have called this Paul's Prayer for Perception in our outline, and that it is. But it is also a prayer for persistence that they wouldn't fall by the wayside, that there would be lasting fruit. But I can tell you today there is no church in Ephesus. There is no trace of a church in Ephesus. Something happened along the way so that the lamp stand was taken away. The people fell by the wayside. They lost their testimony. What happened? That's what we are going to find out.

The "hope of his calling" takes our thoughts back to the Selection by the Father (3-6). When we get to 4:1 we are supposed to walk worthy of the calling with which we were called? What calling? In 1:4 Paul tells us that we were chosen to be holy and blameless before God. That is already true in our **Position**, but our hope is that some day that will be true in our **Condition**. Ephesians 5:25 uses these same two words in reference to how a husband is to love his wife. How? As Christ loved the Church. How was that? In several ways, but one of them was by the washing of the Word to make a glorious bride who was "holy and without blemish." This would be a reference to progressive sanctification, **Condition** not **Position**.

So that is the hope of our calling, to be holy and without blemish. We are reminded of 1 John 3:2-3, where the children of God have the hope of being like Jesus when we see him at his return. John says that those who relish this hope purify themselves. The longing hope for his return is a purifying hope. Right now, in my current **Condition** I wallow around in the mud, at least in my mind. I hate it; it disgusts me; I long to get rid of the Sin Nature that drags me down like gravity. At times the struggle makes me weary. Now that I am seventy years old I still wake up wrestling with some of the same mental attitude sins I had before I was a Christian. It doesn't mean I am a defeated Christian. I don't sense that. I'm just weary of the struggle.

I once read a book on progressive sanctification written by a well-known theologian. He claimed that the longer we spent walking by the Holy Spirit, the weaker our Sin Natures would become. I read that forty years ago. For decades I have been waiting for mine to get weaker. Of course, there are those who would say that I am simply not a Christian. A true Christian wouldn't have such a struggle with his Sin Nature, not after being a Christian over fifty years. I asked one NT professor about Romans 7:24 where Paul cries out for deliverance and refers to himself as a wretched man. He told me that was a description of Paul when he was still Saul of Tarsus. I suggested it might be a Christian longing to be permanently separated from his Sin Nature. He said, "That's a pretty dismal view of the Christian life, isn't it?" I prefer what James D. G. Dunn said on Romans 7:24 when he claimed any Christian who cannot identify with the wretched man of Romans 7:24 is simply out of touch with reality or is self-deluded.[17]

Paul, on the other hand, became more and more aware of the depths of his depravity as he grew in Christ. At the end of his life he claimed, "I am the chief among sinners." We don't think this meant he was more sinful than anyone on earth. We propose that the closer he got to Jesus, the more he realized how far he had to go. The closer we

---

17 James D. G. Dunn, http://www.presenttruthmag.com/archive/XXXI/ 31-8.htm, accessed September 9, 2016.

get to a mountain, the smaller we are in our own eyes.[18] I would suggest that the closer we get to Jesus, the more we despise our Sin Nature and its attempts to enslave us. We long to be delivered and stand before Him holy and without blemish. But that will only happen as we get our eyes off our miserable **Condition** and focus on our wonderful **Position**. Paul knows that one way to do that is by dwelling on our hope in the next world.

Peter also knew this truth. In 2 Peter 1:12ff he is stirring up his readers by turning their attention to prophetic truth. He has challenged them to go up the stairsteps to maturity in 1:5-7. Now he wants to help motivate them to do that very thing. So he reminds them of his own experience at the Mount of Transfiguration when he saw a foreshadowing of Christ's return to set up his kingdom. That event changed his life. No longer could he live for the things of this world, something Christ had accused him of in Matthew 16:23. But not everyone got to have the Transfiguration experience. No matter. Peter says they have a more sure word of prophecy, the written Word of God with its kingdom promises. And he says his readers do well to pay special attention to these prophetic promises until the day dawns and the morning star rises in their hearts. In fact, he says they should focus on these prophetic promises like a light in a dark place.

What is the morning star, and when will the day dawn? In the OT the coming of the day was a reference to the day of the Lord, which included both the darkness of the Tribulation period (Joel 2:2; Amos 5:18) but also the light of the millennial kingdom (Isa 60:19-20). But darkness proceeded light; night before day. And the morning star announced the coming of the day. The morning star was Venus, a planet that looked like a star, the last "star light" visible before the coming of day. Again, in the Revelation the morning star was the

---

18 Although some suggest the "historical present" for Paul's statement (meaning he is speaking of his days before he became a Christian), that is not grammatically possible since the historical present is never used with a first person subject.

Messiah, Jesus (Rev 2:28; 22:16). But Peter doesn't say to focus on these prophetic promises until the morning star (Jesus) comes. He says to focus on them until the morning star arises in your hearts. Uh, oh. Sound familiar? "Hearts"—2 Peter 1:19. In other words, a prophetic focus will help make Jesus the number one priority in your life. We live for his kingdom, not ours. We seek first the kingdom of God and his righteousness. That's what happened to Peter, and that is what he wanted to pass on just before he died.

I can't overstate it enough. Moral transformation is a **heart** issue. Peter wanted the morning star to arise in their **hearts**. Paul wanted the eyes of his readers **hearts** opened. Christianity is not a head-trip. It's a matter of the **heart**. I am not sure Jesus will be the Lord of someone's life until he is the Love of his or her life. This is where the disconnect comes in the lives of those who believe as they should but behave as they should not.

Paul wants their hearts opened up to the hope of their calling, yes; but he also wants their hearts opened to appreciate the riches of the glory of His inheritance among the saints.

II. HIS HERITAGE   18C

. . . what are the riches of the glory of His inheritance in the saints . . .

We have seen this word "inheritance" before (1:11, 14). But in each of the previous uses, inheritance refers to something the saints have—"our inheritance." This time Paul speaks of "His inheritance." What is his inheritance? It's the saints. And what Paul wants is for his readers to have the eyes of their hearts opened to appreciate the "riches of the glory" of God's inheritance in the saints.

This goes back to the work of the Father through the Son in 1:7-12. Just as the "hope of his calling" looks to the Father (1:3-6), this looks to the Son. How, we ask? It goes back to the work of the Father to bring all things into one in Christ: "that in the dispensation of the fullness of the times He might gather together in one all things in

33

Christ. (v. 10)" It is hard for us to imagine the racial, sexual, and class barriers broken down by the cross. Paul gets more specific about this in 2:11-22. In a way, he is going to help answer his own prayer by enlightening his readers to just what Christ did to break down these barriers in 2:11-22.

The racial riots of 2015-16 in America remind us that racism is still alive and sick here in America. And we are not alone. I am writing these words from Lake Chapala near Guadalajara, Mexico. I am being hosted by a wonderful couple that opens their lovely hacienda to people like me. My host, Mo, is from South Africa. Most of his family lives there. I asked him why he doesn't want to live near his family, and he said it isn't safe. "If you go to visit, you have to go in the day time. And you have to go prepared to spend the night. You can only leave when it is daylight. At night there are marauding gangs of boys who will kill for a wristwatch, or even a pen. They kill you first and then take whatever you might have on you."

As horrible as that sounds, and there are worse places, Jesus broke the greatest racial barrier known to man, the barrier between the Jew and the Gentile. He broke down all barriers to make every believer one in Him and one with each other. That included the gender barriers. One reason Christianity spread so quickly is that Jesus elevated women. Everywhere he went he honored women. This was new. It would still be new in many parts of our chauvinistic world today. Paul wants us to begin to wrap our hearts around this incredible accomplishment of Christ when he put all men and women of every race and tribe together into one Body, the Church. He wants us to appreciate the riches of the glory in his inheritance in the saints.

I live with a saint. You probably do too. But the saint I live with is also an angel. The longer I live, the more I love and appreciate my wife. I told her if this salvation by faith alone in Christ alone doesn't work out, I am going to draft behind her at the pearly gates. If anyone gets in by good works, it will be Betty. I travel a lot, and people often ask me if my wife ever goes with me. The answer: no. She is so busy with our school, our church, Eagle Forum, and our children and grandchildren she would feel like a bump on a log on one of my trips.

In the county where I live (Montgomery County, Texas) I am known as "Betty's husband." Most people don't know who I am, and that is fine with me. But they all know Betty. I can't tell you the number of times people have come up to me and said, "Do you know you are married to the most wonderful woman?" And they go on and on. I just stand there like a dumb clunk nodding my head in agreement. Yes, I realize there won't be any marriage in heaven, and Betty will be up there seated next to Jesus. Unless my eyesight improves I probably won't even be able to see her I'll be so far away. So I have a prenuptial agreement with her (that means before our marriage to Jesus when he comes): she gave me permission to name drop. "Yes, I knew Betty in our former life. We were rather close, actually."

You say, well lots of men are crazy about their wives. I know, but it is her saintly qualities I admire most. I have watched her when the chips are down. She walks with Jesus—consistently. That's the Holy Spirit in her. But she is not alone. One of the privileges I have as I travel is meeting saints from all over the world. It doesn't seem to matter their nationality, their class, their race—we sense an instant spiritual rapport. We are one.

I get to speak in a lot of African-American churches. In one of these churches there was a duet just before I spoke—two men. One of them was a student at our school. As he sang, he just sort of rocked side-ways, back and forth, back and forth. The guy next to him had a lot of soul, a lot of rhythm. So when the pastor got up to introduce me, he said if our school can't teach a man better rhythm than this poor guy just rocking back and forth, back and forth, he wasn't sure if the church could continue to support him with tuition money. Of course, he was just teasing. So when I got up, I said, "Pastor, what you don't understand are baby steps. In the first year we teach them how to rock back and forth (I mimicked our student's rocking best I could). But in the fourth year before they graduate we teach them how to do this: I did the moonwalk halfway across the stage. The congregation fell out to see this old, awkward, rhythmless, white man moonwalking across their stage. But we were one. And it was glorious.

As Paul tells us in 1 Thessalonians 4:9, he has no need to teach his converts how to love one another. He says we are God-taught how to love each other. It is an amazing thing God has done through Christ during this dispensation of the fullness of times, or what many call the Church Age.

There is one other aspect to Paul's prayer. Our Hope was tied to the work of the Father in 1:3-6; His Heritage is tied to the work of the Son in 1:7-12; and now Our Help is tied to the work of the Holy Spirit in 1:13-14.

III. OUR HELP   1:19-23

> [19] and what *is* the exceeding greatness of His power toward us who believe, according to the working of His mighty power [20] which He worked in Christ when He raised Him from the dead and seated *Him* at His right hand in the heavenly *places*, [21] far above all principality and power and might and dominion, and every name that is named, not only in this age but also in that which is to come. [22] And He put all *things* under His feet, and gave Him *to be* head over all *things* to the church, [23] which is His body, the fullness of Him who fills all in all.

There is an old rule in Bible study: that which gets the most ink is being emphasized. For example, what would you say is the emphasis of the NT? If you said Jesus, you would be right. How do we know? He gets the most ink—four gospels and some. Here in Paul's prayer that which gets the most ink is this section on power. The uses of "His . . . His . . . He . . . He . . . His" in 1:19-20 certainly point to the power of the Father. But the Father and the Son chose to send the Holy Spirit to help (Jn 16:7) us and to empower us (Acts 1:8). And since the previous two aspects of Paul's request can be tied to the sections in the introduction on the Father and the Son, I think the strong implication is that this power can be tied back to the power of the Holy Spirit that sealed us in 1:13-14.

Paul's main point here is the power we have. It is the same power that raised Christ from the dead, brought him from earth to heaven, and put all his enemies under his feet—every principality, power, might, dominion (order of fallen angels: Col 1:16; 2:15). Paul wants the eyes of our hearts opened to how much power is available to us. Let's go to the physical world to get a little glimpse of this.

2015 was the 110th year anniversary of e = mc². In 1905, Albert Einstein came out with five papers that changed the world as we then knew it. It was called his miracle year. The genius was not in the algebra of e = mc²; it was recognizing a direct relationship between energy and mass. They were interchangeable, different phases of the same thing, like water and ice. Mass (at rest) was frozen energy.

In fact, there is so much energy or power stored up within the nucleus of atoms that the energy stored inside a major league baseball could run the average car at sixty miles an hour without stopping for five thousand years.[19] That's a lot of power. But do you realize we have more power available to us than that. How so? Because God's spiritual power trumps physical power. Remember the storm on the Sea of Galilee and his disciples were afraid? Jesus told the wind and the waves to be still. Instantly there was a calm, and the disciples wondered what manner of man was this that the wind and waves obeyed him.

Do you remember the woman with an issue of blood for twelve years? She touched the hem of his garment and he felt power going out of him and she was healed. Was that physical power? No, it was spiritual power. But the spiritual power trumped the physical world once again.

Do you remember the resurrection account? His physical body becomes a glorified, spiritual body. Einstein's equation says that the body of Jesus (mass) must convert to physical energy before it could become a spiritual body. And when the mass of his body was converted, the ginormous release of energy would have made a great light or sound (think Hiroshima). But we have no record of any such light or boom. That means his body went from physical mass straight

---

19 Brian Greene, "The Famous Equation and You," in *The New York Times*, September 30, 2005.

to a spiritual body by skipping the middle step (energy).[20] Once again, spiritual power trumps the physical laws of the universe. "His mighty power that he worked in Christ when he raised him from the dead." God's mighty spiritual power turned a physical body into a glorified body.

Are you getting the picture? That is the power available to us. Yet I can't even trust him to handle my finances, or my marriage, or my kids, or my health, or you name it. In Philippians 3:10, Paul wants the Philippians not just to know him but also the power of his resurrection. It takes more faith to know the power of his resurrection than to know him in the sense of meeting him as one's Savior. But we won't know that power until we trust him for it. But we can't walk on water until we get out of the boat. We don't need his miracle working power until we get out of our comfort zone. Are you living for comfortable Christianity? Then you may go your entire Christian life without experiencing this kind of power, that is, until your own resurrection or rapture.

CONCLUSION

So what happened to the Ephesians? As we said earlier, there is not a trace of a church ever being at Ephesus during the time of Paul. Perhaps Revelation will give us the answer. In Revelation 2:1-7 John writes to the church at Ephesus. He commends them for their endurance, for their faith, and for their theology. He says they got their theological "I"s dotted and their "T"s crossed. But he had something against them. They had left their first love. He says if they don't repent, he will remove their lampstand from them. In other words, they had it in the head but lost it in the heart. They had drifted away from the devotion for Christ they had when the church started. Perhaps they became ritualistic, just going through the motions.

---

20 Sublimation in H_2O occurs when dry ice goes from a solid to a vapor without becoming a liquid.

Graciously, John tells them how to restore their devotion. He tells them to do the "first works," the things they were doing when their love for Christ was at its peak. Often there is a connection between feeling and doing. George Crane tells of a wife who came into his office with a marriage problem. She was a columnist for a local newspaper as well as a minister, but she hated her husband. She said she did not only want to get rid of him but wanted to get even with him. She wanted to hurt him as much as he had hurt her. So Dr. Crane suggested an ingenious plan.

"Go home and act as if you really love your husband. Tell him how much he means to you and praise him for every decent trait. Go out of your way to be kind, considerate, generous as possible, and spare no efforts to please him and enjoy him. Make him really believe you love him, and after you have convinced him of your undying love and that you cannot live without him, then drop the bomb. Tell him you are going to get a divorce. That will really hurt him."

With revenge in her eyes, she smiled and exclaimed, "Beautiful! Will he ever be surprised!?" And she did it with enthusiasm. For two months she showed love and kindness, listening, giving reinforcement, and sharing. And when she didn't return to Crane, he called her and asked, "Is the divorce final?" "Divorce," she exclaimed. I discovered I really do love him!"

Go back and do the first works. That's what he tells the church at Ephesus. Apparently they didn't listen. Their knowledge never got from their heads to their hearts. And you know what, a head start is not enough.

3

GOD'S POETRY
Ephesians 2:1-10

INTRODUCTION

When I was growing up, my father tried to train me in a variety of things. He was an engineer, a scientist, a builder, a ham radio operator, a pilot, a wine maker, and on it went. One thing he tried to train me in was investing. He traded commodities and stocks. So he had me open my own paper account to get a feel for trading when I was fourteen. He also had me read a book called *The Art of Contrary Thinking*.[21] The idea was to do the opposite of the crowd. Since ninety percent of the people who trade lose money, the crowd is usually wrong. Find out what they are doing and do the opposite. If they are buying, sell; if they are selling, buy.

In a way, Christ was a master of contrarian thinking: the first will

---

21 Humphrey B. Neill, *The Art of Contrary Thinking* (Caldwell, ID: Caxton Press, 1954).

be last; the last will be first. What appears to be a terrible trial is a blessing. What you can see is temporary, and what you can't see is permanent. Your happiest moments on earth may come when you are persecuted for your faith.

Jill Brisco, wife of Stuart Brisco,[22] shared a story about a couple in Britain that went childless year after year. The husband was a factory worker, and he was working among socialists and communists that did not believe in God. He told them he believed God would give him and his wife a child and that he had been praying for a child for over ten years. His fellow workers would just laugh at him and from time to time mock him by asking, "Got your child yet? Wife pregnant?"

Well, finally this man's wife became pregnant. He was overjoyed and shared this joy with his fellow workers. But the child was born with Down syndrome. As this man was going to work, he was praying, "God, give me wisdom. Give me wisdom as to how to share this news to honor your name." So when everyone at work found out about it, they said, "Oh, so that's your God. So this is the child that your God gave you. Some kind of God." He thought for a moment and opened his mouth and said, "I'm just so glad God gave this child to me instead of you." He knew the art of contrarian thinking. He realized that what appeared to be a difficulty was a great opportunity.

Paul had a thorn in the flesh. He prayed three times that it be removed. God said, "My grace is sufficient for your need. What is a thorn in your life is going to turn into an open public display of my grace." And that is the thesis of what I am trying to teach in this lesson: *The Art of Contrary Thinking*. That situation in your life, that disease in your life, that thorn in your flesh, that boss that just won't leave, that husband or wife that is so difficult for you—these are gifts of God's grace in your life. It is part of the very purpose for which He created you.

---

22 An international Bible teacher, Brisco turned Elmbrook Church in Brookfield, WS, into the largest church in Wisconsin as its senior pastor for thirty years.

It's been said that there is no greater pressure than a great potential. It could also be said that there is no greater loss than a wasted potential. Although that point could be argued, we will probably agree that there is much sadness in a wasted potential. Of course, *potential is tied to purpose.* We must know our purpose before we can discover our potential. This presumes that we were created by design for a specific purpose. And that is what God is trying to get across to the Ephesians. They were created and saved for a purpose, and until they discover that purpose, they will never become a Purpose Driven Church.

What was true for them is true for us today. We were created for a purpose and have the potential for an eternal impact. But before we can begin to reach or even realize our potential, we must understand our purpose. That is what we are going to discover in Ephesians 2:1-10. We have finished what we might call the introductory matters of Ephesians and in the opening verses Paul talked about the fact that God's great purpose is not about you. It is about the praise of the glory of his grace. He realizes this is such a difficult concept for most people to grab hold of that he says, "I am going to pray about it." So he gets on his knees in 1:15-23 and prays that the eyes of their hearts might be open, that the facts and theology he presented in the introduction (1:3-14) might get from their heads down into their hearts. He knew only then would their **Position** ever affect their **Condition**. So now he is ready to begin the body of his letter, the Creation and the Conduct of the Church.

This letter is about a Purpose Driven Church. Chapters two and three are about its creation. In these two chapters there are three primary players: God, Christ and Paul. Paul talks about God's role in creating the church; Christ's role in creating the church; and then Paul's role in this mysterious dispensation, this age of grace, the entity we call the church.

Here we want to look at God's role (2:1-10). And breaking this section down we have his Prospects for Salvation (2:1-3), his Procedure for Salvation (2:4-6), and his Purpose for Salvation (2:7-10). He talks about what we were in the past, what we are in the present, and what we will be in the future. But behind it all, he's taking us all the way back to the introduction, to the praise of the glory of his grace.

EPHESIANS
"The Purpose Driven Church"

SALUTATION   1:1-2

INTRODUCTION—"Spiritual Blessings in the Heavenlies"   1:3-14

   (Paul's Prayer for Perception)   1:15-23

BODY   2:1-6:9

  I. Creation of the Church (Its Position)   2:1-3:21

    A. God's Role   2:1-10

      1. Prospects for Salvation   1-3

      2. Procedure for Salvation   4-6

      3. Purpose for Salvation   7-10

    B. Christ's Role   2:11-22

    C. Paul's Role   3:1-13

    (Paul's Prayer for Possession)   3:14-21

  II. Conduct of the Church (Its Condition)   4:1-6:9

CONCLUSION—"Spiritual Battles in the Heavenlies"   6:10-20

FAREWELL   6:21-24

I. PROSPECTS FOR SALVATION   2:1-3

And you *He made alive,* who were dead in trespasses and sins, [2] in which you once walked according to the course of this world, according to the prince of the power of the air, the spirit who now works in the sons of disobedience, [3] among whom also we all once conducted ourselves in the lusts of our flesh, fulfilling the desires of the flesh and of the mind, and were by nature children of wrath, just as the others.

The first observation we need to make is that the words *"He made alive"* are in italics, which means there are no Greek words in the original text behind these words. Some might even suggest that the translators are betraying their theology by sticking these words in the text, meaning, many theologians think we must be regenerated (born again) before we can believe. Much of that approach comes from their understanding of the word "dead."

I listened to a debate between James White and Dave Hunt on Calvinism.[23] During the first twenty-two minutes of the debate White made reference to this verse at least four times. What he was trying to establish as the foundation for his Calvinistic point of view is that spiritually speaking every man or woman is a spiritual corpse before regeneration—dead. Once the word corpse is on the table, the logic flows from there.

Can a corpse eat? No. Can a corpse talk? No. Can a corpse breathe? No. Can a corpse think? No. Can a corpse **believe**? No. This is a primary recruiting tool used by Five Point Calvinists. If a man or woman is a spiritual corpse, and if a corpse is completely incapable of eating, speaking, breathing, thinking, or believing, then one is completely incapable of believing before regeneration.

Sounds quite logical, and it is. The problem with this interpretation is the misuse of the word "dead." White is using "dead" here in the sense of "inactive" like a dead church or youth group. This completely overlooks the word "in." We are in a book about **Position** (Ephesians 1-3) and **Condition** (Ephesians 4-6). Chapter one begins with all the spiritual blessings we have "in Christ" in heavenly places. But chapter two begins with our **Position before** we were baptized by the Holy Spirit into Christ. We were dead <u>in</u> sin. This kind of death is not talking about a spiritual corpse but rather a spiritual separation. Our human spirits were separated from God. Physical death is a

---

23 http://www.youtube.com/watch?v=q61K6ZITck4, accessed October 9, 2014.

44

separation—the material part of man from the immaterial. Spiritual death is also separation—the spirit of man from God. Physical life comes when God breathes the breath of the spirit of life into the material part of man. And spiritual life (post-Pentecost) comes when the Holy Spirit unites with our human spirit. Life is union; death is separation.

It is easy to show that the human spirit of an unbeliever is quite active and functional even though it is separated from God. In Genesis 41:8 we are told that Pharaoh's spirit was troubled within him. In 1 Kings 21:5 we are told that Ahab's spirit was sullen. In 1 Chronicles 5:26 it says God stirred up the spirit of Tiglath-Pileser. In 2 Chronicles 36:22 God stirred up the spirit of Cyrus the Persian to free the Jews. In Daniel 2 it says Nebuchadnezzar's spirit was troubled and anxious and in 5:20 it was hardened with pride. Surely we would argue that none of these mentioned was a believer. But their spirits were not corpses. They were quite active. They were separated from God, but they were capable of a number of activities.

Zechariah 12:1 says the Lord forms the spirit of man within him. To what purpose? To be a corpse? No, the spirit of the unbeliever has many functions, as we have seen. I would even argue that our conscience is a function of our human spirit, and this is precisely where the Holy Spirit convicts the world of sin, righteousness, and judgment.

In Luke 16:19ff Jesus tells the story of the rich man and Lazarus. The rich man dies. His body is buried. His spirit goes to hell. While in hell, the spirit of the rich man can see, feel, talk, and think. Does this sound like a spiritual corpse to you? Not exactly. The only possible response to this is to say the spirit of the unbeliever is a corpse while his body is alive on earth, but then is regenerated when sent to hell so it can function as observed. Wait a minute. You've got a regenerated spirit in hell? Not likely.

So, we would propose that Ephesians 2:1 is a statement of the unbeliever's **Position**, not his **Condition**. Later on (2:2-3) we get into his **Condition**, which appropriately was a reflection of his **Position**.

When we get to Ephesians 2:4-6 we will explain the Procedure for Salvation.

As far as the **Condition** of the unbeliever is concerned, it, as we have said, reflects his **Position**. If he is separated from God, how could we expect him to live a godly life? Just as the word "in" is often a clue that we are talking about **Position**, the word "walk" usually indicates our **Condition**. These prospects for salvation "walked" according to the course of this world, according to Satan, according to the lusts of their flesh. They were "by nature" children of wrath.

In other words, by nature they were thoroughly depraved. Every aspect of their being—body, soul, and spirit—was degraded since Adam passed down the results of his sin to all members of the human race. Adam was thoroughly depraved. That doesn't mean he was as bad as he could be, but it does mean he was as bad off as he could be until he was reconciled to God. As we have shown above, total depravity does not mean total inability. The spirit of the unbeliever is alive and active, even though it is separated from God. There is nothing the unbeliever can do to bridge the separation between himself and God. Just one sin is one too many since Psalm 5:4 says evil cannot dwell with God. There is no sin in heaven. That's why Satan and company had to go. And it is why all our sins must be wiped away for us to be reconciled to God.

Queen Victoria was on a tour of a paper mill. She didn't want to draw attention to herself, so she went *incognito*. The guide led the group from one room to the next until they came to a large room just filled with garbage. There were workers sifting through the garbage and boxes and cans and all sorts of refuse. The workers were holding little bags, and they were pulling out of the garbage rags, just filthy rags. Out of curiosity, the Queen asked, "What are they doing?" the tour guide said, "From those rags we make the finest paper in the realm." Then they went on.

When the tour guide found out that it was the Queen herself that asked that question, he went and got a box of the fine, fine paper and sent it to her with a little note to take it to the light of the window. So she opened it up and took out one of those fine linen like pieces of paper, walked over and held it up to the window. Through the light of the sun, she could see the impress of her own image, the image of the Queen.

And that is precisely what God has done. He has gone out to the refuse of the world and pulled us out like dirty rags and from them he intends to make the finest linen of the realm. Someday in his kingdom he can hold it up, and through the light of the Son of God we can see his image. That is the raw material of 2:1-3, the raw material God wants to work with in order to make his greatest work, his *magnum opus*.

Paul now moves from the Prospects for Salvation (2:1-3) to the Procedure of Salvation (2:4-6).

II. PROCEDURE FOR SALVATION 2:4-6

⁴ But God, who is rich in mercy, because of His great love with which He loved us, ⁵ even when we were dead in trespasses, made us alive together with Christ (by grace you have been saved), ⁶ and raised *us* up together, and made *us* sit together in the heavenly *places* in Christ Jesus . . .

So, if we find the Prospects for Salvation in 2:1-3, what is the Procedure? How does God do it? Notice first of all this procedure for our salvation is born out of a marriage of mercy and love. And he makes it clear that this love is not based on anything we could bring to the table because it says he loved us even when we were dead in trespasses. By repeating the word "love" in v. 4 Paul emphasizes God's love for sinful people. Good thing. That's about the only option out there.

The next word we need to highlight is the word "together." We find it three times in 2:5-6. Each time it is the little Greek preposition *syn* attached as a prefix to the words for being made alive and being raised up and being made to sit. It's like the English word *syn*thetic. The *syn-* means "together" and the "thetic" comes from the verb "to put." So synthetic means "to put together." Why belabor this?

Because we were dead in our trespasses, meaning **separated** from God. But now we are **"together"** with him. No more separation: made alive **together** with him, raised **together** with him, and seated **together** in heavenly places in Christ. It's our new **Position** after we have been saved: in Christ. No longer **separated**; now we are **together**.

This is the short version of Romans 6:3-11 where we are crucified with Christ, buried with Christ, and raised with Christ. Ephesians 1 and Romans 6 may well be the strongest chapters in the Bible when it comes to laying out our **Position** in Christ. Both of them argue that our new **Position** gives us the potential and the expectation of a new **Condition**.

Now right in the middle of this discussion on our new life in Christ, Paul throws out a little teaser. In the NKJ it puts it in a parenthesis: "by grace you have been saved." Whoa. Paul just sort of slipped that one in there. We can't wait to learn more about this salvation by grace. This, of course, is exactly what he does in the very famous verses, Ephesians 2:8-9, but we aren't there yet. Right now we just know that we have a brand new **Position**—in Christ. According to Ephesians 1:8 we have a **Position** in a new family by virtue of adoption.

My wife and I have two daughters. The first was unable to have children, so she and her husband decided to adopt. After three arduous and failed attempts to adopt here in the States, my daughter (Christie) and her husband (Scott) decided to go to Russia. The procedures were difficult and expensive, but doable. The first step was to make a trip to Russia to visit the orphanages to see if they could find a child they wished to adopt. At the time (2002) it cost $25,000 for the first child and $5,000 for the second. So, Scott and Christie decided to go for two. After choosing a boy and a girl from different orphanages but just two months apart in age, they were ushered into a courtroom where the judge read the medical rap sheet on each child. They let it be known that these children were up for adoption because they had medical issues and were not wanted by either their parents or the state.

Of course, the adopting parents had no way of knowing if the medical issues were real or trumped up to give the orphanages a legal sanction to put the children up for adoption. However, after hearing the issues, the prospective parents then flew back to their home country to decide if they wanted to go on with the adoption. They had to wait about a month, enough time for their emotions to subside so they could make a rational decision. Thus, if any medical issues did pop up later, the Russian government could always say, "We told you so."

Well, according to a study done by Buckner Baptist Benevolences in 2002, most orphans in Russia don't live to "graduate."[24] But of those who do, thirty percent turn to crime (boys join the mafia and girls become prostitutes); sixty percent end up jobless and homeless; ten percent commit suicide; and over fifty percent spend time in prison. Knowing that the two children they had picked out would not have much of a chance in life, if they lived to "graduate," Scott and Christie decided they had the opportunity to bring salvation to these kids on two levels: physically and spiritually. So they adopted them, brought them to America, and now the children (Drew and Grace) are thirteen years old.

I have learned so much about God's love for us through this adoption process. God came from a foreign country to adopt us. He could see that I had a lot of defects, but he chose me anyway. He paid the price to bring me home. And despite some of my ongoing problems, he still loves me and will always express that love if I will receive it.

So in this section we learned about God's procedure for delivering us from the penalty of sin, or what most people call salvation. It involves putting us together with Christ by grace and grace alone. But let's learn some more about this in 2:7-11. Here we learn about the Purpose for our Salvation.

---

24 http://www.helporphans.org/pages/countries/russia/russiaorpha nages.html.

III. PURPOSE FOR SALVATION 2:7-10

> [7] that in the ages to come He might show the exceeding riches of His grace in His kindness toward us in Christ Jesus. [8] For by grace you have been saved through faith, and that not of yourselves; *it is* the gift of God, [9] not of works, lest anyone should boast. [10] For we are His workmanship, created in Christ Jesus for good works, which God prepared beforehand that we should walk in them.

We have called this section the "Purpose for Salvation." For good reason. In English, v. 7 begins with "that," and rightly so. It is the Greek word *hina*, which usually signifies purpose or result. It is that IN THE AGES to come his grace would be on display. The plural word AGES would suggest there is more than one age to come. For a dispensationalist, the next age is the Millennium (1,000 year reign of Christ), but the age after that is the New Jerusalem where saints spend eternity.

But don't miss what we are saying here. You may never know the great purpose for your life while you are in this age. You might; you might not. This is Paul's point: The ultimate purpose will be revealed in the next age. And whatever it is, we know for sure it will be a testimony of God's grace. The word "show" implies that God wants to show off, so to speak, his trophies of grace. Every believer will be a trophy of grace. And those who have chosen to live for him will be billboards for his grace in this life and monuments to his grace in the next.

When v. 8 begins with the word "for," we know Paul now wants to support the statement he has just made about showing the exceeding riches of his grace toward us in the world to come. "For by grace you have been saved"—the exact phrase he dropped on us back in v. 5. It is what Greek grammarians call a perfect periphrastic construction. It is a construction used for emphasis. The only reason I bring that out is to point out the great emphasis he puts on the finished work of our salvation. The perfect tense speaks of completed action in the past with present results. This word "saved" is in the perfect tense.

This tells us that our salvation is a completed act of God. There is no more to do. It is not some sort of linear process by which our ultimate entrance to heaven or the New Jerusalem depends on how much we have become like Christ during this life. That's **Condition**. This is **Position**—you have been saved (completed act; done deal; no more to do). And to make all this highly emphatic Paul adds another word in this construction that is not necessary. He just does it for emphasis. It is all by God's grace.

But now Paul adds something to the phrase about our salvation he did not mention in v. 5. He says **"through faith."** It is faith that unlocks the storeroom of God's grace. Some want to teach that faith is a gift God gives to those who have been regenerated. There is zero biblical support for that notion. The word "born again" or "regenerated" is only used three times in the Bible (1 Pet 1:3, 23; Tit 3:5). The word faith is nowhere to be found in those three passages. How could anyone possibly determine from these passages that regeneration precedes faith? No, that understanding is merely a logical deduction from the misunderstanding that "dead" in 2:1 makes us spiritual corpses that cannot breath, think, or believe. The Bible never teaches initial faith is God's gift.

Now, back in Ephesians 2:5 it repeats the fact from 2:1 that we were dead in our trespasses and sins, but this time it does say that **God made us alive**. Though it does not use the word regeneration here, I am fine with "made alive" functioning as an equivalent. But it does not tell us *how* we are made alive. Here in 2:8 Paul tells us *how* we are made alive—by grace through *faith*. If this is *how* we are made alive, or regenerated (by faith), then it is very hard to understand how the result (regeneration) can precede the means (faith). If the result is regeneration, and the means is faith, it is nonsensical to say the result can precede the means.

If faith is the means by which Jesus chooses to accomplish a miracle, it is very difficult to understand how the miracle could occur before the faith. In Matthew 9, a woman comes with an issue of blood. She reaches out to touch his garment, and when He saw her, He said, "Be of good cheer, daughter; your faith has made you well." And the woman was made well from that hour. Although we know it was Jesus who healed her, he chose to use her faith to do it, so he says, "Your faith *has made* you well" (emphasis mine). Faith here is the cause, not the result. She was not made whole before she believed. She was made whole when she believed, and according to Jesus, it was her faith that made her whole.

Nowhere does Ephesians 2 say the Ephesians were made alive before they believed. It simply says they were dead in their trespasses and sins when God made them alive. Then it goes into the process by which they were made alive—salvation by grace through faith. Friends, I implore you, do not be deceived by the "corpse caper" and don't let your congregations or friends fall for it either. Notice how quickly commentators jump on the corpse illustration:

John MacArthur on Eph 2:1:

> One of the first indications of physical death is the body's inability to respond to stimulus, no matter what it might be. A dead person cannot react. He no longer responds to light, sound, smell, taste, pain, or anything else. He is totally insensitive . . . He has no capacity to respond . . . Men apart from God are spiritual zombies . . . Twenty **corpses** on a battle field might be in many different stages of decay, but they are uniformly dead (emphasis mine).[25]

Again, in his book *Saved Without a Doubt* MacArthur says the natural man is "dead in trespasses and sins" and is "no more able to respond to God than a cadaver. How can a person who is dead in sin, blinded by Satan . . . exercise saving faith? A **corpse** could no sooner come out of a grave and walk."[26]

---

25 John MacArthur, Jr., *Ephesians*, The MacArthur New Testament Commentary (Chicago: Moody Press), 53-54.

26 _____, *Saved Without a Doubt* [Colorado Springs, CO: Chariot Victor, 1992), 58-59.

John R. Stott:

> ... spiritual death is the separation from him which sin inevitably brings: "Your iniquities have made a separation between you and your God. ..." Therefore, "they are as unresponsive to him as a **corpse** (emphasis mine)."[27]

Harold Hoehner concludes that "...those who are spiritually dead ... are separated from God. ... Dead people cannot communicate ..."[28]

The entire illustration of the corpse comes from a failure to understand that the word "dead" in 2:1 is not describing their **Condition**; it is describing their **Position**—separated from God. But by grace through faith they are saved. But what about faith? Many use this passage to prove that faith is a gift God gives us. Right after the word "faith" the text says "and that not of yourselves; it is the gift of God." They equate "faith" and "that." In other words, faith is not something coming from within the person, but rather it is something God gives to them.

But that explanation is grammatically impossible. In the Romance languages (Greek, Latin, Spanish, English, German, and French, for example) there is agreement between gender and number. For "that" to refer back to faith it must be feminine because faith (*hē pistis*) is feminine. But that (*touto*) is neuter (a noun or relative pronoun or demonstrative pronoun must be either masculine, feminine, or neuter). Neuter does not agree with feminine. "That" cannot refer to "faith." Now, actually, I hate slowing things down to get into this Greek grammar because I know it bores most people to death. But, folks, so much bad doctrine comes from not paying close attention to the original text. I wouldn't do this if I didn't think it crucial.

---

27 John R. W. Stott, *The Message of Ephesians* (Downers Grove, IL: InterVarsity Press, 1979), 72.

28 Harold W. Hoehner, *Ephesians*, 308.

Some will say that if faith is something man brings to the table, then it diminishes God's sovereignty. It makes the salvation process dependent on men instead of wholly dependent on God. But faith is simply a capacity to receive truth and put our trust in it. Unbelievers demonstrate faith all the time. Whenever an unbeliever gets in his car to drive away, he is demonstrating faith. When an unbeliever gets in an airplane to fly away, he is demonstrating faith. When an unbeliever sits in a chair, he is demonstrating faith. Though we do not teach that an unbeliever would believe in Christ on his own (it takes divine illumination, conviction, persuasion, and wooing), at the point of faith there is no credit for us. There is no diminishing of God's sovereignty, no diminishing of his glory. Faith is defined in John 1:12 as receiving: "To as many as received him, to them he gave the right to become the children of God, even to those who believe in his name." Now there is your definition of receiving: even to those who believe on his name. Now you can flip it around: that's the definition of believing. Receiving is believing and believing is receiving. There is no credit, no merit, no work when you receive something that is a free gift. You just receive it.

Let's say a missionary I know is in bad need of a car, and I am led to buy one for him. I pay for it, drive it over to his house and offer him the keys. If he receives my offer and takes the keys, does he get any credit for this transaction? Of course, not. I paid the price in full. All he did was to believe my offer and receive my gift. It would actually diminish my glory, so to speak, if he refused my gift because then my love for him would not reach it fullest expression.

During the Civil War in America, in a border town between the states, there was a lot of bitterness. A lot of POWs, a lot of atrocities against the Yankees and vice versa. So one day the Yankees decided they were going to put a halt to the abuse of prisoners. And the way they were going to do it was to kill ten of their POWs and keep killing them day after day until the killing stopped on the other side. They announced they would put twenty names in a hat. Ten names would have death on the other side and ten would say life. As soon as they pulled out ten names that said "Death," those named would be killed.

54

So they passed the hat around, and slowly but surely, people were drawing their names out. A middle-aged farmer with three children drew his out and gasped. The next fellow was an eighteen-year-old full of life. He pulled his out and it said "Life." He could tell by the gasp of the farmer that his said "Death," so he looked at the farmer and said, "Switch papers with me." The farmer said, "I couldn't do that." "Don't argue with me and switch the pieces of paper." And so they did. That next morning that eighteen-year-old and nine others were shot to death. The ten who drew "Life" lived to the end of the war and were released.

Now if you went into the home of that farmer, with his three kids, and said, "What did you do to deserve life?" What would his answer be? He'd say "Nothing. The only thing I did was receive the offer given to me." And that is all God asks us to do. There is no merit in there; there is no credit for us. There is no diminishing of his glory. As a matter of fact, it is a magnification of his glory. He offers us the greatest deal in the world, and it is a free gift.

Often people will ask me why we refer to God's grace as "free." "Isn't that redundant?" they ask. "I thought the definition of grace says it is an undeserved favor. If it is undeserved, doesn't that make it free?" Well, of course, it does. But God seemed to know in advance that everyone who names the name of Christ would camp on God's grace. The Roman Catholic Church talks about grace more than the Protestants. But they also say there are seven things we have to do to get God's grace and stay in God's grace (the seven sacraments). Many of the Calvinists don't like to refer to their foundation as the Five Points of Calvinism. They like to speak of these points as "the graces of God."

So God wanted to qualify this grace process a bit. So he says, "It is not of yourselves; it is the gift of God." Now that word for gift signifies something absolutely free, no strings attached. It is used in adverbial form in Revelation 21:6 when God says anyone who thirsts can come and drink of the water of life **freely**. No strings attached. The same adverb is used in Romans 3:24, which says, "being justified **freely** by His **grace** . . ." We will see the juxtaposition of "free" and "grace" once again in Ephesians 3:7. And we find it three times in Romans 5:12-21 (15, 16, 17). But what has happened down through the centuries was the very thing the Holy Spirit was trying to safeguard by coupling the word "free" to the word "grace." The flesh of man wants to get into the salvation act somehow or another, so he keeps attaching strings to this wonderful offer of "free grace."

Some tie strings to God's free grace on the front end—a front-end load (commission) in financial jargon. That front-end load might be water baptism, submission to the pastor, financial gifts, keeping certain rules or laws, good standing with the church, surrendering to Christ as Lord of your life, and so on. Others like to back-end load the good news. You must behave in a certain way after you have received Christ or you never received him in the first place. God himself talks about "free grace" to make it clear that there is no front-end load and no back-end load on his wonderful salvation process. **"Not of works, lest any man should boast."** There probably has never been a more clear statement of the contrast between faith and works than this one. There are others in Galatians and Romans to be sure, but none more explicit than this one. We won't be sitting around boasting about how we got to heaven; we will sit around boasting about how he got us to heaven in spite of our many failures.

Rather than a focus on our workmanship in heaven there will be a focus on his workmanship. **"For we are his workmanship."** He is further explaining why we won't be boasting about our good works in heaven. And now Paul is getting around to the full purpose for which we were created and saved. It is that we might be his workmanship and live a life of good works. Some people suggest that Free Grace theologians teach that God is not interested in good works. Yes, he is not interested in our good works to earn our admittance to heaven, but he is very much interested in our living a life of good works.

One of my pet peeves is the emphasis in Western Christianity on the goal of the Christian life being to get to heaven when we die. That comes from Augustine's introduction of Neo-Platonism into Christianity. Entrance to heaven we might call the starting blocks of the race we call the Christian life. Heaven is not the goal line. Now we are talking about the goal line. Actually, Romans 8:29 and Philippians 3:10 lay out the goal line for us: conformity to the life and image of Christ. But it is the good works, the life of Christ-likeness, we live along the way that make up the race. If we just sit around talking about heaven all the time, we are leaving our eyes on the starting blocks instead of the goal line. We are to be looking unto the author and finisher of our faith as we run the race set before us (Heb 12:1).

And will you notice the word "**walk**"? Remember we said as soon as we see the word "walk," the focus has switched to our **Condition**. He "saved" us (justification) from the penalty of sin (**Position**) in order to have an impact on our walk (**Condition**). **Position** affects **Condition**. Not the other way around.

CONCLUSION

My favorite word in this whole passage is the word "**workmanship**" in 2:10. It is the Greek word *poiēma*. I don't need to tell you what English word we get from *poiēma* (poem). This word is only used twice in the NT. Once is in Romans 1:20 in reference to the creation of the universe, and the other is here. Yes, there was a time that the universe was God's greatest work—a display of his mighty attributes of power and intelligence and presence. Until humans. Now mankind is looked at by God as his magnum opus, his greatest work.

And when a person enters the family of faith, the Holy Spirit begins writing a poem about his or her life. Line upon line, day after day, the poem is written. The poem is about our good works prepared for us that we should (not must or inevitably will) walk in them. And at the Judgment Seat of Christ that poem will be read. It is not a list of our sins. They were judged at the cross. This is our life since the cross. This is "God's Poetry."

Perhaps you have made some mistakes in life. God's grace can still be at work to bring your good and his glory out of your mistakes. This is contrarian thinking. Sometimes in our mistakes God finds his greatest opportunity to manifest his grace. Did Paul the Apostle make mistakes? For sure. He was Saul of Tarsus, Saul the Gestapo, killer of

Christians. But that mistake is probably one of the main things that drove him the rest of his life. What about your handicap or your child's handicap? Do you have a child who is ADHD? So was Ross Perot—still is. Thomas Edison was ADHD. What about bipolar? Theodore Roosevelt was bipolar. You can have a handicap, but God made no mistake. Our children are not accidents. Russell Kelfer put it this way:

You are who you are for a reason,
You are part of an intricate plan.
You are precious and perfect in a unique design
Called God's special woman, or man.

You look like you look for a reason,
Our God made no mistake.
He knit you together in the womb.
You're just what he wanted to make.

The parents you had were the ones he chose
And no matter how you may feel,
They were custom designed with God's plan in mind
And they bear the master's seal.

No, that trauma you faced was not easy
And God wept that it hurt you so,
But it was allowed to shape your heart
So that into his likeness you'd grow.

You are who you are for a reason.
You've been formed by the master's rod.
You are who you are for a reason, beloved,
Because there is a God.[29]

---

29 Russell Kelfer, http://library.timelesstruths.org/music/You_Are_Who_You_Are_for_a_Reason/accessed December 19, 2016.

Yes, you are his greatest work. And he is writing a poem of your life. In fact, God is writing two books of poetry. The first deals with the universe—the heavens declare the glory of God and the earth shows forth his handiwork. God wrote his poetry with the pearls of the night. God's second book of poems is about his children. He is currently writing a poem with the lines of your life. Of course, one difference in these two books of poetry is that the universe had little choice in what was written; we do. We might call it interactive poetry. How we respond to life's issues has a great deal to do with the rhyme and meter of God's poem about us. There is no lasting shame or guilt if God's poem about us includes mistakes and even tragedies. The only lasting tragedy would be if we told God to stop writing. Then when we appear before him, and it is our time to step before his tribunal for our poem to be read before all the angels, and God simply says, "Oh, here's Dave, another one of my unfinished poems." Don't go down in God's greatest book of poetry as an unfinished poem.

4

DREAM ON

Ephesians 2:11-22

INTRODUCTION

On August 28, 1963, some two hundred thousand people gathered in Washington for the freedom march. Martin Luther King, Jr. stepped on the steps of the Lincoln Memorial and said:

I have a dream that one day this nation will rise up and live out the true meaning of its creed: "We hold these truths to be self-evident: that all men are created equal." I have a dream that one day on the red hills of Georgia the sons of former slaves and the sons of former slave-owners will be able to sit down together at a table of brotherhood. I have a dream that one day even the State of Mississippi, a desert state, sweltering with the heat of injustice and oppression, will be transformed into an oasis of freedom and justice. I have a dream that my four children will one day live in a nation where they will not be judged by the color of their skin but by the content of the character. I have a dream today.

I have a dream today. I have a dream that one day every valley shall be exalted, every hill and mountain shall be made low, the rough places will be made plain, and the crooked places will be made straight, and the glory of the lord shall be revealed, and all flesh shall see it together. This is our hope. This is the faith with which I return to the South. With this faith we will be able to hew out of the mountain of despair a stone of hope. With this faith we will be able to transform the jangling discords of our nation into a beautiful symphony of brotherhood. With this faith we will be able to work together, to pray together, to struggle together, to go to jail together, to stand up for freedom together, knowing that we will be free one day.

This will be the day when all of God's children will be able to sing with a new meaning, "My country, 'tis of thee, sweet land of liberty, of thee I sing. Land where my fathers died, land of the pilgrim's pride, from every mountainside, let freedom ring." And if America is to be a great nation, this must become true. So let freedom ring from the prodigious hilltops of New Hampshire. Let freedom ring from the mighty mountains of New York. Let freedom ring from the heightening Alleghenies of Pennsylvania. Let freedom ring from the snowcapped Rockies of Colorado! Let freedom ring from the curvaceous peaks of California! But not only that; let freedom ring from Stone Mountain of Georgia! Let freedom ring from Lookout Mountain of Tennessee! Let freedom ring from every hill and every molehill of Mississippi. From every mountainside, let freedom ring.

When we let freedom ring, when we let it ring from every village and every hamlet, from every state and every city, we will be able to speed up that day when all of God's children, black men and white men, Jews and Gentiles, Protestants, and Catholics, will be able to join hands and sing in the words of the old Negro spiritual, "Free at last! Free at last! Thank God Almighty, we are free at last!"[30]

---

30 Martin Luther King, Jr., "I Have a Dream," ttps://en.wikipedia.org/wiki/ I_Have_a_Dream, accessed September 3, 2016.

Now, whatever you may think of Martin Luther King, I think we all have to admit that this dream of his resonates in the heart of every Christian and causes us to want that kind of brotherhood between persons of all races, between genders, between nations, between all people. From Mahatma Gandhi to Martin Luther King to John Lennon, famous people have dreamed of world peace and the brotherhood of man. But these dreams float away like the mist in the wind. We hear more about wars and rumors of wars.

Deep in the darker side of the human heart the need to hate forages around for new victims. Self-loathing turns outward. Anyone different from us is fair game, especially if he/she/they are in the minority—a difference race, a different religion, a different denomination, a different nationality, a different gender. My feelings of inferiority will build a hollow pyramid of pride by putting others down.

Who would have dreamed that forty years after King's speech bombs would be bursting in Belfast, bombs would be bursting on subways, little children would be taught to pack themselves with dynamite and blow their bodies to bits, and towers would come tumbling down? Hatred is the nuclear weapon of the mind, and when it detonates, social order is destroyed, families are torn apart, and genocide is its offspring. But what is the answer, or is there one?

I agree completely with what Ronald Reagan said in a speech he delivered after becoming President, known as his "Evil Empire" speech. In it he said, "While America's military strength is important, let me add here that I've always maintained that the struggle now going on for the world will never be decided by bombs or rockets, by armies or military might. The real crisis we face today is a spiritual one."[31] The landscape of the world has changed since that speech thirty years ago. The Cold War is over. Yes, Russia and Putin are lurking in the shadows, and, according to former world chess champion Garry Kasparov (a Russian), the most dangerous man in the world is

---

31 Ronald Reagan, "The Evil Empire," https://www.youtube.com/watch?v=do0x-Egc6oA, accessed September 3, 2016.

Vladimir Putin.[32] But there is another Evil Empire seeking to destroy all that we hold dear—Radical Islam with its many faces (Hezbollah, Al Qaida, and ISIS). They hate us.

According to James Olson, former Chief of Counterintelligence at CIA headquarters in Langley, Virginia and now a professor at Texas A&M, ISIS is already among us. He said our current government has pulled personnel out of all five protective arms of the CIA. America is porous. With just the American citizens who have converted to the Islamic State, there are enough cells within our country to do major damage to a dozen American cities.[33] Yes, like Reagan, I am for a strong military. But there is something more powerful than bombs. And that's where we come in.

The vision of Grace School of Theology is simple but far-reaching: to train spiritual leaders in every country of the world who can teach others about the love of Christ, a love that cannot be earned and cannot be lost. My friends, I think the Lord has opened a window for us. We can do things through communication to reach the world that were impossible just ten years ago. I think it is our last chance to try to overcome the hatred, the bitterness, the internecine strife, the prejudice, the genocide, the tribalcide, the infanticide, the sex trafficking, the inequities, and the injustices of this world. Bombs won't do it. Bombs can pulverize people, but they are not an antivenin for the poison of hatred. Bombs may destroy cities, but they are not a barricade against the bacteria of bitterness. Bombs may even wipe out a nation, but they are not a vaccine for the virus of vengeance. Only love is more powerful than hatred, bitterness, and vengeance. And everywhere I have traveled in this world, people are screaming out

32 Gary Kasparov, http://www.dailymail.co.uk/news/article-2775295/Gary-Kasparov-declares-Vladimir-Putin-dangerous-man-world-greater-threat-US-ISIS.html, accessed September 3, 2016.

33 James Olson, "The CIA & the War on Terror, The U.S. Response to the Emergence of ISIS. What can we do to keep America safe?" (Conroe, TX, October 2, 2014).

for a love they don't have to earn and a love that they can never lose. There is only one source for that kind of love. We know the source. We have the source. He is "the light of men," but we are "the light of the world." Come. Help us take it to the world.

Take what to the world, you ask? The cross, of course. And that is exactly what Paul does in Ephesians 2:11-22. We said Ephesians 2-3 is about the Creation of the Church. God had a role (2:1-10), Christ had a role (2:11-22), and Paul had a role (3:1-13). In this lesson we focus on Christ's role: Alienation before the Cross (11-12); Reconciliation by the Cross (13-18); and Unification after the Cross (19-22).

EPHESIANS
"The Purpose Driven Church"

SALUTATION	1:1-2
INTRODUCTION—"Spiritual Blessings in the Heavenlies"	1:3-14
(Paul's Prayer for Perception)	1:15-23
BODY	2:1-6:9
I. Creation of the Church (Its Position)	2:1-3:21
A. God's Role	2:1-10
B. Christ's Role	2:11-22
1. Alienation before the Cross	11-12
2. Reconciliation by the Cross	13-18
3. Unification after the Cross	19-22
C. Paul's Role	3:1-13
(Paul's Prayer for Possession)	3:14-21
II. Conduct of the Church (Its Condition)	4:1-6:9
CONCLUSION—"Spiritual Battles in the Heavenlies"	6:10-20
FAREWELL	6:21-24

I. ALIENATION BEFORE THE CROSS   2:11-12

¹¹ Therefore remember that you, once Gentiles in the flesh—who are called Uncircumcision by what is called the Circumcision made in the flesh by hands—¹² that at that time you were without Christ, being aliens from the commonwealth of Israel and strangers from the covenants of promise, having no hope and without God in the world.

In this great book, we are looking at the creation of a mystery unforeseen on in the OT, the mystery of the Church. And in this Church we will see that God is using Christ to create one new man, where racial barriers are broken, where social barriers are busted, and where nationalism is not an issue. We looked at God's role in making the Church (2:1-11). Now we look at Christ's role (2:12-22). And in 2:11-12 he describes the alienation of Gentiles before the cross.

"Gentiles" is a word first used by a Gentile: Alexander the Great. As he conquered the world and went around setting up Greek "city-states" (think of Washington, D.C.) to help Hellenize the world (instill Greek philosophy and way of life throughout the world), Alexander said anyone living outside one of his city-states was a Gentile. There were ten of these city-states around the Sea of Galilee. They were known as the Decapolis (ten cities). About a hundred years after Alexander (d. 321 BC) the Jews in Alexandria, Egypt, asked for a copy of their Jewish Bible in Greek because that was their spoken language instead of Hebrew. So the Septuagint was born as a group of scholars in Jerusalem translated it from Hebrew to Greek. These Jews then picked up the term "Gentile" and used it of anyone outside the commonwealth of Israel, that is, any non-Jew. Thus you had the Jews and everyone else—the Gentiles. As mentioned in an earlier lesson, this is the greatest racial divide in human history.

From Paul's perspective as a Jew, the Gentiles did not have much going for them: without Christ, without covenants (promises from God like the Abrahamic, the Davidic, and the New), without hope, and without God. The two words "without God" translate just one word in the Greek text: *atheoi*. It is the only time this word occurs in the Bible, and it is pretty easy to see what English word comes from it: atheist, which in this context simply means "someone without God." It doesn't mean the Gentiles did not have their gods, but if they did not have a relationship with Yahweh, Paul says they are "without God"—atheists.

Can you remember the time when you were without a personal relationship with God? Perhaps you grew up in a Christian home and cannot remember such a time. That would be the ideal. But those who can remember such a time also probably remember the hollowness and the emptiness; remember the yearning without learning; remember the thirst without being satisfied; remember the hunger without being filled. One of the great atheists of about a hundred years ago was George Bernard Shaw, the playwright. He was a cynic that loved to attack Christianity. He was also a modernist that put his faith in science. At the end of his life, he said this:

> The science to which I pinned my faith is bankrupt. Its counsels which should have established the millennium, led, instead, directly to the suicide of Europe [talking about WWI]. I believed them once [meaning the counsels of the scientific community]. In their name, I helped them to destroy the faith of millions of worshippers in the temples of a thousand creeds. And now they look at me and witness the great tragedy of an atheist who has lost his faith.[34]

Nobody seems to talk about God as much as those who insist there is no God. No one seems more hopeless in this world than those who are attacking the very existence of God. But you don't have to be an atheist to be yearning and separated from God; to be longing and know that there is a huge gap between you and God. And let me say,

---

34 George Bernard Shaw, http://biblioblography.blogspot.com/2009/06/lies-christians-tell-george-bernard.html, accessed September 3, 2016.

my friend, if you sense such a separation between you and God, then pay special attention to the verses to comes. Here is where Paul talks about those who are far off being drawn near (2:13-18). If we had Alienation before the Cross in 2:11-12, here we see Reconciliation by the Cross.

II. RECONCILIATION BY THE CROSS 2:13-18

[13] But now in Christ Jesus you who once were far off have been brought near by the blood of Christ.[14] For He Himself is our peace, who has made both one, and has broken down the middle wall of separation, [15] having abolished in His flesh the enmity, *that is,* the law of commandments *contained* in ordinances, so as to create in Himself one new man *from* the two, *thus* making peace, [16] and that He might reconcile them both to God in one body through the cross, thereby putting to death the enmity. [17] And He came and preached peace to you who were afar off and to those who were near. [18] For through Him we both have access by one Spirit to the Father.

You see, this is what the world is missing. I wanted to study the development of hatred between men, so I bought five books. None of them mentioned enmity between men and God. Oh, they talked about enmity between Catholics and Protestants in some countries, enmity between Muslims and Jews, enmity between Muslims and the rest of the world, but none spoke of the enmity between man and God. You see, the self-hatred that turns outward to other people begins with my own self-loathing, which starts with my enmity with God. We were his enemies. You say, "Well, I didn't know I was an enemy of God." But remember back there when Adam and Eve fell? What was the first thing they did? They hid. They covered up. They were full of shame. They were full of guilt and there was a gap and a distance between them and God. Even though God saw them, they began to lie to him. And when we cross the line willfully, when we go against his word knowingly, (and who hasn't done that before he was a Christian and even afterwards), that is enmity between God and us. The enmity and the transgressions bring guilt, and the guilt brings self-hatred and self-loathing. With enough of it, especially if there is a sense of rejection by society, I may lash out against society.

I remember having a roommate I was trying to witness to in college. One day we went out to play golf and were over at Houston Country Club. I forget what green it was, but there was some thunder ahead and clouds were gathering. My roommate lifted up his putter and said, "All right, God! I challenge you now! Come on down here if you exist! Let's fight!" I slowly backed off the green. It does remind me of the atheist who made the same challenge as he said, "I'll prove that God doesn't exist." He challenged God to come down and fight. When he wasn't struck dead and he said, "See, I told you he doesn't exist." Someone standing nearby said, "No, you just proved he is a gracious God. That's all you've proved."

The enmity we are talking about is mentioned in v. 16, but in v. 17 it says Jesus came and preached peace. The Prince of Peace of Isaiah 9 preached peace. One of the first messianic promises in the Bible came in Genesis 49:10 where it predicts that Shiloh would come to bring justice to the world. Shiloh means peace. In Luke 19:38 the people recognized the Messiah coming on the donkey as predicted in Genesis 49:11 and began shouting, "Peace in heaven and glory to God in the highest." When the leaders still rejected him, he wept over the city and said they should have known the day of their peace: "If you had known, even you, especially in this your day, the things *that make* for your peace! But now they are hidden from your eyes" (Luke 19:42). They should have known the day the Messiah would come because of the prediction of Daniel 9:24-27 that said there would be exactly 173,880 days between the decree of Artaxerxes to allow the Jews to go back to rebuild their temple (March 4, 444BC) and the day the Messiah would formally announce his kingship on his triumphal entry into Jerusalem (March 29, 33 AD). All they had to do was count. But they missed it, and they missed his mission: peace. Back in Ephesians Paul shows us that Jesus is our peace in four ways:

1. "Middle Wall of Partition"—five feet high; separated the Court of the Gentiles from the Holy Place where only Jews could enter. The penalty for a Gentile going beyond the wall was death.

2. Symbolism—like the Berlin Wall it symbolized two different approaches to life (like democracy versus communism); this was the great racial barrier of all time: Jew versus Gentile

3. Reason—for the wall was the Law of Moses which separated the Jews and Gentiles

4. Broken—by the cross; the OT Law was fulfilled and abolished by Christ; he put it out of gear; it has no demands or grip on us. He did not destroy it; he put it out of business, out of gear, stripped it of any authority. We don't need to sacrifice lambs in Jerusalem anymore because the Lamb of God has taken away the sins of the world through his single sacrifice for all time and all people.

Through his sacrificial act, the cross, Christ made one new man. I heard some years ago about a father who had a son who was a senior in high school and just could not decide if he wanted to go to Texas A&M or the University of Texas. For those who don't know, that is the biggest sports rivalry in Texas. Well, this kid was really conflicted, so he wrote down the pros and cons for each university. It so happens he was also an excellent artist. He decided to draw a picture that would depict his internal conflict. This was a picture of Sarge, the A&M mascot. But Sarge had horns coming out of his head. He also turned Sarge into a four-legged animal. On his front feet were Aggie boots, but for his back feet he had hooves. At the bottom of his picture the young artist named this beast "Agghorn." Now I know there are those from each university who want to rend your garments at this blasphemous picture, but shifting gears a bit, if you are able, aren't you glad God didn't make a "Jewtile"? He didn't make a mongrel. He made one new man where all these distinctions were blown away. Galatians says there is no more Jew or Greek. There is no more bond, slave, or free. There is no more male or female in Christ Jesus.

The next section, Unification After the Cross, gives us an even better understanding of this barrier breakdown.

III. UNIFICATION AFTER THE CROSS   2:19-22

[19] Now, therefore, you are no longer strangers and foreigners, but fellow citizens with the saints and members of the household of God, [20] having been built on the foundation of the apostles and prophets, Jesus Christ Himself being the chief cornerstone, [21] in whom the whole building, being fitted together, grows into a holy temple in the Lord, [22] in whom you also are being built together for a dwelling place of God in the Spirit.

One house, one building, one temple, one dwelling place where ultimately we and the angels and God will be together singing his praises forever. Now since I can't sing, he's already told me I can have a motorcycle, and I'll be going around one of Saturn's rings, listening to the glorious music. Oh, won't it be wonderful? And even now, scientists have discovered the benefits of that kind of community.

My sister had a classmate in the Baylor School of Medicine named Dean Ornish, who became famous through his "Ornish Diet." He was quoted by *Newsweek* as saying:

Medicine today focuses on merely drugs and surgery genes and germs, microbes and molecules, yet love and intimacy are at the root of what makes us sick and what makes us well. If a new medicine had the same impact, failure to prescribe it would be malpractice. Connections with other people affect not only the quality of our lives, but also our survival. Study after study have found that people who are lonely are many times more likely to get cardiovascular disease than those who have a strong sense of connection and community. I am not aware of any other factor in medicine: not diet, not exercise, not smoking, not exercise, not genetics, not drugs, not surgery, that has a greater impact on our quality of life, incidents of illness, and premature death. We are hard-wired to help each other. Science documents the healing value of love, intimacy, community, compassion, forgiveness, altruism, and service. That's God's intention. That mankind could live together and that we could be connected and that there could be this dream; that there could be this harmony instead of discord; there could be peace instead of war; there could be forgiveness instead of hatred . . .[35]

Sometimes when people come to our church, they stay a few months and then leave. I may run into them and ask, "Why did you leave?" And they will say, "I never felt connected. I never got connected." Oh, my friends, if anybody should be reaching out to connect to others, it is those of us whose enmity with God had been taken away, and we should then be reaching out one to another.

The Mormons have figured this out. No matter where the Mormons call their home, they reach out to help members of the church who live around them. They have a network of mutual concern. The church members are organized into "wards." Within these wards, meals are brought to new mothers, there is help to find housing for people new to the community, help in unpacking after the move. "Mormons are also linked up with other believers for monthly visits in which the members can offer each other a friendly ear in good times and bad, providing a sense of connection amid the complexities of daily life."[36] There's that word **connection** again.

"One house"—"one building"—"one temple"—"one habitation"

---

35 Dean Ornish, http://www.newsweek.com/love-real-medicine-121033, accessed September 3, 2016.

36 Na., "Religion," in *Newsweek* (October 17, 2005), 60.

where God, the angels, and we dwell forever. That is the dream. The question is, how much of that dream can we realize in the midst of this evil, war-torn, prejudice-riddled earth? The answer to that depends on how far we carry the cross and its message of a love that cannot be earned and cannot be lost. Only the cross can open the gate into the garden of peace. Why? It's because the cross has both a vertical and a horizontal dimension. Vertically, the cross reconciles God to man, and horizontally, the cross breaks down the barriers between men. Only the cross covers both dimensions. But we cannot have horizontal reconciliation before we have vertical reconciliation.

CONCLUSION

I want to suggest to you, in conclusion, that whatsoever a man sows that shall he also reap. Hatred begets hatred. Cruelty begets cruelty. Bitterness begets bitterness. But, conversely, grace begets grace. Love begets love. Forgiveness begets forgiveness. And only through the cross do we find the gateway to the Garden of Peace opened up because only the cross takes away the enmity between God and man. Until that is taken away, my own self-loathing is not taken away. Until I stop hating myself, I am not able to love others as God wants me to love.

In the silver screen version of Andrew Lloyd Webber's *Phantom of the Opera* the Phantom lives a tragic life of hiding from the world in the catacombs below the Opera Populaire, the Paris opera house. Born with a hideous birth defect on his face, the Phantom was part of a circus sideshow as a boy, the object of scorn and ridicule from those who would pay to see the ugliness of this "Child of the Devil." One day he killed the man who had profited from his repulsive appearance and used to beat him on a regular basis. A young ballet student, who had witnessed the killing, helped him escape the police by hiding him under the opera house.

The young boy never leaves the opera house. As he grows up he discovers he has many natural gifts. He is a singer, composer, architect, designer, magician—a polymath, a genius in many arenas.

But because of his ugliness he hides from the world behind a mask of his own making, a white mask that hides the half of his face that is so hideous to behold. He makes a home for himself in the labyrinths under the opera house and subsists by haunting the house and bullying its owners into paying homage to him lest he, the Phantom of the Opera, should bring them to financial ruin by frightening the patrons away.

In his loneliness the Phantom longs to have a normal life and a passionate love with a woman of his dreams, but instead he spends his time staring at his own ugly visage in the many mirrors he has erected on the walls of his lair. His only pleasure in life is his tutelage of the young Christine Daae, who shows promise of becoming a future diva. With his tortured soul the Phantom deceives Miss Daae into thinking he is the Angel of Music her late father promised would come to her after his death. As she blossoms into a talented ingénue the Phantom longs to possess her. He becomes insanely jealous when Christine's childhood sweetheart, Viscount Raoul de Chagny, comes on the scene as a patron of the opera and soon wants to reunite with Christine and have her for his wife.

In the climactic scene of the movie the Phantom has captured Christine and taken her below to his underworld haunt. Raoul discovers the hiding place but is not able to rescue Christine before the Phantom ties him to a grate to force Christine to choose between the two suitors. By this time Christine has ripped the mask off the Phantom to expose him as he really looks—nothing to hide behind. He hates her for exposing his ugliness, but at the same time he loves her and longs to have her as his bride. He puts her in a *lose-lose* situation. If she goes with the Phantom, Raoul lives, but she loses him and has to spend the rest of her life with this "Child of the Devil." If she rejects the Phantom, she loses, for then Raoul dies at the hands of his rival. What will she choose?

In her spell-binding response Christine slowly descends into the water and walks slowly but deliberately toward the Phantom. As she approaches him, she is singing, "Pitiful creature, may God give me strength to show you that you are not alone." Then as she comes close and gazes into his eyes, beautiful Christine stretches up and gives the Phantom a passionate kiss on his lips. The Phantom is shaken. He has never experienced this kind of grace, this kind of love, a love that would reach out and embrace him in all of his ugliness, exposed for all the world to see, but most of all for *her*—his beloved—to see. How could she do this?

As though something within him has been set free, the Phantom sets Christine and Raoul free to live their lives together. He prepares to escape the police who are now descending into his hideaway. But before he goes, the Phantom goes around his bedroom and his dressing room breaking every mirror that has held him captive all these years. No longer is he a prisoner of his own ugly image. No longer will he behold his own repulsive defect in the mirror day after day, night after night, year after year. Christine has set him free. Her unconditional love has opened a door.

The Phantom escapes his dungeon. The police never capture him. But he lives on. And his love and gratitude for Christine Daae never dies. We know this because at the end of the movie when Raoul, now an old widower in a wheel chair, visits her grave to pay his respects, he finds a single rose with the ring of the Phantom on its stem, the ring the Phantom had intended for Christine, had they become one.

Of course, *The Phantom of the Opera* is pure fiction. But the truth of the matter is that each of us comes into this world with a defect (our Sin Nature). This defect is so ugly, so depraved and hideous, that we do our best to hide it from the world. We adopt various masks so people will not see how ugly we really are on the inside. But we know. And as we focus on our rotten **Condition** day after day and month after month, our defect wraps its tentacles around us like a giant squid sucking the life right out of us. And we continue to hide, afraid that someone will discover our secret self and turn from us with loathing and disgust.

But Jesus comes along to love us in a way we have never experienced. While we were still ugly (Rom 5:8), he proved his love for us by giving his life for us, going to death row in our place. Our defect did not fool him. He knew about it the whole time. We could not hide it from him. Like Christine (is it a coincidence that the first part of her name is Christ?), he prayed that God would give him the strength to show us we are not alone. There is One who loves us and wants us as his bride—all in spite of our ugliness.

We have no reason to believe the Phantom ever lost his defect. Half of his face would be ugly his entire life. But he was no longer a prisoner of his defect. Christine's love set him free. Just so, Jesus' love and the law of the spirit of life in Christ Jesus is setting us free from the ugliness of our defect (Romans 8), which never completely leaves us in this life. Because of his love we can smash the mirrors, which multiply our wretched **Condition** in our own minds. We no longer have to focus on our miserable **Condition**; we are free to enjoy our wonderful **Position** as the betrothed of the incomparable Son of God.

We can "Dream On." The dream Martin Luther, Jr., shared in Washington so many years ago has a long way to go. In some respects racism seems worse than fifty years ago. This much Ephesians tells us. The key to breaking down racial barriers is the breaking down of a spiritual barrier, the barrier between God and man. Christ accomplished that through the cross. In Christ there are no racial barriers. Spiritual freedom precedes racial and ethnic freedom.

And as we focus our attention on this wonderful **Position** and the blessings that accrue to our **Position**, it begins to affect our **Condition**. Slowly but surely the Master Artist, the Holy Spirit, transforms our **Condition** until it conforms with our **Position**, all the while touching up his portrait until we look more and more like the Son of God who lives in us. Through his living in us we can extend our arms of love and peace to all men and women regardless of color, ethnicity, or nationality. Let freedom ring!

5

FREE GRACE

Ephesians 3:1-13

INTRODUCTION

God calls us to be billboards of grace. Now the word "billboard" does not occur in the Bible, but there are a lot of word images, metaphors for the believer: ambassador, farmer, parent, nurse, soldier, builder, but one of the most interesting is the one we will look at in this lesson. It is the world "steward." Perhaps you are more familiar with the word "stewardship." We are to be good "stewards" of what God has given us. And specifically Paul thinks of himself as a steward of the same thing that was given to the servants in Luke 19. Perhaps you remember that parable. It is translated in most modern translations as "mina." That was three months worth of wages in Jesus' day. I read thirteen translations on that word, and some of them translated it as a gold coin or just coin, but in all cases it was a sum of money. The important thing is this: unlike other parables where the master gives several talents to one, not as many to another, and one to a third, he gives each of the ten servants the same amount of money. Then he tells them to go invest it. He comes back and asks for an accounting, what they did with it. Of course, one of them didn't invest at all; the master chastises him. Point being that each servant was a steward to that sum of money that was given to him. He was expected to do something with it. There was responsibility that went with the gift.

But what was that gift? What was that sum of money given by the master: All got the same thing. What would it be that all believers received that is exactly the same? Is it time? Obviously not. We don't all have the same amount of time, either to live or the same amount of time that is free to serve as we go through this life. Is it money? Well, it couldn't be money, because we have different amounts of money depending on how we have been blessed or what we have inherited or the job we have. So it is not money. Is it gifts? Well, the Scripture clearly teaches we have different gifts, so it couldn't be the same gift. What then is it? That's what we intend to find out in Ephesians 3:1-13. For here Paul talks about what was given to him. As we go through this, let's see what it is that every Christian has been given.

Paul starts off explaining his role in the Creation of the Church. We have seen God's Role in 2:1-10 and Christ's role in 2:12-22. Now we are ready for Paul's Role in the creation of this mystery unforeseen in the OT, something called the Church. We will see the Revelation of Free Grace in 3:1-7 and the Responsibility for Free Grace in 3:8-13. The underlying message in all of this is stewardship. What I am trying to say is that with revelation goes responsibility. To whom much has been given much is required.

Toward the end of my seminary years I was studying for the MEDCAT exam with the intention of fulfilling the vision I thought God had given me in college, which was to be a medical missionary. I had spent some years learning the Bible. Now it was time to learn medicine. I already had verbal acceptance to two med schools, but still had to go through the formalities. Then one day Dr. Charles Ryrie asked me what I intended to do after seminary. He invited me to his office to talk about it. I shared my dream to be a medical missionary. He nodded his head and said, "I think that is a good thing. We need lots of committed Christian laymen. BUT . . . if God has led you to finish this school, I think you have more (then he use the R word on me, and it wasn't Ryrie) responsibility than that." It took him all of five minutes to talk me out of something I had been planning years to do. Essentially he used Paul's argument on me. *With revelation goes responsibility.*

EPHESIANS
"The Creation and the Conduct of the Church"

SALUTATION 1:1-2

INTRODUCTION—"Spiritual Blessings in the Heavenlies" 1:3-14

    (Paul's Prayer for Perception) 1:15-23

BODY 2:1-6:9

  I. Creation of the Church (Its Position) 2:1-3:21

    A. God's Role 2:1-10

    B. Christ's Role 2:11-22

    C. Paul's Role 3:1-13

      1. Revelation of Free Grace 1-7

      2. Responsibility for Free Grace 8-13

      (Paul's Prayer for Possession) 3:14-21

  II. Conduct of the Church (Its Condition) 4:1-6:9

CONCLUSION—"Spiritual Battles in the Heavenlies" 6:10-20

FAREWELL 6:21-24

I. REVELATION OF FREE GRACE 3:1-7

For this reason I, Paul, the prisoner of Christ Jesus for you Gentiles—[2] if indeed you have heard of the dispensation of the grace of God which was given to me for you, [3] how that by revelation He made known to me the mystery (as I have briefly written already, [4] by which, when you read, you may understand my knowledge in the mystery of Christ), [5] which in other ages was not made known to the sons of men, as it has now been revealed by the Spirit to His holy apostles and prophets: [6] that the Gentiles should be fellow heirs, of the same body, and partakers of His promise in Christ through the gospel, [7] of which I became a minister according to the gift of the grace of God given to me by the effective working of His power.

"For this reason." Paul is using a word play here. The word for "reason" is the word *charis*, the same word we use for "grace." But it can mean a number of things, among which are "cause, reason, credit, gift." The translator just as easily could have said, "For this cause, for this purpose." We have said this is a book about the Purpose Driven Church, and that we have purpose driven lives. We are about the praise and the glory of God's grace. We are to be billboards of his grace. Paul says specifically, "I, the prisoner of Jesus Christ, for this purpose, for this cause." He wakes up every morning with a purpose, every morning with a cause, something to live for. Do you have such a cause? I think you have got it, but does it have you? You have it, but do you own it? Do you wake up in the morning thinking this is my purpose for being? Whatever your purpose for being it certainly goes beyond your job. It certainly goes beyond just getting through the day. There is a great, grand, and glorious purpose Paul knew about for his life.

"If indeed you have heard about the dispensation of grace." I certainly had not heard about it when I was in high school. I hadn't even heard about it when I was in college. A "dispensation" sounded like a disease. Instead of "dispensation" just think "administration." The underlying Greek word—*oikonomia*—means the same thing. The Bible appears to reveal seven different administrations in God's governance of men. Each administration had a different President. There was President Adam's first term in the Garden of Eden; his second term outside the Garden. Then there was President Noah;

President Abraham; and President Moses. So five administrations until Jesus. Now we live in administration where the Holy Spirit is the President, also called the Age of Grace. Our president in the next administration, often called the Millennium, will be President Jesus. Some might argue that just as President Adam had two terms, in the Garden and out, so President Jesus has two terms, this age and the age to come. I like thinking of the Holy Spirit as our reigning President since he is operative in a special way during this administration not seen before or afterwards.

Some Bible teachers say this is a relatively new (1850) way of looking at the Bible. Not so. During the first four hundred years of church history, all the Church Fathers looked at it this way. The difference is that they thought each administration was a thousand years long. A man named Augustine came along and changed this way of looking at the Bible, but you need to know that until about AD 400 this was the normal approach. They may have named the Presidents a little differently, but they were all agreed on the last two: Church and Millennium, each to be 1,000 years long. We have simply returned to the way the early fathers looked at human history.

At any rate, Paul calls this administrative period a "mystery." That word in its NT use referred to truth that had not been revealed in the OT. The Church Age, or the Age of Grace, or this dispensation. So what was the big mystery? Simply that Gentiles and Jews could be on an equal standing with each other. Something missed in our English is the repetition of the little Greek word *su-*. It is attached to the word "heirs," "body," and "partakers." It's like the English word "co-" and on co-captains or co-chairs—equal status, footing, privileges. This meant the Gentiles had an equal opportunity to go to heaven, to have a Messiah, to have their sins forgiven, to count for God's kingdom— unheard of. It's like Branch Rickey giving Jackie Robinson equal status, salary, and privileges as his white players, only this barrier busting went way beyond the American game of baseball.

Paul was Branch Rickey to the Gentiles. Paul was a minister according to the "gift of grace" of God given to him. The title of this lesson is: "Free Grace." This is where it comes from. As in Ephesians 2:8-9 the word "grace" is set beside the word "free gift." God is emphasizing that the grace of his gospel is a free gift, no strings attached. You say, "Well, I have always known that." Wonderful. You are in a small minority of those who name the name of Christ. The church I pastored in The Woodlands, TX, "adopted" the former Soviet State of Georgia for a special missions emphasis. Instead of going shallow (a missionary or two) they decided to go deep (invest $100,000 a year and start as many churches as possible). Within a few years they had started twenty house churches. One day, one of our missionaries sent me a picture of a line of about ten Georgian Orthodox priests marching along. There was no explanation, so I asked the significance of the picture. I was told they were headed to one of our house churches to pound on the windows during the worship service. Our message of free grace ran so counter to their theology they wanted to do all they could to disrupt it. I asked what they taught to receive eternal life. Here is the answer I got:

1. Belong to the Georgian Orthodox Church.
2. Repent and turn from all your sins.
3. Come to the church and study for one year.
4. Pass a theological test.
5. Be water baptized.
6. The local priest must decide to let you in.
7. For the rest of your Christian life the local priest has the power to take your salvation away.

You say, "Well, that's just Georgia." Well, not far away is Albania. One of our missionaries wrote me to say he and his wife were the only "free grace" voices in the whole country. I myself went to nearby Bulgaria to speak to seven hundred pastors. All seven hundred thought they could lose their salvation. Does that not sound like there was a string or two attached to their ticket for heaven?

Still others will say, "Not in America?" Here is a message

delivered on television in Houston, TX, not long ago—"Eleven Tests to Determine if You Are a Christian":

1. Have you enjoyed fellowship with the Father and with his Son Jesus Christ?
2. Are you sensitive to sin?
3. Do you keep his commandments?
4. Do you eagerly wait Christ's return?
5. Do you reject this evil world?
6. Do you see a pattern of decreasing sin in your life?
7. Do you love other Christians?
8. Do you experience answered prayer?
9. Do you experience the ministry of the Holy Spirit?
10. Do you discern between spiritual truth and error?
11. Have you suffered rejection because of you faith?

This list is what we call back-end loading the gospel. It is saying, if you have truly received Christ, these are the things you will be doing or will be happening in your life AFTER you have become a Christian. These are all good things, but if you say they **have to** be there or I am not a Christian, you just made them necessary for my salvation. And who could measure up? Do **YOU** keep his commandments? "Well, most of them." Which ones do you break? Surely no big ones like murder or adultery. But Jesus said anger with one's brother without a cause falls into the same sin category as murder, and lusting after a woman in one's heart falls into the same sin category as adultery. And what about that little problem called pride. How are we coming along with that one? May I suggest to you that if this is the list you are going to use to determine your entrance to heaven after you die, you will never know where you are going until you get there.

Are we saying a person could receive Christ as a free gift and live like hell? Oh, they could, but they shouldn't (Paul wrote Romans 6-7 to answer that question). *With revelation goes responsibility.*

II. RESPONSIBILITY FOR FREE GRACE   3:8-13

⁸ To me, who am less than the least of all the saints, this grace was given, that I should preach among the Gentiles the unsearchable riches of Christ, ⁹ and to make all see what *is* the fellowship of the mystery, which from the beginning of the ages has been hidden in God who created all things through Jesus Christ; ¹⁰ to the intent that now the manifold wisdom of God might be made known by the church to the principalities and powers in the heavenly *places*, ¹¹ according to the eternal purpose which He accomplished in Christ Jesus our Lord, ¹² in whom we have boldness and access with confidence through faith in Him. ¹³ Therefore I ask that you do not lose heart at my tribulations for you, which is your glory.

Once again we slow down to highlight the word "that." Paul says this grace was given "that." The word signifies **purpose**. Paul lived a purpose driven life. He had a reason to get up in the morning. He had a purpose. But what about you and me?

Remember that parable in Luke 19 where all ten servants got one mina, a sum of money. When the nobleman returned and asked for an accounting, one had made ten minas, another five minas, and another had not used his mina at all. The nobleman was very angry with the servant who did nothing with the mina given to him. But what was the mina? There is only one thing God gives to every Christian other than the free gift of eternal life. It is the gospel itself. In 1 Corinthians 9:17 Paul speaks of the gospel when he says he has been entrusted with a "stewardship," the same word used here in Ephesians 3:2 and 9. We are stewards of the gospel itself. Like the mina God expects us to do something with this gospel, to share it. *With revelation goes responsibility.*

In 2 Chronicles 7 we find four lepers who are starving. The enemy was inside the city with all the food, while the lepers were stuck outside the city starving. They finally said to themselves, "We're going to die out here. There is no food. Let us go into the city." But one of them retorted, "You go into the city and you'll get killed." "Well, we could die there or die here. Let's at least die eating." So they charged into the city. Unknown to them, the Lord had gotten there ahead of time and chased the enemy army out, leaving a whole city stocked with food.

So the lepers sat down and began to stuff themselves. Then one of them says, "This isn't right. Here we are stuffing our stomachs while our friends out there are starving. **This is a day of good news and we remain silent.**" The gospel is "good news." Woe be unto us if we remain silent. On the other hand, being a good steward doesn't mean we should be obnoxious. If someone gave you a million dollars to invest for him or her, it might help to get some training in how to invest money wisely. It is the same with sharing the gospel. A little training goes a long way. My first attempt was with my best friend on the basketball team in college. He got so mad at me he wouldn't even walk with me from the parking lot back to our dorm. So I remained silent for over a year. Finally I got a little training and actually discovered that most people are eager to talk about spiritual things if you learn to open the door in a non-threatening way. Most churches that believe the gospel can train you.

When we are faithful in our stewardship of the gospel we become partners with God in his **eternal purpose**, according to v. 11. God wants purpose driven churches full of people with purpose driven lives. And what greater purpose could there be than aligning our lives with an **eternal purpose.** There are many wonderful purposes we can choose for our lives. We might purpose to become an excellent football coach, a successful businessman, a college professor, or an accomplished dentist. But unless these pursuits are aligned with an **eternal purpose**, they will perish with the sands of time. Fortunately, in God's economy every worthwhile temporal pursuit can also line up with his **eternal purpose**.

I had lunch recently with a man who had made seven billion dollars in shale oil. He set up a foundation to give most of his money away and remarked, "My wife and I simply view ourselves as stewards of God's resources." A prayer partner friend was ready to retire from medicine almost fifteen years ago when he realized he could align his practice with an **eternal purpose**. There are very few patients that pass through his office without hearing about the good news of Jesus either verbally or through a book he gives them as they leave. This doctor lives a purpose driven life, but his purpose for living is not measured by temporal accomplishments but rather by unobtrusively sharing with people the good news, the gospel.

Paul's concluding words regarding his own role in the Creation of the Church point to his tribulations. He does not want his converts to lose heart at his suffering. Rather he says it is their "glory." How different from the prosperity gospel we hear so much about today. Paul did not glory in his riches, but in his tribulations. I shared the gospel once with a man who was the CEO, President, and COO of one of the largest oil field service companies in the world. He trusted Christ and became a faithful servant in our church. After he retired he built a fabulous home in Carlton Woods, which is an elite section of The Woodlands, TX. The homes probably average three million each, maybe higher.

One evening my friend was at a social gathering to welcome newcomers to Carlton Woods. One of the newcomers turned out to be a minister. When asked where his church was, the minister said it was on the other side of Houston in a rather poor area. My friend couldn't constrain his curiosity: "Why are you living here if your constituency is centered forty miles away?" "Oh," responded the minster, "My congregation rejoices that I live a luxurious life here in The Woodlands. You see, we see material success as a measure of spiritual success. We believe Jesus was a wealthy man. I can't show people how to be successful materially and spiritually if I don't set the example for them." How different from Paul, who asked his constituency to glory not in his wealth but in his tribulations. In another place (Phil 2:17) Paul says he rejoices to think that his life might be poured out as a drink offering to the Lord. And he asks his readers to rejoice with him.

CONCLUSION

In an art gallery in London hangs the most famous painting of Sir Frederick Watts. As you look at the picture you see a man in a casket. It is an open casket. He is lying there peacefully. His life is over. It is a shrouded form, and at one particular end of the casket is a table. An open Bible sits on the table. Then back in one corner is his armor: shield, sword, and helmet. Over in another corner, draped on a chair, is a royal robe, for this was a man of nobility. Leaning in another corner is a lyre, or a guitar. And over the whole room are roses—roses that have been scattered and strewn across the room. But the man can no longer read his Bible; he can't don his armor; he can't smell the roses; and he can't play the guitar. There is a plaque on the wall behind the casket. In German it says, "What I spent I had; what I saved I lost; what I gave I have." It's Watt's way of saying that this life is a stewardship; and there is no more fundamental stewardship than the stewardship of the Gospel, especially the Gospel of Free Grace.

6

FILL 'ER UP, PLEASE

Ephesians 3:14-21

INTRODUCTION

In his book *Tribe*, Sebastian Junger discusses a rather overlooked feature that occurred during the settling of America by Europeans.[37] In their struggle with the American Indians many white European children and women were taken into captivity. Subsequently some of the captives were rescued. But to the shock and dismay of the rescuers most of those rescued, who had lived with the Indians for a significant period of time, did not want to return to their European way of life. Something in their tribal existence with the Indians met their human needs in such a way so superior to their civilized lifestyle that they were willing to sacrifice family relationships and creature comforts to live like Indians. What was it?

The most feared tribe among the Plains Indians was the Comanche tribe, as described by S. C. Gwynne in his excellent chronicle, *Empire*

---

37 Sebastian Junger, *Tribe* (New York, NY: Hachette Book Group, eBook edition, 2016).

of the Summer Moon.[38] He tells the true story of the kidnapping of Cynthia Ann Parker in 1836. Cynthia Ann was just nine years old when she was captured. The Indians killed most of her family on their farm in Grosbeck, Texas. She was hauled off by the Indians to be used later as a bargaining chip for weapons, horses, or for slave labor.

Over the next twenty years the settlers sent many rescue teams looking for Cynthia. As the years went by she became the wife of one of the Comanche chiefs and had three children. Then she was finally rescued. Her rescuers cleaned her up, dressed her up, and put her on display. Everyone wanted to take a peek at the "white squaw." But it was obvious she missed the Indian way of life. At the first opportunity, she tried to escape. Cynthia wanted nothing to do with the white, Christian way of life forced upon her. She tried to escape over and over. Her relatives just kept moving her further and further east, making it harder for her to get back to her tribe. They said her two sons were dead. So she just stopped eating. She's starved herself to death. People were mortified that this young white woman with her Christian background would trade it to live with some wild, heathen, and murdering, nomadic savages. And we have to ask ourselves, why? What did Cynthia Ann Parker find among Indians she was willing to die for?

According to USA Today, an average of twenty veterans a day committed suicide in 2014.[39] There were 7,403 deaths. For men between the ages of 18 and 29 the suicide rate is four times the national average. For women of the same age it is over twice the national average. Interestingly enough, the Post Traumatic Stress Disorder that precedes most of these suicides occurs with the same frequency among returning non-combatants as combatants. What is it that throws these veterans into a depression so deep they opt for self-annihilation?

---

38 S. C. Gwynne, *Empire of the Summer Moon* (New York, NY: Scribner eBook, 2009).

39 http://www.usatoday.com/story/news/nation/2014/01/10/suicide-veterans-rates-high-prevention/4393547/, accessed September 3, 2016.

We know the answer must have something to do with our needs. Some fundamental need is satisfied in tribalism or war settings that goes unmet in "civilized" settings. If we walk through Maslow's hierarchy of needs, we see that right after we have our needs for food, water, and safety met, our greatest need is love. Without love we will always feel insecure, helplessly adrift in the white water of life. When we sense that no one cares, we can easily stop caring ourselves—about ourselves . . . about others. But is the answer that simple? These people just need to be loved? Well, it could be.

Since God made us, he knows about our need for love. Although this letter from God to the Ephesians is primarily about a Purpose-Driven Church, most people cannot clearly find and fulfill their purpose until they know they are loved. So, before moving onto the significance of his readers in Ephesians 4-6, Paul prays for their security, a security based on knowing experientially how much they're loved.

We see the same thing in Paul's development of the Book of Romans. The first part of the book deals with their need for Security (1-11); the second part of book deals with their need for Significance (12-16). Finding eternal security and eternal significance—that's what Romans is all about. When it comes to security, Paul finds his primary source not in the love from people, but in the love of God. In no uncertain terms he says nothing can separate us from the love of God in Christ Jesus (8:31-39). With that statement he seals up our eternal security and is then ready to move on to our need for significance. Chapters 9 through 11 answer a challenge from an imaginary objector, who does not think we can count on the love of God if we reject him. For his proof he points toward Israel. His claim is that when the leaders of Israel rejected Jesus, God rejected the nation of Israel. Paul writes three chapters of inspired Scripture to prove that God did not reject Israel. And the point is, if Israel is secure, then so is anyone who's been grafted into Israel, like all the Gentile believers in Christ. With eternal security firmly stated (Rom 8:31-39) and defended (Rom 9-11), Paul is ready to discuss eternal significance. This will be found as we understand the Body of Christ and find our place in it.

Paul does exactly the same thing in the Book of Ephesians. After explaining the wonderful heavenly blessings we have in Christ in heavenly places (1:3-3:13), he seals off the section on our eternal security with this prayer about God's love for us (3:14-21). Then, just as he did in Romans, Paul moves on (4-6) to the Body of Christ so his readers can find their eternal significance.

So in his first prayer Paul prayed that our spiritual eyes might be opened to the resurrection power available to us (1:15-23); now in his second prayer Paul wants us to have our eyes opened to just how great God's love for us really is. In our analysis of this prayer we want to look at Paul's Posture (14-15), his Petitions (16-19), and his Purpose (20-21). Let's start with his posture.

I. PAUL'S POSTURE IN PRAYER 14-15

[14] For this reason I bow my knees to the Father of our Lord Jesus Christ, [15] from whom the whole family in heaven and earth is named, . . .

"Bow my knees." If you were to visit Israel today, you would see Jewish people dressed in black garb standing at the Western Wall praying. In fact, at all their holy sites you would see the religious Jews standing while they pray. They usually have a slight rocking motion that accompanies their prayers as well. I have yet to see anyone in Israel praying on his knees. Perhaps that's something they do in private.

In my own prayer life, most of my prayers are done while I'm sitting. But when occasion calls for it, I get on my knees. What occasion might that be? Well, it could be any occasion, but usually it's an occasion of dire need. Praying on one's knees spoke of great sincerity and earnestness. Our posture in prayer can be an indication of the seriousness of our situation. We think of Elijah in 1 Kings 18:42 when he "bowed down on the ground, and put his face between his knees" to pray for God's victory over Ahab and the prophets of Baal. We also remember Daniel whose prayer habit was to kneel in prayer three times a day with his windows open for all to see (Dan 6:41). And later on when Daniel realizes from Jeremiah 25 that the seventy years of captivity are almost over, he set his face toward the Lord God to make request by prayer and supplications, with fasting, sackcloth, and ashes (Dan 9:10).

From these examples we can see that there is no prescribed posture for prayer. Some knelt, some put their head between their knees, some faced toward Jerusalem, and some employed sackcloth and ashes. To postulate a formula for prayer, whether in our posture or our prayer itself, borders on the rituals we associate with magic. It would appear there is great freedom in whatever posture in prayer we might assume. Nevertheless, there do seem to be times when our posture reflects the seriousness of our situation. Paul was serious about his prayer for us.

So much for Paul's posture in prayer. What about his prayer itself?

II. PAUL'S PETITIONS IN PRAYER 16-19

Much like his first prayer (1:15-23) Paul wants the **Condition** of his readers to conform to their **Position**. He has been teaching positional truth for almost three chapters. He is ready to transition from **Position** (1-3) to **Condition** (4-6). This prayer is his transition. He's going from Head Knowledge to Heart Knowledge, **Position** to **Condition**. He prays for their Em-Powering by the Spirit (16), their In-dwelling by Christ (17-19a), and their Up-Filling by the Father (19b).

A. Em-Powering—by the Spirit 16

. . . that He would grant you, according to the riches of His glory, to be strengthened with might through His Spirit in the inner man, . . .

"His Spirit"—Paul's mind is back to 1:3-14 where we saw blessings from the Father (3-6), the Son (7-12), and the Holy Spirit (13-14); now Paul moves in reverse order through the Power of the Spirit, the Love of the Son, in the Fullness of the Father. We are about to enter a beautiful castle of divine riches available to us via our Position in Christ. All the riches of the Godhead are at the disposal of every child he ever created. Any attempt to describe the depth of these riches leaves one with an overwhelming sense of inadequacy, kind of like an ant trying to hug Mt. Everest. Specifically, in his reference to the Holy Spirit Paul again focuses on the power of the Spirit as he did in his first prayer (1:15ff). With this power the Christian has divine enablement to do the impossible, to accomplish the supernatural. Why? Simply because we have a supernatural being living inside us with his supernatural power available to live a supernatural life.

And where does this power operate? Is there a divine fireworks display for all the world to see? Not exactly. This power operates in what Paul calls the "inner man." Because this supernatural power strengthens the "inner man" the Christian has the ability to persist and endure all the stress this world has to give without fracturing. We can't think of the "inner man" without also thinking of Paul's words to the Corinthians:

> [7] But we have this treasure in earthen vessels, that the excellence of the **power** may be of God and not of us. [8] We are hard-pressed on every side, yet not crushed; *we are* perplexed, but not in despair; [9] persecuted, but not forsaken; struck down, but not destroyed—[10] always carrying about in the body the dying of the Lord Jesus, that the life of Jesus also may be manifested in our body. [11] For we who live are always delivered to death for Jesus' sake, that the life of Jesus also may be manifested in our mortal flesh. [12] So then death is working in us, but life in you . . .
>
> [16] Therefore we do not lose heart. Even though our **outward man** is perishing, yet the **inward *man*** is being renewed day by day. [17] For our light affliction, which is but for a moment,

is working for us a far more exceeding *and* eternal weight of glory, [18] while we do not look at the things which are seen, but at the things which are not seen. For the things which are seen *are* temporary, but the things which are not seen *are* eternal (2 Cor 4:7-18).

Here the "outward man" is perishing, passing away. But the "inward man" is being renewed daily. Clearly the outward man is the physical body. The inward man must then be spiritual. One is temporal; the other is eternal. One is outer; the other is inner. What is this "inner man" of which Paul speaks? Does the non-Christian have this inner man, or is it something created by God when a person is regenerated, born again? Could we think of this inner man as a capacity or dimension that can be filled or empty? Could this inner man be the "God shaped vacuum" attributed to Blaise Pascal: "There is a God shaped vacuum in the heart of every man which cannot be filled by any created thing, but only by God, the Creator, made known through Jesus"?

Actually, Pascal never wrote the words "God shaped vacuum," but what he wrote was even more profound:

> What else does this craving, and this helplessness, proclaim but that there was once in man a true happiness, of which all that now remains is the empty print and trace? This he tries in vain to fill with everything around him, seeking in things that are not there the help he cannot find in those that are, though none can help, since this infinite abyss can be filled only with an infinite and immutable object; in other words by God himself.[40]

What Pascal and most especially Paul were trying to say is that man is more than material. As such he cannot be satisfied with material

---

40 Blaise Pascal, https://www.evangelismcoach.org/2009/god-shaped-vacuum-exist/, accessed September 3, 2016.

things. In fact, strange as it may sound, an emptiness in the inner man is actually one of the causes of posttraumatic stress disorder (PTSD). In his book, *Tribe*, Junger speaks of extrinsic values versus intrinsic values. By intrinsic values he refers to the feeling of competence, the feeling of authenticity, and the feeling of connectedness.[41] By extrinsic values he is describing an acquisitive society where self-worth is measured in terms of getting more and better: a bigger and better house, a bigger and better job, a bigger and better car, a bigger and better retirement account, and so on. Although there is nothing inherently wrong with bigger and better things, they're usually acquired through competition. If I win, I have more than you. A competitive society promotes the rugged individualism that says I don't need you and you don't need me. A psychic isolationism can envelop an individual such that he feels very alone and doesn't know where he belongs. When God created man, he created a communal being, where interdependence and a sense of belonging are vital for fulfillment.

Military service strips away acquisitive distinctions and individualism. It all starts with boot camp. The new recruit has his head shaved and wears the same clothes as everyone else. He soon learns that it's all for one and one for all. A band of brothers may develop such as A Company in World War II during the Normandy Invasion. According to Stephen Ambrose those men experienced something intrinsic during war they never found again and spent the rest of their lives looking for. What was it? Obviously with their lives at stake they discovered an interdependence like no other. Every man had to do his part and had a vital part in the mission. Competitiveness and acquisitiveness are foreign concepts that have no meaning in a struggle for survival.

Studs Terkel quotes from a former gunner in the 62nd Coast Artillery named Win Stracke in his book *The Good War*:

For the first time in our lives . . . we were in a tribal sort of situation

---

41 Junger, 66.

where we could help each other without fear. There were 15 men to a gun. You had 15 guys who for the first time in their lives were not living in a competitive society. We had no hopes of becoming officers. I liked that feeling very much... It was the absence of competition and boundaries and all those phony standards that created the thing I loved about the Army.[42]

When veterans come home to a competitive society where their self-worth and significance are measured by extrinsic, material acquisitions, the adjustment is just too overwhelming for many of them. Some of them can't even find jobs, let alone compete. Suddenly their lives seem to have no meaning and no purpose. They don't belong to anything, and in many cases no one seems to care.

According to Junger, "America's great wealth, although a blessing in many ways, has allowed for the growth of an individualistic society that suffers high rates of depression and the anxiety. Both are correlated with chronic PTSD."[43] Instead of finding a job so they can contribute in a meaningful way to society, the minimum wage jobs they are offered make it next to impossible to raise a family. It's much easier to take the lifelong disability offered to them by the government.

Though we would never equate the intrinsic values recognized by Junger with the fruit of the Spirit, nevertheless, he does identify three "feelings" considered more necessary to happiness than external values like beauty, money, and status. In a way he is saying that it is what's on the inside that counts. In this prayer Paul acknowledges the same. He does not pray for beauty, money, or status. He prays for something internal, something to fill up the inner man. He prays for what the unregenerate man longs for, strives for without knowing, and in some cases would rather commit suicide than to keep on living without. He longs to be filled with God on the inside. And, as we shall see in the last half of Ephesians, all the values Junger highlights in the tribal experience are provided by the church. By church I don't refer

---

42 Ibid., 216.

43 Ibid., 236.

to the Country Club down on 1st and Main. No. I'm referring to A Company, a band of brothers and sisters, where each member belongs and is needed for the success and survival of the "tribe."

Sometimes students at our seminary, Grace School of Theology, want to know why the modern church differs so much from the first century church. What happened to the interdependence and the sharing in a sacrificing of one for all and all for one? Some would say it's because we do not recognize the full gospel in the sense of utilizing the sign gifts described in the Book of Acts and 1 Corinthians. But may I remind you that the pastoral epistles (first and second Timothy and Titus) were written specifically to tell believers how to conduct themselves in the church of God (1 Tim 3:15). But the sign gifts are never mentioned in these epistles.

Could it be that part of the vitality of the early church was because the church was at war? Most of the epistles were written during Nero's persecution of the church (AD 54-68). The church was fighting for its very survival. If they didn't hang together they wouldn't make it. Real corruption in the church didn't begin until Constantine recognized Christianity as an official religion of the realm. As Howard Hendricks used to say, "The greater the heat, the greater the expansion." Perhaps the best illustration of this principle is modern-day China. According to Tom Phillips there are 100 million Christians in the underground church in China.[44] And it's growing at ten percent per year. At that rate, by 2030 China will have the largest contingency of Christians in any nation in the world. Is it a coincidence that this phenomenal growth is accompanied by persecution?

Contrast that to the church in Western civilization. There is no persecution of Christians in Germany or Spain or Canada or America. I'm not referring to the encroaching anti-Christian agenda of those who would like to eliminate our first amendment rights. I'm talking

---

44 Tom Phillips, http://www.telegraph.co.uk/news/worldnews/asia/china/ 10776023/China-on-course-to-become-worlds-most-Christian- nation-within-15-years.html, accessed September 4, 2016.

about the kind of persecution that would put you in jail. If and when that comes to the West, you just might see a revival of first century church Christianity.

And so before going into specific instructions on how to win the war (4-6), Paul prays for God's band of brothers and sisters that they might be fortified in the inner man by God's the Spirit, God the Son, and by God the Father. We have seen his prayer for empowering by the Spirit. Let's look at his prayer for an indwelling by Christ.

B. In-Dwelling—by Christ   17-19a

> [17] that Christ may dwell in your hearts through faith; that you, being rooted and grounded in love, [18] may be able to comprehend with all the saints what *is* the width and length and depth and height—[19] to know the love of Christ which passes knowledge; . . .

This is where Paul shifts from **Position** to **Condition**. He knows Christ dwells in the hearts of his readers because they're already believers. They are seated in Christ at the right hand of God the Father. He doesn't have to pray for Christ to dwell in their hearts. He already does. So what's this all about? Perhaps the word "dwell" can help us. This is not the normal word used of a temporary dwelling such as we saw in 2:19 with the word for sojourners/foreigners/aliens (*paroikoi*). No, this is the word for a permanent dweller, an owner, a possessor (katoikeō).

Perhaps the best illustration of this is found in the little book *My Heart, Christ's Home.*[45] The idea is that Christ might be in our hearts without possessing our hearts. He entered our hearts by faith, and now he must possess our hearts by faith. In Romans 1:17 it says, "the righteousness of God is revealed from faith to faith; as it is written, *'The just shall live by faith.'*" The just are not the unjust. The just are

---

45 Robert Boyd Munger, *My Heart, Christ's Home.*

believers. The victorious Christian life is a life of faith. It takes faith to apply the principles of our **Position** to our **Condition**. It takes faith to believe that we are new creatures in Christ. It takes faith to believe that my sinful nature has been deposed and I no longer am its slave. It takes faith to believe all my sins are forgiven—past, present, and future via my **Position** in Christ. And it takes faith to give my whole heart to the one who already lives in me. That's what Paul is praying for.

In other passages like Philippians 1:1, Paul sees himself as a slave, owned by Christ. Here he becomes a home, a dwelling place, which Christ purchases and moves into in order to possess. Rather than being possessed by a demon, we are to be possessed by Christ. With my heart as Christ's home, Paul sees the entire home filled with the love of Christ: 1) After laying a firm foundation of love, Paul speaks of 2) The dimensions of the house (width, length, depth, height) of Christ's love.

The words "to know" further underscore the fact that Paul's focus has switched from **Position** to **Condition**. It's the Greek word *ginōskō*, which is the Greek word for experiential knowledge. He doesn't want his readers to know about this in their heads; he wants them to experience this in their hearts.

Love may just be the greatest of our inner needs. The first needs listed by Maslow are physical needs: food, water, and safety. The next need in the hierarchy is love or a sense of belonging. Of course, the two go hand-in-hand. If one feels love, he senses that he belongs. And here Paul prays his readers might "comprehend" the dimensions of Christ's love. The word translated "comprehend" (*katalambanō*) or "grasp" means "to seize, to make one's own, or attain," when used in an active sense. In other words, it carries with it something a little more aggressive than just an intellectual understanding.

Paul describes this love as though there is a house with a foundation and walls and a basement, perhaps, and more than one story. All facets of this love surpass the understanding of human intelligence. In so many ways, God's love does not make sense. The cross itself may be the foundation of God's love. The voluntary sacrifice of an innocent person for the sake of paying a penalty deserved by guilty people does not make sense. The forgiveness of future sins through that same sacrifice does not make sense. The imputation of the perfect righteousness of the innocent into the account of the guilty does not make sense. And on it goes. But as we view this beautiful diamond of God's love for us through Christ from angle to angle, facet to facet, dimension to dimension, we become filled with the fullness of God.

Victor Hugo tried to paint a picture of God's love in his book *Les Miserables*.[46] The foundation of God's love was laid by the priest who did not turn Jean val Jean into the gendarmes when he stole some silver from the parish manse. In fact, he stunned Jean val Jean by telling him he had forgotten to take some of the silver and gave him another candelabra right in front of the police. Then he whispered in Jean's ear, "Go and do likewise." The transforming effect of God's love began to do its work. Jean could not comprehend that kind of love. He decided to spend the rest of his life doing good for others. He became a wealthy industrialist and provided jobs for hundreds in his home town—the **width** of God's love.

Then Jean had the opportunity to help one of his employees, a poor woman whose misfortune it was to have been taken advantage of through a summer love, the only legacy of which was a young child, Cossette. Fired without cause Fantine went to the streets. Jean rescued her—the **depth** of God's love. After Fantine died, Jean adopted Cossette as his own, but his love was so possessive he would not give her the freedom to live her own life and find her own love. But the love of God kept growing in him until he actually risked his life to rescue Cossette's young love, Mario, from death in the French Revolution—the **length** of God's love. Finally, when he had his nemesis, Javert, the inexorable personification of the law, in his sights, he lets him go, knowing that mercy triumphs over judgment—**height** of God's love.

Such is the transforming power of the love of God. That's why the

---

46 Victor Hugo, *Les Miséserables* (New York, New York: Signet Classics, 2013).

mission statement of our school centers on the love of God, a love that cannot be earned and cannot be lost. That kind of love doesn't make sense. That's why it must be "grasped." We must reach out for supernatural comprehension of a supernatural love, perhaps the only thing more powerful than hatred. I am convinced a peace-loving world will never win the war against ISIS by bombs. Like the Greek Hydra, we can cut off one head and two will come up in its place. But through the love of Christ we have a chance.

A volunteer with Global Mission Outreach told me that ISIS recruited 50,000 volunteers during a three-month period. But during that same three months their mission, which utilizes a satellite 24/7 transmitting the gospel message around the world, had 3,000,000 indications of people receiving Christ as their Savior and hope. Many of these were in Muslim countries where the people were responding to the poison of hatred spread by ISIS by saying, "Enough of this hatred; show us a better way."

Again, "to know" = *ginōskō* = the Greek word for **experiential** knowledge. Paul furthers his transition from **Position** to **Condition**. This love of Christ is not sitting up there in heavenly places alone. It is right here on planet Earth available for us to experience. Ironically, Paul wants us to know the love of Christ that cannot be known. In both cases the word for knowledge is *ginōskō*. I think this is Paul's way of saying we will never plumb the depths of God's love.

In the days before sonar there was a man named Fridtjof Nansen, an arctic explorer. He liked to record the depth of the ocean as he voyaged through uncharted waters. He did this by means of a Plumb Bob. He tied weight onto the end of a piece of long string or rope to measure the depth of the ocean. At one particular spot the Plumb Bob did not hit the bottom, so he recorded in his ledger, "Deeper than that." The second day he tied more rope onto his Plumb Bob but still didn't hit bottom, so he recorded, "Deeper than that." On the third day he took all the available rope on the ship, tied it together, lowered the Plumb Bob, and did not hit bottom. He recorded, "Deeper than that," and sailed away from that spot never knowing the depth of the ocean. So it is with the love of Christ. We can never plumb the depths of his love. We shall always sail away not knowing just how deep his love for us really is. All we can say is, "Deeper than that." As the songwriter put it:

> To write the love of God
> Would drain the ocean dry.
> Nor could the scroll contain the whole
> Though stretched from sky to sky.

The end result of the Em-powering by the Spirit and the In-dwelling by Christ will be the Up-filling by God the Father.

C. Up-filling—by God   19b

. . . that you may be filled with all the fullness of God.

"That" signifies a **purpose** or **result** clause. Though the Greek construction used here (*hina* + the subjunctive) usually means purpose, it can also mean result. It would seem that verses 17-19a focus on the love of Christ. Therefore, I would suggest that the result of grasping and experiencing the love of Christ is that we are filled with the fullness of God. Here we cannot but think of John 17:3, which says, "And this is eternal life, that they may know You, the only true God, and Jesus Christ whom You have sent." Again, the word for "know" is *ginōskō*. Henry Blackabee correctly translates this *Experiencing God*.[47] When we experience the love of Christ, we have experienced God. And this is "eternal life."

More often than not, the emphasis on "eternal life" in the NT is not on quantity but quality. After all, unbelievers exist forever. Believers exist forever. So linear time is not the issue. It is the quality of our existence that makes the difference. The unbeliever exists forever without God; the believer exists forever with God. We might say that

47 Henry Blackabee, *Experiencing God* (Nashville, TN: B&H Publishing Group, 2008).

"eternal life" is the "abundant life" Christ came to offer (Jn 10:10b), and this life lasts forever. But the quality of this life can increase. The more of God we experience, the more of life we enjoy. That is one reason the Christian life can be the most exciting, fulfilling life anyone could live, whether he is in Communist China or the United States of America. This life is experienced on the inside, not the outside, the inner man, not the outer man.

The "fullness" (*plērōma*) of God has puzzled theologians for centuries. It's another one of those concepts so huge we have trouble getting it into our little, finite minds. We might best understand the fullness of God as simply a summation of his character qualities.[48] We know that some of these qualities cannot be developed in us, such as omnipresence. But many of his attributes can be developed within us. The NIV and NASB[49] probably render the best understanding here. "All the fullness of God" is preceded by a three letter Greek word: *eis*. Rarely does this word mean "with." It usually speaks of a goal and can be translated "with a view to," that is, with a goal in mind. So it's not that we are filled **with** the fullness of God, but we are filled with Christ's love with a goal in mind: the fullness of God, or his character formed in us.

Another Christ-like character taken from the world of fiction is Melannie in Margaret Mitchell's *Gone with the Wind*. She always seemed filled with the love of Christ, and, as such, she radiated many of the character qualities of God himself. She always saw and believed the very best about every person, whether it was Madam Belle Whatley or even her jealous and scheming sister-in-law, Scarlett. Her radiant smile seemed capable of melting an iron fortress of self-centeredness. And so it is as Paul shifts away from the first half of his letter to the Ephesians. Grounded in their **Position**, Paul can't wait to see the truth transferred into the **Condition**.

---

48 See Hoehner, 301-04.

49 NASB has "that you may be filled **up to** all the fullness of God"; the NIV says "that you may be filled **up to the measure** of all the fullness of God."

Almost fifty years ago my pastor at the time, Neil Ashcraft, told a story about his first visit to the Puget Sound. He was pastoring in the Oakland area and went to visit a friend in Washington, who lived right on the Puget Sound. Neil had never seen the Puget Sound. He always heard how beautiful it was, so he couldn't wait to get to his friend's home and get down to the edge of the water. But he said it was a great disappointment. In fact, he said it was ugly. There was a lot of mud, broken branches, and just a bunch of junk. Neil's friend could see the disappointment written on his face. He smiled and said, "Oh, you don't understand. Right now the tide is out, and this place really does look ugly. But we'll come back when the tide is in. It is one of most beautiful places on the planet."

So it is when the Christian is walking according to the flesh. The tide is out, and everything looks pretty ugly. There's mud and brokenness and a lot of junk. That's how it is when we as God's children are filled with ourselves. Gifted though we may be, it's hard for others to see Christ in us. But when we are filled with Christ's love, then an ongoing work is taking place on the inside to make us more and more like Christ. That's when the tide is in, and it's one of the most beautiful sights on earth.

As we come to the end of this great passage, it just may be that the best is yet to come. We saw Paul's Posture in Prayer, his Petitions, and now let's look at his Purpose in Prayer.

III. PAUL'S PURPOSE IN PRAYER   20-21

> [20] Now to Him who is able to do exceedingly abundantly above all that we ask or think, according to the power that works in us, [21] to Him *be* glory in the church by Christ Jesus to all generations, forever and ever. Amen.

"Exceedingly abundantly" = *hyper* + *ek* + *perissou* = above + beyond + abundantly. All three Greek words are combined here to make *hyperekperissou*. There is no single word in Greek more effusive in its expression than this one. It is the equivalent of supercalifragilisticexpialidocious. In other words, God can answer our prayers "exceedingly above and beyond" anything we could have imagined. All of us can probably give examples of prayers where God answered us in ways far greater than we thought possible. Sometimes, however, the timing and the manner in which God answers these prayers will surprise us. There is no better example than the prayer of Christ on the cross predicted in Psalm 22.

In Psalm 22 we have a righteous man calling for help. We know it is a righteous man because in the first verse are the words of Christ on the cross: "My God, my God, why have you forsaken me?" We can understand when the prayers of an unrighteous man go unanswered. But the prayer of a good man? Christ was praying for deliverance from the cross. He couldn't bare the thought of separation from his Father. He had already been rejected by the disciples, his best friends on earth, and the nation. But his own Father? If he took the sins of the whole world on his back, he would be separated from his Father for the first time. Sin causes a separation between the sinner and God because God is perfectly holy. He cannot fellowship with sin. So God the Father told God the Son, "No. No, I am not going to deliver you from the cross." So Christ died. Apparently, the prayer of a righteous man, a good man if there ever was one, went unanswered. Until you get to Psalm 22:22ff.

Here the petitioner is praising God. He is saying God is not deaf that his prayer went unheard, and God is not dead that his prayer went unanswered. God did hear, and God did answer. But he answered the prayer in a better way and at a better time. If he had taken Christ down from the cross in his mortal body, that body still would have died one day. But through the death and subsequent resurrection, Christ was given an immortal body and is the first fruits of all believers who will receive a similar "glorified" body to enjoy forever. So the prayer was answered in a better way. But it was also answered at a better time. If Christ had been taken down from the cross before his death, there would have been no substitutionary atonement for the sins of all mankind. Since he was the God-man, he was the only one who could offer a sacrifice sufficient to pay for the sins of the entire human race.

But by answering his prayer through the resurrection, now all have the opportunity to enjoy eternal life by believing in his person and his work.

But notice that Jesus never saw his prayer answered in this life. He prayed on Good Friday, but his prayer wasn't answered until Easter Sunday. With a foot in both worlds, Jesus could look back after the resurrection and say, "Wow. What an answer—at a better time and a better way. You have answered exceedingly above and beyond anything I could have hoped or wished for." So too we will see the answer to many of our prayers in this life until we reach the next. And when we do, we will probably be surprised at how many of our prayers have been answered at a better time and a better way.

"To Him be the glory"—it's not about us, is it? So many of our prayers are like Old MacDonald's wife: "Gi' me, gi' me here, gi' me, gi' me there; here a gi' me, there a gi' me, everywhere a gi' me, gi' me." Then we wonder why these prayers go unanswered. Paul's prayer lines up with God's will—the maturity of these believers through progressively becoming more like Christ. Who gets the glory for all that? God, of course. As we saw way back in 1:14, it's all "to the praise of his glory." Our existence is not anthropocentric, meaning God does not exist for us. It is theocentric, meaning we exist for him.

CONCLUSION

We began this lesson with the observation that a disproportionate number of veterans, both combatant and non-combatant, commit suicide. Short of suicide depression appears to be endemic among those who return from war. Why, we asked. Similarly, we asked why so many white settlers preferred the tribal life of "uncivilized" Indians to that of "white, Christian" society. In fact, as early as 1612 the Spanish observed with amazement that forty or fifty Virginians had married into the Indian tribes. They had been in America only a few years.[50]

---

50 Junger, 38.

Emigration invariably went from the civilized to the tribal, not vice versa.[51]

In 1753 Benjamin Franklin wrote, "When an Indian child has been brought up among us, taught our language and habituated to our customs, if he goes to see his relations and makes one Indian ramble with them, there is no persuading him ever to return."[52] By contrast, when white captives were freed from the Indians, it was almost impossible to keep them at home. "Tho' ransomed by their friends, and treated with all imaginable tenderness to prevail with them to stay among English, yet in a short time they become disgusted with our manner of life . . . and take the first good opportunity of escaping again into the woods."[53]

A French émigré named Hector de Crèvecoeur lamented in 1782: "Thousands of Europeans are Indians, and we have no example of even one of those Aborigines having from choice become European. There must be in their social bond something singularly captivating and far superior to anything to be boasted of among us."[54]

The question for Western society isn't so much why tribal life might be so appealing—it seems obvious on the face of it—but why Western society is so unappealing.[55] The answer seems to be wrapped up in the communal nature of man. God made man to be a communal being. According to Junger, both agriculture and industrialization increase man's capacity for accumulation.[56] The accumulation of personal property allows people to make more and more individualistic choices about their lives, and those choices reduce any group efforts toward a common good. As society modernizes, people find themselves able

---

51 Ibid., 23.

52 Ibid., 23-24.

53 Ibid.

54 Ibid., 37.

55 Ibid., 49.

56 Ibid., 54.

to live independently from any communal group. A person living in a modern city or suburb can, for the first time in history, go through an entire day—or entire life—mostly encountering complete strangers. They can be surrounded by others and yet feel deeply, dangerously alone.[57]

Apparently, as affluence and urbanization rise in a society, rates of depression and suicide tend to go up rather than down.[58] Rather than buffering people from clinical depression, increased wealth in a society seems to foster it. According to a global survey of the World Health Organization, people in wealthy countries suffer depression as much as eight times the rate they do in poor countries.[59] Apparently financial independence can lead to isolation, and isolation can put people at a greatly increased risk of depression and suicide.[60]

Soldiers in war form little bands of brothers. It's a modern form of tribalism with its struggle for survival and its lack of focus on accumulation. These little tribes find a communal experience almost completely lacking in our modern, civilized society. Some of their deepest internal needs are met through their tribe in a way that rugged individualism cannot: the sense of belonging, the sense of being needed, the sense of competency, and a sense of purpose. Love.

Let's not be confused. In no way am I suggesting we should all go to the Middle East to fight ISIS so we can get our communal needs met. Nor am I suggesting we should become nomadic Indians. I'm simply observing what PTSD and the appeal of tribalism are telling us. Man's primary needs our internal, not external. All our external needs can be met, while at the same time we can be greatly depressed. I would suggest that tribalism and the bonds of war only partially fulfill some of man's innermost needs.

---

57 Ibid., 55.

58 Ibid., 56.

59 Ibid., 58.

60 Ibid., 60.

As Pascale noted, only God is able to fill up the vacuum within the heart of man. And it is through the local church that God has made a way for the communal needs of man to be met during times of war or peace. There he can find a sense of belonging. There he can find his ability (spiritual gift[s]) to contribute to a great cause: the kingdom of God. There he can discover that others need him. And when his spiritual gifts are being used, he will experience a sense of competence. But it all begins with the love of Christ. This is man's greatest source of security. And before man can feel significant, He needs to feel secure. That's why Ephesians 3:14-21 precedes Ephesians 4.

7

US-US

Ephesians 4:1-6

INTRODUCTION

Sholom Aleichem, a writer and humorist, tells a story about the court-martial of a young soldier charged with failing to fire his weapon during a battle.[61] The soldier freely admitted that he was ordered to shoot when he saw the enemy.

"Then why didn't you shoot?" someone asked. "But I never saw the enemy," the soldier explained. "I just saw people." You see, in order to see an enemy, an US-THEM mentality must be developed. Once the US-THEM distinction is made, all sorts of ghoul and evil can be front-end loaded onto THEM until WE can actually justify in our minds the need to kill THEM.

In July 1941, we are in a little town spelled Jednwabni, Poland,

---

61 Rush W. Dozier, Jr., *Why We Hate* (New York, NY: McGraw-Hill, 2002), xi.

population 3200 people, half Jews and half Gentiles. The halves are not segregated but intermingled, living right next to each other. Of course, this is WWII, two years after Hitler's invasion. However, there are no Nazis in this little town. But in one day the Gentiles killed every single Jew except seven—roughly 1600 people in one day.[62] All the adult Gentiles participated in one form or another. It was not the result of a madman like Hitler; he had nothing to do with it. It was the result of extreme hatred, prejudice, and bigotry. We cry out, "What kind of past led to that kind of cruelty?"

Perhaps we are tempted to say, "Well, that's Europe. They have always been cruel to the Jews." Maybe. But sixty-five years ago a young American soldier entered a bus in Montgomery, AL, from the front instead of the back. That was a mistake. You see, the color of this soldier's skin was black. Blacks were not allowed to enter a bus in Montgomery, AL, from the front. A policeman clubbed Thomas Brooks to the ground and shot him dead.[63] That's why it took so much courage for Rosa Parks to refuse to give up her seat to a white man five years later in Montgomery, AL. She helped inspire the Civil Rights Movement. How do we explain this kind of insanity? US-THEM.

Again, we may be tempted to say, "Well, that was a long time ago. The world is a much more civilized place today." Really? Boka Haram, a militant Muslim group in Nigeria, is using little kidnapped girls as suicide bombers to kill Christians (summer, 2014).[64] US-THEM. Shiites blow up Sunnis in Yemen. US-THEM. ISIS beheads Christians in Iraq. US-THEM.

---

62 Willard Gaylin, M.D., *Hatred* (New York, NY: Perseus Books, 2003), 1-2.

63 Ellis Cose, "A Legend's Soul is Rested," in *Newsweek* (November 7, 2005).

64 Alexander Smith, http://www.nbcnews.com/storyline/missing-nigeria-schoolgirls/boko-haram-appears-be-using-abducted-girls-suicide-bombers-experts-n284456, accessed September 4, 2016.

We could multiply the examples. Wherever humans congregate the US-THEM mentality develops. Freud attributed it to what he called the *thanatos*, one of the three strongest urges in the human being, the urge to kill. As Christians we recognize hatred as a work of the flesh, meaning the sin factory living inside each one of us. That Sin Nature within us will scan for THEM. Who exactly are THEM? Pretty much anyone you are against without a cause. Could be people with a different skin color. Could be people of a different political party. Could be your next-door neighbor whose dog keeps doing its business in your yard. God forbid, it could even be someone in your own church. In general, anyone who is not a member of your "in-group."

God sent the Letter to the Ephesians express mail through a deliveryman named Paul. Its intent was to pulverize the US-THEM mentality. Ephesians calls purpose-driven people to become part of a purpose-driven church to enter into this dark, hate-filled, vengeful world to be lights and billboards of his grace, to be advertisements for his love. As Paul wrote to the Corinthians, "to show them a better way" (1 Cor 13). But love and unity are difficult to achieve if we are full of US-THEM distinctions. We often stereotype THEM by universalizing the things we don't like about some individuals among THEM. Soon we are prejudiced against THEM. Anger, hate, and violence are the children of prejudice.

I was raised in a liberal Methodist church in Nashville, TN. Never heard the gospel there. No one in my family had a personal relationship with Christ. But I very well remember the day my mother gathered my three sisters and me into the living room of our home to warn us. "What's up, mom?" Now I consider my mother a well-educated, highly intelligent woman. Here was her answer: "Children, I need to warn you that some Baptists are buying the property across the road." She was silent as that somber truth weighed in on us. Our response was pretty much the same: "And so?" "Well, children, Baptists are strange people with some strange beliefs. Just be on the look-out." "OK, mom...we'll be careful." Until we moved further out from Nashville a few years later, I always looked at that Baptist house kind of the way Scout and Jim looked at Boo Radley's house in *To Kill a Mockingbird*. No telling what kind of evil incantations those Baptists were up to.

We are now ready for our big transition. Transition from what to what? From **Position** to **Condition**. Remember, we have said that the first three chapters of Ephesians are about **Position**, but the last three are about **Condition**. Oh, yes, the salient message of the book is about the Creation (1-3) and the Conduct (4-6) of the Church, but the connection between **Position** and **Condition** is too obvious to ignore. So let's review our basic premise: nothing in your **Condition** can ever change your **Position**, but focusing on your **Position** can greatly improve your **Condition**.

The first part of that statement is about "eternal security." We need the assurance that nothing we ever do in the future can change the fact that we are seated in heavenly places at the right hand of God the Father **in Christ**, and nothing can pluck us out of his hand (Jn 10). We are a bunch of forever-forgiven sinners. We could spend the rest of our lives trying to plummet the depths of that kind of love, but we will never get there. However, a deeper and deeper understanding of that kind of divine love can free us up to love other people, to turn the US-THEM tendency to US-US. Other human beings are not the enemy. At the end of this book Paul points his finger at the enemy. It is principalities and powers and the rulers of darkness in heavenly places, that is, demons. There is the US-THEM. It is US against THEM—the demons. We do not wrestle against flesh and blood. Within the human race it should be US-US. But only the cross can get us there. Let's see how.

EPHESIANS
"The Creation and the Conduct of the Church"

SALUTATION — 1:1-2

INTRODUCTION—"Spiritual Blessings in the Heavenlies" — 1:3-14
(Paul's Prayer for Perception) — 1:15-23

BODY — 2:1-6:9
  I. Creation of the Church (Its Position) — 2:1-3:21
  II. Conduct of the Church (Its Condition) — 4:1-6:9
      A. The Goal: Maturity of the Body — 4:1-16
          1. Through Unity — 1-6
          2. Through Diversity — 7-11
      B. The Means: Maturity of the Individual — 4:17-6:9

CONCLUSION—"Spiritual Battles in the Heavenlies" — 6:10-20

FAREWELL — 6:21-24

The answer to the US-THEM mentality is unity. Christ established the potential for that unity when he broke down the wall of partition between the Jews and the Gentiles. This destroyed all human distinctions. Without distinctions there can be no US-THEM. But the potential established and the potential realized are two different things. Nevertheless, what is true in our **Position** can become true in our **Condition**.

I. OUR CALL TO UNITY   4:1-3

A. The Walk   4:1

I, therefore, the prisoner of the Lord, beseech you to walk worthy of the calling with which you were called . . .

"**Therefore.**" We can't underestimate the importance of this word as it makes the transition from heaven to earth, from **Position** to **Condition**. It is the swing word taking us away from the message of chapters 1-3 into the message of chapters 4-6. "Therefore" also let's us know that these are not two separate messages. They are connected. There would be no second message without the first. The second is based on the first. Our expected **Condition** is based on our exalted **Position**. Paul wants the realities of our heavenly blessings to be reflected in the realities of our earthly existence. So he calls us to unity in vv. 1-3 and then gives us the basis for unity in vv. 4-6. In the first sixteen verses of this chapter he is going to start talking about unity and diversity within the same body. That body is made up of individuals each with different gifts. There is unity, but there is diversity in this wonderful mystery unforeseen in the OT, the Body of Christ, the universal Church.

"**Beseech.**" Paul does not command us. He does not say, "I draft you." He does not say, "I threaten you." He says, "I beseech you, I invite you, I encourage you, I urge you." It is a volunteer army. It is one where you will pay a price. It is one where there will be meaningful misery, or as Chuck Holten says in his book *A More Elite Soldier*: "Are you willing to be an elite soldier for God? It's not all guns and glory. It is a life of purpose-filled privation, meaningful misery, postponed payment. It is never easy, but always worth it. Pursuing God's purpose is by definition the hard road, the path that few will be willing to follow."[65] Some will have ears to hear.

"**Walk.**" When Paul says that word "walk," he is talking about our conduct in life, the way we live our lives. He says this walk is to be **"worthy of the calling with which you were called."** This high calling in Christ Jesus is that God has selected us to be part of an elite group of troops of special people, a holy people, a kingdom of priests, but sent as missiles into a dark world, not to destroy it but to heal it and

---

65 Charles W. Holten, *A More Elite Soldier* (New York, NY: Multnomah Books, 2003).

to light it up. But again, though all of God's children are called to walk this walk, it is still an invitation. You do it because you want to, not because you have to. But be aware. Once you cross that line to join his army, the world is watching.

A preacher decided on his day off to do a little work around the house instead of playing golf. So he got out his tools and was putting some siding on the house. A little boy from across the street wandered over, sat down, and crossed his legs. He just watched the preacher work on the siding, not saying a word. The preacher thought to himself, "Maybe the boy just wants to learn a little about carpentry, and he probably admires me because I am a preacher." When he couldn't stand the silent treatment any longer, the preacher said, "Well, young man, why don't you come over here so I can teach you a little bit about carpentry?" The little boy said, "No, thanks. I know you are a preacher and I just want to see what you say when you hit your thumb with a hammer." Well, I don't know what the preacher would have said, but I do know this, the world is watching.

A London pastor got on one of those double-decker buses, paid his fair, sat down, and then looked at his change. He realized the bus driver had given him too much. In our money it was only about a quarter, not much, and he thought to himself, "No big deal." But then he thought, "Well gosh, it is really not mine. Maybe it is the Lord's blessing for that good sermon I gave last night." But then he thought, "I better give it back." So when he got off the bus, he went to the bus driver and said, "Sir, you made a mistake. You gave me a little too much change, so here is the extra quarter." The bus driver said, "That was no mistake. I was sitting in church last night when you preached on honesty. I just wanted to see if you practice what you preach." The world is watching.

In the movie "Back to the Future" a mad scientist souped up a Delorian with the ability to take off like a drag racer until it hit the necessary threshold to go back or forward in time. Every time this feat was accomplished, the Delorian left some scorch marks on the road where it was before its transition. The only evidence of this unseen reality was the scorch marks. In his book *Disappointment with God*, Philip Yancy asks, "If the unseen world really is making contact with the seen world, the natural world, where are the scorch marks, the sure sign of the supernatural presence?"[66] I like that. Scorch marks. If the supernatural has really intersected with my life, where are the scorch marks? What is left that the world can see to say something supernatural has happened here? Something has gone on here I can't explain from natural causes. Those scorch marks are lights in the darkness. Those are billboards of God's grace. Those are advertisements of his love.

Robert McQuilkin, former president of Columbia Bible University, once remarked, "What is the average Christian experience? Church members typically behave like moral, upright non-Christians. They are decent enough but there is nothing supernatural about them."[67] Nothing supernatural. We are called by the Apostle Paul and by the Holy Spirit to walk "worthy of the calling to which we were called." That's the call. Thankfully Paul tells us how to do it. If we find the walk in v. 1, then we find the way in vv. 2-3.

B. The Way   4:2-3

> [2] with all lowliness and gentleness, with longsuffering, bearing with one another in love, [3] endeavoring to keep the unity of the Spirit in the bond of peace.

Will you notice this call to unity does not say we have to achieve unity, accomplish unity, or develop unity? He says, ". . . keep the unity." In our **Position** in Christ, we are united. It is only the devil that divides and conquers. It is the devil that wants to split us up, and

---

66 Philip Yancy, *Disappointment with God* (New York, NY: Harper Paperbacks, 1991).

67 Robert McQuilkin, in a commencement address at Dallas Seminary, May, 2000.

it is the devil that fills us with prejudice and bigotry and anger and hatred and snobbiness.

There is a Way to War and a Way to Peace. Paul gives us the Way to Peace. Four words: lowliness, gentleness, longsuffering, and love. Let's look at them more closely.

1. "Lowliness" = tapeino + phrosuneis = humble + attitude = a humble attitude

"Lowliness" is a word that speaks of humble thinking. Jesus was lowly—humble thinking. I like a word from John Stott on this.[68] He thinks it is the "key" to unity. He said the greatest single secret of concord is humility. It is not difficult to prove this in experience. The people we immediately and instinctively like and find it easy to get along with are the people who give us the respect we consider we deserve. Well, the people we immediately and instinctively dislike are the people who treat us like dirt. If, however, we give them our respect by recognizing (and here is the key) their intrinsic God-given worth, we shall be promoting harmony in God's new society. You see, humble mindedness is not putting myself down. It isn't going around saying, "Ah, shucks," every time you get a compliment; it is not that. It is lifting others up and not falsely so. It is recognizing, as Stott says, the intrinsic value in every single human being and knowing God is absolutely colorblind. Not one of these distinctions made on earth register with him. All created, equally loved, all the same. "Lowliness" of mind; that is where it starts.

2. "Gentleness" = praute-tos = meekness = not fighting for one's rights

---

68 John Stott, https://www.pinterest.com/langhampartners/john-stott/, accessed September 5, 2016.

3. "Longsuffering" = makro + thumias = long + anger = a long fuse

4. "Love" = agape- = selflessness

In contrast to this Path to Peace is the **Way to War**:

Us-Them > Superior to Them > My Rights Violated > Anger/Envy > Hate

The Way to War comes from an US-THEM attitude. It starts right there. Now they say little children don't have those attitudes. I think back to nurse Nelly in *South Pacific*. She finds the love of her life, Emile, a Frenchman living on one of the Polynesian islands during WWII. American soldiers and nurses are stationed on the same island trying to figure out what the Japanese are going to do next. Emile courts Nellie without letting her know he had been married before to a Polynesian girl. They had two children together before Emile's wife died. Nellie is all ready to marry Emile when she finds out about the little children, who are a little darker color than Emile and Nellie. It throws Nellie for a loop. Her prejudice from her background slips its ugly hand around her heart and squeezes out her love for Emile like a ghastly skeleton squashing a gourd on Halloween. She can't believe the conflict within her. Where did she learn US-THEM? Where did she learn to hate? She finally concludes she had been *taught* how to hate. Little kids don't really make distinctions between US and THEM until about age seven. And then they catch the attitudes of their parents. These attitudes filter down until the children are *taught* to make these distinctions.

Out of the distinctions comes an air of superiority, the thinking WE are better than THEY—whatever our group, nation, or race. Then, if it just so happens that we find our rights violated, some sort of offense, that leads to anger, and anger leads, or can lead to hatred.

Now I want you to notice how easy it is to fall into this stuff. I thought I was pretty much free from all this even before I became a Christian, but my wife disagreed. She sent me this thing from the internet and introduced it by saying, "You have a problem with women drivers. US (men drivers)-THEM (women drivers). I only had a little prick of the conscience until I read her Internet ditty. It was about ATM machines and instructions from a bank on how to get money out of an ATM machine from your car. It says: "Drive up to the cash machine; put down car window; insert card into the machine; enter pin; enter amount of cash required; withdraw; retrieve card, cash, and receipt; put window up and drive off." I read that and thought, "Well, yeah, that's what you do." But then I saw the directions for female drivers:

> Drive up the cash machine; reverse and back up the required amount to align car window with the machine; set parking break and put the window down; find handbag; remove all contents onto the passenger seat to locate card; tell person on cell phone you will call them back and hang up; attempt to insert card into machine; open car door for easier access to machine due to its excessive distance from the car; insert card; reinsert card the right way; dig through to find diary with your pin number written on the back page; enter pin; press cancel and reenter correct pin; enter amount of cash required; check make-up in rear-view mirror; retrieve cash and receipt; re-check make-up; drive forward two feet, reverse back to cash machine; retrieve card; give dirty look to irate male driver behind you; restart stalled engine and pull out; redial person on the cell phone; drive two or three miles; release parking break.[69]

I emailed my wife to ask her how this reminded her of me. She said to refer to step 23—"give dirty look to irate male driver behind you." I can't imagine. Be sure to remember my wife sent this to me, not I to her.

---

69 http://wilk4.com/humor/humorm370.htm, accessed September 5, 2016.

The Way to War is the world's way. It leads to division, factions, sects, prejudice, bigotry, abuse of women and children, hate crimes, genocide, and war. But let's go back to the **Way to Peace:**

Us-Us > Humble-Minded > Yield My Rights > Slow to Anger > Love

We notice in God's sovereignty and by the inspiration of the Holy Spirit, the Way to Peace is the opposite of the Way to War. It all begins with US-US. There is no US-THEM in this dispensation. That's what Paul was saying in chapter three. "God so loved the world that he gave us his only begotten son . . ." That's US-US talk. God loves everyone the same—no distinctions. But do you know there are whole groups who name the name of Christ who think God only loves the elect and hates the non-elect.[70] They even think God's hatred and God's love bring equal glory to God. And, in actuality, since these people believe God's love will bring only about ten percent of created humans to heaven while his hatred will send ninety percent to hell, you could say that, according to this view of Christianity, God's hatred brings more glory to him than his love. That's US-THEM theology.

Someone will surely observe that the NT makes a distinction between believers and unbelievers, and the appeal in Ephesians 4 is for unity among the believers, not the believers with the unbelievers. In fact, 2 Corinthians 6 tells the believers to separate from the unbelievers in matters of worship. True, but the difference between the US-THEM mentality and the US-US mentality is the former looks at unbelievers as potential enemies, while the latter looks at unbelievers as potential friends. In other words, God loves the unbeliever just as much as the believer. That's why he sent us out as billboards of grace. That's why

---

70 See Theodore Beza's chart exalting the hatred of God to the same level as the love of God, David R. Anderson, *Free Grace Soteriology* (The Woodlands, TX: Grace Theology Press, 2012), 370, in *Summa Totius Christianismi*, Quellenverzeichnis Nr. 6., translation mine.

the world needs to see our scorch marks, so they can learn about the specific love of God for them when we bring them to understand God's love. To pull this off there must be humble-mindedness where no one feels superior to anyone else. This attitude must be backed up by a willingness to yield one's rights instead of fighting for them (I refer to personal rights, not the rights of other people that may need defending). A slowness to anger and a selflessness reinforce the attitude of humble-mindedness. The ultimate fruit is love, a fruit of the Holy Spirit.

This is not easy. It is walking by the Spirit instead of walking by the flesh (Rom 8:1-6). "Endeavoring" (the first word in v. 3) is the same word used in 2 Timothy 2 when it says, "Study to show yourselves a workman." It is also used in Hebrews 4:11 when it says, "Labor to enter the rest." Labor, study, endeavor—it doesn't say this is easy. It doesn't say this is natural. It says this is supernatural. If you really slow down to think, you might be surprised at how much of the US-THEM mentality is in us. It is really sickening. Of course, our flesh manufactures it, and the only way to counteract it is by the power of the Spirit. Only the fruit of the Spirit can replace the works of the flesh. Right in the middle of his listing of the works of the flesh (Gal 5:19ff) we read: hatred, contentions, jealousies, outbursts of wrath, selfish ambitions, dissensions, heresies, envy, murders. Almost all of those come from US-THEM thinking. But the fruit of the Spirit express US-US thinking: love, joy, peace, longsuffering, kindness, goodness, faithfulness, gentleness, self-control. We have been called to live a supernatural life. A supernatural life requires supernatural power. Our only hope is the substitutionary life of Christ: Christ in you, the hope of glory (Col 1:27). Walk by the Spirit and you will not fulfill the lusts of the flesh (Gal 5:16).

In 4:1-3 we have looked at our "Call to Unity": the Walk (v. 1) and the Way (vv. 2-3). But what is the basis for unity?

II. OUR BASIS FOR UNITY   4:4-6

> [4] *There is* one body and one Spirit, just as you were called in one hope of your calling; [5] one Lord, one faith, one baptism; [6] one God and Father of all, who *is* above all, and through all, and in you all.

OK. Get ready for a shocker: **the basis for Christian unity is not love.** Pretty much all we hear these days is how we are to love one another. That is certainly biblical, but it is not the basis for unity. I can love all kinds of people of different denominations or even different religions or no religion. But that does not mean I can work with them in a Christian project. The basis for Christian unity is not love; **it is what you believe.** This passage does not teach unity at all costs. It does not say if they don't believe Jesus rose from the dead and if they don't believe Jesus died in my place on the cross that I should yoke together with them and go praise God. Paul teaches just the opposite in 2 Corinthians 6. But he does say if certain basic beliefs are there then you are already united and should strive to keep the unity. So what precisely does Paul think are the basics?

1. One Body (the universal church)

2. One Spirit (the Holy Spirit)

3. One Hope (eternal life through Christ)

4. One Lord (Jesus, the Son)

5. One Faith (in Christ as God and Savior)

6. One Baptism (of the Holy Spirit)

7. One God (the Father)

So there you have it. If we can agree on the basics, why divide over the other things? You say, "Well, Dave, I just don't have a clue about what you're talking about." May I stop preaching and go to meddling a little bit? Undoubtedly, the most divisive item in evangelical churches today is the music. In the last church I pastored we had people leave because there were not enough hymns. We had people leave because there were too many hymns. We had people leave because the music was too loud. We had people leave because it wasn't loud enough. You think I'm kidding? Wait. I'm not through. We had people leave because the contemporary music wasn't upbeat enough. And we had people leave because the contemporary music was too upbeat. I know, I know, you are wondering if we had any people left. Actually, we did, but it's a wonder.

The fellowship (this group of thousands of churches refused to be called a denomination) I am in now used to have about 4,000 churches. They lost about forty percent over the King James Only issue. Others have split over wine versus grape juice. And on it goes. Do we not realize, my friends, that unity is one of the highest priorities for God's people, especially in the church? Right out of the box, when Paul shifts from **Position** (Eph 1-3) to **Condition** (Eph 4-6), he addresses unity: strive, work, labor to keep the unity. It's like he is saying, "The unity is already there; just don't mess it up."

So in 4:1-3 we began the transition from our **Position** to our **Condition** with a Call to Unity. Then we briefly looked at our Basis for Unity (4-6)—what we believe.

CONCLUSION

To do our part to help the unity Christ desires, we must transform the **US-THEM** thinking into **US-US** thinking. **US-THEM** thinking says our group or race or nation is superior. **US-US** thinking says all people are created equal and, therefore, have equal value. The **US-THEM** approach views those outside our elite group as potential enemies. The **US-US** approach views those outside our group as potential friends.[71] The first says the rights of those in my group

---

71 Obviously we are not applying this to those who would destroy innocent lives, like ISIS and its ilk. Saving innocent lives is the highest priority (see the Egyptian mid-wives).

supersede the rights of people outside my group. The second says all groups have equal rights. The first says all lives are expendable, but the second says all lives are sacred. **US-THEM** thinking says if I help the members of my group, I will become a better person. **US-US** thinking says if I help the members of my group and the people outside my group, I will become a better person.

OK, that's all well and good, but how do you get to **US-US** thinking? How do you get rid of **US-THEM**? Interestingly enough, even unbelievers have observed that people in a battle lose the **US-THEM** thinking within their team. They have the **US-THEM** thinking toward the people they are fighting, but within themselves the distinction dissolves. That is especially true of war. When your life depends on the man next to you, concerns about color of skin or political views or even social status disappear.

That is even true on athletic teams. Watch any Super Bowl championship or NBA championship or World Series championship celebration and you will see a melting pot of joy, every person of every race hugging one another and jumping up and down. Sadly, it has taken America a long time to get there. I remember when I came to go to school in Texas. Our school (Rice University) was part of the Southwest Conference. There were no blacks playing in the SWC—not in football, not in basketball, not in track.

Then Southern Methodist University stepped out and signed a gifted black student to play wide receiver—Jerry Levias. When he joined the team, his own teammates spit on him. When he went to the showers, they all emptied the stalls. The student trainers would not tape his ankles. At one game, the Cotton Bowl, there were death threats, so he had to be taken on and off the field very quickly, shuttled by other players to protect him, and during the huddle he would kneel down for further protection.[72]

We have come a long, long way from Jerry Levias to Vince Young

---

72 Alexander Wolf, "Ground Breakers," in *Sports Illustrated* (November 7, 2005).

and Reggie McNeal. Even Alabama, where so much of the extreme racism exploded, started a black quarterback this past season (2016). The stands are filled with people of all different races cheering and yelling together for their team because they recognize a team effort.

As Christians we should do them one better. After all, we have the Father, the Son, and the Holy Spirit in common. With these three comes supernatural power, the very power Paul was praying his readers' hearts would be open to comprehend. More than that. We are in a battle. We should be pulling the rope the same way—together. Yes, there is an **US-THEM**. But the **THEM** are not other humans; it is spiritual warfare. Our guns should be aimed at the demonic forces in heavenly places.

Someone who knows me is sure to ask, "But, Dave, what about all those denominations you have preached against all these years?" Well, I confess that early in my ministry I had a lot of heartburn toward denominations since I thought it went directly against Jesus' prayer in John 17 that all his disciples should be one. To be identified as a Methodist, Presbyterian, Baptist, Episcopal, etc., seemed counter to that prayer as I understood it. In fact, when Betty and I left my first church to go to another, they had a roast. All in good fun. But one of the funniest things they did was a takeoff on *Gone with the Wind*. They cooked up a play in which Betty and I were the stars, but my name was Rutt instead of Rhett, and Betty was Starlett instead of Scarlet. Of course, we were in the audience watching all this unfold.

Right in the middle of this little spoof, a rather hefty lady came running down the center aisle yelling, "Oh, Pastor Rutt, Pastor Rutt... de Baptists is coming, de Baptists is coming!" OK, guilty. There was a time when I was stuck in **US-THEM** thinking, where the **THEM** was anyone not part of my church. I have repented. I fully realize there are wonderful Christians in almost all the groups that name the name of Jesus. Though we might differ on some of the basics, which would keep us from yoking together for service, they are not part of the **THEM**. The only **THEMs** out there are demonic and the devil himself. Beyond that it is **US-US**? Everyone in the human race not part of "my" group is a potential friend and team member. Jesus made that possible. When unbelievers look at the Church unified and fighting together against demonic forces, they should see scorch marks all over planet earth.

There are two more things that help develop the **US-US** thinking. One of them is **the same attitude** toward the team. Peyton Manning and Tom Brady are great, Hall of Fame quarterbacks. Though I prefer the private life of Manning over Brady, when it comes to winning Super Bowls, we have to tip our hat to Brady. One year after Peyton Manning signed his 98 million dollar contract with a 34.9 million dollar signing bonus, in the spring of 2005, Brady did something so unusual it caught the attention of the nation. After winning three Super Bowls, Brady was arguably the most valuable quarterback in football, but he purposely signed a contract half the value of Manning's. When asked why, he wouldn't give an answer, but his father spoke up for him. He said, "Tom is so interested in this team's winning more Super Bowls that he knows they could never win if one player takes seventy percent of the money available."[73] He put his money where his mouth was. Team spirit and team attitude. Others are more important than I am. I offer my gifts, my service, my time for the good of the team. That develops **US-US** thinking.

Finally, we need **the same goal**. Probably the most famous run in all of football history was in the 1929 Rose Bowl. Georgia Tech is lined up against the University of California. The score is 7-6 in favor of the University of California. One of the players from the University of California named Roy Reagles picks up a fumble from the Georgia Tech team. You were allowed to run it once you picked it up in those days, so he goes right and then fakes and goes to the left; he swirls this way and that. Finally, he sees daylight and aims for the goal line sixty yards away . . . the wrong goal line. One of the players on his team named Binny Long realizes what is happening and takes off after him. Reagles is a center, while Long is a half-back on the offensive side when they play offense, so he is faster than Reagles. He catches

---

73 *Sports Illlusrated* (November 7, 2005), 49.

his own teammate at the three yard line and turns him around before he can cross the goal line for the other team. But Georgia Tech is already there. They tackle Reagles and put him on the one yard line. The whole fiasco turns into a safety (two points) in favor of Georgia Tech, who wins 8-7.

From that point on, Roy Reagles was known as Wrong Way Reagles.[74] I actually kind of sympathize with Roy. I have run the wrong way a few times in my life. But we need to have **the same goal and the right goal** in mind. And that goal is to shatter the power of darkness; to bust through the powers of the devil; to go forth as elite soldiers on a platoon that is willing to pay the price, that is willing to go into meaningful misery and postponed reward in order to cross that goal line.

Remember when Moses was walking along and saw the burning bush? The bush was burning but it wasn't being consumed. So Moses said, "I will turn aside and I will look at this bush that is burning and not being consumed." That is what God wants for you and for me: to be burning bushes, bushes on fire for him, on fire because of the trials and tribulations that come, the undeserved and even the deserved suffering, but not being consumed. Then the world will stop and say, "I see a bush that's burning but it is not being consumed with bitterness; it is not consumed with hatred; it is not consumed with prejudice and bigotry. Let's go see what that's all about." Talk about scorch marks!!

---

74 Na., "Roy Riegel's Wrong-Way run to Daylight," in The New York Times (January 1, 1929), http://www.nytimes.com/1993/03/28/obituaries/roy-riegels-84-who-took-off-in-wrong-direction-in-rose-bowl.html, accessed September 5, 2016.

8

CAPTURED BY GRACE

Ephesians 4:7-10

INTRODUCTION

In an old movie, Billy Crystal is playing the part of a father that is invited to school where his young son and other fathers have gathered to hear about the work of their fathers. He happens to be a bored baby boomer. He sells radio advertising for a living. His turn comes to share. He starts off and then suddenly goes into a deadpan monologue that sort of bewilders the children. He says:

> Value this time in your life kids because this is the time in our life when you still have choices. It goes by very fast. When you're a teenager, you think you can do anything and you do. Your twenties, however, are a blur. In your thirties you raise your family and make a little money and think to yourself, 'What happened to my twenties?' In your forties you grow a little potbelly, you grow another chin, the music starts to get too loud, one of your old girlfriends from high school becomes a grandmother. In your fifties you have a minor surgery; you call it a 'procedure,' but all your friends know it is surgery. In your sixties you have a major surgery,

the music is still loud, but it doesn't matter because you can't hear it anymore. In your seventies you and your wife retire to Fort Lauderdale. You start eating dinner at 2 o'clock in the afternoon. You have lunch around 10 o'clock in the evening and breakfast the night before. You spend most of your time wandering around malls looking for the soft yogurt and muttering, 'How come the kids don't call?' The eighties? You will have a major stroke and you end up babbling with some Jamaican nurse who your wife can't stand but who you call mamma.[75]

One of those kids listening to that monologue by Billy Crystal could have easily raised his hand and said, "What's the point?"

It was Helen Keller who said, "Many persons have a wrong idea of what constitutes true happiness. It is not attained through self-gratification but through fidelity to a worthy purpose."[76] Purpose-Driven people are not living just to survive or for their own enjoyment. They want to have an influence that lasts. They want their lives to be more than just another piece of sand on the seashore of human history. They want to have an influence that shouts to the world, "It mattered that I lived! It mattered that I lived!"

George Bernard Shaw, though a cynic, spoke these words about purpose in life: "This is the true joy in life, the being used for a purpose, recognized by yourself as a mighty one; the being thoroughly worn out before you are thrown on the scrap heap; the being a force of nature instead of a feverish, selfish little clod of ailments and grievances, complaining the world will not devote itself to making you happy."[77]

The Ephesians are not wanting for a purpose; not after reading

---

75 Chuck Colson, *The Body* (Dallas, TX: Word Publishing, 1992), 168-69.

76 Helen Keller, http://www.quotationspage.com/quote/1964.html, accessed September 11, 2016.

77 George Bernard Shaw, http://www.goodreads.com/quotes/tag/george-bernard-shaw, accessed September 11, 2016.

this letter. It is about a Purpose-Driven Church made up of Purpose-Driven People. We have seen that the greatest influence on the world is made by a united team effort more than the genius of one individual. Teams, not individuals, win Super Bowls. So we need UNITY. But the best teams are made up of gifted individuals who are specialists at their positions. So we also need DIVERISTY. If UNITY asks, "Where are we going?" then DIVERSITY asks, "Where do I fit in?"

EPHESIANS
"The Creation and the Conduct of the Church"

SALUTATION	1:1-2
INTRODUCTION—"Spiritual Blessings in the Heavenlies"	1:3-14
(Paul's Prayer for Perception)	1:15-23
BODY	2:1-6:9
I. Creation of the Church (Its Position)	2:1-3:21
II. Conduct of the Church (Its Condition)	4:1-6:9
A. The Goal: Maturity of the Body	4:1-16
1. Through Unity	1-6
2. Through Diversity	7-16
a. Distribution of Spiritual Gifts	7-10
b. Description of Spiritual Gifts	11
c. Development of Spiritual Gifts	12-16
B. The Means: Maturity of the Individual	4:17-6:9
CONCLUSION—"Spiritual Battles in the Heavenlies"	6:10-20
FAREWELL	

Let's review. Ephesians 1-3 is about our **Position** in the heavenlies; Ephesians 4-6 is about our **Condition** on earth. The first three chapters are about our blessings in heavenly places; the next three chapters are about how to bring those blessings home, how to get them from our heads to our hearts. God's plan to accomplish all this was the Creation of the Church (1-3). With the Church created (1-3), a new way of life was possible (Conduct: 4-6). In Ephesians 4:1 we begin our new Conduct with a new possibility: unity. Through the Creation of the Church, unity has been achieved in our **Position**: no distinctions—racial, social, or gender. But what is true in our **Position** needs to be worked out in our **Condition**: unity. Paul does not say to *create* unity. We already have it. God created it when the Holy Spirit baptized us into the universal Church, the Body of Christ. That church includes Martin Luther and Paul and Billy Graham and you and me. But within this universal church are local expressions of it, and within these local expressions we often find jealousy, envy, and self-seeking. Paul says, "Put all that away." Learn how to love each other through humility (lowliness of mind), gentleness (not fighting for your rights), and longsuffering (slow to anger).

But to reach to our full purpose, we need more than unity. We also need diversity. So unity (vv. 1-6), but diversity (7-16). Diversity through the Distribution of Spiritual Gifts (7-10), the Description of Spiritual Gifts (11), and the Development of Spiritual Gifts (12-16). In this lesson we will just look at the Distribution of Spiritual Gifts: God's Plan (7-8) and God's Purpose (9-10). So what is God's Plan in regard to spiritual gifts?

I. GOD'S PLAN   7-8

[7] But to each one of us grace was given according to the measure of Christ's gift. [8] Therefore He says:

> "When He ascended on high,
> He led captivity captive,
> And gave gifts to men."

"To each one of us." Here the emphasis goes from the team to the individual members of the team. No one is left out; no one is overlooked; there are no Munchkins in the Body of Christ; every person is of equal value; every person is important. I almost entitled this lesson "Each One" because that is one of the great messages of this chapter. God didn't leave any believer out. He gifted every single person who trusted in Christ as his or her Savior, and he did it through his grace. He reached out in his grace to save us, and he reaches out in his grace to sanctify us. By grace we came to faith in him as our personal Savior, and by grace we live this life of personal sanctification. He didn't have to give us gifts, but he wanted to. He wanted to give us something that was special; he wanted each person to be absolutely unique and have a place, a part in this great plan of his. He says each one was given according to the measure of Christ's gift.

Call it OPERATION GRACE. Once more Paul couples "grace" (charis) with the "free gift" (dorea) as he did in 3:7 and 2:8. We didn't deserve salvation, and we don't deserve sanctification. He employs us by grace and empowers us by the same grace. "Free grace"—that's God's plan. We can never deserve salvation, and we can never deserve sanctification. You will wear yourself out trying to be saved, and you'll wear yourself out trying to be sanctified—if you are trying through your own efforts or through the flesh. And so he says, "I have gifted you and placed you in a body where through ministry to one to another in community, through the Holy Spirit, you can grow up." That is what vv. 12-16 are all about: growing up and coming to maturity in Jesus Christ.

"**When he ascended on high.**" This part of a difficult verse we can figure out. After being resurrected, Jesus teaches the disciples for a few weeks. Then in Acts 1 we see him going up into the clouds. The angels say he will come back through the clouds just as he went up, but we know from earlier in Ephesians 1 he went up into the heavenly city, the New Jerusalem, the city that is coming, that already is (Heb 12:22), and he sat down at the right hand of God the Father.

Somehow, and we will never figure this out, but, spiritually speaking, he took everyone who ever had or would believe in him with him—"**he led captivity captive.**" It is the picture of the conqueror of a city setting its citizens free and leading them back home to the city of the conqueror. At the cross Christ conquered his enemy, the devil, and set the devil's captives free. He took those who were held captive by their sin nature. He took those that were held captive by traditions that beat them down. He took all those who were held captive by the things that would keep them from a personal relationship with their creator. He swooped them up and took them home with him and together they are seated at the right hand of God the Father in heavenly places in Christ.

Having ascended, in Acts 2 Jesus sent the Holy Spirit down, and the Holy Spirit "**gave gifts to men**." Who has a gift? Every believer (1 Pet 4:11). If that is true, when does he get the gift? The moment he or she believes. That is when he or she is baptized by the Holy Spirit, and that is when he or she is put into the body of Christ. That is when he or she is given a potential to have an impact forever.

Diana grew up on Stanton Island of New York. In 1999 at age thirty-three she was diagnosed with leukemia. They said she had about nine months to live. Well, she began writing out her will. Normally, looking for a bone marrow donor, they search for someone in the immediate family. They checked all the relatives, but no one qualified to be a bone marrow donor. However, they said they would keep searching.

Time went by and as it went by, Christmas was here. Diana always liked to sit under the big, beautiful Christmas tree at Rockefeller Center. It was sort of a symbol of hope. It had been put up during the depression years. It was so brightly lit with so many lights—just a symbol of hope for lots of people. As it turned out, Diana got a call in February 2000, two months after Christmas, and they said of the four million people who had registered as bone marrow donors, potentially, they found only one match. They called the person, and the person said he would think it over.

A month later, on March 27, 2000, this person agreed to donate bone marrow. The doctor said before putting Diana under that she had six hours for the bone marrow to graft, and if it didn't, they couldn't bring her back and she would die there on the operating table. So she said her prayers and prepared to die. Two hours into it she started feeling strong and the doctors said it looks like it's grafting. It turned out a great success, and Diana was restored to health. She was so full of joy that she wanted to tell the world and wanted to thank person who gave her the bone marrow, but they are always anonymous.

Diana pleaded, "Isn't there some way I can thank this person?" She didn't know if it was an old or young person, man or woman. They said she could write a note and they would pass it on. So she wrote a note and they passed it on. There was no response for months. I think nine months after she wrote the note a man called. His name was David Mason from Massachussetts, thirty-four years old. They exchanged pleasantries and then he called again and again for three months.

Then on December 23rd of 2003, unexpectedly, David showed up at her front door. It wasn't love at first sight, but they began seeing each other, and almost exactly a year later, just before Christmas, under the Christmas tree at Rockefeller Center, David the donor proposed to Diana the receiver.[78]

When I read that story, I thought, "My gosh, that's God's gift; that's God's grace." There we were running around with this dreaded deadly disease of sin in our bloodstream—something we inherited, a sinful nature that would influence all of us to sin and be separated from God. Who could help us? Who could save us? Out of all the human beings who ever lived, only one was found who could qualify. Only one was found who could be a worthy substitute. He died on that cross, and his blood was the substitute to give us life. But even after having done that for me two thousand years ago, I read about it and I believed it growing up, but I didn't really know this person. It was a provision that was out there and then one day, I started getting telephone calls through the Bible, and I was getting messages about his love for me and his grace and his acceptance. As I started coming home, suddenly there was a knock at the door and there he was and he was asking me out and wooing me in a love relationship. He persuaded me that he could be my personal Savior. And over time he slowly unveiled for

---

78 Gary Sledge, "Perfect Match," in *Readers Digest* (December, 2005).

me my own uniqueness and how he could use that for his glory. That's God's plan. That's God's gift. That's God's grace. Have you received it?

We have looked at God's Plan in 4:7-8; what about God's Purpose (9-10)?

II. GOD'S PURPOSE   9-10

> [9] (Now this, *"He ascended"*—what does it mean but that He also first descended into the lower parts of the earth? [10] He who descended is also the One who ascended far above all the heavens, that He might fill all things.)

God not only had a plan; he also had a purpose. Since v. 8 is somewhat obscure, the Holy Spirit gave us vv. 9-10 to explain v. 8. But when I read this explanation, it gets more confusing. Nevertheless, he goes into a parenthesis and says, "Now this, He ascended, what does it mean?" See, he knew we would be a little confused. But then "he also first ascended into the lower parts of the earth." Well, what does that mean? The lower parts of the earth have interpreters divided. Some think it just means he descended from heaven to earth, died, was buried, rose again, and then ascended from earth back to heaven.

Others think he descended from heaven to earth, but when he died, he went on down to the parts under the earth, to Hades where the fallen angels that possessed human beings before the Genesis Flood are kept chained in gloom. In this view his resurrection and ascension began from hell in order to prove that Christ had authority over all things: things under the earth, on the earth, and above the earth. His resurrection and ascension traversed the full gamut of all spiritual authority, both demonic and otherwise, so that some day every knee will bow and every tongue confess that he is King of kings and Lord of lords. I lean toward that latter view, although it is not something I would go to the wall for because the main point of these two verses is not verse 9; it is v. 10.

I said that in vv. 7-8 you have God's plan: Operation Grace. But in vv. 9-10 you have God's Purpose. Where do I see his purpose? It is in v. 10: "He who descended is also the one who ascended far above the heavens **that**. . . ." With the word "**that**" he tells us he is about to tell us the purpose of all this. He says Christ ascended far above all the heavens that "**he might fill all things**." It doesn't say fill all the universe; it says fill all things. But where does that come from and what does that mean? We had this word *plēroō* (fill) in 3:19 and 1:23. In the latter it meant fill the Church and in the former it means fill their cups with love. In this passage I think it means fill us up with a special purpose for living. It is to give us full significance in life.

I like the word "fulfill." It gives you fulfillment, and you will notice that this fulfillment is going to be connected to spiritual gifts. May I be bold enough to say we will never find complete fulfillment in this life through our physical gifts and abilities? God gave those to us. He gave you some natural talents at physical birth. They also are to be used for his glory, but you will never find complete fulfillment through those gifts. You have to add the spiritual gifs to the natural talents. It is the combination that leads to complete fulfillment.

Let me illustrate it this way. If I have a car with eight cylinders, and four of those cylinders are firing, just possibly my car may be able to chug down the street, but it won't be operating as it was designed. It won't be humming down the street. And if God has given you eight cylinders, and you are only running on four, then you will only be half fulfilled. Or if you are running on six, you will be one quarter unfulfilled. He wants us to discover and develop our spiritual side and our spiritual gifts that we might be completely fulfilled.

My conclusion to all this is that we will find our greatest sense of purpose and meaning when we are involved in Christ's mission to take captivity captive. Through his ascension to sit at the right hand of his Father, he has provided forgiveness to all who have or will believe in him by virtue of their **Position** in him. This includes people who have not even been born. But now he has given us a mission. He wants us to help free people from spiritual slavery in their **Condition**. What he has already done in the heavenlies we get to participate in on earth: take captivity captive. He sent us his Holy Spirit to show us how and to empower us for the mission. Let me tell you about some of the captives.

When I was in India I learned that one third of the population is considered subhuman. The highest caste is the Brahmin caste. I met a woman from that cast that had become a Christian. I asked her what she was doing with her time. She said she was working with women in rural India. Helping them with what? "We are trying to stop infanticide." Infanticide? Who is killing whom? "The mothers are killing their daughters." Oh, how could that be? How do they do it? "They poison them." How? "In the food." Oh, come on. How could a mother with her mother instincts systematically kill her daughter? Nundini replied, "They view it as a mercy killing. 'Rather you die now, little one, than grow up a woman like me in India.'" Those people are captives. The government won't help them for fear of interfering in their karma, which might cause those who interfere to come back in the next life as a roach.

"What's wrong with these people?" we ask. It all seems somewhat incredulous. Don't they live in the civilized world? Well, what about the civilized world? In 1990 a man named Breese came out with a book called *Seven Men Who Rule the World from the Grave*.[79] Those men are Charles Darwin, John Dewy, Sigmund Freud, Soren Kierkegaard, Karl Marx, Lord Maynard Keynes, and Julius Welhausen. Let's just take a look at one of them—Karl Marx.

Karl Marx and his sidekick Engels took the dialectical materialism of Hegel and applied it to society. Hegel ruled out the supernatural and believed the material world could spiral up toward Utopia through thesis, antithesis, and synthesis; each synthesis was an improvement over the preceding thesis. So Marx pitted the working class (thesis) against the nobility (antithesis) to help society evolve into a classless utopia (synthesis). But the rights of the individual were absorbed by the higher goal of a classless society.

---

79 David Breese, *Seven Men Who Rule the World from the Grave* (Chicago, IL: Moody Press, 1990).

Now be sure to notice how close this is to what Christ accomplished in breaking down the wall of partition between Jew and Greek and thus dissolving all distinctions. But in the Body of Christ the individual is never lost. Every individual has infinite worth since Christ died for each person. But pull the supernatural out, and the individual has no inherent value. He exists for the good of the state. If he cannot serve the state, he is expendable. In some sense, the thinking of Karl Marx still rules the world, but wherever it goes, Utopia is sure not to follow. Marxism becomes a nice tool for the sinful nature of man to exploit people for the good of the few. Sooner or later, as the individual is forced to serve the state, tyranny results.

Friedrich Hayek was an economist that spent the first half of his life in Germany and Austria. He watched Hitler bring in his "Utopia." He wrote a book that was intended for a small audience: *The Road to Serfdom*.[80] Published in 1945 they made only five thousand copies. It became a cult classic in America, selling five hundred thousand copies in America alone in its initial wave of distribution. In his book Hayek explains how Marxism leads to socialism, which leads to communism, fascism, or Nazism, and then tyranny—serfdom. He spent the last half of his life in England and America trying to warn those countries of what was to come if they continued down the Marxist path.

The Bolsheviks in Russia were the first to try to put shoe leather on Marxism. Much new information has revised the estimates, but all agree that Stalin had at least ten million people starved, shot, or sent to work themselves to death in the Gulags.[81] All for the good of the state, of course. Chiang Kai-shek followed by Mao Zedong tried to bring Marxism into China. Over forty million people died of

---

80   F. A. Hayek, *The Road to Serfdom* (Chicago, IL: University of Chicago Press, 2007).

81   Timothy Snyder, http://www.nybooks.com/articles/2011/03/10/hitler-vs-stalin-who-killed-more/, accessed September 11, 2016.

starvation in the Chinese utopia.[82] Pol Pot went to school in Paris and was indoctrinated to Marxism. He brought it home to Cambodia and killed a million to one and a half million of his own people.[83]

But Marxism lives on. I am told by those better informed than I that the seedbed for Marxism in America is among the tenured professors at our universities. And guess who their subjects are? Our children. These are the captives, people captivated by a great ideal, a classless society. But because they discount the supernatural, they do not realize that fallen man is incapable of harnessing his greed for power and control over other human beings. Marxism winds up in tyranny. How many examples do we need to get the picture?

God has created a classless society within his Church. And he has sent us forth like lights in darkness to free the captives. That is his great purpose for our lives. And we will find our fullest meaning and purpose in life when we are part of that program. It doesn't have to be a big part, but be a part of it.

CONCLUSION

1. **Give spiritual gifts the priority.** When you get to the Judgment Seat of Christ, he is not going to ask you if you were a plumber or a computer technician. If you are, he wants you to do even that work as though you were working for him. But the main question he will ask, if he asks any questions, will be, "What did you do with the spiritual gift I gave you? And what did you do with the spiritual opportunities I gave you?"

This was a hard one for me. Always in school my math and science aptitude and performance outstripped my literary side. I chose my college based on its math and science reputation. I planned

---

82   http://www.independent.co.uk/arts-entertainment/books/news/maos-great-leap-forward-killed-45-million-in-four-years-2081630.html, accessed August 8, 2016.

83   http://www.history.com/topics/pol-pot, accessed September 11, 2016.

on medical school. During seminary I served as a Youth Pastor for Scofield Memorial Church in Dallas. My pastor was resigning at age seventy-two, and he and his wife wanted me to put my name in the hat to be the next pastor. He thought I had some speaking ability that could be developed. I was always scared of public speaking and had only preached three times. So as I prepared to apply to med school he said, "Dave, I respect whatever decision you make. But if you go to med school, I think you are burying a gift in the sand." Obviously, since I still remember his comment, the advice stuck with me. Little did I know at that time I would spend my career primarily in a pulpit. Part of my leading was a sense that spiritual gifts took precedence over natural. Often times they overlap or complement. Someone good at math might make a good accountant, but in heavenly accounting God will be looking beyond the natural abilities he gave us to the spiritual. Blessed is he or she that gets to use both.

2. **There are no Munchkins in the Purpose-Driven Church.** One night I was flipping channels when one of my wife's least favorite movies popped up: *The Wizard of Oz*. She said, "Oh, don't watch that; It is full of witches and evil." So she went to the mall, and I . . . well, you know how it goes. Here comes Dorothy's house out of the tornado, and it plops on the wicked Witch of the West. Dorothy is walking along and out come all the Munchkins. They are so happy because Dorothy has killed a wicked witch. She is their Savior, and they declare an Independence Day with singing and shouting and celebration. Of course, Dorothy and the Munchkins are a fairy tale. In the reality of God's Purpose-Driven Church there are no Munchkins. Only giants. Every member of God's Church is a giant, but he or she may not know it. Each member has a gift and has been "called" to the ministry.

Sometimes people will ask me about my call to the ministry. I answer their question with a question: "OK, but tell about yours first." They usually don't know what I am talking about, so if there is a Bible around, I take them to 1 Peter 4:10, which says, "As each of you has received a gift, let him so minister." There it is. Every believer has at least one gift, and he is called to use his gift to minister to others. No

Munchkins. All giants. All equally important. All gifted children. All called to minister.

George was a pharmacist when I met him. He was new to my church, but it was clear he had a hunger for the Word of God. He would call me over to his pharmacy during the day while he was working. I would sit on a stool behind the counter and watch George count pills for a prescription on his left side while he had his nose in a Bible on his right side. He would ask Bible questions while he filled prescriptions for people who came in. He was a gifted teacher and evangelist, so about the tenth time he called me over, I said, "George, has it ever occurred to you that you are in the wrong business?" Long story short, at age thirty-nine and with two kids in high school, George packed up and headed for seminary. Four years later he was pastoring a start-up church in San Antonio, TX. Twenty years later he retired from NE Bible Church. His son, Robert Paul, followed his dad to seminary and is now his father's pastor. George was a good pharmacist. He could easily have continued dispensing pills his entire career while he taught Sunday School or home Bible studies on the side. But he decided if he wanted to maximize his life and gifts for the kingdom, he needed to go all the way. Either way, had George stayed on as a pharmacist or gone on to become a preacher, he would never be a Munchkin in God's kingdom.

3. **It's never too late.** Charles met his future wife, Ruth, in Dallas while delivering a UPS package. He spent his career with UPS. Toward the end of his career he made a trip to Lake Chapala, Mexico, to minister to some orphans. He fell in love with them and discovered, even at his age, they loved him. Charles just had a way with young boys. So when he was able to retire, he made plans to move to Mexico and live with the orphans. UPS said if he would work another year and a half, they could double his retirement benefits. He said, "No thanks. I think we can make it fine as it is." So Charles and Ruth packed up and moved to Lake Chapala.

Along the way Charles discovered he had a teaching gift as well as a love for orphans. He became quite a Bible student and teaches a men's study on Tuesday mornings and the primary adult Sunday

School class in his church on Sundays. You can tell from the glow on his face that Charles has found his ultimate fulfillment in using his spiritual gifts, even if it took a while to discover them. It's never too late.

Viktor Frankl, the Austrian psychiatrist and holocaust survivor said this: "Everyone has his own specific vocation or mission in life. Everyone must carry out a concrete assignment that demands fulfillment. There he cannot be replaced nor can his life be repeated. Of us, everyone's task is as unique as his specific opportunity."[84]

When Billy Crystal finished his monologue with the kids, his final words were: "Any questions?"

---

84 Viktor Frankl, https://www.goodreads.com/author/quotes/2782.Viktor _E_Frankl?page=2, accessed September 11, 2016,

9

GIFTED AND TALENTED
Ephesians 4:11

INTRODUCTION

Some of you will recognize the name of Phillip Johnson as a professor and famous author. As a professor at the University of California at Berkley for many, many years, his specialty was criminal law. In his mid-40s the university gave him a sabbatical for a year. He went to the University of London. One afternoon as he was wandering about on some of the lush green hilltops outside London with his wife, Kathy, he said, "I'm afraid I have used a first-class mind for only a second class occupation. I am looking for something more significant to do for the rest of my life. I pray for an insight. I'd like to have an insight that is worthwhile. I don't just want to go through my life as an academic who writes papers and spins words." He was getting off a bus on his usual trek toward the university college when he passed by a scientific bookstore. Not being able to resist the draw to go inside the bookstore, he said:

> I couldn't go in without fondling a few things. I went by and saw the powerful and compelling argument for Darwinian

evolution by Richard Dawkins called *The Blind Watchmaker*. I devoured that book and then got another called *Evolutionary Theory in Crisis* by Michael Denton. I read these books and I guess almost immediately I thought, 'This is it. This is what it all comes down to. The understanding of creation.'[85]

He spent all the rest of his sabbatical devouring books dealing with evolution. Finally he looked at his wife and said, "I think I understand this stuff. I think I know what the problem is. However, I am not about to take it up professionally; I would be ridiculed. No one would believe me. They would say, 'You're not a scientist; you're a law professor.' It would be something once you got started with it, you would be involved in a life-long, never-ending battle." He concluded with these words: "That was, of course, irresistible. I started work the next day." And the rest is history. He has not given up his law profession, but as a noted apologist for Christianity, he has found his mission in life.

What I am trying to suggest in this letter written to a Purpose-Driven Church made up of Purpose-Driven people at Ephesus is that at physical birth God gave us certain natural talents and abilities. They may be physical, they may have something to do with athletics or they may involve your inner self: your mind, your emotions, or your will. You may use those talents to make a living. You may use those talents to raise a family, but somewhere along the line, if you have trusted Christ as your Savior, something brand new comes; a new capacity; a new ability; a new talent, if you want to call it that. But instead of being something physical or mental, this is something spiritual. The two often dovetail. They usually don't contradict one another, so God will complement our natural talents with these spiritual gifts to make a package. But if all we do in life is discover various natural talents and never go on as Christians to develop our spiritual abilities and

---

85 Tim Stafford. "The Making of a Revolution," in *Christianity Today* (December 8, 1997).

talents, I am suggesting that would be like Phillip Johnson before his sabbatical. We may be successful. Perhaps we have made a good living. Perhaps we are using the natural talents God gave us, but we are missing out on that which is the most fulfilling of all, a chance to add to something that will last forever.

What I am talking about is his Church. I don't mean a local church at 1st and Holcomb, although the local church is part of the Universal Church. The Universal Church includes local churches all over the world, ever since the Day of Pentecost, for that is when his Church began. The Universal Church will not be burned up; it will be snatched up—the Rapture. To contribute to this Universal Church, whether it is through Young Life or through raising a family in a godly way, through serving in a local church, whatever it may be, is going to be a contribution that will give you a lasting sense of significance because that will be a work that will last forever. Now God didn't intend for this kind of work on his behalf to be drudgery. He wanted it to be a joy. So he gave us these gifts to enjoy when we use them. In the secular world, the old saying from a father to a son was, "Son, find something you enjoy doing and see if you can get paid for doing it. Then you will never work another day in your life." The point being, even if it's your career, if its something you just love to do, it doesn't seem like work.

In the spiritual realm, God is saying the same thing. Find something you love to do that God blesses and you will probably find your spiritual gift. And so this lesson is on finding our spiritual gifts. We have seen in the Book of Ephesians, the first three chapters deal with our **Position** in heavenly places in Christ. Now the last half of the book deals with our **Condition** and how some of the spiritual gifts he's given us can impact planet earth for eternity.

In the first part of chapter four, we saw that the greatest impact will come from a team effort, not just from an individual or two. But as the team comes together it needs to be unified, not splintered. Nevertheless, we saw that great teams have individual specialists. People are fulfilling different parts of the team; one person is a tight end, another is a quarterback, and still another is a linebacker, according to each individual's ability. And, of course, spiritually speaking, that is what Paul is about to get into—the individual players that are a part of a team. So there is unity, but there is also diversity, and they work together to complement each other. So in verse 7-16, we are talking about the diversity in the Body of Christ. We saw the Distribution of Spiritual Gifts in 7-10; now we are going to look at the Discovery of Spiritual Gifts in v. 11.

> [11] And He Himself gave some *to be* apostles, some prophets, some evangelists, and some pastors and teachers, . . .

Before using this verse as a springboard to discuss the Definition, the Description, and the Development of spiritual gifts, let me clarify something with regard to pastors and teachers. Years ago a famous pastor without a lot of training in the koinē Greek of the NT used a particular grammatical rule[86] to come up with what he called the pastor-teacher gift. Now, according to him, part of your life quest was to find the pastor-teacher who is right for you. If you could find this guy, he could take you on to spiritual maturity. In fact, only this guy could take you on. Poor you if you never find him. You could never be a mature Christian. There was just one who was right for you.

Due to his limited training this famous pastor did not know one of the three exceptions to the rule he was using. One of those exceptions is that it never applies to nouns in the plural. You see the word "pastor<u>s</u>" and the word "teacher<u>s</u>"? Both of these nouns are plural, meaning more than one. Therefore, the two nouns cannot be linked together. There is no such gift as "pastor-teacher." In the Universal Church (and that's what he is referring to in these verses—the Body of Christ) there are pastors and teachers. Of course, since the elders in the church were to pastor the flock (Acts 20:28; 1 Pet 5:2) and some of them were to teach the flock (1 Tim 5:17-18), we can deduce that

---

86 See Granville-Sharp's rule in Dan Wallace's *Greek Grammar Beyond the Basics* (Grand Rapids, MI: Zondervan Publishing House, 1996), 271-72, 284.

all the elders were to shepherd (pastor) the sheep, but not all elders were teachers.

Rarely do you find one person with both gifts. Teachers are usually book-people. They have trouble getting out of the office to be with people. Pastors are usually people-people. They have trouble tearing away from people long enough to get into their books to come up with a decent sermon. Every now and then you find one person with both gifts, but even then, there is no such single gift as pastor-teacher. And this is good. God did not design even the local church to depend on one person. Most local churches of any size have both pastors and teachers, and they all work together to edify the local body and the Universal Body of Christ. So let's look first of all at the Definition of Spiritual Gifts.

I. DEFINITION OF SPIRITUAL GIFTS

A. What They Aren't

1. **Church Office.** There is a difference between an office and a gift, biblically speaking. There are only three or four church offices mentioned in Scripture: Apostle (only 13 that we know of: 11 + Matthias [replacement for Judas] + Paul), elder, and deacon. I think a good case can be made for the deaconess, but it is not as clear as the others. Now here is what is unique about the office that is not true of the gift. An office has **authority** and **locality**. Elders have the spiritual authority in a local church (Heb 13:7; 1 Pet 5:1-4). Evangelists do not. But you cannot be an elder at 1st Baptist in Houston and 1st Baptist in Dallas at the same time. The elder's authority is restricted to a certain locality. Neither of these distinctions is true of a spiritual gift. If I have the gift of evangelism, I can exercise it all over the world. It is not limited by locality. But the gift of evangelism has no authority. I cannot command people who listen to receive Christ. I can invite them; I can try to

persuade them; but I cannot command them. So a gift is not a church office. Much confusion and disappointment has developed over the centuries by turning a gift (pastor) into an office.

2. **Natural Talent.** Gifts are not offices; nor are they natural talents. Natural talents come at physical birth. Spiritual gifts come at spiritual birth. When we receive Christ, we get at least one spiritual gift (1 Pet 4:10).

3. **A Ministry.** If you are a leader of a Small Group at church or an Adult Sunday School teacher, those are ministries, not spiritual gifts. You might use the spiritual gift of teaching in one of those ministries, but the ministry itself is not a spiritual gift.

B. What They Are

1. **God-given—1 Corinthians 12:11**

2. **Abilities to minister—1 Peter 4:10**

3. **To the Body of Christ (the Church)—Ephesians 4:12**

4. **Received at our spiritual birth—Romans 12:3; 1 Corinthians 12:11; 1 Peter 4:10**

So, when we read these together, spiritual gifts are God-given abilities to minister to the Body of Christ received at our spiritual birth. They are God-given. We don't get to choose our own spiritual gifts. The Holy Spirit gives them to us according to his will. They are abilities to minister to the Body of Christ. Someone might be a good algebra teacher, but when he tries to Sunday School, nobody seems blessed. He might be a good teacher of algebra, but he doesn't have the spiritual gift of teaching.

Someone might ask if you can receive a spiritual gift after you have been a Christian ten years. Well, God can do whatever he wants. If he leads you to a ministry ten years after you become a Christian, and a certain gift is needed for that ministry, God can certainly give it to you. But we know he gives you at least one spiritual gift when you become a Christian.

I want to say something more about the purpose of these gifts. As far as we know no spiritual gift was given for the purpose of self-edification. Ephesians 4:12 tells us that the spiritual gifts were given for the edification of the body. However, the side benefit of using any spiritual gift is self-edification. If you have the spiritual gift of evangelism, you might spend all afternoon witnessing door to door but not lead anyone to Christ. Nevertheless, you will probably come back higher than a kite. Why? Because the side benefit of using your spiritual gift is self-edification. But that's just a side benefit. No gift was given for the purpose of self-edification. If I use my spiritual gift only for my self- edification, God would say that's not why I gave you that gift. You are given the gift to build up the Body of Christ.

II. DESCRIPTION OF SPIRITUAL GIFTS

A. Sign Gifts—Hebrews 2:4

The sign gifts or miraculous gifts described in Scripture are: signs and wonders, healings, tongues (which is the supernatural ability to speak a foreign language you've never studied in order to lead someone to Christ), and interpretation of tongues. I want you to go with me to Hebrews 2:3-4. These particular gifts we know for certain from this passage were given to confirm the beginning of the new spiritual work we call the Church. In Hebrews 2:3 it says, "How should we escape if we neglect so great salvation which at the first began to be spoken by the Lord?" He is talking about the beginnings of Christianity. He is talking about a new spiritual thrust in God's program for salvation. "At the first, began to be spoken by the Lord," and that was confirmed in two ways: 1) Confirmed by those who heard him (those who walked with him and heard his messages); 2) "God also bearing witness."

God himself confirmed the beginning of this work with signs and wonders, with various miracles, gifts of the Holy Spirit, according to his own will. That was the purpose of raising someone from the dead. That was the purpose of a miraculous healing. That was the purpose of speaking in tongues. It was to confirm the man and the message—to confirm something new. Those miracles were done by the power of Jesus. Jesus raised Lazarus from the dead, Peter raised the dead (Acts 9:40-42), and Paul raised the dead (Acts 20:9-12),[87] all to convince the people that this was a special new work from God.

The miraculous gifts are mentioned in only two NT books between Acts and Revelation: Galatians and 1 Corinthians, which were early books. They are never mentioned in all the later books, even the ones instructing the believers how to conduct themselves in church (1&2 Timothy and Titus). It could well be that after the confirmation of this new work by these miraculous gifts, they were no longer deemed necessary for their original purpose (confirmation).

We know from church history that they died out some time between AD60 and AD150 because Montanus was accused of heresy when he claimed to have brought them back in AD150. He couldn't have been accused of bringing them back unless they had died out. Of course, even if they died out, there is nothing to say God cannot bring them back whenever he wished. We know that miraculous gifts will come from both God through the two witnesses (Rev 11) and Satan through the Antichrist (Rev 13) during the Tribulation Period.

And since today is probably the latter rain spoken of by James (Jas 5:7) when a great harvest of new believers will be added to the Church, it wouldn't surprise me if God brought the miraculous gifts back to help bring in his latter day harvest before the return of the Lord. I have looked for them expectantly and diligently, but have yet to witness or even hear of those who have witnessed what took place during the ministry of Jesus on earth and during the first twenty years of the early church.

---

87 There is some debate over whether Eutychus had really died.

Last week I went to eat lunch with a missionary from Cambodia. He went on for a half an hour talking about Pol Pot in Cambodia and Laos and Vietnam and all the Christians springing up. He said there were 100,000 new Christians in Vietnam just since the fall of the Iron Curtain and the lack of funding they had from the Russians. He said now there were pockets of Christians springing up from Cambodia all over the place. "It's an outpouring! It's the latter rain!" he claimed. And we have already referenced the 100,000,000 Christians in the underground church in China, and the number is growing at a ten percent a year clip.

In the midst of all this, I would expect the miraculous gifts to confirm this outpouring. I just haven't seen them yet. I talked to missionaries in India, and they haven't seen them. According to a friend of mine who was head of all the Wycliffe Bible Translators in Papua New Guinea, where they had reached all eight hundred language groups over twenty years ago with the gospel, none of the translators were given the gift of tongues to help them in their evangelistic efforts, nor had they heard of anyone receiving such a gift. I find that somewhat surprising.

So what about the gift of healing? Proof of that gift was the need to raise someone from the dead in front of an unbelieving audience. That's what Jesus did, and many believed in him because of this miracle (Jn 11:45). The same thing happened after Peter raised Dorcas (Acts 9:42)—many believed. Are today's miracle workers raising people from the dead? I think we would've heard about it, if it had happened. If you had the gift of healing, someone could touch your clothes and you would be healed, or even the cast of your shadow was sufficient to heal. I haven't heard credible reports of any of that happening these days.

The person with the gift of healing could heal anyone of anything providing the person had faith. After watching ten healings in a row I'm pretty sure I would have faith. Also, he could heal them all instantaneously and a hundred percent. We're told in James 5:15 that the prayer of faith will heal the sick, but that's a group of elders praying for someone who's called for them. There is a big difference between faith-healing and a faith-healer. I know God can heal anyone at anytime. God is the same yesterday today and forever. He can do that, but that's not the same as giving individuals these sign gifts.

B. The Speaking Gifts

The Speaking gifts are teaching, encouraging/exhorting, preaching, mercy, apostle, evangelist, pastor, knowledge, and wisdom.[88] Let's talk a little bit about the difference between teaching and preaching. Teaching is simply the transference of knowledge from one head to another. Preaching is designed to change the will. The preacher calls for a response. Preaching in the church age is called the gift of prophecy. Even in the Old Testament, prophecy was more forth-telling than fore-telling. Forth-telling was expanding on the truth God had already given in his Word. And that's what we call preaching. Sometimes great preachers are not good teachers and vice versa.

You notice we listed apostle as a spiritual gift. That's because Ephesians 4:11 does. But we also said apostle is an office. How can it be both ways? Actually the NT uses the word apostle in three ways. One is the office, of which they're only thirteen. Remember Jesus promised the twelve they would be sitting on twelve thrones ruling over the twelve tribes of Israel during his kingdom reign. Those are positions or offices only twelve men can hold. The gift of apostleship was different. It was similar to being a missionary. The word apostle and missionary mean the same: "sent one." So an apostle is one who is usually gifted in starting churches. Those were people like Apollos or Barnabas (Acts 14:14). They had the gift of being apostles, but not the office.

There was one more type of apostle mentioned in the New Testament. Paul called Epaphroditus an apostle in Philippians 2:25.

---

88 Some also include a word of wisdom or a word of knowledge.

In that context an apostle was someone who was sent as a messenger. So in summary we have the office, the gift, and the function.

C. Serving Gifts

The serving gifts are named: administration, helps, serving, giving, leading, and faith.

I want to show you something very interesting about these serving gifts. Let's go to 1 Corinthians 12:31, which says, "But earnestly desire the best gifts." That seems to go counter to everything he has been teaching in this chapter. It sounds like he's been saying that no gift is better than another. So why would you conclude by saying desire the best gifts? So I want to approach this verse in a little different way.

Let's compare verse 28 with 29 and 30. Here is verse 28: "And God has appointed these in the church: first apostles, second prophets, third teachers, after that miracles, then gifts of healings, helps, administrations, varieties of tongues." Now here are verses twenty-nine and thirty: "Are all apostles? *Are* all prophets? *Are* all teachers? *Are* all workers of miracles? Do all have gifts of healings? Do all speak with tongues? Do all interpret?"

As you compare these verses, you will notice some gifts mentioned in verse 28 that are not mentioned in verse 29 or 30. Can you spot which ones are not mentioned? There are two gifts mentioned in verse 28 that are omitted in verses 29 and 30. Those are the gifts of helps and administrations. If you lose a preacher, the church can keep going. Paul has been using the human body to illustrate the church. He's been saying some parts of the body we can do without, and the body will keep on living. You can lose a toe, a foot, even a leg, and keep living. You might even lose your ability to see or to speak or to hear and keep living. Those are what we might call the glorious gifts of the body. They're seen and heard. But the mouth and eyes have some silent partners they cannot do without. If you take away the stomach, or the lungs, or the heart, the body will die. These are the more necessary parts of the body.

So it is with the local body of Christ. The gifts of helps and administrations are the unseen partners of the hand and foot and mouth. If I may put it this way, they're the guts of the church. Lose them and you don't have a church. So I would call these the more necessary gifts: helps and administrations. And I think that is what the end of the chapter is saying: seek the more necessary gifts.

So Paul has made a stunning point. These Corinthians were chasing after the glamorous gifts. He says if you want to chase after gifts, go after the unseen gifts. Go after the gifts without glamour, go after the more necessary gifts, go after helps and administrations.

III. DISCOVERY OF SPIRITUAL GIFTS

A. Try it; you'll like it.

1. **DO.** Do something, anything; it doesn't matter what; just try something. Go pick up trash in the parking lot. Go work in the nursery. That's always a good place to start. I remember once we had a shortage in the nursery. I had a co-pastor that was preaching in the morning, while I preached at night. So on Sunday mornings I volunteered for the nursery. It was kind of fun. We had a shortage of binkies (little rubber things for the babies to suck on when they weren't sucking a milk bottle), so I rolled up my sleeve and discovered I could fake out these little babies for ten to fifteen minutes at a time. You will discover your spiritual gift trying things. Just go do that. A rolling stone collects no moss. Start rolling for Christ. He will show you your spiritual gift.

2. **DESIRE.** What do you long to do? Is there something in your heart that has been stirring? Try something like you might try different sports. Just keep trying until you find something you desire. Suddenly you find yourself practicing. You'll be practicing at all hours. You're wife will say, "Where are you!?" Your answer: "I'm practicing!"

People will see your sweat and say, "You're sweating," but you won't even notice the sweat because you are doing what you want to do. I like the word **passion**. You might actually be gifted in a number of areas, but one of those areas is going to be your passion. Follow your passion and you will probably discover your primary spiritual gift.

3. **DELIGHT.** When you're using your gifts, you will discover an inner joy. It may well be at the delight of your life. Most people with the spiritual gift of teaching spend a lot of time studying the Bible. In preparing for their lessons they themselves are fed by their study. They enjoy the preparation. But their greatest joy comes from actual teaching. I have often heard a teacher say, "I just love it when I see the eyes of the students light up. It tells me they got it. There is nothing more rewarding for a teacher than that." So find out what brings you the greatest joy as you serve Jesus. That is probably your gift.

B. Try it; we'll like it.

1. **Discernment—we'll see it in you.**

John Champagne was a short little guy from New Hampshire. He was the general manager for AAA in the Greater Houston Area. He made lots of money and had a beautiful home on a local lake. Then he became a Christian. Because of his experience with AAA I thought he might have a gift of evangelism. He did. But I also discovered another gift John had. He had a gift of mercy. I never wanted to follow John after he visited someone in the hospital. He was such an encouragement to people when he got on his knees beside their bed to pray for them that I would've sworn he could levitate people while they were lying in their hospital beds. If I walked in after John had just come out, there was always a big letdown. I do not have the gift of mercy. John did, and all of us saw it in him. We told him about it, and visiting the hospital became one of the joys of his life.

2. **Direction—we can guide you.**

Sometimes a person who loves to study will think he has the gift of teaching. But when he tries to teach, he discovers his audience doesn't have the gift of listening. That's a problem. The local body of Christ will confirm your gifting. I remember a time a man came to me and told me he had the gift of preaching. He wanted to know if I let other people preach in the church. I said, "Yes, occasionally. I have trained a number of men to preach in the church, and when I go on vacation, they take over."

I suggested that he serve in the church for a while as a teacher or leader of a small group. He said, "No, my gift is preaching. I need to join a church where they will let me preach." He really had everything upside down. It just wasn't the right focus. Not that he couldn't preach had he been part of our church, but that his preaching was a condition for belonging to the church. Probably not the best approach.

I prefer the approach of one little fella that ardently wanted to be part of a school Christmas play. His mother thought he was perfect for one particular part in the play. But when he went for the tryouts, he wasn't gifted in that area and did not get the part his mother felt he should have. She thought, "Oh boy, this is going to be tough." So she went to pick him up after the tryouts, and he came running out to the car. She was afraid he was going to start crying. But he had a big smile on his face and said, "I got a part, mom!" She asked what is was, and he said, "I got chosen to clap and cheer!" All right, that's the right attitude. They chose me to clap and cheer. Who knows where that might lead? God says, "If you are faithful in little things, I will entrust to you the true riches."

CONCLUSION

1. The life of a church is directly proportionate to how many are using their spiritual gifts.

Want to visit a dead church? Just go find one where the staff does all the work and you'll have a dead church. Why? Because the staff is invariably going to be a small minority of the church, right? That means the vast majority are just kind of sitting, soaking, and souring. Doing nothing. They are not using their spiritual gifts and, just like the human body, if they are not moving at all, you might say, "They are close to death." The more people discover their gifts and get active, the more alive that church is.

That reminds me of one American pastor that visited a friend in Switzerland and went to the Sunday evening service. He got there a little early and didn't see anyone. It was getting dark, so he thought maybe he'd gotten the hour wrong, so he said to himself, "I'll wait a while." Suddenly, it looked like fireflies were descending on him. People were carrying their lanterns, walking down from the Alps to the little church. They brought their lanterns and came in and just lit the church up. After the service they went home with their little lights, and like fireflies, they just disbursed out into the night. Is your lantern lit? You're not hiding it under a bushel, are you? The more people who don't use their gifts in the church, the closer the church is to *rigor mortis*.

2. Don't use gifts as an excuse for not serving.

This is probably the biggest downside to teaching on spiritual gifts. When people start looking for their gifts, and try different things out, and discover they don't like something, they conclude that's not their spiritual gift. Then when they're asked to help in that area, they refuse based on the fact that it's not one of their spiritual gifts. I don't know how many times I have heard someone say, "I'm sorry, I would just love to help out, but you know, that's not my spiritual gift." After about ten of those calls you want to scream.

Can you just imagine the Upper Room? There is Jesus not far from the cross and all around him are these guys still hung up on who's going to be the greatest. He is still going to try to teach them how to be humble. So they come in and they've got the table set and everything's beautiful except for the dirty feet and basin of water. And Jesus says to Peter, "Hey, Pete, it's about the dirty feet. You are one of the servants. Could you start washing our feet like you are supposed to do?" "Oh, Lord, not my spiritual gift. Ask John." (I said use your imagination here.) So Jesus asks John, who replies, "Oh, Lord, it's not my spiritual gift either." Of course the Lord, knowing the future and knowing the Holy Spirit is going to give spiritual gifts, also knows that foot washing is not listed among the nineteen gifts. So he says, "Oh, gosh guys, you are right. Foot washing is not a spiritual gift, so I guess we can just live with dirty, smelly feet." No, that's not how it happened, is it? Jesus got up and showed them how to serve. He did what was needed. He had some speaking gifts last I remember. He also had some of those miracle working gifts, last time I checked. But he wasn't above doing service tasks that just had to be done. You may not have the gift of helps, but everyone can help.

3. Don't rob God of his joy.

One more excuse I've heard from people over the years for not stepping forward to help is that they would mess things up. "Aww, I'd mess it up. I would do something wrong. This is a holy calling, and I'm just not worthy. I would mess it up." You know, there is a lot of joy we get from serving, but you know who else gets joy when we serve? Right up there. Reminds me of a father that was a single parent. He had done his duties in the kitchen. Everything was cleaned up, so he left the kitchen to make sure his kids were getting their homework out of the way before bedtime. After helping one of them with some math, he came back into the kitchen only to discover his little seven-year-old daughter had just made a mess of everything. There was flour here and a mess there. Sugar was on the floor and utensils everywhere. He had a flash of anger. He said to himself, "That little twerp! I can't believe her!"

And then he got near the breakfast table and looked down. His little sweetheart had scrawled with little chocolate fingers a message on the breakfast table. It said, "I'm making something for you, daddy. Your angel." It took his eyes off the mess and put them on the one he loved, his child. She was trying to do something for him. What joy, he said, flooded his heart. Then he thought about our heavenly father and how we as his children are serving and invariably, from time to time, make a mess. But he looks down from heaven and says, "He is trying to do something for me," and bring him great joy. Think about this. I would propose to you that there is no exhilaration in this world like doing the will of God by the gift of God through the Spirit of God for the glory of God.

Betty and I were walking one night as we usually do in the evening. We started talking about various things in our respective lives and how easily the flesh can pull us back to "It's all about me" thinking. Like disappointments, hurts, and things that come along to take you back to yourself. And she said, "You know, it's really been just since Jimmy (our first born son) was killed that I realized it's not all about me and that it really is all about God. It really is all about his glory. Now as I do the various things through the day and through the week, whether it is in church or outside of church, I try to focus on his glory and all I want to do with my life is to glorify him. No, I'm not doing it perfectly, but it is my desire. It is all about him." That's it folks. There is no exhilaration in the world like doing the will of God by the gift of God through the Spirit of God for the glory of God.

10

WINDS OF DOCTRINE

Part 1 – Freed to Grow Mature

Ephesians 4:12-16

INTRODUCTION

Sometimes children reflect reality in ways that are quite unexpected. One little eight-year-old was playing with his tinker toys in the living room, while his family sat around and watched. He started building a church, and when the church was over half finished, he looked at his family and said, "Shh, quiet." His father just swelled up inside because of the new found reverence his child had for church. Then he asked, "Son, why do you want us to be so quiet?" His son said, "Many people are sleeping in church."

Now preachers have a unique perspective from the pulpit. It is quite easy to see those whose eyes are shut whether they're sleeping or not. I remember visiting one family that wanted to join the church. I listened to the testimony of each child and their mother. Then I came to their father. The family sat near the front of the church. In three minutes into every sermon this father's eyes were shut. So I just had to ask him, "Why do you come to church so faithfully? Are you missing rest?" He said, "I'm not sleeping. Since I'm a lawyer, I like to think about the things you're saying so I can figure out how to refute them." I thought, "Well, that's an interesting approach."

Now to be honest with you, I'm not concerned about the eyes that are shut. I am concerned about people sleeping with their eyes open. I sometimes wonder if we have trained ourselves to be bored in church, and if it's boring here, what will it be like in heaven? I remember reading about a little boy that asked his father what heaven would be like. His father said, "Well, son, it will be like one long church service." His son replied, "Then, dad, I don't think I want to go." Is heaven losing its appeal? And is heaven what it's all about, anyway?

In retirement Barbara Walters had four shows she wanted to do. One of them dealt with life after death. So she went around the world interviewing religious people.[89] In America she interviewed both Jews and Christians and found the distinction between the two interesting. But she said the answer was the same for every Christian. When she asked, "What is the goal for Christianity?" they all said, "It's so you can have life when you die. It's so you can go to heaven when it's all over. That's the goal of Christianity." She said she did not find an exception to that answer. Is that what you think the goal of Christianity is? Not according to the Book of Ephesians. I challenge you to read the entire Book of Ephesians (or the Bible) to find a single verse that says the goal of the Christian life is so we can go to heaven when we die. There isn't one. Of course it does talk about being saved by grace through faith (Eph 2:8-9), but even that passage doesn't focus on going to heaven when we die. It focuses on the good works we're supposed to do after we are saved (2:10).

---

89 Barbara Walters, http://www.beliefnet.com/faiths/2005/12/heaven-is-a-place-where-you-are-happy.aspx, accessed September 11, 2016.

It's almost a paradox. We are told we cannot earn our way to heaven, that we cannot be saved by doing good works, but then it says, after we have received the free gift of salvation, we are suppose to live a life of good works (2:10). Why? Because it's not about you! It's about him! And from the beginning of this book to the end of this book, it's about the glory of God. This time we have on earth in these temporary bodies is our only chance. It's our one shot—our only opportunity to see how much glory we will bring God forever and ever. So, day-by-day, week-by-week, year-by-year, this life is about him. The glory of God is the end game. His glory should penetrate every area of our lives.

The problem is, we have a huge gulf, a huge divide, a Grand Canyon, a great dichotomy between the spiritual and secular. Even Christians seem to think Sunday's for God and the rest of the week is about my secular endeavor. They don't mix the two. As one congressman said recently, "I got into politics in 1973 after the abortion decision because I thought that was the fastest route to freedom."[90] Well, we have won some legislative victories, but we have lost the culture. One mother came up to me and said, "You have no idea how early we lost the culture. My little girl's in the fifth grade, and she was seated at lunch with a bunch of other fifth grade girls, and they were talking about abortion. One girl said, 'Well, it's only a baby.'" That's a 10-year-old girl, folks! Where did she get that? The other girls were in agreement.

So in this section of Ephesians 4 we want to explore with you the moral state of the Western world and how we got where we are. In verse 14 of our text it says we should no longer be children. He wants us to grow up. And one of the marks of the child, a spiritual child in terms of spiritual immaturity, is that he is tossed to and fro and carried about by every wind of doctrine. Here is an example of a wind of doctrine taught by Peter Singer, a Princeton professor, in an

---

90 Nancy Pearcey, *Total Truth* (Wheaton, IL: Crossway Books, 2004), 19.

article he wrote called "Heavy Petting."[91] Singer justifies bestiality in certain cases this way: "My agenda is to undermine biblical values. We have been raised on a Judeo-Christian ethic that says God created man alone in his image and that we are higher than the animals. Evolution has proven that categorically wrong. We're just the highest animal." And then he goes into some of the gross ramifications of that conclusion. That is our culture.

One impressionable 18-year-old went off to a Christian college. In her first biology class her teacher drew a heart on one side of the board and drew a brain on the other side of the board. Then in the heart she wrote Christianity and in the brain she put science and said the two don't mix. What's that message? That message is that you park your brain out in the lot before you come through the doors of the church. That's as far from Christianity as you can possibly imagine. John 1:1 says in the beginning was the Word. The "Word"—*logos*—is a concept that spoke of reason, sensibility, and logic. Since logic and reason existed before the creation of this universe, in the biblical view, then everything in this universe has the stamp of God's reason, God's logic, and God's mind. The idea that Christians park their brains when they open their Bibles is an anathema. We're going to show that the two (reason and faith) should run together and they were never intended to be separate. In fact, that was part of Paul's prayer back in chapter one. He wanted the great truths of positional truth to get from his readers heads to their hearts. But notice these truths were in the head first.

We are in the section on spiritual gifts because we have left the three chapters about our **Position**, and now we are in the three chapters about our **Condition**. We are going into the marketplace. We are taking theology out of the pew and into the office. It's coming out of the pew and going into the home. It's coming out of the pew and going into the playground. It is everywhere we go 24/7. In order to do that, Paul says God has created a wonderful entity, unforeseen in the

---

91   Peter Singer, "Heavy Petting," in *Nerve* (2001).

Old Testament, something he calls the Body of Christ, something he calls his Church. This Church has unity (4:1-6) and diversity (4:7-16). We have to act as a team to have the greatest impact, but the team has individual members. Each one is to do his part. Large or small, each member is significant, very significant.

EPHESIANS
"The Creation and the Conduct of the Church"

SALUTATION	1:1-2
INTRODUCTION—"Spiritual Blessings in the Heavenlies"	1:3-14
(Paul's Prayer for Perception)	1:15-23
BODY	2:1-6:9
I. Creation of the Church (Its Position)	2:1-3:21
II. Conduct of the Church (Its Condition)	4:1-6:9
A. The Goal: Maturity of the Body	4:1-16
1. Through Unity	1-6
2. Through Diversity	7-16
a. Distribution of Spiritual Gifts	7-10
b. Description of Spiritual Gifts	11
c. Development of Spiritual Gifts	12-16
B. The Means: Maturity of the Individual	4:17-6:9
CONCLUSION—"Spiritual Battles in the Heavenlies"	6:10-20
FAREWELL	

From the outline above we can see that we are going to focus on the **Development of Spiritual Gifts.** We will look at the Process of Development in verse 12, the Product of Development in verse 13, and finally the Purpose of Development in verses 14 through 16. First the Process.

I. PROCESS OF DEVELOPMENT   12

[12] for the equipping of the saints for the work of ministry, for the edifying of the body of Christ, . . .

A. "For the equipping of the saints"

The word "**equipping**" (*katartismon*) is used in a number of ways: 1) In Matthew 4:11 it is used for mending nets that have been broken; 2) In Galatians 6:1 it is used for resetting a bone that has been broken in order to restore it to its former use; 3) In this context he might have a voyage in mind because it talks about waves and winds. So Paul's use here may be limited to fully equipping a ship for its voyage. Paul might even have all three uses in mind. An unknown author said this about the church: "It is not a gallery for the exhibition of eminent Christians, but it is a school for the education of the imperfect ones, a nursery for the care of the weak ones, a hospital for the healing of the ones with 'assiduous care.'"

That's what the church is all about; it is to heal; it is to mend broken people; and it is to equip them for an impact on planet Earth. Adam was given what many theologians call a cultural mandate. Now you know what "culture" is, and a "mandate" is just a command. The command was to go into the entire world. The command was to take dominion over the earth and over the animals and the sky and the seas. That was the cultural mandate. But what do we find Christians doing? Pulling out of the world; coming together in holy huddles; leaving their possible sphere of influence to impact this world for Jesus Christ and for God. So Paul says we are to be equipped. But equipped for what? Before we figure that out we better figure out just who is being equipped in this passage.

Who are the saints in this verse? Hopefully you won't tell me the saints are the church staff. The church staff is found back in verse 11. It is the job of the church staff to train the church members for the work of ministry. In this passage the "saints" are the church members. The staff is the pastors and teachers (v. 11). The pastors and teachers are to equip the church members for the work of the ministry. But just what is the work of the ministry?

B. "For the work of the ministry"

People seem to think the work of the ministry is inside the church walls. Well, that's part of it. But that's just on Sunday. It should be all week long, and all day long, ministering to your children, your wife, your husband, your students, your fellow employees, whoever they are. That's the work of the ministry. And it is the job of the apostles, the prophets, the evangelists, the pastors, and the teachers (v. 11) to equip you, the saints, to do the work of the ministry (v. 12). But why?

C. "For the edifying of the Body of Christ"

Why do the work of the ministry? The text says it is for the edifying of the Body of Christ. Guess what? God hasn't given these gifts to edify you as an individual. Remember, self-edification is a byproduct of using one's spiritual gift. The primary use of spiritual gifts is to build up others, not ourselves. As we said in the very first lesson, it's not about you. So many people come to church to get instead of to give. God says that is an inversion; that is a perversion. And self-serving rarely yields happiness, joy, or fulfillment. Serving others does.

II. PRODUCT OF DEVELOPMENT 13

> [13] till we all come to the unity of the faith and of the knowledge of the Son of God, to a perfect man, to the measure of the stature of the fullness of Christ;

The product? Well, what is the product? What's it all about? So we can go to heaven when we die? Not exactly! That's not mentioned in this verse. What's it all about? "To come to the unity of the faith and the knowledge of the Son of God." That word "knowledge" (*epignōsis*) is not just the beginning knowledge that helps me come into God's Forever Family. It's full knowledge; it's intimate knowledge. It's the deepest experience with our Lord Jesus Christ. And then it says to a "perfect man." It's not talking about sinless perfection. It is the same word used in James 1:4 when it says our trials help make us mature. It is used in Galatians 3:3 when talking about going on to maturity in the Christian life. It's used in Colossians 1:28 when Paul says he warns every man and teaches every man in all wisdom that he may present every man mature before God." It is to go on to Christian maturity.

Finally, if we still don't understand it, the text says to the "measure of the stature of the fullness of Christ." He is the standard. We are built up to be like him. In the magazine *The Last Days Newsletter*, Leonard Ravenhill talks about a tour of Luther's travels he once took over Europe. They came to a small village out on the countryside, and as they were walking along the bus, they saw an old man sitting on some stones near the village. One of the tourists somewhat frothily asked, "Any great men born in this village?" The old man looked at him and answered, "Nope, just babies."[92] Snobby question . . . profound answer.

It is the same in the Christian life. Any great Christians out there? We are all born babies, and we have to grow. It is about growing into the likeness of the Lord Jesus Christ. Someone once said, "We dwell upon the impartiality of the soul and forget the vehicle of service of God now is the body. And if we fail to serve God and the body now, we shall never be able to make it up for what we failed to do now." Colossians 3:21 says, "Whether you eat or drink or whatsoever you do, do to the glory of God." That is talking about right now.

Well, what's the purpose of all this development? If we saw the process in verse 12 and the product in verse 13, then in verses 14 through 16 we shall see the purpose.

---

92 Leonard Ravenhill, http://www.sermoncentral.com/illustrations/sermon-illustration-sermoncentral-staff-humor-7937.asp, accessed September 5, 2016.

III. PURPOSE OF DEVELOPMENT   14-16

[14] that we should no longer be children, tossed to and fro and carried about with every wind of doctrine, by the trickery of men, in the cunning craftiness of deceitful plotting, [15] but, speaking the truth in love, may grow up in all things into Him who is the head—Christ—[16] from whom the whole body, joined and knit together by what every joint supplies, according to the effective working by which every part does its share, causes growth of the body for the edifying of itself in love.

Paul expresses the purpose of development of spiritual gifts first of all negatively and secondly positively. Let's look at the negative side.

A. Negatively Expressed   14

Paul uses four negative expressions or phrases to describe Christians who can't tell the difference between the sound biblical doctrine from unsound:

1. "Children"—immature

2. "Tossed to and fro"—a sign of immaturity; no doctrinal depth or stability

3. "Wind of doctrine"—the philosophies of men change like the wind. So too do many young Christians. They grab on to the next "hot" preacher or teacher without ever understanding his doctrinal foundations.

4. "Deceitful plotting"—there truly is a conspiracy to undermine biblical values and absolute truth.

Make no bones about it. There has been a conspiracy, and there has been one for a long time, to undermine biblical values and question Western Christianity. I'm not talking about the international bankers. I'm talking about the educational system designed to undercut and undermine values. In our educational system it puts values on one side and facts on another side, and they put a wall between the two.

On the left side we have revelation; on the right side we have reason with no connection between the two. We want to try to expose that deception. In coming lessons we will go all the way back to the days before Christ and come right up to the present-day. The dichotomy we hear most often today is couched in these terms: spiritual and secular. Spiritual values are put on the left side; secular values are put on the right side. Where did that idea come from? We shall soon find out, but right now let's look at the positive goal Paul has in mind.

B. Positively Expressed   15-16

1. "Speaking the truth in love"—we can't speak the truth if we don't know it.
2. "Grow"—have you stopped growing?
3. "Every joint . . . every part"—when I don't do my part, I am stunting someone else's growth.

The Santa Fe Trail is an old movie loaded with some of the early stars of Hollywood: Errol Flynn, Ronald Regan, Olivia de Havilland, and others. It centers on the battles in Kansas led by John Brown the abolitionist against the "slavers." How much is fact and how much is fiction is hard to tell at times, but clearly John Brown was trying to free the slaves through violence. He was convinced that violence was the only means to freedom. The sins of our nation could only be purged by blood.

John Brown probably spoke a lot of truth. I don't currently know of anyone that would defend what we did to the Negro race as a moral good. But I think we can also agree that John Brown did not "speak the truth in love." Sometimes truth is like snow—the softer it falls the longer it stays. Using the truth as a club or a battering ram will backfire more often than not. That's what happens to a lot of kids raised in homes where the truth is crammed down their throat. A little love combined with the truth goes a long way.

So what is the goal of the Christian life? To go to heaven when we die? That's Western Christianity but it's not biblical Christianity.

We might call heaven the starting point, but it is not the goal line. But how did heaven as the end goal of the Christian life become the focal point of Western Christianity? Our starting point is centuries before Christ. Since we are talking about winds of doctrine that can lead us astray, I will call each influence a hurricane. The first hurricane we will look at I will call Hurricane Plato. We want to look at some of the damage from **HURRICANE PLATO**.

First of all, Plato viewed heaven as a place that was spiritual and it was good. His forms and ideals are in heaven. He saw all spiritual things as good. He viewed material things as evil. For example, since your body is a material thing, he thought it was evil. This is what philosophers call an ethical dualism: spiritual/material; good/evil. Now Plato did not believe in a personal God. He thought that good and evil were both eternal. He also thought our souls were. But to come to completion our souls needed to spend a certain amount of time in the human body. Of course the soul was good but the body was evil. So what was the goal of life on earth? Life's goal was to get the soul out of the body so it could go back in a completed state to the spiritual world. That was salvation according to Hurricane Plato.

That was over 350 years before Jesus Christ, but Hurricane Plato was still swirling around the educated world centuries after Christ. A man named Plotinus taught a new form of Hurricane Plato, which philosophers called Neo-Platonism. It was just Plato with a new face. But these winds of doctrine began swirling around a Christian by the name of Augustine (d. 430). **HURRICANE AUGUSTINE** absorbed Neo-Platonism wholesale. Augustine combined Neo-Platonism with his background in Manichaeism and Stoicism to weave Christianity into a new tapestry that combined biblical teaching with Greek philosophy.[93]

Part of this Greek philosophy, which was completely anti-biblical, was that material things are a hindrance to spirituality. Plotinus, for example, never bathed because he had so little regard for his body. He

---

93 See Chapter 1, footnote 9.

also taught celibacy. But his goal was the same as Plato's: to release the soul from its prison, the body. Well, Plato didn't make it completely clear how to get the soul out of the body (though he made a run at it through his allegory about the Cave). Augustine spelled it out for us. Here are the steps:

1. Asceticism—that's a big word, but all it is talking about is the denial of material things: meat, wine, personal property, and sex. Augustine started a monastery in Northern Africa. He even taught that sex within marriage was always sin, even for procreation. Sex outside of marriage was a mortal sin; sex inside of marriage was a venial sin.

2. Contemplation—this is where you go into solitude. You pull away from relationships. You become a Desert Mystic. You go off by yourself. The hope was to have a beatific vision, essentially a vision of God. Plotinus claimed to have had four of these during a six-year period. He described it as "the alone going up to the Alone." Augustine never had such a vision, but that's what he was searching for, and that's what he was trying to train other monks to have.

3. Sacraments—there were four sacraments recognized by Augustine (three more have been added since that time). Here are the four recognized by Augustine:
   - Water baptism
   - Mass
   - Confession
   - Perseverance—you must be faithful until the end of your life; you must die in a state of grace.

So this is the goal! All of life is centered around reaching that one goal. What's that goal again? To go to heaven when you die. To get your soul out of its prison, the human body, so it can go up to heaven.

Catholics and Protestants alike talk almost exclusively about this end goal.

There was a lot of fallout and collateral damage from these hurricanes. For example, because Christians have been largely taught that the material world is evil, they tend to retreat instead of transform. They pull out of society instead of being inside of society. Jesus says we are to be in the world but not of the world. Jesus said we are to be salt and light so unbelievers can see our good works so that someday they will glorify God who is in heaven. How? Because they're attracted to the light. But if you put your light under a bushel, the unbelieving world will never see it. So the whole idea of pulling away, even in relationships, is collateral damage from Hurricane Plato and Hurricane Augustine.

Another example of collateral damage is the emphasis in Western Christianity on justification to the gross neglect of sanctification. In other words, most of the emphasis in Western Christianity is on how to get to heaven when you die, as opposed to growing in Christ right now until you become a mature Christian—the measure of the stature of the fullness of Christ.

In her book *Total Truth*, Nancy Pearcey talks about her upbringing in her denomination and says:

> Every sermon came back to justification by faith. I thought we were fighting the Reformation every Sunday. Most churches are strong when talking about conversion but weak on teaching about how to live after conversion. Think of an analogy. In one sense our physical birth is the most important event in our lives, the beginning of everything else. But, in another sense, our birth is the least important event, because it is merely the starting point. If someone were to mention everyday how great it is to be born, we would think that is a little bit strange. Once we have come into the world, the important task is to grow and mature. By the same token, being born-again is the necessary first step in our spiritual lives, yet we should not focus our message constantly on how

to be saved. It is crucial for churches to lead people forward and to spiritual maturity, equipping the saints to carry out the mission God has given to us in the cultural mandate to take possession of the world.[94]

CONCLUSION

Let me pause here and say if none of this makes any sense to you, it could be that you have never taken that first step, or that you never had a spiritual birth and that you have never been born again. You cannot get into the race without getting into the starting blocks. So first of all, the decision you need to make is, "Do I trust the claims of Jesus Christ? Do I believe that on the cross he died in my place in order to pay the penalty that I deserve for my sinfulness?" God says if you are persuaded of this truth about Jesus then Jesus will be your Savior and you will be God's child—forever. He offers you the free gift of eternal life. You can do that right now while you're reading this book. But again, that's just the starting point. It is the beginning of the race.

Here is one more fallout from these two hurricanes: Christianity is good for getting you into heaven, but pretty irrelevant for the rest of your life. There is a certain lawyer that comes to church on Sunday. He is a deacon in his church and also teaches a Sunday school class. So he reserves Sunday for the Lord's work. But during the week he does his work. And his work is to break contracts. His law firm is hired by corporations that discover that certain contracts are not beneficial to the bottom line. These are contracts they have signed and contracts they have negotiated. So this particular lawyer has been hired specifically all day long to look for "loopholes" in these contracts. His job is to figure out how these corporations can break these contracts. This lawyer sees no contradiction between what he

---

94 Nancy Pearcey, 49-50.

does on Sunday and what he does during the week. On Sunday he is simply a deacon and a Sunday school teacher. But during the week he simply does his job.

A gal named Sarah, a born-again Christian, goes to church every Sunday right here in the state of Texas. She is in a small group with Christian friends, but during the week she works for an abortion clinic. When young ladies come to the abortion clinic, her job is to show compassion for them and counsel them on the potential aftermath of having an abortion and how it might come to haunt them later on in life. When asked how she can go to church on Sunday and be part of a small group another day of the week while working for an abortion clinic, she says, "Well, I don't see any contradiction. This is a choice these girls are making. I don't have any right or control to tell them what to do with their own bodies, but as a Christian, I feel it is my job to show them compassion. So I try to inform them of all the ramifications of having an abortion."[95]

Contrast that to Sealy Yates, another lawyer.[96] Sealy actually gave his life to be a preacher at age fourteen. However, through aptitude tests he was counseled that he did not have the abilities to be a preacher. They told him to be a lawyer. He goes to law school, passes the bar, gets married, has a child, has the American dream, and gets depressed—morbidly depressed. He couldn't figure out why he was depressed. "I've got everything I've worked for." Suddenly it dawned on him that he thought he was doing second-level work for God, or no work for God during the week at all. He thought if you are really serving God, you're a missionary or pastor or on a church staff—doing something for God full-time. That's the top level. Then the lower levels are these other things you do in life to make money.

Kelly said, "I was depressed for I had given my life when I was fourteen to go to the top level, and now I realized I was at a lower level." What Kelly was telling us is that he had a dichotomy between

95 Pearcey, 31.

96 Ibid., 63-66.

the spiritual and secular, between faith and reason, between values and facts. As Pearcey points out, he had not integrated total truth in his life. Fortunately Sealy saw the light. Now he realizes if what the Bible claims is true, then Christ is with us all day long, every day of the week, every week of the year. That's exciting. That means there is no excuse for being bored. You can get up every day with a mission. There is something to do. Today I can be a mirror of God's grace. Today I can glorify God! Wow! Awesome!

So what is the goal of the Christian life? If you tell me it's to go to heaven after we die, I think I will fall over dead right now. That's the starting point, not the goal.

11

WINDS OF DOCTRINE

Part 2 – Freed to Fly

Ephesians 4:17-24

INTRODUCTION

There's not much debate—we've lost our Christian culture. Prayer was taken out of the public schools in 1962. Then in 1963 Madeline Murray O'Hare took Bible readings out of the same schools. The Ten Commandments was removed from some courtrooms, and "Merry Christmas" was taken out of the stores. What's next?

Historians are calling us "Post-Christian" America. That's right, we are no longer the most Christian nation in the world. That honor probably goes to South Korea. I recently met a couple from New Zealand—Kiwis. They came to America as missionaries because we are the largest English speaking mission field in the world.

How did it happen? What went wrong? Can we recover? Does anyone care? We are proposing that cultures change when belief systems change, when our world views change. It was a new belief system that changed Russia from a God-fearing culture isolated from the rest of the world to a godless, materialistic culture trying to revolutionize the world.

So, what about us? How have we drifted so far from our religious roots? What "Winds of Doctrine" have infected the lifeblood of America and driven us into spiritual anemia? That's what we want to find out.

EPHESIANS
"The Creation and the Conduct of the Church"

SALUTATION	1:1-2
INTRODUCTION—"Spiritual Blessings in the Heavenlies"	1:3-14
(Paul's Prayer for Perception)	1:15-23
BODY	2:1-6:9
I. Creation of the Church (Its Position)	2:1-3:21
II. Conduct of the Church (Its Condition)	4:1-6:9
A. The Goal: Maturity of the Body	4:1-16
B. The Means: Maturity of the Individual	4:17-6:9
1. Through Personal Sanctification	4:17-5:14
a. Walking in Life	4:17-32
1) Old Life versus New Life	4:17-24
2) Old Lips versus New Lips	4:25-32
2. Through Personal Submission	5:15-6:9
CONCLUSION—"Spiritual Battles in the Heavenlies"	6:10-20
FAREWELL	6:21-24

Now we begin to see our **Position** affecting our **Condition**. What's true in our **Position** can come true in our **Condition**, progressively. A change in our **Condition** will show up when we exchange old habits and ways of living with new habits and ways of living that bring glory to God. So we want to see what Paul says about leaving the old life behind (4:17-19) and living a new life (4:20-24).

I. LEAVING THE OLD LIFE   4:17-19

[17] This I say, therefore, and testify in the Lord, that you should no longer walk as the rest of the Gentiles walk, in the futility of their mind, [18] having their understanding darkened, being alienated from the life of God, because of the ignorance that is in them, because of the blindness of their heart; [19] who, being past feeling, have given themselves over to lewdness, to work all uncleanness with greediness.

"No longer walk"—Paul calls for a change in lifestyle; he calls for conversion. A person can be "born again" but not converted. How so? Because conversion speaks of a change in lifestyle. Every converted Christian is born again, but not every "born again" Christian is a convert. The word "convert" comes from the Latin *converto*, which means "to turn around, to revolve, to turn in the opposite direction." The Greek equivalent would be *epistrephō*, which means "to turn around."

When John the Baptist challenges the Pharisees in Matthew 3:7-9 to "bear fruits worthy of repentance," he is speaking of a turn-around in their lives. He is not talking about what is in their hearts. Only God can see in their hearts. The Pharisees may have repented (many did over the course of Christ's ministry; see John 12:42-43), but John can't see it because repentance is a matter of the heart. God can see the root; men can only see the fruit. John is simply saying the obvious: a change of heart should result in a change of life.

I must admit to some irritation when I read or hear about people criticizing those of us who teach "free grace" by accusing us of teaching a life without repentance and without good fruit. How ridiculous. The normal Christian life is for a born-again Christian to grow and mature in Christ. You can't do that without spiritual growth and good fruit. But that is not the question. The question centers on the abnormal Christian life, or is there such a thing? Can a born-again person enter darkness for an extended period where no good fruit is observable and still be headed for heaven?

The Arminians resolve this difficulty by saying such a person loses his or her salvation unless he or she repents and comes back to the straight and narrow. The Catholics say such people are running well and on the way to being fully justified when they die, but, alas straying off the beaten path of righteous living puts them in danger of hell-fire. The Calvinist resolves the difficulty by simply concluding the person never was born-again to begin with. And you get into all the discussion about "how long" a period of no fruit, or what kind of fruit are we talking about, or how much fruit—*ad infinitum ad nauseum*. Well, this is not a theological textbook, so we aren't going to try to unravel this Gordian knot here.

But let's be clear on this point: **a change of heart calls for a change of lifestyle.** The interests of the unbeliever are different, his way of thinking is different, and his passions are different. Paul speaks of the "futility of their minds" when referring to the minds of unbelievers. That word **"futility"** (*mataiotēs*) can also mean "purposelessness" or "emptiness" (BDAG[97]). According to another Greek dictionary it "suggests either absence of purpose or failure to attain any true purpose" (MM[98]). Although used by Paul (Rom 8:20; here) and Peter (2 Pet 2:18), it is rarely used at all in secular Greek. It describes so well what we might call the "lost generation," the generation usually identified with postmodernism. It is a generation without purpose or meaning in life because they, like Camus, view this life on this planet as "absurd."

---

97 Walter Bauer and Frederick William Danker, *A Greek–English Lexicon of the New Testament and Other Early Christian Literature,* 3rd ed. (Chicago: University of Chicago Press, 2000–2002).

98 George Milligan and James Moulton, *The Vocabulary of the Greek Testament* (Grand Rapids: W.M.B. Eerdmans Publishing, 1930).

Camus' philosophy of "absurd" was born out of the existentialist movement beginning with Søren Kierkegaard (d. 1855) but popularized after WWII when the atom bomb and the Holocaust sent the intellectual world into a black hole completely devoid of light when it came to purpose and meaning in life. The "absurd" refers to "the conflict between (1) the human tendency to find inherent value and meaning in life and (2) the human inability to find any."[99] Paul would describe this as *mataiotēs*. All this changes when someone passes from death to life through the portals of Christian faith. But we are getting ahead of ourselves.

Do you see where those with an unconverted lifestyle have gone astray? It starts with **"their mind,"** their thinking, their mindset, their belief system, their worldview. That's why we here at Grace School of Theology believe the only way to change the world is to change their thinking. And that kind of change won't come by passing through town with a gospel crusade. That's a good beginning, but lasting change takes more than that. It requires education—and a lot of it. And that education has to be indigenous. The people with roots in their respective countries have the best chance of changing the minds of their own people.

That's why we are investing dollars in Nepal to create a branch campus of our school, not so Americans can go there and teach, but so Nepalese teachers can impact their own countrymen. And it's happening. All our courses are being translated into Nepalese so these people can get quality, accredited education in Christian thinking. It has the potential to change their nation. That excites me and gives me purpose. Doing God's kingdom work gives a person a reason to live and excitement for each day, a **purpose** for existing. Yes, I agree with Camus; life on this earth with its suffering, inequities, and injustice is completely absurd—without Christ.

Paul continues his description of the old life with the old way of thinking as having their understanding **"darkened."** This word for

---

99 https://en.wikipedia.org/wiki/Absurdism, accessed September 12, 2016.

darkened (*scotóō*) in the perfect tense points toward a state of darkness, and it all began with wrong thinking, wrong understanding.
Their "**ignorance**" again is a failure to properly understand.

But what if no one has explained the Christian worldview
to them? I well remember sitting on the Mao Zedong statue at
one of the leading universities in Shanghai, China, talking to
students that wanted to practice their English. It's what they called
their "English Corner." One student that wanted to become a
professional translator told me, "We have a crisis of belief here in
China. We don't believe in Buddhism anymore—too old fashioned.
We don't believe in the government anymore after Tiananmen
Square. We don't know what to believe." I hurt for that man.
He was crying out for meaning and purpose in life—something to
believe in.

Paul further describes the mental state of the unbeliever as a
"**blindness of their heart.**" The word for "blindness" is *pōrōsis*, which
is also used for the paste that forms around a break in a bone in
order to make new bone; thus "hardness" is probably best here. This
indicates that the unbeliever has seen the light but rejected it over and
over until his heart is hardened (see Rom 1:18ff). I find this especially
true of people that have received *gnosis*, the word from which we
get Gnostics, those with higher knowledge. Higher than what? Well,
higher than ours, that's for sure.

I once had Eugene Merrill, a renowned OT scholar, tell me that
during the summer he would often visit and stay at Tyndale House at
Cambridge University, a nook for biblical scholars from around the
world to come and research. He said he would sometimes run into
former students of his that wouldn't even acknowledge his presence,
let alone have a conversation with him. Why? They had received
gnōsis. Something in their graduate education led them to believe
they had risen so far above Dr. Merrill's level of understanding (he
has two PhDs, by the way) that they could not stoop down to his
level to engage in a conversation. And these are not unbelievers, but
it illustrates the effect of *gnōsis* on the heart. Of course, 1 Corinthians
8:1 tells us that *gnōsis* puffs up. Well, it can also harden. It can cause

pōrōsis of the heart. Here is Simon and Garfunkel's expression of purposelessness in life:

> From the moment of my birth
> To the instant of my death
> There are patterns I must follow
> Just as I breathe each breath;
> Like a rat in a maze the path
> before me lies,
> And the pattern never alters
> until the rat dies.[100]

Evolution is one of the many areas of knowledge in which the fact/value dichotomy is most obvious. Evolution is presented as an assumed fact; religion is only a value. As Nancy Pearcey so well explains,[101] the contemporary university pundits don't care what you believe anymore. To them it is completely irrelevant because they have relegated all religion and philosophy into the upper story of values, which are different for different people. All they care about are the facts (lower story). The science of facts (even if merely alleged and unproven) cannot be disputed.

Unfortunately, as the evolutionist philosopher Michael Ruse, states, "Evolution came into being as kind of a secular ideology, an explicit substitute for Christianity . . . I must admit that . . .the biblical literalists are absolutely right. Evolution is a religion. This was true of evolution in the beginning and it is true of evolution still today."[102] But if evolution is a religion, doesn't it belong on the upper story along with all other religions if we are going to be consistent?

---

100   http://www.quotesfromlyrics.com/simon-and-garfunkel-quotes/, accessed September 18, 2016.

101   Pearcey, 176-77.

102   Michael Ruse, "Saving Darwinism from the Darwinians," *National Post* (May 13, 2000), B-3.

Richard Dawkins shows how far the high priests of science will go in their blindness with this comment in his book *The Blind Watchmaker*: "Biology is the study of complicated things that give the appearance of having been designed for a purpose."[103] Wonderful. He looks into the light: there is design and purpose in the arrangement of cells. But alas, what seems to be purpose is only an appearance, not reality. My, my. And this is intelligence?

Such people are described by Paul as **"being past feeling."** The word used here is *"apalgeō,"* which means something that is "calloused" or "insensitive." It's like coming out of the darkness into the light. At first our eyes are sensitive to the light, but then they get used to it. Or we could turn that around. This "insensitivity" is like leaving the light and entering darkness. At first we may feel completely overwhelmed and lost, but then our eyes adjust to the darkness.

I talked to a young man that confessed to having been a pornography addict with a hundred dollar a day habit. He began selling drugs to pay for his pornography habit. When I talked to him he had been "clean" for ten years and helped other guys struggling with the problem. He described his initial shock at looking at all the explicit pictures of both normal sex and perversions. He was just a high school kid. This is where he learned about sex—online. All kinds of sex. He talked about the growing insensitivity after the initial shock. And then he described the insatiable hunger for more and more things to titillate his senses. I won't go into all the phases he described, but basically he became insensitive to one phase so he would go on to another one, each phase more ribald than the last. Finally, he realized there was no end to all, and he was hopelessly lost with a $2500 a month habit funded by selling drugs.

---

103 Richard Dawkins, *The Blind Watchmaker* (New York, NY: Norton, 1986), 1.

We are reminded of oft quoted words of Alexander Pope:

Vice is a monster of such awful mien
that to be hated needs but to be seen
but seen to oft familiar of face
we first endure, then pity, then embrace.[104]

Paul himself portrays the problem with these words: **"Lewdness . . . uncleanness . . . greediness."** I think the NIV (not my favorite translation) hit the nail on the head this time: "sensuality so as to indulge in every kind of impurity, with a continual lust for more." Those last words, "a continual lust for more," describe the Greek word *pleonexia*, which seems to speak of a person who cannot be satisfied with whatever. They have to have more and more.

I once talked to a very successful lawyer that had enough money to retire before he was forty. I asked him if he enjoyed practicing law. He said, "No, I hate it." So, why not give it up and find something you enjoy. He said he liked hanging around the office so he could seduce the girls that worked there. He said it was his goal to seduce every girl in the office. He had a beautiful wife. So I asked him, "Your wife is so beautiful. What do you get out of chasing all these girls?" He said, "Oh, it's not the sex. It's the chase. It just makes me feel like a conqueror. I can't seem to get enough. I don't really know what's wrong with me. It will probably ruin my marriage." He was right. His marriage did dissolve. *Pleonexia*.

The sad thing here, among other things, is that this young lawyer was only talking to me because he was wondering if I could help him figure himself out. Actually, when you think about it, sin is spiritual insanity. We were designed for a different kind of life. You remember all the pictures from the Valdez oil spill. The most pathetic were the birds tarred and covered with oil. How tragic. Those birds were designed to fly. But they were all black and covered with tar. When

---

104 Alexander Pope, http://www.goodreads.com/quotes/94296-vice-is-a-monster-of-so-frightful-mien-as-to, accessed September 18, 2016.

the world sees a Christian covered with tar and squawking, "I'm a Christian, I'm a Christian," they look at us with pity and disgust. Such a contrast between what we say we believe and how we are actually behaving. We are behaving as though we are still unbelievers. We need to change our clothes. That's what the next section in Ephesians 4 is about.

We have seen that Paul expects us to leave the old life (17-19). Now we are to be living the new life in Christ (20-24).

II. LIVING THE NEW LIFE   4:20-24

20 But you have not so learned Christ, 21 if indeed you have heard Him and have been taught by Him, as the truth is in Jesus: 22 that you put off, concerning your former conduct, the old man which grows corrupt according to the deceitful lusts, 23 and be renewed in the spirit of your mind, 24 and that you put on the new man which was created according to God, in true righteousness and holiness.

The words **"put off"** and **"put on"** are key to this text. These are the words for taking off one set of clothes and putting on another. As he calls us to walk worthy of the calling by which we were called (4:1), Paul pictures a change of clothes. No longer should the child of God wander around wearing the filthy rags of the days when he lived in darkness. Now he should step into the light and put on a fresh set of clothes that he might be presentable for a visit to the king.

"So learned" uses a word for discipleship: *emathete*. It means "to learn," but it is very similar to the word for "disciple" (*mathētēs*). A disciple is a learner. Then Paul says, "If indeed you have heard Him and have been taught by Him." These are more words indicating what they had learned. We must remember that Paul had spent three years discipling these Ephesian believers. Can you imagine? Three years with the apostle Paul. That would have to be almost as good as three years of seminary! Ha, ha. The point is that these were not new believers. They had learned a lot, probably from the best teacher in the Christian world. But some of them had not been applying what they had learned. Sounds familiar?

In seminary, it sometimes felt like our instructors had opened a little hole in the top of our heads and stuck a funnel in and then began pouring knowledge into the funnel. But they often told us it would probably take ten years for our walk to catch up with our talk. It's one thing to know it; it's another thing to apply it. Notice, however, Paul never disparages knowledge, as some people like to do. After all, you can't apply it until you know it. And if you know the wrong thing, then imagine how far off your application will be. But these believers knew the right things. Now it was time for them to show what they had learned.

One of God's amazing creations is the butterfly. They have the most phenomenal color designs. And they flit around the air light as a feather. But it didn't start out that way, did it? The beautiful butterfly used to be an ugly caterpillar. Instead of soaring in the heavens, the caterpillar crawled around in the mud. If you were to stick a caterpillar in front of me and tell me it could fly some day, I'd either say you were crazy or, "That would take a miracle." Yes, to fly, the crawling caterpillar would have to basically become a new creature. Voila!

That's Paul's appeal. He tells his readers they are no longer caterpillars. The Holy Spirit has made them into new creatures designed to fly in the heavenlies. But most Christians see themselves as forgiven caterpillars instead of emerging butterflies. The issue is who we are, and in light of that, how we should then live. We are to live in sharp contrast to who we were; we are to live in total conformity to who we are.

It's interesting that the caterpillar was always designed to become a butterfly. Jonathan Edwards wrote a book called *Images of Shadows of Divine Things*. His thesis is that God created the natural world in such a way that in every aspect it reflects the realities of the spiritual world as described in Scripture. So what we call natural revelation is full of pictures of spiritual revelation, or what is contained in the Scriptures. In fact, Edwards uses the butterfly as one of the examples. Think about it. Of all the ways God could have created the butterfly, he choose this arduous process of starting out as a caterpillar crawling in the mud, going into a cocoon, and finally a butterfly. This is the process of metamorphosis, exactly what 2 Corinthian 3:18 describes regarding the believer and his own metamorphosis from what he was without Christ into the very image of Christ.

But imagine two caterpillars crawling along. They see a butterfly overhead. One of the caterpillars remarks, "That is an incredible creature, the most beautiful creature I have ever seen." The other caterpillar responds, "Yes, that is what's known as the butterfly. It is one of God's most beautiful creatures." They both kept watching it until the butterfly goes out of sight. Then the other caterpillar said, "That may be a beautiful creature, but you'd never get me up in one of those things."

It reminds me of the scenario I witnessed while hiking in NE Oregon one summer. I was walking along a gorgeous mountain stream as the path I was on slowly went higher and higher into the forest. I was watching the path in front of me carefully so I wouldn't stumble. Then about ten yards ahead I saw a flurry of activity in the middle of the path, near the ground. Curious, I went ahead slowly. Then I saw it was a bunch of butterflies in a bit of frenzy. I'd never seen anything like that before. Each butterfly was different. Each had an exquisite color design of incredible beauty. I got closer to see what all the commotion was about. Suddenly, the source of excitement became clear. The butterflies had found a pile of manure in the middle of the trail. They were having a feeding frenzy. As I looked at the fresh, gooey pile of excrement and all God's beautiful creatures vying for their share, I felt a little nauseous. Something just wasn't right about that picture.

There is also something wrong with the way we believers so often try to get our nutrients for life from the manure of this world. Here are these beautiful creatures grabbing for all the *skubala* (Paul's word for manure in Phil 3:7) their hands can hold and then wondering why they are never satisfied. James calls it "friendship with the world." The problem here in the West is that the world has so much to offer that really looks good. And it actually may be good. But it's a matter of the heart. Trying to love the world and love God at the same time is risky business. James doesn't even think it is possible. In a stunning rebuke he calls it unfaithfulness to God—spiritual adultery (James 4:4). There is just something wrong with the picture of people who claim to be sold out to God but are at the same time seeking satisfaction in this world. It's like a bunch of butterflies in the slurpy, gooey . . .

Paul chooses a picture not quite so repulsive to get his point across. Clothes. The Germans have a saying: *Kleider machen Leute.* It means, "The clothes make the man." Napoleon put it another way: "Every man becomes his uniform." I think the idea is that if we dress well, we will think well—of ourselves. If we think well of ourselves, we will be better people. Well, that's not quite what Paul has in mind. He is not saying we can change from the outside in. No, he is saying a change has taken place on the inside that should now show up on the outside. Again, **we should no longer live the way we used to live because we are no longer who we used to be.** A new man requires a new wardrobe.

The clothes of the old man (all we were before knowing Christ) grow tattered and old even as the corruptible man grows old. His lusts are **deceitful.** Men lust after sex, money, and power. But the satisfaction from these things wanes as the corruptible man gets older and older. I had dinner with a billionaire one evening. He had all the trappings of wealth but he seemed miserable. His lips painted a picture of his misery. He had nothing good to say about anything or anybody. Turned out he was a white supremacist. But his health was slowly giving way. His power was gone because he could no longer work. He retained an office at the headquarters of the company he built, but he had no say-so. Age had diminished his physical prowess so there was little satisfaction in things of the flesh. All he had left was his money. To his credit he had formed a charitable foundation, but he missed the joy and satisfaction that comes from philanthropy because he had turned the foundation over to others to administrate.

Paul says, "Wake up. Can't you see these lusts are deceitful? They promise satisfaction but bring only an aftertaste of emptiness." Take off those dirty rags. Put on the new clothes of the new man:

righteousness and holiness. Just as the new man is incorruptible, so are his clothes. Holiness doesn't wear out. Righteousness doesn't need to go to the dry cleaners. These clothes will last forever. As such, the satisfaction they bring does not fade away. Mick Jaeger of the *Rolling Stones* used to sing:

> I can't get no satisfaction
> I can't get no satisfaction
> 'Cause I try and I try and I try and I try
> I can't get no, I can't get no . . .

The lyrics of the song move from what advertisers offer on the radio to clothes to girls. Mick just can't find satisfaction anywhere. Neither can anyone else . . . in the things this world has to offer.

Of course, the beauty of living for Christ is the promise of renewal. Paul tells us to be **"renewed in the spirit of our minds."** He moves from the corruptible to the incorruptible. That which is incorruptible lasts. Therefore, it can bring lasting satisfaction. I recently had my fifth attack of diverticulitis. Quite painful. So is the treatment. No problem with the antibiotics. It's the diet. They put you on a liquid diet. Four sheets of paper to tell you what you can and cannot eat: broth, jello, pudding. As my wife was reading through the list, I was slowly gagging to death. But then she spoke two words that brought refreshment to my soul: ice cream. I have long been a recovering addict from Homemade Blue Bell Vanilla ice cream. The Hebrew for this ice cream is none other than manna. You remember that manna was white like vanilla. If you got more than your share, it melted. Clearly, Homemade Blue Bell Vanilla Ice cream is the only thing along with the quail that could sustain a generation forty years in the wilderness.

But I said "recovering" addict. You see, I used to be able to buy two half gallons of Blue Bell for five bucks—on sale, of course. But over the years the price went higher and higher. This offended me. Blue Bell was not a want; it was a need. That they would keep jacking up the price on something I needed for survival was offensive to me, so

I went cold turkey. After a period of withdrawal I found I could exist without Blue Bell. Really. But when I heard the doctor had actually prescribed ice cream for the healing of my ailing diverticula, no price was too high; $7.50 a half gallon—no problem. I had Blue Bell for breakfast, lunch, dinner, and snacks. What was I supposed to do, eat jello?

But, you know, strangest thing. After all that Blue Bell, day after day, meal after meal, even my taste buds became cloyed. Suddenly, jello started looking pretty good. But isn't that just the way it is with the things of this world? Get enough of them and they lose their appeal.

But not the things of the Spirit. As we feast on the things of the Spirit, our minds are renewed day by day. And we become what we think about—inside out. That's God's way. Our clothes on the outside become an expression of what's on the inside. And once you have tasted the deep things of the Spirit nothing in this world can substitute. I have a friend that has done well in business and loves cars. Every six months it's a different Maserati or Porsche or Lamborghini or Ferrari. I drive a twenty-year old Buick (and proud of it, I might add). A couple of months ago my friend asked my wife and me if we would like to come out and take a drive in his new Rolls Royce. He said there were only five like it in the whole world. Of course, we accepted.

But, you know, as I looked at his stable of fancy cars, though enjoyable, I just have no hunger for those things. I don't judge my friend. He loves cars. There was a time I did too. I can still remember when I earned enough one summer during college to go out and pay cash for a brand new Firebird. I thought that car was really something. I thought I was really something. But it brought no lasting satisfaction to me. In time the car wore out and actually became quite ugly. No lasting satisfaction. So I drive my old Buick. Tonight I drive into the wealthiest part of Houston to visit a donor to our school. I'm not sure they will let me in with my old Buick, but we'll try.

There is nothing wrong with being blessed from our careers and owning nice houses and nice cars and what-have-you. But the issue is the heart. Our God is a jealous God. That's just another way of saying God loves us more than anything or anyone in the world. When we make him second or third or fourth in our lives, it says we don't love him as much as he loves us, and it hurts him. The greatest commandment isn't about loving God for nothing.

CONCLUSION

We began this study asking what "Winds of Doctrine" have blown Good Ship Christian so far off course in America that this is no longer considered a Christian nation. We looked at a couple of those winds: **HURRIANCE PLATO** and **HURRICANE AUGUSTINE**. Now we want to look at another hurricane:

HURRICANE ARISTOTLE (D. 322 BC)

Aristotle was a student of Plato for about twenty years, only going off on his own after Plato died. As such he was greatly influenced by Plato's philosophy of forms and ideals. But as he branched out on his own he became less interested in forms and ideals in an unseen world and more interested in the world he could observe. He became our first scientist, writing hundreds of works about things he observed in the world around him. He rejected the philosophy of dualism taught by Plato, which said the spiritual world is the intrinsic good while the material world is intrinsically evil. Just as the caterpillar moves from crawling into the chrysalis and finally the butterfly, that process cannot be viewed as evil. The material thing is moving toward its own ideal form, its *telos* (end goal). Surely that is a good thing.

So with his empiricism, Aristotle laid the groundwork for what developed into the "two story" approach to knowledge spoken of by

Francis Schaefer.[105] I am oversimplifying a bit, but Thomas Aquinas (d. AD 1274) was the first influential man in the church to popularize Aristotle's approach to knowledge and logic. A cache of Aristotle's works were discovered in Spain and translated by a team of Muslims, Jews, and Christians.[106] The Muslims were needed because they are the ones who preserved Aristotle's works for centuries. They had been lost to the Greek/Latin speaking world but translated for preservation into Arabic. They regarded Aristotle as the "First Teacher."

The great discovery is made in the twelfth century. Aquinas comes on the scene roughly a century later. He falls in love with Aristotle's thinking. Of course, Aristotle is not a Christian or even a believer in God. So faith was not one of his centers of inquiry. His god, you might say, was reason. Observation through his senses was the conduit for knowledge. But Aquinas was a man of faith. But he loved Aristotle. So he tried to combine faith and reason. In doing so, he became a pioneer in the two-story approach to knowledge. Faith was on the upper story, while reason resided down below on the first story. How to reconcile faith and reason—that was a conundrum that preoccupied both scientists and theologians for centuries.

The problem with the division between faith and reason is that there was no connection between the two in the minds of the scientific and theological thinkers of the day (Roman Catholic scholars). As the disconnect grew wider, faith was an area of knowledge overseen by the priests, while science was explored by laymen. The priests had access to the heavenly; the laymen could only work with the earthly. This ultimately led to the distinction between the sacred and the secular, and, in time, the church and the state.

This sacred/secular distinction leads to the "be holy on Sunday

---

105 Francis Schaeffer deals with the divided concept of truth in *Escape from Reason* and *The God Who is There* (in *The Complete Works of Francis A. Schaeffer* [Wheaton, IL: Crossway, 1982]).

106 Richard E. Rubenstein, *Aristotle's Children* (Orlando, FL: Harcourt, 2003).

but live anyway you like the rest of the week." Sunday is sacred; the rest of the week is secular. It was always hard for me as a young Christian seeing and watching people that reaffirmed what they believed every Sunday (the Apostles Creed, for example), but played by a different set of rules during the week. The disjuncture between what we believe and how we behave didn't make any sense to me until I began to recognize the sacred/secular compartmentalization of life. How Christians behaved during the week was part of their worldview; it was part of what they believed. Holy behavior was reserved for Sunday.

As Nancy Pearcey has so well documented in her two books *Total Truth* and *Saving Leonardo*, this same dichotomy morphed into a split between the facts (lower story) and values (upper story). The facts are observable, quantifiable, and verifiable. Values are relative, grey, and unverifiable. The man of prejudice says, "Don't bother me with the facts, my mind is made up." The man of science says, "Don't bother me with your values, my mind is made up." People living on the lower story don't care what people on the second story believe. It doesn't matter because those are just values. The cry of the existentialist is: "What's right for you isn't necessarily what's right for me."

Of course, this disjuncture between the Upper Story (values) and the Lower Story (facts) explains why Intelligent Design is not allowed in the classroom. They mistakenly view ID as religion, and in their two-story system, the educators have religion on the upper story of values, while science is on the lower story of fact. We can verify science; we cannot verify religion. Therefore, since ID implies an Intelligent Designer (God), they throw it into the sphere of religion. Too bad they cannot recognize the obvious, as Michael Ruse did, that evolution is also a religion.[107]

So, how did we get where we are in 21st Century America? The "Winds of Doctrine." Not too hard to figure out, is it? And now this facts/values dichotomy has encroached on our First Amendment

---

107   See footnote 4.

rights through the misguided application of separation between the church and the state. The church has no right to impose its **values** on other members of the state, we are told. Just saying a prayer before a football game has been tagged a violation of civil rights. How absurd. Perhaps Paul Harvey said it best:

> I don't believe in Santa Claus, but I'm not going to sue somebody for singing a Ho-Ho-Ho song in December. I don't agree with Darwin, but I didn't go out and hire a lawyer when my high school teacher taught his theory of evolution.
>
> Life, liberty or your pursuit of happiness will not be endangered because someone says a 30-second prayer before a football game. So what's the big deal? It's not like somebody is up there reading the entire book of Acts. They're just talking to a God they believe in and asking him to grant safety to the players on the field and the fans going home from the game.
>
> "But it's a Christian prayer," some will argue. Yes, and this is the United States of America, a country founded on Christian principles. According to our very own phone book, Christian churches outnumber all others better than 200-1. So what would you expect—somebody chanting Hare Krishna?
>
> If I went to a football game in Jerusalem, I would expect to hear a Jewish prayer. If I went to a soccer game in Baghdad, I would expect to hear someone pray to Buddha [I think he meant Allah]. And I wouldn't be offended. It wouldn't bother me one bit. When in Rome . . .
>
> "But what about the atheists?" is another argument. What about them? Nobody is asking them to be baptized. We're not going to pass the collection plate. Just humor us for 30 seconds. If that's asking too much, bring a Walkman or a pair of earplugs. Go to the bathroom. Visit the concession stand. Call your lawyer.
>
> Unfortunately, one or two will make that call. One or two will tell thousands what they can and cannot do. I don't think

a short prayer at a football game is going to shake the world's foundations.

Christians are just sick and tired of turning the other cheek while our courts strip us of all our rights. Our parents and grandparents taught us to pray before eating, to pray before we go to sleep. Our Bible tells us to pray without ceasing. Now a handful of people and their lawyers are telling us to cease praying. God help us. And if that last sentence, offends you, well, . . . just sue me.

The silent majority has been silent too long. It's time we let that one or two who scream loud enough to be heard know . . . that the vast majority don't care what they want. It is time the majority rules! It's time we tell them, you don't have to pray; you don't have to say the pledge of allegiance; you don't have to believe in God or attend services that honor him. That is your right, and we will honor your right. But by golly, you are no longer going to take our rights away. We are fighting back, and we WILL WIN!

God bless us one and all . . . especially those who denounce him. God bless America, despite all her faults. She is still the greatest nation of all. God bless our service men who are fighting to protect our right to pray and worship God. May 2006 be the year the silent majority is heard and we put God back as the foundation of our families and institutions. Keep looking up. Paul Harvey—Good Day!

12

WINDS OF DOCTRINE
Part 3 – Freed for Interdependence
Ephesians 4:25-29

INTRODUCTION

Stephen Covey begins his best selling book *The 7 Habits of Highly Effective People* with some laments from frustrated, discouraged people. Listen to some of them:

1. My marriage has gone flat. We don't fight or anything; we just don't love each other anymore. We're going to counseling; we've tried a number of things, but we just can't seem to rekindle the feeling we used to have.

2. I want to teach my children the value of work. To get them to do anything, I have to supervise every move ... and put up with complaining every step of the way. It's so much easier to do it myself. Why can't children do their work cheerfully and without being reminded?

3. My teenage son is rebellious and on drugs. No matter what I try, he won't listen to me. He pierces every piece of flesh he can find. What can I do?

4. I've set up and met my career goals and I'm having tremendous professional success. But it cost me my personal and family life. I don't know my wife and children anymore. I'm not even sure I know myself and what's really important to me. I've had to ask myself—has it been worth it?

5. I've taken course after course on effective management training. I expect a lot out of my employees, and I work hard to be friendly towards them and treat them right. But I don't feel any loyalty from them. I think if I were home sick for a day, they'd just spend most of their time gathering at the water fountain. Why can't I train them to be independent and responsible—or find employees who can be?[108]

Changes need to take place if these people are going to find the fulfillment in life they're looking for. And coming back to a case for change from the inside out, he says the self-help books that teach us how to manipulate others with external people skills will fail in the long term with those that are closest to us. Our wives, our children, our work partners or employees can see through the external veneer to the selfish motives behind our techniques. They know when they are being loved or being used. Sooner or later trust breaks down in these relationships. People who are economic successes often find themselves domestic failures. They can manage their money, but they cannot manage their relationships.

Covey challenges his readers to work on character before community. He wants us to develop seven habits to bring us fulfillment

---

108 Stephen R. Covey, *The 7 Habits of Highly Effective People* (New York, NY: 1989), 23-24.

in life. Now, obviously I am not teaching a Stephen Covey course. But I noticed something straight from the book of Ephesians when I saw how he divided his seven habits into three tiers. Here are the three tiers: Dependence—Independence—Interdependence.[109] We all come into the world dependent. We couldn't take care of ourselves if we had to. We are especially dependent on our mothers. Hopefully our parents want us to become independent some day. What joy and rejoicing my wife and I had when our third child finally moved out of the house. We celebrated his independence. We called it Independence Day for him and for us. Independence is good. Independence is a step toward individual maturity. In America, especially, we celebrate independence. The Declaration of Independence. But independence can go too far. We pride ourselves on our rugged individualism. Unfortunately individualism can lead to isolationism. We like the sense that we don't need to depend on other people to make it through life. But individualism and independence can be stumbling blocks on the road to *interdependence*. When we read the word *interdependence*, we may shy away, thinking this is a step backwards. This is going back to dependence. But according to Covey, it is only on this third tier he calls *interdependence* that we find fulfillment. Why? Because we cannot find fulfillment in isolation. We must learn to relate. God made us that way. As we mature in life we need to move away from Dependence to Independence to Interdependence.

According to Ephesians chapter 2, we come into this world dependent, and I don't mean just physically. We are spiritually dependent as well. We come into this world with a sinful nature. We sin and Paul describes us as children of wrath. We are slaves of this sinful nature. We can keep from sinning some of the time, but not all of time. We are involuntarily dependent on our sinful nature.

But through Christ we have been set free from our sin nature by virtue of our **Position** in him. We have a new sense of independence. No longer do we have to serve the sinful nature. Unfortunately,

---

109 Ibid., 60.

for so many Christians in our western culture, here is where our rugged individualism gets in the way. Because most of us can live financially independent of other people, we so easily can let that independence bleed over into the spiritual realm. We may tip our hat to God on Sundays when we go to church, but then live completely independent of one another during the week. We drive home after church, drive into the garage and go into the house, but we left Jesus back in the car. We may do the same thing on Monday morning— listen to Christian radio or an audio book about Jesus on the way to work, but leave him in the parking garage. We are not taking him with us into the community, into the marketplace, or into our homes.

Ephesians is a book about total truth, truth that travels with us 24/7, truth that permeates every area of our lives. God created us in his image. And only in Christianity do we find a Godhead with three persons—Father, Son, and Holy Spirit. They have been living in community, loving each other and practicing relational virtues since eternity past. When we were created in his image, he created us to be like him—interdependent. That's how he made us. Therefore, it is absolutely impossible for a person to be completely fulfilled in isolation. He can find partial fulfillment, but not total.

We train our kids to win championships, but they may lose at relationships. They may succeed at their finances but fail in their families. They go full bore when it comes to competition, but they shut down when it comes to community. All this goes against the way they were made. It leaves them lonely and confused, often isolated and depressed. Covey says good character precedes good community. And Paul says the same thing in the book of Ephesians chapters 4 through six.

Paul spent three chapters on our independence from the sin nature. But now he calls for us to live in accordance with our newfound independence. He wants us to live a life free from slavery to the sin nature. But as he says in Galatians 5, we are not to use our new independence as an opportunity to feed our lusts, but rather to serve one another in love. Do you see what's happening here? Now Paul is moving from independence to interdependence. That's why chapter 4 starts out with the body of Christ. He simply claims we can't go to the highest tier of maturity alone. God is saying spiritual maturity only comes for those who move from independence to interdependence. We can't grow up without reaching out. Our vertical growth is in direct proportion to our horizontal. Have you ever wondered how we could possibly develop the fruit of the Spirit in isolation? The Holy Spirit in us develops most of the fruit as we relate to other people.

In Ephesians 4:13 Paul gives us the goal of the Christian life. The goal of the Christian life is not to go to heaven when we die. Receiving Christ as our Savior is the greatest gift we will ever get. But God calls us to run a race. Receiving Christ would be the starting blocks of this race but not the goal line. The goal line is to become like Jesus, to develop into the measure of the stature of the fullness of Christ. Until we develop into this mature man Paul talks about, we are subject to every wind of doctrine. He likens us to little children blown about by the wind of the sea. So what I want to do in this lesson and in succeeding lessons is to go through the text, first of all, and then go over some of the winds of doctrine that so easily keep us from going on to maturity. So first of all, let's look at our passage for this lesson, Ephesians 4:25-29.

In our last lesson we talked about our old life versus our new life. Now we want to talk about our old clothes versus new clothes. Remember, nothing in our **Condition** can change our **Position**, but our **Position** can change our **Condition** for the better. In accordance with what's true in our new **Position** in Christ, we should wear the proper clothes. Instead of the rags of a spiritual slave we should wear the new clothes of spiritual royalty. So Paul uses this image of clothing in order to urge us to disrobe and rerobe. He wants us to take off the clothes of our former life before we knew Christ and put on new clothes that reflect who we truly are in Christ. He wants us to get a new wardrobe in verses 25 to 32. We might have called this lesson: the Lion, the Lamb, and the Wardrobe. In these verses he talks about new outerwear and new underwear. New outerwear is what we are looking at in this lesson. In our next lesson we will look at new underwear. We'll look at our new outerwear regarding our Witness in verse 25, our Wrath in verses 26-27, our Work verse 28, and our Words in verse 29. As we look at these new clothes, we need to be very much aware that God is taking us from independence to interdependence. These are building blocks for good relationships.

EPHESIANS
"The Creation and the Conduct of the Church"

SALUTATION   1:1-2

INTRODUCTION—"Spiritual Blessings in the Heavenlies"   1:3-14
   (Paul's Prayer for Perception)   1:15-23

BODY   2:1-6:9
  I. Creation of the Church (Its Position)   2:1-3:21
  II. Conduct of the Church (Its Condition)   4:1-6:9
    A. The Goal: Maturity of the Body   4:1-16
    B. The Means: Maturity of the Individual   4:17-6:9
      1. Through Personal Sanctification   4:17-5:14
        a. Walking in Life   4:17-32
          1) Old Life versus New Life   4:17-24
          2) Old Clothes versus New Clothes 4:25-32
      2. Through Personal Submission   5:15-6:9

CONCLUSION—"Spiritual Battles in the Heavenlies"   6:10-20

FAREWELL

I. REGARDING OUR WITNESS   25

²⁵ Therefore, putting away lying, "Let each one of you speak truth with his neighbor," for we are members of one another.

We are to "take off" (v. 22) the dirty clothes of the old man and "put on" the clean clothes of the new man (v. 24). The four character qualities mentioned in vv. 25-29 are external while those that follow in vv. 30-32 are internal. So, to maintain Paul's imagery, we speak of our outerwear and our underwear—external actions and internal attitudes. In this verse he says to "take off" lying. It is an ugly rag from our old wardrobe. It is not becoming to a Christian.

Now when Paul says to stop lying, he's talking about the very first requirement for building a good relationship—trust. If you can't trust someone, it's very difficult to have a good relationship with him or her. Trust precedes love. Susan has been happily married for twenty-five years. But then she discovered her husband subscribing to pornography sites on the Internet. She was so angry she picked up his computer and threw it downstairs. He asked for forgiveness and said he wouldn't do it again. But the pornography spam kept hitting their Wi-Fi site at home, so she knew he was still watching it. One day she walked in while he was looking at gayboys.com. She really got scared and confronted him. He said there was not a problem. She knew he was lying. Trust flew out the window, and riding on its wings was love. She said she had not been intimate with her husband for over a year. She said trust precedes intimacy.

That's a marriage relationship, but we could expand this application to all human relationships, couldn't we—your boss, your co-workers, your elders at church, your best friend? Trust is one of the building blocks of good relationships. Lying destroys trust. When we make promises we don't keep, they will begin to question our credibility. If they don't believe you, they can't trust you. So Paul wants liars to take off that stained garment. Then he goes on to anger management.

II. REGARDING OUR WRATH   26-27

[26] *"Be angry, and do not sin"*: do not let the sun go down on your wrath, [27] nor give place to the devil.

Uh, oh. Here is my biblical justification to get angry. Look, it is a command: "Be angry." Well, wait a minute. Let me suggest an alternative translation here: "If you become angry, then do not sin." Although all anger is not sinful (Jesus got angry), it usually is. Anger can pop up so quickly we often do not know its root. When my rights are violated, my goals are blocked, or my feelings are hurt, the resulting anger is usually a form of self-defense and is usually sinful.

Uncontrolled anger can mow down personal relationships like a strike at the bowling alley. I watched a sad movie about Beethoven. It was so sad because he was never able to establish solid human relationships because of his father's blocked goal. His father's goal was to make money from his gifted son like Mozart's father did. But Beethoven was not a piano prodigy. People even laughed at him. So his father got angry, not at the people who laughed, but at his son. So in a fit of rage he beat his son's head over and over, causing Beethoven to become more and more deaf as the years went by. Much of his music was about his own anger and bitterness towards his father and his frustration over his inability to hear and to establish healthy human relationships, especially with a family.

How many cases of child abuse stem from the anger of a father? Jeff Eckert talks about the "father wound" that so many people carry around, a wound that continues to fester and spread its germs to succeeding generations.[110] But feelings are hard to control, and they are self-generating. Yet the thrust of this verse is anger management.

One misapplication of this verse is to think all problems need to be resolved before going to sleep at night. That can lead to even more problems because late at night is when we are tired. Trying to hash through difficult issues when tired can lead to losing patience and getting even more angry. We need to remember the Jewish day ended at sundown. The verse seems to be saying, "Let the day of your anger be the day of your reconciliation." Otherwise the devil gains a

---

110 Jeff Eckert, http://newlife.com/what-is-the-father-wound, accessed September 5, 2016.

foothold in my life, a foothold that can turn into a stronghold. My anger (*orgē*) can turn to wrath (*parorgismos*—bitterness). Bitterness can poison my whole family tree. If we take a literal application, then we should resolve our issues before sundown. The main idea is to not let our anger simmer. When we stuff it, that is when anger turns to bitterness.

So Paul says a little anger management will go a long way in building good relationships. Now he goes into our Work.

III. REGARDING OUR WORK   28

> [28] Let him who stole steal no longer, but rather let him labor, working with *his* hands what is good, that he may have something to give him who has need.

Most of the skills in the first century were manual. Not a lot of white-collar workers. I had a church member once who spent his career with an oil company that moved him and his family around a lot. His observation was that most of our church was made up of "white-collar migrant workers." Ephesus didn't have that kind of worker, but it did have a lot of loafers that sponged on the Christian society. Unfortunately, they also had a lot of thieves. So he's just talking about basic honesty—another building block for good relationships. And that goes back to trust, doesn't it? If a man will cheat at work, he could very well cheat on his wife. Both involve a lack of honesty.

On the other hand, one of the best ways to build relationships is through our money. Jesus tells us to learn how to make friends with our money so that when our life is over and we are ushered into heaven, we will have some friends there to greet us—people we have helped along the way with our money (Luke 16:9). But if we don't know good money management, we won't have extra money to use for the needs of others, will we?

Our Witness, our Wrath, our Work—wearing the right clothes in all these situations can help us build good relationships. But Paul mentions one more—our Words.

IV. REGARDING OUR WORDS   29

²⁹ Let no corrupt word proceed out of your mouth, but what is good for necessary edification, that it may impart grace to the hearers.

When I was a new Christian, I thought this verse meant we were to stop cussing, if we did that in the first place. The NKJ translated the Greek word *sapros* as "corrupt," and the NIV says, "unwholesome." But the best way to understand a word sometimes is to study its opposite. If the opposite is clear, it informs us about that which is less clear. The word (*oikodomēn*) translated "edification" (NKJ) or "building up" (ESV) is clear. It means to use our words to build people up. And what is the opposite of building people up? It is to tear them down, of course. Lots of people are experts at tearing people down with their words. How many children have labored in vain to get a word of praise out of their fathers?

It is harder for most of us to build people up with our words than to tear them down. We are quick to find fault, but slow to find favor. Perhaps nothing destroys good relationships faster than hurtful, unkind, cutting words. On the other had, who doesn't want to be around someone who builds them up. I remember one pastor that was especially good at building up his staff. One of his staff members was talking to me one time about his boss and said, "Well, who wouldn't want to work for someone who makes you feel good all the time."

One of the great principles John Maxwell has contributed to human relationships is this comment: "When I meet someone for the first time, I immediately look for ways to add value to them."[111] For him that meant looking for something within the other person that was praiseworthy or a skill they might develop. Maxwell thought we added value to the other person by verbalizing this trait or skill in a positive way. I have an aversion to insincere or manipulative flattery,

---

111 John Maxwell, *Developing the Leaders Around You* (Nashville, TN: Thomas Nelson Publishing, 1995), 181-96.

but even the great guru on human relationships, Dale Carnegie, said to "be lavish in your approbation and sincere in your praise."[112]

But someone will surely object, "But what if there is nothing praiseworthy, or what if they don't deserve to be praised?" Wait a minute. What are we to be mirrors of? The grace of God, right? The verse goes on to say by building others up, even those who don't deserve it, we are ministering "grace" (*charis*) to the hearers. Wow. It could be something said to encourage someone who has directly hurt us by saying something ugly or gossiping about us. Or as Jesus might have said, if we just go around patting our friends on the back, how are we any different from unbelievers? It takes the Holy Spirit working in us, that is, supernatural power, to do something supernatural. It's natural to pat our friends on the back. It is supernatural to pat our enemies (someone who has hurt us) on the back. Mirrors of God's grace.

God, through Paul, wants us to go on to maturity—Christ-likeness. That will only happen as we move from spiritual independence to spiritual interdependence. That means we need to know how to relate to other people, especially in the Body of Christ. For proper relationships with each other we need to be wearing the right clothes, the right outerwear and the right underwear. In this lesson we looked at the right outerwear regarding our Witness, our Wrath, our Work, and our Words. In the next lesson we will take a closer look at our "underwear."

As something of an excursus, we have also referred to "Winds of Doctrine" that can keep us from going on the maturity. In fact, a mark of immaturity is to be blown about by every wind of doctrine. In order to deflect gale force winds of false doctrine we need a storm shelter of healthy doctrine. So let's look at another one of these hurricanes that has blown much of our Christian "fleet" off course.

---

112 Dale Carnegie, *How to Win Friends and Influence People* (New York, NY: Gallery Books, 1936), 220.

HURRICANE ROUSSEAU (D. 1778)

1. **Creation—man is born good.** Man is not only good, he is free, autonomous, and independent. But if man is good, how do we explain evil in the world?

2. **Fall—Society has corrupted man.** Social relationships oppress and corrupt man (you see how this is just the opposite of biblical teaching?). The conventional relationships of marriage, the family, and the church are evil. They hamper man's freedom to develop himself into all he can be. In his most famous work, *The Social Contract*, Rousseau begins by saying, "Man is born free, and everywhere he is in chains."

3. **Redemption—the State will free man from social conventions that imprison him.** The State can liberate us from social oppression by destroying all loyalties except loyalty to the State itself.

4. *The Social Contract*—**the State must dissolve all social bonds (marriage, family, church, marketplace, etc.) so the "New Man" can choose his own contracts.**

5. **Autonomous Self—the "New Man" must be free to reach his maximum potential.** Autonomy expresses our true nature. Lone, solitary, autonomous individuals whose only motivating force is self-preservation (*amour de soi*). Social relationships are not ultimately real. They are confining. They interfere with our natural ability to create ourselves, to develop and transform ourselves.

   Of course, this is directly in conflict with the biblical worldview. Do you remember back in the Garden before the Fall? God put one man and one woman in a marriage relationship that was intrinsically good. No evil. No sin. God put his blessing on this institution that he created. Why? Because we are created in his image (*imago dei*). Through this divinely instituted relationship we express the same virtues God has expressed: love, submission, self-sacrifice, empathy—all these virtues are developed in community. They are only enjoyed in a relationship. And so the marriage relationship is the foundational relationship of all society. "Relationships are part of the created order and thus are ontological real and good."[113] Only in relationships where individual desires are sacrificed for the common good (whether it is in a marriage, a family, a church, a society, a state, or a nation) do we develop the virtues that prepare us for eternal use in the Kingdom of Christ and of God.

Are we surprised, then, that this most fundamental relationship of society is being attacked with fervor in Western culture? It's not just America. It's all of Europe and North America. But in America, strangely enough, the battle has shifted into the arena of the Constitution and the Supreme Court. The "separation of church and state" has been adopted by those who want to ban the church from having any influence over the state, when actually the original intent of the statement was to keep the state from interfering in matters of the church. As such there has been a line of demarcation between God and Caesar, a line never to be crossed by Caesar. God defined marriage. But now Caesar is reaching across the line of demarcation to redefine marriage: one adult human plus one adult human. The Supreme Court has been trying to force the states to redefine marriage. Instead of a union between one man and one woman, no longer does the couple need to be two people of the opposite sex.[114] Charles Krauthammer, in one of his acerbic commentaries, says polygamy will be next.[115] He claims the same arguments used to take away the 1 Man + 1 Woman = Marriage equation can be used to take

---

113 Pearcey, 138.

114 http://www.heritage.org/research/reports/2015/03/memo-to-supreme-court-state-marriage-laws-are-constitutional, accessed September 6, 2016.

115 Charles Krauthammer, *Things That Matter* (New York, NY: Crown Forum, 2013), 720 in the eBook.

away 1 + 1. Now that the government (Caesar) has crossed the line to dissolve the gender distinction, it is only one step away from saying it can be 1 +2 or 1+ 3, or whatever.

But who needs marriage anymore, anyway? Just cohabit. We can keep populating the earth that way, can't we? Or can we? Once society crumbles, rule of law goes with it.

6. **Rousseau—is the one that influenced revolutionaries like Robespierre, Marx and Lenin, Mussolini, Hitler, Stalin, Mao Zedong, and Pol Pot.** It shouldn't be too hard to extrapolate from what we have said which world leaders fell under the spell of Rousseau. Jean Jacque Rousseau had to flee Paris. He had to hide out in Switzerland because his teachings were so heretical. But people picked up on them. The first one was **Robespierre.** He incited the French Revolution in the 1790's. Then along came **Marx and Engels** (around 1750). They followed in the line of Rousseau and Robespierre. Marx and his wife were also banned from Paris because of their seditious teaching and relocated to London. The rest of the rogues we know all too well.

7. **The Irony—blind loyalty to the State leads to loss of individual freedom.** Robespierre trumpeted freedom and autonomy for the individual. But in the totalitarian state, individual rights are yielded for the benefit of the State. And the totalitarian state is a terrorist state. When I taught in Almaty, Kazakhstan, (2000) it had been about ten years since the fall of the Soviet Union. I asked some of my students: "What do you think of democracy?" The answer: "It is good for Adam." What does that mean? "It is good for fallen man. You see the Red Mafia everywhere. Our President was the head of the KGB in our country before democracy began. Now he is running the country, and he is running it into the ground. The oil from the Caspian Sea has a pipeline into his bank account. As the French philosopher de Tocqueville said after visiting America in 1832, 'Democracy works in America

only because of its spiritual values.' Without those spiritual values democracy is easily corrupted."

So I asked, "Would you rather go back? You have 50% unemployment here." They said, "No way." Why? "Because the old system was a terrorist state. One in four was an informer. Family members betrayed family members. We lived in constant fear. What we have now is flawed, but it is better than that." That is the way it will always be when fallen man governs the State in a totalitarian way.

8. **It is through the protection of "Group Rights" (family, marriage, church, nation) that we protect "Individual Rights."** Nancy Pearcey boldly claims: "I suggest that the assumption of autonomous individualism is a central factor in the breakdown of American society today."[116] Michael Sandel says the background belief of modern liberalism is the concept of the "unencumbered" self—by which he means "unencumbered by moral or civic ties they have not chosen."[117] This is why relationships and responsibilities are often considered separate from and even contradictory to our essential identity—why individuals often feel they need to break free from their social roles (as husband, wife, or parent) in order to find their "true self."

This is why more and more young couples choose to live together without marriage, which is not considered by them something good in and of itself. In fact, in light of the prevalence of divorce, marriage is viewed by many of them as an economic risk. According to the National Marriage Project at Rutgers University, "Today's singles mating culture is not oriented to

---

116 Pearcey, 141.

117 Michael J. Sandel, *Democracy's Discontent: America in Search of a Public Philosophy* (Cambridge, MA: Harvard University Press, 1996, 6, 12.

marriage. Instead it is best described as a low commitment culture of 'sex without strings, relationship without rings.'"[118]

One college freshman at one of our well-known universities here in Texas was shocked by the availability of condoms for freshmen at advertised spots on campus. Even more shocking to him was the practice of "hooking up," which, according to him, was trial sex before dating. Shack up and then decide if you want to date each other. No, we're not in Kansas anymore, Toto.

9. **In other words, God has created us to find fulfillment in relationships: Interdependence is greater than Independence.** Of course, this is precisely what Ephesians is teaching us. At the foundation of any good relationship is trust. So how does our passage begin? Truth telling; anger management; honesty; encouragement. This is relationship building at its best. As Covey would say, from the inside out; right character precedes right community. Yes, Covey has the right idea. He knows the way. But does he know the means?

CONCLUSION

We are created in God's image. Now our quest is to be conformed to that image. That's our goal. That's the end product. It's not to go to heaven when we die. It is to become progressively like Christ as we run the race. Remember, the Trinity is interdependent. He made us to be interdependent. But the qualities for successful interdependence are developed from the inside out. Ezra Taft Benson said, "The Lord works from the inside out. The world works from the outside in. The world takes people out of the slums. Christ takes the slums out of people, and then they take themselves out of the slums. The world

---

118   Elana Ashanti Jefferson, "Sex 101:College Students Increasingly Casual About Bedfellows, Just as Casual About Condoms," in *The Denver Post* (October 24, 2002).

would mold men by changing their environment. Christ changes men who then change their environment. The world would shape human behavior, but Christ can change human nature."[119] Good character precedes good community.

Do you remember how the rotten apple forms, other than just falling from the tree and lying on the ground? If you see a wormhole, it didn't come from the outside; it came from the inside. Early on a large insect plants a seed right in the blossom. As the apple forms around the seed, the larva hatches, the worm grows, and out it comes. That's the way our Sin Nature works. But God can counteract that. He doesn't do it through our self-discipline. He does it by planting his seed on the inside (1 Jn 3:9). God's seed cannot commit sin because it is not in his genetic code. Sin is not in his genes. This seed can grow stronger and stronger as we feed it, until one day it is stronger than the Sin Nature. God's seed can overcome the worm. Unfortunately, we won't be dewormed until Christ's return or we die, but there is hope for victory in the meantime. It all starts by trusting in Christ as one's Savior. That is when the divine seed is planted.

The wind of doctrine that interferes with our spiritual growth and going on to maturity in Christ is the doctrine of the autonomous self—independence at any cost. The message from Ephesians in this lesson is simple: **Independence is good; Interdependence is better.**

Some years back my son-in-law was promoted to a managerial position at his Fortune Five Hundred company. In doing so, he jumped over several others who had seniority. A company VP explained: "We promoted you early because we recognize in you a team player. We aren't looking for John Waynes around here. We want men who are good at relationships and team-building."

There were two other managers that were his peers in this division of the company: one from Canada and one from Australia.

---

119 Ezra Taft Benson, http://www.goodreads.com/quotes/31260-the-lord-works-from-the-inside-out-the-world-works, accessed September 6, 2016.

212

Each of these men made it clear he had no faith in God. But each also expressed that they were lonely. One of them said, "It is my goal for this year to find one male friend outside this company." The other one remarked, "I've noticed that religious people seem to find friends and community wherever they move. Isn't that interesting?" My son-in-law just smiled.

Yes, he smiled at work while I was at his home playing with his children, my grandchildren. You see, they can barely exist without Papa. They would wake me up in the morning, and I would break out in song: "It's a happy day, I'll thank God for the weather; it's a happy day, just living it for my Lord." My three-year-old grandson would raise his hand authoritatively and affirm loudly: "No sing-ging. No sing-ging." But he loves me.

It was time to go to the airport to return home from visiting our grandchildren. We got there, and Betty and I were just hugging them and tears were coming down. We didn't want to go; they didn't want us to go. Some lady kept saying, "You wanna check in early? You wanna check in here?" We were still crying. "You wanna counselor?" These are the bonds of family. This is the way God made us. This is what it's all about.

13

WINDS OF DOCTRINE

Part 4 – Freed to Change Clothes

Ephesians 4:30-32

INTRODUCTION

Stephen Covey has a follow-up book to his best-selling Book *Seven Habits of Highly Efficient People*. It's how to apply those habits to families. In a personal message to the readers he quotes Barbara Bush as she addresses the Graduating class of Wellesley College:

> As important as your obligations as a doctor, lawyer, or business leader will be, you are a human being first, and those human connections—with spouses, with children, with friends—are the most important investments you will ever make. At the end of your life, you'll never regret not having passed one more test, not winning one more verdict, or not closing one more deal. You will regret time not spent with a husband, a child, a friend, or a parent . . . Our success as a

society depends not on what happens in the White House but on what happens inside of your house.[120]

Covey closes his personal message by saying, "I am convinced that if we as a society worked diligently in every other area of life and neglect the family, it would be analogous to straightening deck chairs on the Titanic."[121] And as I have traveled around this world a bit, I have noticed a huge difference in the emphasis on the family from culture to culture. What's going on in America and the assault on the family is unprecedented in most countries. In fact, when I was in India the divorce rate was two percent. The divorce rate in America is now forty percent for first-time marriages, and sixty percent for second marriages where there's a blended family.

Just two percent in India. I had trouble believing that, so I sat down with an Indian couple that had been converted from Hinduism to Christianity. I asked them how they got together. They said their respective parents arranged the marriage. So I asked if the first time they have seen each other was when they went to the altar. They said, "No, they were allowed five minutes alone with each other before the wedding arrangements were made to make their decision." Didn't waste much money on dating, did you? But how could you tell if you love each other in five minutes? "Oh, we didn't love each other when we got married. It was completely arranged." Okay so, tell me, do you love each other now? "Oh yes, for sure." Okay, you were not Christians, and you didn't have the Holy Spirit, so how does that work? They said, "It's really not that hard to understand. You see, when we married, it was not two people coming together; it was two clans—150 people in each clan. And the night before the wedding all the bride's brothers take the groom out to dinner. And they'll agree that the groom will take care, good care, of their sister. Do you understand?" they asked.

---

120 Stephen R. Covey, *The 7 Habits of Highly Effective Families* (New York, NY: Franklin Covey Company, 1997), 2.

121 Ibid.

"Oh, I get it," I replied. "But what happens if down the road there is no abuse, but the couple starts having serious problems?" "Oh," they said, "That's no problem. You see, because this is an arranged wedding, both sets of parents feel responsible for the success of the marriage. So both sets of in-laws have agreed to move in with the young couple until their problems are solved." Hmmm. I'm just guessing it doesn't take a couple long to solve their problems, possibly even before the in-laws arrive. What do you think?

You know, all the mother-in-law jokes come out of India. They are outsourced. What do you do if you miss your mother-in-law? You reload and try again! What do you have when your mother-in-law is covered in concrete up to her shoulders? Not enough concrete! Can you believe they tell these jokes? The patient says, "Doctor, last night I made a Freudian slip. I was having dinner with my mother-in-law, and I wanted to say, 'Could you please pass the butter?' But instead I said, 'You silly cow, you have completely ruined my life.'"

Now I have an absolutely wonderful mother-in-law, yes, a wonderful mother-in-law. I really do. She is one of the five people in this world I admire the most. But our families are under attack. I have a proposal. It's more of an opinion than a proposal. It seems to me, with our very mobile society, that the extended family doesn't have the influence in this country that it had in days gone by. And because of that I think our individual families are exposed.

You've heard it said families that pray together stay together. I would suggest that as a general rule clans that live together stay together. I live in Houston. I have one sister in Oregon, another sister in Alabama, and a third sister in Kentucky. My parents spent most of their life in Tennessee. What about your family? Those extended families play a vital function in the health of an individual family. They can give solidarity, strength, and a place to retreat. They can give counsel and comfort. They can offer moral support. Sometimes grandchildren look up to their grandparents with a sense of awe—like mine do (just kidding). Now, I know a lot of you do have families, extended families, that live close together. But I'm just guessing the majority of Americans don't. So what am I suggesting? Should we all uproot and move close together? Well, you know that's not going to happen in America. So what's God's answer to all this? You know where I'm going. The church is God's extended family. That would be my thesis as we go through this lesson from Ephesians 4:30-32.

Now we are in a section on interdependence. We said that dependence is good; independence is better; but interdependence is best. Energy is good; synergy is better. The intelligence of one person is good; group-think is better. And that's what Ephesians is trying to say, but it includes the spiritual side, doesn't it? It says you can never be what God created you to be by yourself. It just isn't possible. The Father, the Son, and the Holy Spirit are interrelated and interdependent. He made us like them. He made us in his image. Therefore, he made us to interrelate and he made us to be interdependent. But if we're going to do that successfully, we need to know how. That's where Ephesians chapter 4 is trying to help us.

It is through the Body of Christ. And the universal Body of Christ has many local expressions. Each local church is an expression of the Universal Body of Christ. And within each local body of Christ God desires that we learn the virtues of the Godhead by being interdependent so we can go on to maturity. Last week we looked at our outer clothes, our outerwear; this week we will look at our inner clothes, our underwear. In his mind Paul sees the image of changing clothes. We saw that in verses 22 and 24. We are to take off the clothes of the old man and put on the clothes of the new man? We began to do that in 4:24-29. These are the things that are to be taken off; these are things that are to be put on—the pants, the shirt, the belt—things that people can see. Those are actions, for the most part. Now we want to look at attitudes. Attitudes are in on the inside. That's why, in keeping with Paul's imagery, we call these attitudes our underwear. That's what we're going to cover in this lesson on 4:30-32.

We are going to look at Holy Grief in 4:30 and then Holy Garments in 4:31-32a. Finally, we will close out the chapter by looking at our Holy Gratitude in 4:32b. So, Holy Grief, Holy Garments, and Holy Gratitude. Let's start off with Holy Grief in verse 30.

I. HOLY GRIEF 30

> [30] And do not grieve the Holy Spirit of God, by whom you were sealed for the day of redemption.

This verse just sort of jumps out at us. You're talking about outerwear and underwear, external actions and internal attitudes. All of a sudden we see this verse about grieving the Holy Spirit. Wow, what's that doing there? Theologians love this verse because it's a great place to help prove the doctrine of the Trinity. Here we can show the Holy Spirit isn't just some impersonal force. Forces like gravity don't have feelings. But the Holy Spirit has real feelings or he couldn't grieve. Therefore he must be a person. We can't grieve atomic energy. We can't upset electricity. Yes, the Holy Spirit is a real person, and he has humbled himself to come and live inside of us to empower us for a victorious Christian life.

And isn't this a great statement of eternal security? Think you can lose your salvation? Be pretty hard to do when God himself has sealed you until the day of redemption. A seal was placed on a crate of fruit for protection as it was being shipped, as we saw back in chapter one. To break that seal someone or something would have to be more powerful than the omnipotent God. However, isn't it amazing that someone that powerful can be hurt by little ol' you or little ol' me?

When I got into the third grade, I decided math was boring. So I decided not to go to school during math. Instead I went to a field near our home to build a fort. Apparently a neighbor saw me and called the school principal. She drove by to pick me up. She asked me if my mother knew what I was doing. "Of course," I said. She said we should probably go to her office to call my mother. As we started walking down the hall and getting close to her office, I decided to run for it. I had mapped out the northwest part of this town through the sewers, so I went down a manhole where I knew she couldn't follow me. I went through the sewers to the north part of town just beyond the local racetrack. I came out near an apple orchard with lots of empty apple crates, so I decided I would have to build a home here. But as

I was putting apple crates together for my new home, I disturbed a bunch of bees.

This wasn't working out as well as I had intended, so I decided to run away. I would go to Grammy's house because I knew she loved me. I went out to the only road to Grammy's and began to hitchhike. A man picked me up and asked me where I was going. "I'm going to Norwalk," I replied. You know how far that is? "Yes," I said. "It's 98 miles." Do your parents know you're doing this? "Of course," I lied. He thought maybe we should call them on the phone. He began slowing down to turn in the driveway at a farmer's house. I had seen Roy Rogers jump off a horse. So as the car slowed down, I opened the door while the car was still moving and jumped out. I began running through the farmer's fields, while the farmer and the man who picked me up got a tractor to chase me. Each time I climbed a fence I thought, if they catch me, I'll have to go to prison. But they're getting closer with the tractor, so I ran into a clump of trees in the middle of his farm where the tractor could not go. Then the farmer's wife drove out to where I was hiding, got out of the car, and began crying. I couldn't stand, even at that age, watching a woman cry. So I came out of the trees, and they called my mother. Then they took me home. My mother came to the door, and guess what? She was crying. I've never forgotten that. I can still see her crying that day over sixty years ago.

Can you see the Holy Spirit crying? Do you enjoy causing someone you love to cry? If I had trouble watching my mother cry, what about the Holy Spirit? And to think he would make himself that vulnerable that I could make him cry. He only cries because we hurt him. And that just says how much he loves us. It's the people we love the most that have the greatest potential to hurt us. And what is it that causes him to cry? That takes us to the next verses: Holy Garments.

II. HOLY GARMENTS   31-32A

[31] Let all bitterness, wrath, anger, clamor, and evil speaking be put away from you, with all malice. [32] And be kind to one another, tenderhearted, forgiving one another, . . .

Paul starts off with unholy garments. Then he moves to holy garments. Yes, unholy garments—that's what makes the Holy Spirit cry: bitterness, wrath, anger, clamor, evil speaking, and malice. These are dirty, smelly, ugly rags—the clothes of the old man. Take them off, barks Paul. Since most of this list of new clothes deals with internal attitudes as opposed to external actions, we liken them to our underwear. All of these repulsive rags come from our failure to interrelate in a healthy way.

As you look back at these unholy garments, can't you just hear some of the ugly, vindictive, revengeful things said in the midst of a power struggle? How swift we are to choose sides and to believe lies about our brothers or sisters. Taken to the extreme these ugly attitudes can wind up in murder. I was reading about female suicide bombers. A lot of them have been working for the Taliban and Al Qaeda, but now we have them in Chechnya. Some of the Chechen women who have lost husbands or sons in war want to live only long enough to take revenge. The first attack by a "black widow," in the summer of 2000, killed 27 members of the Russian special forces. Over a four-month period in 2003, Chechen women performed six out of seven suicide attacks on Russian targets, killing 165 people. Women bombers allegedly brought down two Russian airliners in 2004, killing all 90 passengers and crew.[122] Their motivation? Vengeance, bitterness, malice—pay the ultimate price to get even with your enemy.

God is saying I can break through that, I can stop the cycle, I can break the family feud, I can stop the interracial feuds, and I can stop the international feuds. I can even stop ISIS because I offer a stronger weapon than hate. I offer love. Here are the clothes of love: kindness, tenderheartedness, and forgiveness.

"Kindness"—*chrēstoi*. This is one of the fruits of the Holy Spirit mentioned in Galatians 5:22. If you pronounce that Greek word, you can hear how much it sounds like Christ. In fact, some of the

---

122 Newsweek, December 12, 2005, 32.

people in Greece confused the two words and were calling Christians Chrēstians. The word could also be translated "gracious." A believer should be "grace-oriented." Since we are designed by God to be billboards of his grace, we should look at opportunities that come our way to do just that. Every time we are mistreated we have another opportunity to dispense his grace by offering the person who hurt us an undeserved favor. It is an opportunity to let the world see something supernatural. Rather than putting on bitterness, you put on graciousness.

And then the word "tender-hearted"—*eu* + *splanchnoi* = deep feelings = empathetic = feel for the other person in his/her situation; seek to understand before seeking to be understood. This is Covey's fifth habit. Get in their shoes. Try to see things from their point of view. See if you can feel their feelings. Then you will be a long way home toward properly relating to that person. Part of this word was used to describe Jesus' feelings when he saw the leper in the third stage of leprosy. Jesus was "moved with compassion." That's this word. In fact *splanchnoi* refers to his insides, his viscera, his intestines. It moved. He felt the suffering of the leper. Can you get into someone's shoes to that point? Can you feel what they feel? That's what this word is saying we should do.

Finally, Paul says that we should forgive one another. This is not a normal word for "forgiving" in the New Testament, which is *aphiēmi* (used about 100x in the NT); this is *charizō* (used 8x in the NT). It literally means "to **cause** grace." Cause grace. Create grace. Be proactive with grace. What is the Greek word for grace? *Charis.* Our word "forgive" even hints at the grace underlying *charizō*: for + **give**. For-giveness is a gift. It is giving something that is probably undeserved. Maybe they knew what they were doing when they hurt you; maybe they didn't. Either way, **cause grace**. Create some grace in their lives. Let them experience an undeserved favor. Mirrors of grace. Forgiveness is right at the top of the list of the ways we can reflect the grace of God.

But why should I do that? Look what they did to me. They don't deserve grace. Well, duh. That's what grace is—some kindness that is **undeserved**. We have seen Holy Grief and Holy Garments. The chapter closes with Holy Gratitude.

III. HOLY GRATITUDE   32B

. . . even as God in Christ forgave you.

Do you have any gratitude for what Jesus did for you on the cross? Of course you do. It would be pretty much impossible not to be thankful for what he has done, if indeed you have experienced his loving forgiveness for all your sins. Well, what has that person done to you that compares to all the things you have done to hurt Christ? It's a thimble full of water next to the Pacific Ocean. If God has forgiven me the Pacific Ocean, can't I find it in my heart to forgive a thimble full of water?

That's Jesus' argument back in Matthew 18. Here is a servant who has been forgiven a huge debt he could never repay, but he turns around and won't forgive his own servant of a small debt. Doesn't make much sense, does it? We have experienced grace; so let's be dispensers of grace. We have been forgiven all our sins; so let's forgive a few sins. In the parable the ungracious servant is thrown into the dungeon and turned over to the tormentors. We don't think the dungeon is hell, and we don't think the tormentors are demons. No, the torment comes in this life when we don't forgive. The bitterness over the suffered wrong begins like a mustard seed. Over time it grows into a mustard tree. Hebrews 12 talks about a root of bitterness that can grow into a tree with many branches, sending its poisonous, rancid sap into each branch, only to produce the rotten fruit of singed relationships:

> [14] Pursue peace with all *people,* and holiness, without which no one will see the Lord: [15] looking carefully lest anyone fall short of the grace of God; lest any root of bitterness springing up cause trouble, and by this many become defiled;

Notice a root of bitterness can spring up when we "fall short of the grace of God." Because we have experienced God's grace we should be dispensers of God's grace. If we have any gratitude at all for his grace, then forgive the other person. It pretty well takes all our excuses away, doesn't it?

You see, I thought I was a pretty good guy—considerate, sensitive, kind, loving, . . . until I got married. It didn't take long to discover that I'm selfish, self-centered, pigheaded, and on it goes. The late Michael Novak has observed:

> Marriage is an assault upon the lonely, atomic ego. Marriage is a threat to the solitary individual. Marriage does impose grueling, humbling, baffling, and frustrating responsibilities. Yet if one supposes that precisely such things are the preconditions for all true liberation, marriage is not the enemy of moral development in adults. Quite the opposite. . . .[123]

You see, what we're saying is that it's only in the context of getting close to people that we need the virtues of the Godhead. Again, it is in the context of rubbing shoulders with people that have sin natures just like our own that we need to practice extending grace toward one another. Novak goes on and says:

> Being married and having children has impressed on my mind certain lessons, for whose learning I cannot help being grateful. Most are lessons of difficulty and duress. Most of what I am forced to learn about myself is not pleasant. . . . My dignity as a human being depends perhaps more on what sort of husband and parent I am, than on any professional work I am called upon to do. My bonds to [my family] hold me back (and my wife even more) from many sorts of opportunities. And yet these do not feel like bonds. They are, I know, my

---

123 Michael Novak, "The Family out of Favor," in *Harper's Magazine* (April, 1976), 39.

liberation. They force me to be a different sort of human being, in a way in which I want and need to be forced.[124]

During one of my messages I offended someone in the congregation. I probably did that every Sunday. But this person had the Christian character to go home and type me an email explaining how I had offended her. I returned her email saying, "I am so glad you have the Christian character to be forthright about how I offended you. Lots of people would have just slinked off without a word. Please forgive me." She came back and asked, "Will you and Betty come over for dinner?" That's what it's all about. You see, your Christianity really isn't tested as long as you live in spiritual solitude, as long as you are a lone wolf Christian. Lone wolf Christians never learn these lessons.

CONCLUSION

In the home and in the church; in our physical family and in our spiritual family—that's where our enemy, the devil, concentrates his attack. And that is where these verses (4:30-32) are desperately needed—right in the center of our closest human relationships. "Okay," some of you are saying, "I'm closer to my friends at work than my family members or my friends at church." Well, to be honest, that's a warning sign. You are probably closer to them because you spend more time with them. It's hard to have a relationship with someone unless you spend time with him or her. Could it be you are spending too much time at work and not enough time with your physical family and your spiritual family? Just asking.

Yes, the physical family and the spiritual family. These are the foundations for our freedom, both in our nation and our souls. It shouldn't surprise us to realize the family unit is under attack. Just as I write this the Supreme Court of the United States has approved the marriage of homosexuals. Caesar has crossed the line of demarcation

---

124 Ibid., 42.

between God and the state by redefining marriage. Caesar is not supposed to cross the line into God's territory, but now they have. It's not the first time. The twenty-sixth of forty-five stated goals to communize America was: "Present homosexuality, degeneracy and promiscuity as 'normal, natural, healthy.'"[125]

As I am working away here in Mexico, some people here have asked me why the home school movement has become such a big thing in America. I told them about a documentary my wife and I watched called *Indoctrination*. It actually filmed a thirty-year-old teacher showing marriage options to third graders. Using flannel graph to keep the kids attention, this male teacher showed these little kids how as they grow up they should experiment with different relationships (boy-girl, girl-girl, boy-boy) to find their own sexual orientation. I watched with my mouth agape. The little kids have no idea at age eight what the guy is talking about. They are looking around like any group of eight year olds, but the guy drones on. What's the point? Indoctrination. Starting at a very young age these kids are indoctrinated to options that would not have been discussed a generation ago. By the time they hit puberty, they are ready to experiment with consciences already seared by society. That's not the only reason, but it is one reason the home school movement has exploded in America.

Here were the top disciplinary problems in public school back in 1940: talking out of turn, chewing gum, making noise, running in the halls, cutting in line, dress code infractions, and littering. Here are the top ten problems in public school in 1990: drug abuse, alcohol abuse, pregnancy, suicide, rape, robbery, and assault. That was over twenty-five years ago. Now you can add at least one more to the list: homosexuality. One of the students in Grace School of Theology is a high school football coach. I just happened to mention the first few homosexuals I ran into over the course of my life—all men. He popped

---

125 Greg Swank, http://rense.com/general32/americ.htm, accessed September 6, 2016.

up and said, "That's not the problem we run into in our school." Of course, I asked what he ran into. "It's lesbianism. The guys who are homos in our school are still in the closet, but the girls are kissing, hugging, and fondling themselves right in the hallways." I asked when that had started. He said about ten years ago when some TV shows came on that made lesbianism look chic, something every girl should at least try.

Would you agree that the traditional family unit faces a frontal attack? Look at these statistics:

- Illegitimate birth rates have increased more than four hundred percent.

- The percentage of families headed by a single parent has more than tripled.

- The divorce rate has more than doubled.

- Teenage suicide has increased almost three hundred (three of my older daughter's high school classmates committed suicide).

- The number one health problem for American women today is domestic violence. Four million women are beaten each year by their partners.

- One-fourth of all adolescents contract a sexually transmitted disease before they graduate from high school.[126]

You might comment, "I find your focus on the family strange in a passage that never mentions husbands, wives, or children." Fair enough. However, this passage is focusing on the church family—how to relate to each other. If these verses apply to the church family, I would suggest they are also appropriate for our personal families

---

126 Covey, 17.

as well. It's all about relationships, close relationships. For those kind of relationships, you have to learn to wear the right kind of clothes: outerwear and underwear that is appropriate for close relationships. You can't get close to someone you don't trust or someone who is judgmental. You would be afraid to share your struggles and failures.

Not long ago I was driving along with a friend in his seventies. I asked, "What is one of your biggest struggles as you get older." He just said God had given him the gift of contentment and he really didn't have any struggles. I knew better because through other sources I knew he was addicted to pornography. So I changed the subject, realizing he wasn't ready to open up. There was silence for a few miles. Then he said, "You know, to give you an honest answer to your question, I would have to say my biggest struggle as I am getting older is knowing how to relate to my wife." Then he began to open up. The next morning he went with me to a men's breakfast where I was to bring a fifteen to twenty minute devotional. I talked about "God's Cures for Loneliness." Of course, the number one cure is a spouse. But I find so many men who can't open up to their wives about their deepest struggles, one of which is usually lust. So I made the point that one of God's alternative cures when a man can't talk to his wife is some trusted brothers in Christ. Afterwards my friend said that was exactly what he needed to hear. You see, he is a loner. He doesn't open up to anyone. But he is on the way. He has taken the first step, as we shall see later on in Ephesians 5.

In order to get really close, we have to open up. We have to get beyond the masks most of us wear in public, whether it is at church or at work or on the tennis court. Here is what one soul wrote about masks:

Don't be fooled by me. Don't be fooled by the mask I wear. For I wear a mask. I wear a thousand masks—masks I am afraid to take off, and none of them is me. Pretending is an art. It's second nature with me. But don't be fooled. I give the impression that I am secure, that all is sunny and unruffled with me within as well as without—that confidence is my name and coolness is my game—that the waters are calm and I am in command and need no one, but don't believe it. Please don't. My surface may seem smooth, but my surface is my mask, my ever varying and ever concealing mask. Beneath lies no smugness, no coolness, no complacency. Beneath dwells the real me in confusion, in fear, in loneliness. But I hide this. I don't want anyone to know it.

I panic at the thought of my weakness being exposed. That's why I frantically create a mask to hide behind, a nonchalant, sophisticated facade to help me pretend, to shield me from the glance, the glance that knows. But such a glance is precisely my salvation, my only salvation, and I know it. It is the only thing that can liberate me from myself, my own self-built prison walls, from the barriers I so painstakingly erect.

But I don't tell you this. I don't dare. I'm afraid to. I'm afraid your glance won't be followed by love and acceptance. I'm afraid you will think less of me, that you'll laugh, and your laugh will kill me. I'm afraid that deep down inside I am nothing, I am just no good and you will see it and reject me. So I play my games, my desperate pretending games with the facade of assurance on the outside and a trembling child within. And so begins the parade of masks, the glittering but empty parade of masks until my life becomes a front.

I idly chatter with you in the suave tones of surface talk. I tell you everything that is really nothing, nothing of what is crying within me. So when I am going through my routine, don't be fooled by what I am saying. Please listen carefully and try to hear what I am not saying, what I would like to be able to say, what for survival I need to say, but I can't say. I dislike the hiding, honestly I do. I dislike the superficial, phony games I am playing. I would really like to be genuine.

I would really like to be genuine, spontaneous, and me, but you have to help me. You have to help me by holding out your hand even when that is the last thing I seem to want or need. Each time you are kind and gentle and encouraging, each time you try to understand because you really care, my heart begins to grow wings, very small wings, very feeble wings, but wings. With your sensitivity and sympathy and your power of understanding, I can make it.

You can breathe life into me. It won't be easy for you. A long conviction of worthlessness builds strong walls, but love is stronger than walls. And therein lies my hope. Please try to beat down those walls with firm hands, but with gentle hands, for a child is very sensitive, and I am a child. Who am I, you may wonder. I am someone you know very well. I am every man, every woman, every child, every human you meet.[127]

We want to continue our sidebars on various "Winds of Doctrine" that have blown so many Christian ships off course during the last couple of centuries. Few have had more catastrophic consequences than the teachings of Charles Darwin. So let's spend some time looking at Hurricane Darwin. Remember, Paul warned his readers in Ephesians 4:14 that they should no longer be children, tossed to and fro and carried about with every **wind of doctrine**, by the trickery of men, in the cunning craftiness by which they lie in wait to deceive. These hurricanes are the major winds of doctrine that have carried the Christian ships of who knows how many believers away from sound doctrine that can lead them to Christian maturity.

HURRICANE DARWIN

Part 1

I think Charles Darwin was the most influential person of the 19th century. Let me say a couple of things about his assumptions. He was influenced by Immanuel Kant, who actually wrote more about science than philosophy. Part of his understanding of the universe is that it is infinitely old and infinitely large. Don't forget about the

---

127 Unknown.

infinitely old part. Without a universe that is nearly infinitely old there would not be enough time for evolution. As Hugh Ross claims the current estimate on the age of universe is 14.3 billion years old, a mere drop in the bucket of the time required for evolution.[128] You need near infinite time for enough random mutations to evolve into the human race—survival of the fittest. So these are two (infinitely old and infinitely large) of the three assumptions required by Darwin for his hypothesis. The third one is that the process is slow and gradual.

Now you will notice I don't call this a theory as we shall see. According to the scientific method, evolution doesn't even qualify to be called a hypothesis, let alone a theory. Darwin finished his *On the Origin of the Species* in 1859.[129] It was a rush job because someone else was hot on his heels. He said, "If anyone could show that evolution did not take place through gradual, almost infinitesimal changes that are positive changes, which could move the organisms up the ladder from lower to higher, then my theory fails." And so, we're going to talk about six problems with his theory. We'll start with what Darwin himself admitted was most problematic about evolution: the fossil record.

1. The Fossil Record. If we are going from down on the lower part of the tree up to the higher part of the tree, if we are ascending up through genus and family, etcetera, then there should be some transitional forms. If something came out of the sea and its fins turned to wings and it started to fly, there would be some transitional fossil forms. THERE ARE NONE. Not one. And, if it is a gradual process taking place over a period of time, then it is going on now. We can go back in the fossil records a long, long time. There should be some transitional forms. THERE ARE NONE.

---

128 Hugh Ross, *The Creator and the Cosmos* (Colorado Springs, CO: NavPress, 1995), 57, 106, 149.

129 Charles Darwin, https://en.wikipedia.org/wiki/Charles_Darwin, accessed September 6, 2016.

A second problem for the fossil record is that the evolutionary tree has no trunk. Have you ever seen a tree with just branches and no trunk? Well, he has a trunk, but there's nothing on it. The evolutionary tree says we are slowly going up, developing from simplicity to complexity, but the fossil record shows a tree with no trunk. At a macro evolutionary conference in Chicago the paleontologists (people who study old things) finally conceded that the gaps in the fossil record will never be filled. Almost all of them have given up on evolution. After over a hundred years of observation no fossil form to fill the transitional gap has ever been observed. Apparently, the fossil records will never support evolution. Hence, if Darwin were alive today, he would have to admit that his so-called theory is wrong.

2. The Hot Big Bang. In 1916, when Einstein came out with his general theory of relativity, it predicted the universe is expanding but slowing down in its expansion—expanding but decelerating. Those are the properties of an explosion. If I take a hand grenade and pull the pin, we will get an explosion. The material of the hand grenade will expand, but because of gravity and the friction from the air, the expansion will slowly decelerate.

Now, Einstein did not like the implications of the Big Bang. If there is an explosion, then someone had to pull the pin. This implied the existence of a Prime Mover, a Supreme Intelligence (Einstein never accepted a personal God). So, in an attempt to avoid the Prime Mover conclusion, he came up with his static state view of the universe and then the oscillating state of the universe with antigravity, which he later admitted was foolishness. Finally, in 1929 Hubble (of Hubble telescope fame) persuaded him that what his theory of general relativity predicted was true: the universe was expanding like an explosion.[130] That is when Einstein gave up and concluded there had to be a Prime Mover, a Supreme Intelligence. He defended this position until his death in 1955. His fellow scientists did not like his

---

130 Ross, 49-62.

conclusion, so they discarded the static state theory of the universe and came up with the steady state view. According to this view, new stars were always coming into existence to replace those that had burned out. But as the years went by the astronomers proved that all the galaxies are of the same age, pointing thus back to a common origin in time.

All this was put to rest April 24, 1992. Again, this is the conclusion of Hugh Ross, former professor at Cal Tech with a PhD in astronomy.[131] Because of our atmosphere, we can't see as clearly as someone in space or on the moon. So COBE (Cosmic Background Radiation Explorer) was sent out there to increase our powers of observation. COBE was sent out to observe radiation (light) coming from the edges of the universe. It looked a little too smooth when observed from planet earth. There should have been some ripples and bending of the light as it came to us from so far away. The results came in on April 24, 1992. Yes, just as predicted, there were ripples and bending. Boom. The cynics disappeared. Even Stephen Hawking said, "It is the discovery of the century if not of all time." It establishes the age of the universe at about 14.3 billion years old.

For those who want to hold to a young earth, that is no problem. God can create with age. When he created Eve, she wasn't a little baby that Adam had to feed until she grew into maturity. Furthermore, in his book *Starlight and Time*, D. Russell Humphreys has done a wonderful job, with favorable peer review, establishing the age of the universe depends on the point of view of the observer and where we pin point the center of the universe.[132] If our galaxy is near the center, then an observer on earth as it was created would say it only took six twenty-four hour periods to create the earth. On the other hand, an observer today on the edge of the universe could accurately say the universe is 14.3 billion years old. There is no contradiction here since

---

131 Ibid., 19-29.

132 D. Russell Humphreys, *Starlight and Time* (Green Forest, AR: Master Books, 1994).

the speed of light is constant (Einstein's principle of invariance) and time is relative.

If the universe is 14.3 years old when seen from the edge of the universe, that is not in conflict with our faith or Genesis 1. If anything, it confirms our faith since even 14.3 billion years is a drop in the bucket compared to the amount of time needed for evolution to have taken place. I went to a lecture by Hugh Ross in my old chemistry lecture hall at Rice University. He said, "When I go to campuses to debate, the astrophysicists don't show up anymore. They know that current theories on the age of the universe simply do not allow enough time for evolution to have happened. The only people who show up are the biologists that have yet to take into account what is going on in other disciplines." I would love to get Francis Collins[133] and Hugh Ross in the same room to listen to them have a discussion on these issues. I am a theologian, well aware I don't have the educational background to speak with any authority or credibility on evolution. I am left with reading what the authorities themselves have to say. I wish we could get them together.

If we define science as Webster does, that is, a discipline governed by the process of the scientific method, then Darwinianism is not science. Our kids need to know that evolution is not science. If we remember the scientific method, it all begins with observation. Observation leads to a guess, a hypothesis. The hypothesis is taken into a controlled environment where it can be tested over and over. From these tests a theory can be postulated. If the theory works without exception, we have a law. But on several fronts we lack the observations necessary to make even a hypothesis, let alone a theory.

I read the brief on the trial against Intelligent Design in the

---

133 Francis Collins . . . I did run into Hugh Ross at an ETS conference in 2015 and asked if what the chances of getting Collins and him into a room together. He said that had already been done. He said he came up with nine observations Collins could not explain through his view of theistic evolution.

classroom in Philadelphia. The case was won against ID before the trial began. It all hinged on the new definition of science: science includes anything derived from natural causes. That rules out supernatural causes, or religion. But evolution takes more faith than Christianity. If Christianity is a religion that should not be allowed in the classroom, then so is evolution. Either neither should be allowed or both should be allowed.

The evolutionary lie produces independence from God and from each other, leaving us with no purpose in life. Only if God created us in his image via intelligent design do we as his children and church mirror the loving interdependence of the Godhead—Father, Son, and Holy Spirit—with the purpose of becoming like Christ, full of grace and truth.

14

WINDS OF DOCTRINE
Part 5 – Freed to Imitate Christ
Ephesians 5:1-6

INTRODUCTION

Well, you probably have heard of the story of the beautiful blonde that was driving down the road in her brand-new 500 SL, but she was going a little too fast. Alas, she was pulled over by a motorcycle cop. It just so happens the motorcycle cop was also a beautiful blonde. She asked to see the other blonde's driver's license. The blonde driver practically emptied her purse trying to find her drivers license. Impatiently, the blonde motorcycle cop said, "It's the little square thing with your picture on it." Finally, the blonde driver saw her little, square pocket mirror, looked at it, saw her reflection, and handed it to the beautiful blonde motorcycle cop. The blonde motorcycle cop looked at the pocket mirror, saw her own reflection, handed it back to blonde driver, and said, "OK, you can go. I didn't know you were a cop." Awwhhheee.

What do you see when you look in the mirror? You know, we do it several times a day, don't we? It's always fun to watch people as they go by a mirror. They kind of get sneaky about it, don't they—kind of give a little furtive glance out of the corner of their eye to see how they look at that moment in time on that particular day. What do you see? It can get kind of scary as we get older. Of course, what we see in the mirror may depend on whether we are looking with our physical eyes or our spiritual eyes.

If we are to be mirrors of God's grace and Christ-likeness, then our spiritual eyes will see an emerging butterfly instead of a forgiven caterpillar. Once we enter God's kingdom, we have been accepted for flight school. But whether we learn to fly or not depends largely on whether we focus on our Savior or on ourselves. The more we focus on him the more we see him in the mirror and the more we reflect his character to the world. As we think about him, we become givers; as we focus on ourselves, we become getters. That's what our passage is all about in Ephesians 5:1-6.

EPHESIANS
"The Creation and the Conduct of the Church"

SALUTATION   1:1-2

INTRODUCTION—"Spiritual Blessings in the Heavenlies"   1:3-14

    (Paul's Prayer for Perception)   1:15-23

BODY   2:1-6:9

    I. Creation of the Church (Its Position)   2:1-3:21

    II. Conduct of the Church (Its Condition)   4:1-6:9

      A. The Goal: Maturity of the Body   4:1-16

      B. The Means: Maturity of the Individual   4:17-6:9

        1. Through Personal Sanctification   4:17-5:14

          a. Walking in Life   4:17-32

          b. Walking in Love   5:1-6

            1) Emulating Selfless Sacrifice 1-2

            2) Eliminating Selfish Sensuality 3-6

          c. Walking in Light   5:7-14

        2. Through Personal Submission   5:15-6:9

CONCLUSION—"Spiritual Battles in the Heavenlies"   6:10-20

FAREWELL   6:21-24

We have seen that the goal of the Christian life is not to go to heaven when we die. Of course we want to go to heaven when we die, but it just isn't the emphasis of the Bible. How many verses can you find in the OT about going to heaven? How many verses can you find in Ephesians about going to heaven? It is very important how we get there, and Ephesians has something to say about that in 2:8-9, but the end game is not 2:8-9; it's 2:10—to live a life of good works so we can bring glory to our spiritual parents: the Father, the Son, and the Holy Spirit. That is what the last half of Ephesians is all about. The first half talked about our **Position** in Christ—we were created like beautiful butterflies to fly. The second half of Ephesians is about our **Condition** on earth, to teach us how to fly. God did not create butterflies to crawl around in the mud like caterpillars. That's what we were when we were dead in our trespasses and sins (Eph.2:1). But through Christ we have been transformed through the new birth. Now we are butterflies. But wouldn't it be tragic if a butterfly never got out of the mud? Paul teaches us how to fly in the last half of Ephesians.

Ephesians 5:1-6 picks up right where he left off in chapter four, of course. In that chapter we were learning Interdependence, how we need each other if we are going to get off the ground. We can never soar in the heavens by ourselves. We won't get off the runway. Chapter five continues the lessons on Interdependence. Here we learn that selfishness will never yield Interdependence, so Paul wants us to say yes to selflessness (vv. 1-2) and no to selfishness (vv. 3-6).

I. SAY YES—TO SELFLESSNESS   5:1-2

5 Therefore be imitators of God as dear children. ² And walk in love, as Christ also has loved us and given Himself for us, an offering and a sacrifice to God for a sweet-smelling aroma.

As we have seen so often, the word "therefore" is a connector taking us back to the final verses of Ephesians 4. He is still trying to teach us to be interdependent. And apparently a key component of interdependency is the virtue of forgiveness. Paul seems to be saying we can never move into interdependence without forgiving others. We are like all those white and red blood cells trying to navigate our way along a vein or artery. Everything is cool until we come to an intersection. Ever seen a film of this? The cells all start bumping into each other as they try to get through the intersection. It's the same with horizontal relationships, isn't it? It might be in the church or the family or at work or the athletic field. Because of our inherent selfish, sin natures we bump into each other. You just can't get through the intersection whole without being able to forgive other people.

To become interdependent we need to take away the masks we so often wear in public and get honest. But getting honest with each other involves opening up. But when we open up, we are vulnerable to being hurt. Then what? If we can't forgive, we can't move on. But when we do forgive, we become imitators of Christ—"Father, forgive them, because they don't know what they are doing." When we are imitators of him, we become mirrors, reflectors of who he is. We are to forgive as Christ forgave and to love as Christ loved (v. 2).

Notice Paul says to be imitators as dear "children." All children tend to imitate their parents, even their grandparents. I remember going over to see my grandchildren some time back when Drew was just eighteen months. He could walk by then. I was still having trouble with my hip at that time and walked with a pronounced limp. As soon as he saw me coming, Drew began to drag his right leg behind himself, trying to imitate my limp with a gross exaggeration, I might add. It was funny to watch. The point? Kids imitate their parents. They imitate not only our actions, but also our attitudes. They pick it up in the atmosphere.

Here we are told to imitate God, to love as he loved. The "love" mentioned here is *agapē* love, the very essence of which is sacrifice. Instead of finding ways to get, this loves looks for ways to give. Instead of selfishness, it is the very picture of selflessness (see 1 Cor 13). The words here for "offering," "sacrifice," and "aroma" call up the image of the sacrificial altar used in worshipping God. He suggests that Christ himself became such an offering for us. If we imitate him, we put our own lives on the altar for the purpose of serving others. It reminds us of Romans 12:1 where Paul invites us to place our bodies on the altar as a living sacrifice. That is his opening salvo in Romans 12 in his battle against selfishness—become part of the body. Learn to be interdependent.

A servant today will be a sovereign tomorrow (Rom 8:17). But not all sacrifices are a sweet-smelling aroma. The attitude (motive) for sacrifice is important. He tells us we could give our bodies to be burned, but if we do not make this sacrifice out of love, it profits us nothing (1 Cor 13). At the Judgment Seat of Christ it is this Act-Intention combination that is judged. Or we might say Act-Attitude. A good act cannot be canceled out by a selfish attitude, but the reward for a good act can be canceled out by a selfish attitude. If I give $1,000 to the church, that is a good act. Now, if I do it with the wrong attitude the church doesn't give the money back. The act is still good. But there will be no reward for the act at the Judgment Seat of Christ because of the wrong attitude

So what is the right motive? You know the answer to that, don't you? It's not about us; it's all about him. Ultimately, all we do should be unto the Lord for his glory, not our own. Of course, the sincere desire to help others is also part of the selfless sacrifice.

Ken Blanchard came to Houston to give a motivational speech (Nov 14, 2005). In his talk he mentioned Barbara Glands, who was invited by a grocery chain to come to speak to their employees in order to motivate them to be servants. There were two or three thousand baggers, shelvers, cashiers, and people working in the flower department. They wanted Barbara to pump them up with the idea that everyone of them could make a difference for his or her customer. She always leaves her phone number and email in case anyone wants to get ahold of her. She got a call about two and a half weeks after her talk from a nineteen-year-old bagger named Johnny. Johnny told her proudly that he was a Down syndrome youngster. He said, "Barbara, I want to tell you what has happened to my life since you spoke here. I went home and told my mom and dad that you had spoken to us and said each one of us could make a difference for our customer. I asked, 'How can I? I'm just a bagger.'"

His mom and dad thought and thought and came up with the idea that Johnny loved to collect inspirational sayings. He had been doing it since he was a little kid. So he went into his computer that night, copied in his favorite inspirational saying, put six copies on a page, printed 150 copies, hand cut them, folded them, signed the back of them, and put them into a paper bag that he took to work with him.

Johnny set the bag next to him as he was bagging groceries. When he finished bagging someone's groceries, he would look them in the eye, as his mom and dad had suggested, and tell them that he was going to put his favorite inspirational saying in their bag. "I hope it makes your day a little brighter."

Well, the store manager was making his rounds after Johnny have been doing this for a couple of weeks. He got up front where all the cashiers were and everyone was in Johnny's line. No one was in anyone else's line. The manager began to panic. He tried to get people to move to other lines, but no one would move. They all wanted to get Johnny's saying for the day.

The store manager said he started to get tears in his eyes. One woman grabbed his hand and said, "I used to shop here once a week. Now I stop by here every single day." This kid changed the whole store. In the flower department, if they broke a stem, they made a little corsage and went out and pinned it on some elderly lady or little girl. In the meat department the butcher liked Snoopy. After he wrapped someone's meat, he put a little Snoopy sticker on it and then told them a little story. Now, every cashier has something special he does for his customer. Johnny really made a difference. He wasn't going to get a pay raise for doing what he did. He had no ulterior motive. He just wanted to be a blessing in someone's life that day. He was walking in love, imitating Christ, his Savior. Are you going to be a Johnny today?

So we are to say yes to selflessness, but to say no to selfishness. That's what we are looking at as we move into 5:3-6.

II. SAY NO—TO SELFISHNESS 5:3-6

³ But fornication and all uncleanness or covetousness, let it not even be named among you, as is fitting for saints; ⁴ neither filthiness, nor foolish talking, nor coarse jesting, which are not fitting, but rather giving of thanks. ⁵ For this you know, that no fornicator, unclean person, nor covetous man, who is an idolater, has any inheritance in the kingdom of Christ and God. ⁶ Let no one deceive you with empty words, for because of these things the wrath of God comes upon the sons of disobedience.

Filthy ways lead to filthy words. "**Fornication**" = *porneia*, which is any kind of sexual immorality. It is much broader than just the act. Pornography comes from this word. Do we need to quote the statistics on those addicted to pornography and the damage it does to relationships? And now it appears that women are entering a world that used to be dominated by men. Some estimate that 20% of adult women are addicted to pornography. "**Uncleanness**" refers to any kind of impurity. And "**covetousness**" has at its very root selfishness. It is to desire something that does not belong to me. In this context it can speak of sexual addiction, meaning a person who is never content with what he has in this area. He always wants more. In v. 5 Paul calls this kind of covetousness idolatry. He turns sex into his idol. It is what he thinks about all day long. But filthy ways lead to filthy words.

These next three words in the Greek text occur only here in the NT. Nowhere else. So to understand them better we go outside the NT to see if we can find them used elsewhere in Greek literature. We can. And here is what they mean: 1) "Filthiness" (NKJ)/"Obscenity"(NIV) = *aischrotēs* = cussing; 2) "Foolish talking" = *mōrologia* = a euphemism for lewd expressions; and 3) "Coarse jesting" = *eutrapelia* = dirty jokes. One of the first ways I knew something was different in my life after receiving Christ was the cussing. It just went away. I was like a lot of teenagers. Cussing was just being one of the boys. No big deal.

But it must have been a big deal to the Holy Spirit because he just took it away.

Paul tells us filth shouldn't be coming out of the mouths of saints. Instead of using our tongues for smut, we should use them for giving thanks. They should be used for blessing instead of cursing, for giving thanks to God rather than taking God's name in vain. And now he gives his readers a little motivation to clean up their acts. He issues two warnings: 1) Eternal loss; 2) Temporal loss.

When the text tells us "no fornicator, unclean person, nor covetous man, who is an idolater, has any inheritance in the kingdom of Christ and God," the warning is not exclusion from heaven. This text has been used as a hammer to scare people out of hell. But notice the text does not say no fornicator, unclean person, nor covetous man, who is an idolater, **can enter** the kingdom of Christ and God. It says such a person will not have an inheritance in the kingdom of Christ and God. You ask, "Well, what's the difference?"

If we slide over in our Bibles to Colossians, which was written at the same time and from the same place as Ephesians, we learn in Colossians 3:23-24 that the word "inheritance" refers to our rewards in the next life: "And whatever you do, do it heartily, as to the Lord and not to men, 24 knowing that from the Lord you will receive the **reward** of the **inheritance**; for you serve the Lord Christ." It is another way of referring to the Judgment Seat of Christ where Christians will be rewarded for both their character and their conduct. And, again, these rewards are not for our glory; they are for his. (We find a similar statement in Galatians 5:19-21.)

If this text meant we had to have a clean life in order to enter God's kingdom, then how could Paul in this very letter tell us we enter "by grace . . . through faith . . ."? He would be contradicting himself. Our passage in Ephesians 5:3-6 certainly promotes a clean life, but Jesus cleans his fish after he catches them. With some of these addictions an unbeliever simply does not have the power to clean up his act. It takes supernatural power, the power of the Holy Spirit.

Is this easy-believism? Certainly not. There is eternal loss if the saint chooses to live a raunchy life. But the threat is not loss of an eternal life with God; it is a threat of a wasted life, a life where there are no rewards given to God to glorify him out of a thankful heart. But more than that. There is eternal loss, yes, but there is also temporal loss: "the wrath of God comes upon the sons of disobedience." Now we have been conditioned through the centuries to believe "the wrath of God" refers to hell or the lake of fire. It's hard to show an example of that in the NT. In Revelation 6-19 we see this word (*orgē*) six times. But it does not occur in Revelation 1-5 or 20-22. It occurs in the chapters referring to the seven year Tribulation Period, which is an outpouring of God's anger against man's sin in time, not eternity. If it were going to be used of eternity in hell or the lake of fire, Revelation is the book to do it in, and specifically in Revelation 20-22. Nada. Nothing.

Romans uses this word *orgē* more than any other book of the NT (12x). Its first use is Romans 1:18—"[18] For the wrath of God **is revealed** from heaven against all ungodliness and unrighteousness of men, who suppress the truth in unrighteousness." The important factor to notice is the present tense of "is revealed" (*apokaluptetai*). This wrath is presently being revealed from heaven against the ungodliness and unrighteousness of mankind. This is not referring to something that will take place at the Great White Throne (as a matter of fact, there is no use of *orgē* in the NT which links it directly with the Great White Throne). It is in no way connected with eternal judgment. This is a present time judgment.

Specifically, this wrath is defined in the rest of Romans 1 as three stages of God's giving sinful man over to the control of his sinful nature as he descends the staircase into the basement of depravity. The phrase *paredōken autous ho theos* (God gave them up/over) defines these three stages in vv. 24, 26, and 28. The bottom of the basement is to have a mind that is *adokimos*, "disapproved" or "unable to tell right from wrong." It is total control by the sin nature. That is wrath in Romans 1:18ff. And the gospel of Romans 1:16 includes not only deliverance (salvation) from the penalty of sin (the lake of fire), but also deliverance from the power of sin (slavery to our Sinful Nature = God's wrath in Romans).

So let us try it out in Romans 5:9 to see if it makes any sense. "Much more, then, having now been justified by His blood, we shall be saved from wrath [the control of our sinful nature] through Him." Does that make sense? Perhaps. But does it fit the rest of the context? In Romans 5:10, it says that we were reconciled (past tense) through the death of his Son, but we shall be saved (future tense) through his life. If the meaning of wrath in Romans 5:9 is the same as the wrath in Romans 1:18, then the saving in Rom 5:9 must also refer to being saved from the tyranny of the sin nature in our lives. And this does make sense.

We were saved from the penalty of sin by His death, but we shall be saved from the power of sin by His life. We gained eternal life as He became our substitute in death, but we shall enjoy an abundant life as He becomes our substitute in life. "I am crucified with Christ; nevertheless, I live; yet not I, but *Christ lives in me* . . . ." (Gal 2:20). The hardest thing for a non-Christian to believe in is the substitutionary death of Christ, but the hardest thing for a Christian to believe in is the substitutionary life of Christ. Romans 5:10 is about His substitutionary life. In this "swing section" of Romans the author is turning away from his focus on justification from the penalty of sin to salvation from the power of sin. And being saved in this section is to be delivered from the tyranny of the sin nature in one's life (the wrath of Rom 1:18).

But let's turn this around. To live the substitutionary life of Christ delivers us from the wrath of God (control by our sinful natures), but not living the substitutionary life of Christ leaves us under the control of our sinful natures. That means we are living lives of disobedience. As we continue in disobedience, the power of our sinful nature becomes stronger and stronger in our lives. And that's the wrath of God. It "comes upon the sons of disobedience."

So Paul gives us two good reasons to avoid filthy ways and filthy words: 1) Eternal loss (rewards); 2) Temporal loss (slavery to our sinful natures). Now let's put some leather on the possible outcomes of temporal loss coming from slavery to our sinful natures. 1 Thessalonians 4:3-7 says this:

³ For this is the will of God, your sanctification: that you should abstain from sexual immorality; ⁴ that each of you should know how to possess his own vessel in sanctification and honor, ⁵ not in passion of lust, like the Gentiles who do not know God; ⁶ that no one should take advantage of and defraud his brother in this matter, because the Lord is the avenger of all such, as we also forewarned you and testified. ⁷ For God did not call us to uncleanness, but in holiness.

Essentially, this is God's will on how to find a life partner. The passage begins with the word "sanctification" and ends with the word "holiness." It is the same word in Greek: *hagiosmos*. The NAS translation notes this by translating it "sanctification" both times. The word is used a third time in v. 4—"sanctification and honor." The point is the passage is all about how to find a life partner in a sanctified way. The opposite way is through "sexual immorality" or "lustful passion" (NAS). "That each of you know how to possess his vessel" really means that each person "should learn how to acquire his/her life partner." It is how to find a wife or husband. You can do it through lust or through purity.

I mentioned earlier that the custom at some colleges and universities these days is to "hook up" on the first date in order to determine sexual compatibility before making a decision to date each other. Can you see how that could lead to some very foggy decision making? There is a lot more that goes into a good marriage than sexual compatibility.

My younger daughter went through some bad experiences with boys in high school. So when she hit college, she just decided not to date for the first three years. I was teaching a class in College Station, TX, where she was going to school, so when I went up there once a week, I would take her out to dinner. At the beginning of her senior year we were at dinner and she said, "OK, dad, I'm ready." "For what?" I asked. "To look for a husband. I have made a list of five things I am looking for." "Well, Laura, most people don't get everything on their list. You may have to compromise."

Next thing I know this guy is coming down to visit us. He seemed nice enough, was a dedicated Christian, and won the outstanding cadet that year at Texas A&M and an invitation to the White House. I didn't think much more about him until Christmas break. Laura and I were used to doing Father/Daughter trips together. One year we went scuba diving, another hang gliding, another a music trip to New Orleans then Nashville and Branson. So I asked her what she wanted to do this year, and she said she wanted to go deer hunting. "Deer hunting. Have you ever even shot a rifle?" "No."

Well, I had a place to go if I wanted to, but I didn't want to go out and wound a bunch of animals, so I said, "OK, if you can put three shots out of five into a space this big (I made a circle with my thumbs and fingers) at a hundred yards, we'll go." It just took her four shots. So we had time to drive from Houston to Kerrville for an evening hunt. Now I had always enjoyed these trips with my daughter. It was a special time for us to get away and just share our lives with each other. Only this time was different. This young buck from College Station was texting her every ten minutes. I mean every ten minutes. It was driving me crazy.

We finally reached our destination, and the owner of the ranch put Laura in a blind with a walkie-talkie and me in a blind with a walkie-talkie about a quarter mile away. An hour later I hear a boom, and my walkie-talkie says, "I just shot my first buck." Humph. Lucky. I hadn't shot anything. An hour later it is almost dark and I hear another boom: "I just shot my second buck." I still hadn't shot anything and my daughter who has never hunted has two bucks. Life ain't fair.

So we collect the bucks and start cleaning them. But there is a third buck I was getting ready to shoot. He's texting again. Every ten minutes. "What's with this guy, Laura?" "Oh, he loves me." "He loves you, does he? Have you talked about marriage?" "Oh, he talks about it all the time." "Are you two physically involved?" "DAD . . . DAD! We haven't even kissed, and if we do get married, we aren't going to kiss until the altar." (No wonder the guy was texting every ten minutes.)

I didn't know if they would go on to matrimony (thank God, they didn't; he was a smothering control freak), but I was proud of her commitment. Laura held on to her list of five things she was looking for. I really thought she would never marry. But finally, at age twenty-nine, she found a guy with all five points and some to spare. By the way, Laura went on to seminary after college and then joined Young Life's staff. One of her points was to marry a man who was the spiritual leader in their relationship. They approached their relationship in sanctification and honor.

Say Yes—to Selflessness, but Say No—to Selfishness. Now we listen to these words from God's Word because we believe these words are from God. We believe in God. But there is an influence out there that does not agree with us. And they will do all they can to turn our children into another direction. Now faith and science in the classroom are presented as mutually exclusive. Intelligent design is not allowed in the classroom because it presumes a supernatural cause. Science has been redefined as the realm of natural causes. Actually, I would be okay with the redefinition if supernatural causes were not presented as contradictory to the realm of science. You see, I see no conflict between what we have discovered in science and what we are told about supernatural causes in the Bible. Some of us not only believe they are compatible but revelatory. Being a scientist does not mean we have to throw faith out the window. I have had a number of MIT graduates in my churches, a number of Rice graduates, and even students from Cal Tech, three of the top science schools in our nation. Somehow their science is not incompatible with their faith.

But Charles Darwin wouldn't agree with us. So we want to go a little further with Darwinism as we look at the "Winds of Doctrine" that have blown the ship of faith steered by many, many Christians off course. The Darwinians tell us the world we live in came about by random chance over nearly infinite time. So we want to look at a couple more problems for "Hurricane Darwin."

HURRICANE DARWIN
Part 2

1. **Mutations**. First of all, mutations are somewhat rare, especially a positive mutation. For example, in studying fruit flies it has been observed that a mutation only occurs in 1/1,000,000 fruit flies. Almost all mutations are harmful, that is, they lead to the extinction of that which has been mutated. Most mutations are recessive, meaning they go into hiding in the genetic code and never do come out. Beneficial mutations *within* a species are not what we are talking about when we talk about evolution. Those that want to keep ahold of evolution call beneficial mutations within a species "micro-evolution." But Darwin's evolution is not about micro-evolution. It is all about macro-evolution, that is a lower species moving up the ladder to something higher. You don't evolve by adaptations within a species. That is not evolution. All scientists who have studied the subject rightly believe in adaptation within a species. The adaptations usually occur when the species finds itself in a new environment. It adapts as necessary to survive. For the theory of evolution to work somehow the tadpole has to have zillions of positive mutations that take it from a lower rung on the evolutionary ladder all the way to becoming a man. BUT, no positive mutation going from a lower species to a higher species has ever been observed. NO, NOT ONE.

Let's not miss the word OBSERVED. The first step in the Scientific Method was an observation. Newton observes the proverbial apple falling. From this observation he makes a guess (a hypothesis): bodies with mass attract each other. Into the laboratory he goes to test his hypothesis. He keeps dropping apples. They keep falling. He moves his hypothesis from a guess to a theory. When he tests his theory over and over without finding any exceptions, he poses a law. We call it the law of gravity. But note well, the law of gravity didn't start off as a law. It started off as an observation. If no positive mutation from a lower species to a higher species has ever been observed, evolution, scientifically speaking, doesn't even qualify as a hypothesis, let alone a theory. And yet in most universities it is taught as a fact, a law. It is about as unscientific as we can get. It is a ruse that has done untold damage to modern civilization.

2. **Intelligent Design**. Classrooms in our public schools are not allowed to teach ID because it is not scientific. Excuse me. Intelligent Design is one hundred percent scientific. ID is often equated with creationism, which presupposes a supernatural cause. ID does not presuppose a supernatural cause. It is one hundred percent scientific according to the modern definition of science. According to the Center for Science and Culture:

> The theory of intelligent design is simply an effort to empirically detect whether the "apparent design" in nature acknowledged by virtually all biologists is genuine design (the product of an intelligent cause) or is simply the product of an undirected process such as natural selection acting on random variations. Creationism typically starts with a religious text and tries to see how the findings of science can be reconciled to it. Intelligent design starts with the empirical evidence of nature and seeks to ascertain what inferences can be drawn from that evidence. Unlike creationism, the scientific theory of intelligent design does not claim that modern biology can identify whether the intelligent cause detected through science is supernatural.[134]

Is ID a scientific theory? Absolutely:

> The scientific method is commonly described as a four-step process involving observations, hypothesis, experiments, and conclusion. Intelligent design begins with the observation that intelligent agents produce complex and specified information (CSI). Design theorists hypothesize that if a natural object

---

134 http://www.intelligentdesign.org/whatisid.php, accessed on July 31, 2015.

was designed, it will contain high levels of CSI. Scientists then perform experimental tests upon natural objects to determine if they contain complex and specified information. One easily testable form of CSI is irreducible complexity, which can be discovered by experimentally reverse-engineering biological structures to see if they require all of their parts to function. When ID researchers find irreducible complexity in biology, they conclude that such structures were designed.[135]

Of course, the scientific community couldn't let irreducible complexity go unchallenged, so many attempts have been made to discredit Behe's examples. One counter I read, however, tried to show from gene replication that a flagellum could be created without an outside agent. But it was gene replication, that is, there was already an intelligent designer—the prior gene with its code. Such specious reasoning is not very convincing.

CONCLUSION

Any child will imitate his parents if . . . if . . . if he spends enough time with his parents. We are told to be imitators of God. How much time do you spend with Jesus? How much time do you spend with God? And if you do spend that time, you will imitate him and you will love as he loved.

The special Olympics were held in Spokane, WA, on November 17, 2008 (see YouTube). There were nine kids in the finals of the 100-meter dash. They all got down into the starting position and the gun went off. These nine young people raced out of the blocks as fast as they could, given their respective disabilities and handicaps. About a third of the way down the track, one of the kids tripped and fell on the track. He tried to get up again, but he tripped and fell again. He just lay on the track sobbing.

---

135   Ibid.

The other eight kids were racing toward the finish line. Three of them heard the other kid who fell crying. They stopped where they were. They went back and picked this kid up. And the four of them held hands and walked across the finish line together. The crowd didn't know what to do with that initially. It was beyond their comprehension. And when they realized what had happened, they gave the four kids a fifteen-minute standing ovation.

The truth is all of us as Christians are in a Special Olympics. The Christian life is a race. We are all handicapped in one way or another. And who knows, you may trip up along the way and lie sobbing on the track. Or you may be one of the ones who hear your brother who has fallen crying. But when you pick him up and all of you cross the goal line together, hand in hand—you are all winners. Again, who knows? The longest and loudest ovation from the holy angels may be reserved for you.

In "Snow White and the Seven Dwarfs" the ugly witch asked, "Mirror, mirror on the wall; who's the fairest of them all?" If all you do through life is look at yourself in the mirror, you may become as ugly as the old witch. But if you spend your time serving "the little people," you may become as beautiful as Snow White. And when the handsome Prince returns, he will be proud to have you sitting by his side at the wedding feast of the Lamb.

Selfishness turns ugly; selflessness becomes beautiful.

15

WINDS OF DOCTRINE

Part 6 – Freed to Walk in the Light

Ephesians 5:7-14

INTRODUCTION

Why is it good people sometimes do bad things? It could be from bad communication, even from the pulpit. I read about one preacher who was trying to teach holy living to his people. He thought he needed a prop, so he got a table and put four tin cans on the table. In the first can was alcohol, the second can tobacco juice, the third can cigarette smoke, and in the fourth can was good soil. Then he put a worm in each can. A worm in the can with alcohol, the can with tobacco juice, and so on. Then he proceeded to preach his sermon. As he was drawing his sermon to a conclusion, he went to the four cans. He opened the first can with the alcohol, and sure enough, the little worm had died, of alcoholism, no doubt. The second worm? You guessed it, chewing tobacco can cause cancer—in thirty minutes. And, alas, the third worm died of smoke inhalation.

Of course, the fourth worm was thriving in the good soil, doing quite nicely, thank you very much.

So the preacher looked at his audience and asked, "What lesson can we draw from these four cans?" A little ol' lady at the back of the church raised her hand. When called upon, she said, "Well, preacher, it's pretty clear, isn't it? If we drink, and smoke, and chew all we can, we won't have worms." There's a can of worms for you. Well, sometimes bad communication or miscommunication can corrupt good morals. And you no doubt have heard it said that bad company corrupts good morals. And that is the lesson we learn in Ephesians 5:7-14—bad company corrupts good morals. And corrupt morals lead to worse relationships. And worse relationships lead to works of darkness.

So, there is a progression as we work our way through the passage. Paul has been trying to teach us to go from independence to interdependence. He wants us to become interdependent so we can become mature Christians. Mature Christians will radiate the attributes of God. To radiate the attributes of God is to glorify God. It's to be a billboard for God. It is an open display of his character qualities. Paul wants his Purpose-Driven Church to glorify God. They can't do that through the unfruitful works of darkness. How can we be mirrors of God's grace when we openly or secretly practice the works of darkness? Some of these works of darkness are seen in public, some only in private, and some only in secret, the proverbial closet.

Ephesians says we can only come to maturity through horizontal relationships. But here Paul clarifies. This does not mean horizontal relationships at any cost, especially close relationships where we potentially yoke together for life. So we will see in 5:7-10 that we are not to have close horizontal relationships with workers of darkness, what we might call partnerships. Then in 5:11-14 Paul tells us we shouldn't have fellowship with the works of darkness themselves. So, no partnership with the workers of darkness in 5:7-10 and no fellowship with the works of darkness in 5:11-14. He goes from the bad company to the corrupt morals they can produce. The key to avoiding the workers of darkness and the works of darkness? Walk in the light.

EPHESIANS
"The Creation and the Conduct of the Church"

SALUTATION 1:1-2

INTRODUCTION—"Spiritual Blessings in the Heavenlies" 1:3-14

(Paul's Prayer for Perception) 1:15-23

BODY 2:1-6:9

I. Creation of the Church (Its Position) 2:1-3:21

II. Conduct of the Church (Its Condition) 4:1-6:9

A. The Goal: Maturity of the Body 4:1-16

B. The Means: Maturity of the Individual 4:17-6:9

1. Through Personal Sanctification 4:17-5:14

a. Walking in Life 4:17-32

b. Walking in Love 5:1-6

c. Walking in Light 5:7-14

2. Through Personal Submission 5:15-6:9

CONCLUSION—"Spiritual Battles in the Heavenlies" 6:10-20

I. NO PARTNERSHIP—WITH THE WORKERS OF DARKNESS 7-10

[7] Therefore do not be partakers with them. [8] For you were once darkness, but now *you are* light in the Lord. Walk as children of light [9] (for the fruit of the Spirit *is* in all goodness, righteousness, and truth), [10] finding out what is acceptable to the Lord.

The "them" of v. 7 are the "sons of disobedience" mentioned at the end of v. 6 on whom the wrath of God will come in this life. It's not talking about eternity. In the NT the wrath of God is now . . . in time. The word "partakers" (NKJ) or "partners" (NIV:NAS) is *symmetochoi*, which refers to co-partners. It could apply to marriage, business, best friends, or worship. This is more than a casual association. These are the people you open up to. When you open up, you begin to bond. This doesn't come from talking about the weather. You have to go deeper. So on a deeper level you link up or partner up—whatever the purpose.

The point is obvious: our closest personal relationships should not be with either unbelievers or believers walking in darkness. Light and darkness don't mix. 2 Corinthians 6:14 says, "Do not be unequally yoked together with unbelievers. For what fellowship has righteousness with lawlessness? And what communion has light with darkness?" Yoking was when you joined two oxen together to plow a field. The yoke was for the purpose of working together, for the purpose of serving. The Corinthians were not to be unequally yoked with unbelievers. The word "fellowship" in the NKJ translation is the same word as "partners" in Ephesians 5:7.

"For" in 5:8 tells us why we should not partner with the workers of darkness. "For . . . you were darkness . . . but now you are light **in the Lord**." You **were**, but you **are**. You **were**, but you **are**. He makes an argument based on their new identity *in Christ* (see 1:3-14). A change in their **Position** should bring about a change in their **Condition**. Remember, what they do in their **Condition** can never change their **Position**, but what they are in their **Position** can most certainly change their **Condition**. Because of our new **Position** (in Christ) there should be a change in our **Condition** (our character and conduct). Because we are now light (**Position**), we should no longer walk in darkness (**Condition**). We have a new identity.

When we see that word "walk," we know Paul is talking about our lifestyle. He is saying, "Let your **Condition** reflect your **Position**." In other words, *become* as you *are*. When we walk as "children of light," then we will enjoy the fruit of the Spirit[136] like "goodness, righteousness, and truth." "But if we walk in the light as He is in the light, we have fellowship with one another, and the blood of Jesus Christ his Son cleanses us from all sin" (1 Jn 1:7)—meaning we are in fellowship with him. And if we walk by the Spirit, we will not fulfill the lusts of the flesh (Gal 5:17).

So it's what's on the inside. It goes from the inside out. Batman said, "It's not what's on the inside, but it is the things I do that define what I am." Well, no wonder Batman lives in darkness. That's not what the Scriptures teach. You have had a fundamental change on the inside. You are not who you once were. God has put his seed within you. God's seed is the new nature. It is impossible for it to sin. God put his DNA into that New Nature. Its genetic code will not allow it to sin. And that is the power source for the inner man we need to strengthen day by day so our **Condition** reflects our **Position**. We still have the Sin Nature. The Sin Nature is like a factory. It can produce Human Good or Human Evil, both of which are unacceptable to God. But with the New Nature we have a new identity. Through the Holy Spirit working through our New Nature, we do not have to sin. We may choose to sin, but we do not have to sin. Of course, Paul is arguing that when we choose to sin, we are acting contrary to who we really are, contrary to our new identity in Christ.

I saw one of the most beautiful sights in North America recently in Montana. Beat anything I had seen in the Smokies or Washington or Oregon or California. But the folks in Montana kept telling me I had to come back during the fall. "Oh, you need to be here in the

---

136 Although most modern translations say "light" here instead of "Spirit" (NKJ), 98% of the manuscript evidence supports "Spirit" as the correct reading. Many argue that the Egyptian manuscripts Aleph, Vaticanus, and Alexandrinus (which support "light") should be followed since they are earlier. However, p[46] (which antedates the other Egyptian manuscripts by as much as forty years according to some scholars and contains all of Paul's letters except the pastorals) reads "Spirit."

fall when the leaves change." That's when I would really see beauty. Well, that set me off on one of my mini-scientific lectures about leaves and chlorophyll. I said, "The leaves don't change colors. The colors are there all along. The only thing that happens in the fall is that the chlorophyll falls away, that is, the pigment disappears. During the spring and summer the chlorophyll covers over the colors. The true colors of the leaves are only seen when the chlorophyll goes away." They looked at me with a "Say what?" look on their faces.

But isn't that true in our Christian lives? Your true colors won't be seen until the chlorophyll of the world falls away. The colors are there the moment you become a believer. As we grow in Christ the power of the Holy Spirit manifests the character colors of Christ himself as the pigment of the world falls away. We become like a prism to break up the colors of the spectrum. Through the prism of your New Nature the Holy Spirits let's the light of Christ shine. His beautiful light is broken up into the various character colors of his divine nature. We become reflectors of that character for all the world to see. And in doing so, we glorify him by becoming an open, public manifestation of his character.

So Paul seems to be saying, "Have horizontal relationships, but be careful with whom you form them." It's a plug, is it not, for bonding together with Christians? Is there anyone you open up to? Anyone you share your innermost being with? There is nothing quite like the fellowship with another Christian when you can both open up. This is how we go on to maturity—horizontal relationships; interdependence.

Now Paul moves from the Workers of Darkness to the Works of Darkness in 5:11-14.

II. NO PARTNERSHIP—WITH THE WORKS OF DARKNESS 11-14

[11] And have no fellowship with the unfruitful works of darkness, but rather expose *them*. [12] For it is shameful even to speak of those things which are done by them in secret. [13] But all things that are exposed are made manifest by the light, for whatever

makes manifest is light. [14] Therefore He says:
"Awake, you who sleep,
Arise from the dead,
And Christ will give you light."

The idea here is we are to have no participation in the works of darkness. No sharing when it comes to evil. Rather than getting involved in them we are to expose them. *Elenchō* is the word used for "**expose**" in v. 11. "**Bring to light**" is offered by BDAG as an alternative to "expose." That's what we are to do to the "works of darkness." Now let's be careful here. It does not say to expose people. We have moved from the "workers" to their "works." This is not a Christian witch-hunt in which we go around exposing others we presume to be involved in serious sin. If we know that someone is involved in gross moral sin, then we go to the elders. It is their responsibility to deal with serious sin in the church, assuming we are referring to church members.

No, it is not our responsibility to expose the workers of darkness. Nor does it say we should expose the works of darkness performed by the workers of darkness. What it does talk about is exposing my own works of darkness. *We are going to see this is one of the great promises in the NT for having a victorious Christian life.* Verse 12 says "it is shameful even to speak of those things which are done by them in secret." A friend of mine likes to say we have our Public Self, our Private Self, and our Secret Self.

Our Public Self is on display for everyone to see. Our Private Self may be seen by those close to us: our family and close friends. But then there is our Secret Self seen only by us, God, and the angels. Someone has said that the true test of character is what we do when tempted and we think no one else is looking. This word for "secret" is the word *kryphē* from which we get the English word "cryptic," meaning "hidden." And what does Paul say about these works? They are too shameful even to talk about. These are the works that are to be exposed.

We are to expose the darkness. Why? Because of the great promise in vv. 13-14. In fact, if you get nothing else from this lesson, don't miss the promise of v. 13: "All things that are exposed are made visible [NAS, ESV, NIV]." OK, we understand this. Anything exposed to the light becomes visible. It is the next part of v. 13 that is tricky. I think the NAS and NKJ have nailed it. "Whatever is made visible is light." That is almost it. Here is what I think it says: "Whatever is made visible **becomes** light." **BECOMES LIGHT.** That's it. If it is visible, there is no longer darkness. The light causes the darkness to disappear, to go away. **The light dispels the darkness.** This is one of the great promises for a victorious Christian life, for progressive sanctification.

If we will take the works of darkness (things done in secret when we think no one else is looking) and expose them to the light, the light will dispel the darkness. Your very life will be light. Jesus said to his followers, "You are the light of the world." That's what Ephesians is all about—reflecting his light (his character qualities, his attributes) for his glory. We are just reflectors of his light—moons, not stars. We have no light of our own. But we can reflect his light. "Let your light so shine before men, that they may see your good works and glorify your Father in heaven," (Matt 5:16) exhorted Jesus.

So, practically speaking, what does this look like? For one thing, it means spending time in the light. I would consider a revelation from God to be light. The revelation he has given us is written down. It is his Word, the Bible. When we read or study our Bibles, we are exposing ourselves to the light: "For the word of God *is* living and powerful, and sharper than any two-edged sword, piercing even to the division of soul and spirit, and of joints and marrow, and is a discerner of the thoughts and intents of the heart. And there is no creature hidden from his sight, but all things *are* naked and open to the eyes of him to whom we *must give* account" (Heb 4:12-13). God's Word exposes our Secret Self. There are no thoughts or deeds hidden from him. But that is good news. Why? Because the promise of Ephesians 5:13 is that this kind of exposure to the light will dispel the darkness in our lives. His light works like exposing a cancerous tumor to radiation, or dirt to water. Again Jesus prayed for his disciples, "Sanctify them by your truth. Your word is truth" (Jn 17:17).

But there is another way to "come to the light." We are also told to "confess your sins to one another" (Jas 5:16). By definition our secret sins are done in darkness. But the power of Satan is also in darkness. Our enemy constructs his strongholds in darkness. To break that power, those strongholds, we need to come to the light. Confessing to one another is coming to the light. It breaks the power of darkness. One afternoon a friend I had known for years came by to visit. I assumed it was just a normal fellowship time, but he let me know right away that he was there for a special reason: he wanted to come to the light. "What do you mean?" I asked. He said, "You have been preaching about the power of Satan being in darkness and how we can break that power by confessing our secret sins to a trusted brother. So here I am. I am about to share with you some stuff that could ruin my family if my wife finds out. I hope you are right about what you have been preaching."

It is one of the sobering things about being a teacher or preacher of God's Word. Lives hang in the balance based on what we teach. This brother desperately wanted deliverance from the power of his Sin Nature. He confessed secret sin after secret sin, stuff I really did not want to know about or care to hear about. Nevertheless, we both leaned on God's promises that confession of sin one to another can heal both spiritually and physically (Jas 5:15-16) and when darkness is exposed to the light, the darkness goes away. It was a turning point in his marriage.

Decades ago I read a book by O. Hobart Mowrer, a non-Christian psychologist, called *The Crisis in Psychiatry and Religion*.[137] He concluded that the vast majority of people in psychiatric wards for non-physiogenic reasons are there because of unresolved guilt. I found that an interesting observation from someone who was openly against Christianity. He spotted the problem. I couldn't wait to read his solution. His solution? Return to the confessional. Although he was not a practicing Christian, he saw psychological value in confessing

---

137 O. Hobart Mowrer, *The Crisis in Psychiatry and Religion* (New York, NY: D. Van Nostrand, 1961).

one's sins to another person. Get them out of the closet, out of darkness. Is confession to another person a guarantee of victory? No, but it is a step in the right direction. Depending on the stronghold, other steps may be necessary as well. Confession is a good first step.

Now look at the promise in v. 14. **"Awake you who sleep."** He is talking about spiritual lethargy, spiritual apathy. It is because you know and God knows there is a secret place of darkness where we entertain or produce works of darkness. It's that common knowledge that sucks the vitality right out of our Christian lives. You might call it a spiritual stupor. So Paul says, "Wake up; arise from the dead." Here he means the living dead like the Christian widow of 1 Timothy 5:6. She was dead even though she lived. Why? Because she was living for pleasure instead of Christ. The death she experienced was the agony of spiritual defeat, the depression of knowing what's right but doing what was wrong.

So what happens if you rise up from the dead? Another great promise: "Christ will give you light." Another way to translate this would be, "Christ will shine on you." He will bless you. He will illumine you. He will vitalize your spiritual life.

HURRICANE DARWIN
Part 3

But, of course, there are those who don't believe these promises. In fact, they don't believe the Bible at all or the God of the Bible. We have been talking about the "Winds of Doctrine" that can undermine the faith of a believer. One of those is the teaching of Charles Darwin. So here we look at another weak link or missing link in the logic and science of evolution. We want to look at what we will call "Specific Complexity." As we do this we propose that we can filter the events in our lives through the concepts of chance, law, and design. Each of these concepts has different characteristics. The key word connected to chance is randomness. It happens at random. The key word for law is repetitiveness. That's why the Law of Gravity is a law. Every time you drop the apple, it falls. The falling happens over and over.

It repeats. With design you have an irregular sequence that has been prescribed. You have Specific Complexity.

Well, the evolutionists gave up on chance quite a while back. They realized the odds were so remote that spontaneous generation by chance was impossible. Emile Borel, the statistician formulated a law, call Borel's Law, that any occurrence that has less than 10^{-50} chance of happening just won't happen.[138] The chances of spontaneous generation are much, much less than that. And the chances of macro-evolution, where changes in the DNA structure of life takes us up the ladder of evolution, are even worse. Ain't gonna happen. So these thinkers have given up on chance/randomness as an explanation for evolution. Now they turn to Natural Law.

With Natural Law they are appealing to an argument about certain chemicals being arranged in such a way that they react favorably for the formation of life and going up the scale of evolution. Forget the fact that they have never been able to do this in a controlled setting, aka a laboratory. That is still what they believe. Well, the problem is the DNA code is much better described as a language than as a law. And language is complex, but specifically so. For example, if I take the letters from the game of Scrabble and dumped them out on the table, and you see the word "cat," you could deduce that happened by chance. Now if I take the same scrabble letters and dump them on the table, and every time I dumped them on the table, they spell "cat", you would say we have a law. Repetitiveness: it happens over and over and every time we do it. Chance–randomness; law–repetitiveness. But if we dumped the Scrabble letters on the table and you saw the words, "Betty loves Dave," you wouldn't say, "Luck." No, you would say, "Design."

Now you could spell out that sentence, "Betty loves Dave," or, "Dave loves Betty," in any number of ways. The message does not depend on the medium. That message is not inherent in the Scrabble

---

138   E. Borel, *Probabilities and Life* (New York, NY: Dover, 1962), chapters 1 and 3.

letters. We could write the same sentence with a black felt pen on a white board. We could write it on our computer, or we could write it on the sand. It is the message that is superimposed on the medium. Do you follow that? It requires an outside intelligence to prescribe the sequence. That is specific complexity, and it infers design.

Well, God is telling us in Ephesians 5 that bad company corrupts good morals. But you can flip that around, can't you. Good company produces good morals. I want to illustrate the main message of this passage from the life of Johnny Cash. When I watched the movie *Walk the Line*, it went through his drug addiction and ended with June Carter taking him to church. You really couldn't tell from the movie if Johnny Cash became a Christian. So I did some research and was surprised to find the Cash did have a conversion. He actually went on to go to Bible College and graduated. While in college he became fascinated with the apostle Paul. Both of them seemed to be Type A personalities. Both of them went full bore at whatever they did. Both of them were converted to Christianity in the middle of their lives.

But what I did not know is that after Bible College, Cash went to Jerusalem to learn as much as he could about the Bible and about the Apostle Paul. He studied Josephus and Gibbons and Suetonius and other scholars. Then he wrote the best book on the Apostle Paul I have ever read. You would think a doctoral student had written this book. It is called *A Man in White*.[139] But you know what, he couldn't have done it alone. He started on drugs when he was traveling with Elvis and Jerry Lee Lewis. Bad company corrupted good morals.

When Cash came to Christ, he had to find a new group of friends to keep his head above water. That can be difficult and painful. I found that I actually had to move off campus to an apartment while going to college in order to break away from my old group of friends to find a new group. The *Man in White* is referring, of course, to Jesus, who

---

139 Johnny Cash, *Man in White* (San Francisco, CA: HarperSanFrancisco, 1986).

appeared to Paul on the road to Damascus. In the book Cash wrote this song:

> The friends of the Nazarene became united
>> And I became enraged
> And led a slaughter zealously
>> I found their secret places
> So they were beaten, they were chained
>> But some of them were scattered
>> They were justified in fearing me
>
> And then the Man in white appeared to me
>> In such a blinding light
> It struck me down and with its brilliance
>> It took away my sight.
> Then the Man in white in gentle loving tones
>> Spoke to me
> And I was blinded so I might see
>> The Man in White.

Bad (immoral) company produces works of darkness. Good (moral) company exposes works of darkness by coming to the light.

16

REDEEMING THE TIME

Ephesians 5:15-16

INTRODUCTION

Some years ago my older daughter and family moved to a small town just south of Cleveland, Ohio. Betty and I were eager to visit. The name of the town is Hudson. When we got there my daughter informed me that my hair had gotten way too long. Somehow she has an influence on me, so I said, "Okay, I'll cut it." So I went to the town square and walked around until I found a barber. He said that I'd have to wait two hours, so to kill time I found the city library, went in, and read a little sketch of Hudson, Ohio. I discovered they number among their early citizens a man named John Brown. Now, I'm not a real civil war history buff, but I knew he was an anti-slavery abolitionist so I said, "I think I'll find a biography and read that." So I found a John Brown biography and read it while waiting for the haircut.

John Brown's route in life took him from Ohio to Kansas and back. Then he went down to Harpers Ferry where he was captured by Robert E Lee and hung. At his funeral Wendell Phillips said this, "Some men struggle into obscurity, while others forget themselves into immortality." As I read those words, I thought, "I suppose only God will decide on whether he forgot himself into immortality," but I think I caught the gist of what Phillips was trying to say. I started thinking of biblical characters like Moses and Pharaoh that illustrate Phillips' words.

Can anyone of you name the Pharaoh in charge while Moses was in Egypt? Ramses II. It's not a name that jumps out at us. But he went to great means and struggles to see that his name lived on by means of a tomb with all kinds of treasures in it. Despite his best attempts at immortality, he struggled, you might say, into obscurity because very few people know his name. Moses, on the other hand, relinquished his position and his power and gave his life to serve an obscure race of slaves. Yet I don't think you could go into a country in the civilized world where some of its people haven't heard of Moses. He forgot himself into immortality. And that's really what our passage is about in Ephesians 5:15-16. We are builders for eternity. To each is given a book of rules, a block of stone, and a bag of tools. Each must shape before his or her time is gone a stumbling block or a stepping-stone.

The Bible presents us as builders, builders on a foundation of life. Pretty much all of us make a living, but how many of us make a life? God wants us to do just that in Ephesians 5:15-16. As we get to this part of Ephesians, we are moving away from growing into maturity through personal sanctification. Now we are growing into maturity through personal submission. It is easy to see how becoming more holy will help us become more mature Christians. But it's harder for us to understand how we can become more mature through personal submission. How can submission help me become a mature Christian? Again, we often lose sight of the forest for the trees.

We have suggested before that the two great questions of the universe are:

1. **Who has the right to rule the universe?**

2. **Is God worthy of being loved?**

God created man to answer those two questions. He used the issue of authority and submission as one of his primary ways to answer the first question, "Who has the right to rule the universe?" When I choose respectfully to be submissive to the authorities God has placed over me, then I am saying, "Yes, God, you have the right to rule!" I am also saying, "You are worthy of being loved," because in John 14:21 we are told that through obedience to his commands we prove to God that we love him.

So submission becomes a big theme in Ephesians, and make no mistake about it, maturity in Christ is what God is going for. Understanding the importance of submission to God-ordained authorities is a major pillar in the building of Christian maturity. Back in chapter four, Paul talked about the whole Body of Christ growing up into the measure of the stature of the fullness of Christ, but the Body can't go on to maturity if the individuals don't. One of the many beauties of Christianity is that it offers an equal opportunity for every one of God's children to go on to maturity, assuming they have some time to live after they become Christians. God's plan for the human race is that every person is given the opportunity to have his name written on the walls of immortality. I am not talking about the book of life, which contains the name of every believer. No, I am talking about the Hall of Faith that contains the name of every believer who lives his life to glorify God.

As we enter Ephesians 5:15, we are moving toward this great doctrine of personal submission, but because the concept contained in Ephesians 5:15-16 is so important I want to just cover those two verses in this lesson. We are going to look at the foolish man and the wise man, specifically to see what each does with his time.

I. WALKING LIKE A FOOLISH MAN 5:15-16

15 See then that you walk circumspectly, not as fools but as wise, 16 redeeming the time, because the days are evil.

In 5:15-16, Paul talks about the wise and the foolish. There is a wise man and a foolish man. The foolish man doesn't redeem the time; the wise man does redeem the time. The foolish man doesn't walk circumspectly; the wise man does. But what does that word "circumspectly" mean? "Circum-" reminds us of "**circum**ference" and "-spectly" suggests looking, like "in-**spect**." So, "looking around" gets pretty close. Some other translations say "carefully" or "careful."

That's pretty good, but the Greek word *akribos*, which is translated "circumspectly," speaks of "accuracy," or "exactness." The underlying meaning of accuracy never really leaves. The foolish man does not use the equations of life to come up with the right answer. Or when it's all over, he may look back and say, "Ooops—careless error." It's like looking back over a math test and finding a careless error, only in this case the man's whole life turns out to be one big careless error, not on God's part, but on his. Wow. Think of that. My whole life could be summed up as a careless error if I live like a fool. That doesn't mean God made a careless error when he created me. It means I made a careless error by not living my life wisely to "redeem the time."

The wise man is in contrast to that. He takes the equations of life and works accurately. Part of that is to realize there is intelligent design out there, and if there is design, there is purpose. If there is purpose in the created order, and I am part of the created order, that means there is purpose for my life. Can I find it? That is all over Ephesians. It is written to a Purpose Driven Church made up of purpose driven individuals. That is what God wants us to be.

So if we are going to redeem the time, we better take a closer look at the word "redeem." The word translated here "redeeming" is from *exagorazō*. The "*ex*" means "out of" and the "*agorazō*" means "to buy out." The *agora* in the Greek world was the market place. The word is used in Galatians 3:13 in reference to Christ, who "redeemed" us from the slave block of sin in the devil's marketplace. But here we are talking about redeeming the time. Again, various translations come at the meaning differently: "making the best use of" (ESV); "making the most of" (NASB); or "making the most of every opportunity" (NIV).

I prefer to stick with "redeeming" because of the use of this word in Galatians in reference to Christ's work on our behalf. He paid the price to buy us out of the marketplace to transfer us from this world to the next, from death to life. He says you can do the same thing with time. You can do that with the days of your life. This world is seen as the marketplace, and you can invade the marketplace and buy up the days of your life. It's what Jesus calls "saving your life," a concept he introduced in Matthew 16:24-27. How much of our lives has been saved versus how much of our lives has been lost (wasted) will show up when Christ returns and evaluates our lives (our time on earth) at the Judgment Seat of Christ. The more we save, the more glory we bring to him for all eternity. We will say more about this when we discuss the wise man.

The foolish man doesn't know anything about this. He fritters away the days of his life; here today, gone tomorrow. He may be like the epicurean that eats, drinks, is merry, and thinks this is it. There is nothing more. That is a foolish man. But even some foolish men want their lives to last and their names to live on through future generations. That's what Cecil Rhodes was trying to do when he leased up most of the mineral rights in South Africa and became enormously wealthy with his diamonds. Looking for ways to make his name last, he said, "I think I'll have a country named after me." And so he did. The name of that country was Rhodesia. On his deathbed he asked, "They can't change the name of a country, can they?" Well, I guess they can. There is no country in Africa named Rhodesia anymore. They changed the name to Zimbabwe. Even if you want your name to last, you have to build on the right foundation. That's what the wise man does.

II. WALKING LIKE A WISE MAN   5:15-16

15 See then that you walk circumspectly, not as fools but as wise, 16 redeeming the time, because the days are evil.

The wise man lives "accurately." That is, he uses the equations of life to come up with the right answer. In the context of Ephesians the right answer is to live a purpose driven life, the purpose of which is to use one's time on earth to glorify God. The Scriptures teach there are a number of ways to do just that.

A. A Life of Self-Sacrifice for the Kingdom of Christ— Matthew 16:24-27

> [24] Then Jesus said to His disciples, "If anyone desires to come after Me, let him deny himself, and take up his cross, and follow Me. [25] For whoever desires to save his life will lose it, but whoever loses his life for My sake will find it. [26] For what profit is it to a man if he gains the whole world, and loses his own soul? Or what will a man give in exchange for his soul? [27] For the Son of Man will come in the glory of His Father with His angels, and then He will reward each according to his works.

This is a classic passage on self-sacrifice. So let's be clear from the beginning. If this is a passage about how to go to heaven, then you get there by self-sacrifice. Jesus says in verse 24 we are to deny ourselves, take up our crosses, and follow him. We usually think of crosses as symbols of some sort of self-sacrifice. Of course, Jesus made the ultimate self-sacrifice when he died on a cross. However, we have all heard people mention "the cross they have to bear." By that they usually mean some sort of self- sacrifice short of death. But Jesus had just talked about his own impending death. So, when he faces his disciples and mentions carrying a cross, he's warning them that following him may well result in their deaths. So is that how you get to heaven? Doesn't sound like the free gift Paul talks about in Ephesians 2:8-9, does it?

Now it is interesting to see the connections between verses 24 and 27. Verse 25 starts with "for," and verse 26 starts with "for," and verse 27 starts with "for." In the New Testament, about ninety percent of the time the word "for" is used to give a reason or an explanation for what was just said in the verse before it. That means verse 25 is explaining verse 24, and verse 26 is explaining verse 25, and verse 27 is explaining verse 26. It is a daisy chain of logic stretching from verse

24 to verse 27. Keeping that in mind, when Jesus starts off in verse 24, it's helpful to see where he's going to wind up in verse 27. He begins with a condition for discipleship: self-sacrifice. He winds up in verse 27 with rewards given to those that have been sacrificial. The passage has nothing to do with getting into heaven, but it has everything to do with being rewarded when we get there.

Now what does all this have to do with redeeming the time? Simply this. In these verses Jesus says we can save our lives or lose them. Here's the question of the day: what does the word "life" mean? If I ask a new high school graduate, "What do you want to do with your life?" he doesn't ask me, "What do you mean by life?" He knows what I mean by life. Your life or my life or anyone's life is simply our time on earth, from our birth until our death or the rapture. It is a quantity of time, and we can measure that time in terms of days or months or years. Psalm 90 talks about our time on earth. The Psalmist says we get seventy years to live, eighty if we're blessed. And then he tells us to number our days. The idea is to value our time on earth, for our days are numbered by God.

Jesus is actually saying each day is like a pearl. In other words, each day is precious. And like a pearl each day can be saved or lost. Therefore, he says, "Don't cast your pearls before swine." In Matthew 16, he's saying there is nothing more valuable than our time on earth, at least to us. "For what does it profit a man if he gains the whole world and loses his own life? Or what will a man give in exchange for his life?" The idea is simple: gaining the whole world doesn't do us much good if we're dead.

Someone will surely say, "But my text says 'soul' instead of 'life.'" Yes, but that's in verse 26. In verse 25 the same Greek word, *psychē*, is used twice, but there it is translated "life" by every translation I have checked. And well it should be, because that is what it means about half the time it's used in the New Testament. The strange thing is that the translators translate the word "life" both times in verse 25, but when they get to verse 26, they translated it "soul" both times. We have already explained that verse 25 and 26 are connected by "for." That means verse 26 is explaining verse 25. So when two verses are back to back with the second one explaining the first one, you would expect the same word being used twice in verse 25 and twice in verse 26 would be translated the same way all four times.

Now these translators are not stupid people. What would've caused them to go from "life-life" in verse 25 to "soul-soul" in verse 26? There is only one answer. It is their understanding of the word "saved." We are conditioned in Western Christianity to think the word "saved" means go to heaven. About half of its uses in the New Testament mean just that. But it is often used of physical salvation such as saving the disciples from drowning in the Sea of Galilee: "Lord, save us" (Matt 8:25). Or, healing a woman from an issue about blood (Matt 9:21) is another example of the Greek word *sōzō*, which is usually translated "save."

The word "saved" has many uses other than being saved to go to heaven. Matthew 16 is a case in point. Here the subject is saving or losing our lives, our time on earth. This passage is Jesus' way of saying, "Redeem the time." He is saying what the Psalmist said. Each day of our lives can be saved or lost for eternity. At the Judgment Seat of Christ (v. 27), when we are rewarded for what we have done on earth, we will find out how much of our time on earth has been saved and how much has been lost. Each day that has been saved will go to glorify Jesus forever and ever. Each day that is lost is lost forever—wasted (Eccl. 12:13-14).

B. A Life Built on the Right Foundation (Jesus Christ)— 1 Cor 3:10-11

This well-known passage on the Judgment Seat of Christ tells us how our lives will be evaluated when we stand before him. Only believers show up at this judgment seat. It occurs right after the rapture (see Revelation 4-5 where the twenty-four elders are wearing white robes, are seated, and wearing their crowns). Let's look at the foundation God himself is looking for:

> [9] For we are God's fellow workers; you are God's field, *you are* God's building. [10] According to the grace of God which was

given to me, as a wise master builder I have laid the foundation, and another builds on it. But let each one take heed how he builds on it. [11] For no other **foundation** can anyone lay than that which is laid, which is **Jesus Christ** (emphasis mine).

The beginning of this foundation for an individual is when he takes his sins to the cross to seek God's forgiveness through God's provision, the substitutionary death of his Son on the cross. But that is just the beginning. Jesus is the cornerstone not only of the Universal Church but also our individual lives. We are builders, and each thing we do for his kingdom with the right motive (1 Cor 13:3) becomes another brick in the building, which is our life on this earth. Now let's look at vv. 12-15:

[12] Now if anyone builds on this foundation *with* gold, silver, precious stones, wood, hay, straw, [13] **each one's work** will become clear; for the Day will declare it, because it will be revealed by fire; and the fire will test **each one's work**, of what sort it is. [14] If **anyone's work** which he has built on *it* endures, he will receive a reward. [15] If **anyone's work** is burned, he will suffer loss; but he himself will be saved, yet so as through fire (emphasis mine).

Notice how many times we see the word "work" in this passage. If someone builds on the wrong foundation, his works are burned up. "Works" in this context is used as a figure of speech to refer to our whole life since knowing Christ. If we build on the right foundation, we will receive a reward. He symbolizes those rewards with his reference to gold, silver, and precious stones. And what do we do with gold, silver, and precious stones? We make jewelry, including crowns.

Now some people think the whole emphasis on rewards is selfish. But wait a minute. What do we do with our crowns? If the twenty-four elders in Revelation 4-5 are representative of the church that has been raptured before the Tribulation Period begins, then we cast our crowns at his feet, because he (Christ) alone is worthy to wear them. In other words, much if not most of the emphasis on rewards received for a life well lived, a life built on the right foundation, is on God's glory, not ours. Surely there is nothing selfish about that.

One summer some people from Germany came to visit our church. They were being hosted by a couple that belongs to our church. They asked me if I could take these guys to play golf. While we were waiting to tee off on one hole, they were pointing their fingers at a new home being constructed and laughing. I asked them what they were laughing about. They said, "We've never seen a home built with wood. Wouldn't such a home be completely destroyed by a fire? In Germany we only build homes with stones, cement, and reinforcing steel. They're built to be passed down from one generation to another. Some of them are 500 years old."

That is really what Paul is saying here. If we build a life of wood, hay, and stubble, a fire can easily destroy it. But if we build a life with things that will last like gold, silver, and precious stones, our life won't be lost or destroyed by a fire. Of course, no one's eternal life with Jesus is threatened in this passage. Paul makes clear that even a person who built a life of wood, hay, and stubble will be saved. His life will be lost, but he will be saved. How is that possible? How can a life be lost, but a person be saved? We have to distinguish between the person and the life that person lives. When a person trusts Jesus Christ as his Savior, that person is guaranteed to live with God forever. But the time one has on earth after he receives Jesus, is what is evaluated at the Judgment Seat of Christ. So, redeeming the time means to save that time forever. And that time is your life on earth.

C. A Life Built on Hearing and Doing God's Word— Matthew 7:24-27

Some churches seem to think just getting God's Word into their heads is going to "save their lives" in the sense we have talked about above. Not according to this passage:

²⁴ "Therefore whoever hears these sayings of Mine, **and does them**, I will liken him to a wise man who built his house on

the rock: ²⁵ and the rain descended, the floods came, and the winds blew and beat on that house; and it did not fall, for it was founded on the rock.

²⁶ "But everyone who hears these sayings of Mine, and **does not do them**, will be like a foolish man who built his house on the sand: ²⁷ and the rain descended, the floods came, and the winds blew and beat on that house; and it fell. And great was its fall" (emphasis mine).

Both the wise man and the foolish man go to church, so to speak. More than that. Both of them go to Bible-teaching churches. Both of them hear the Word of God. But one of them acts in accordance with what he hears, while the other one does not. Many Bible scholars believe that James drew much wisdom from the Sermon on the Mount. James devotes an entire section of his letter to exhorting his readers to be doers of the word, not hearers only (Jas 1:19-2:26).

The fact is, it is a risky thing to attend a Bible-teaching church. Why? Because we're responsible for the light we receive. God's Word is light. We will be judged in accordance with the amount of light we have received. That is why Jesus spent the last half of his ministry speaking in parables. When he realized in Matthew 12 the Jewish leaders would never receive him, he mercifully limited the judgment on them by reducing the amount of light they received. Speaking in parables accomplished that purpose. It limited the light received by those determined to walk in darkness, but it increased the light received by those who were already responding to the light (Matt 13:10-15). To receive God's light, his Word, and do nothing about it, is a dangerous thing to do. It has consequences in this life and the life to come. In the life to come you see the consequences at the Judgment Seat of Christ: wood, hay, and stubble—all burned up. In this life we see the consequences when the storms come, when the wind blows, the rain descends, and the floods destroy. Pretty much everyone is going to face a storm or two in this life. The person committed to hearing and doing God's Word will weather that storm. It may hurt him, but it can't destroy him.

These are but three passages that show us how to redeem the time, how to save the days of our lives for eternity. Whole books of the Bible are devoted to this, like 1 Peter and Hebrews. But getting back to Ephesians, Paul says the reason we should redeem the time is because the days are "evil." That's kind of strange. I would think the days would be neutral. It's kind of like money or television. You can use money for good or evil, and you can use television for good or evil. You can use the Internet for good or evil. I would think you could use days for good or evil, but Paul says no, the days are evil. It is as though the days are little pieces of sand in Satan's hour o'clock, and they are just dripping away for his kingdom because he is the god of this world. Unless we are doing something to reach into the hour clock, those days go into his account. We have to redeem them out of his hour clock and put them in a safe deposit box not to be opened until Christ's return. That's what he says we can do; that's how we find the purpose of our life.

The evil of this present world is all but overwhelming; to focus on it too long becomes almost immobilizing. That's the bad news. But the good news is that the days of our lives can shine like the stars against the dark backdrop of this evil world. Remember, Jesus likens the days of our lives to beautiful pearls. Each day is a valuable pearl. To waste on this world is to cast our pearls before swine.

But there are those who say that is hogwash. Life has no meaning or purpose. That's what we hear in our postmodern world. That is another wind of doctrine. In our sidebars we are looking at the various winds of doctrine of our modern society where the pundits of education want us to believe there are no values, no absolute truth, no meaning, and no purpose. One of the most wicked winds Western civilization has ever faced is Hurricane Darwin. Here is our last installment on Hurricane Darwin.

HURRICANE DARWIN
Part 4

Some people will wonder and ask, "Why do you spend so much time on Darwin? What's the matter with poor Darwin? He just observed some things in nature and evolution was probably God's way of bringing forth mankind." That's what Francis Collins, head of the Genome project, has concluded. He is what we call a theistic evolutionist. He claims to be a Christian and a firm believer in evolution as God's means to create the human race.

So here's why I'm spending so much space on Charles Darwin. His impact went far beyond biology, as Nancy Pearcey says in "Biology Today, Tomorrow the World."[140] If we accept biological naturalism, it leads to a naturalistic worldview. During the textbook controversy in Ohio, one of the leaders put it well. He said, "A naturalistic definition of *science* has the effect of indoctrinating students into a naturalistic *worldview*."[141] Everything about one's worldview deals with his understanding of the origins of life. Pearcey says, "Darwinism functions as the scientific report for an overarching naturalistic view which is being promoted aggressively far beyond the bounds of science."[142]

I want to show you how we absorb Darwinism in high school and college, and how it logically works its way out to the rest of our society. I'll do it just with the titles of books:[143]

- Psychology—*The Selfish Gene*

- Morality—*The Moral Animal and Evolutionary Origins of Morality*

---

140 Pearcey, 207-25.

141 Ibid., 207.

142 Ibid.

143 Ibid., 208-10.

- Violence—*Demonic Males: Apes and the Origin of Human Violence.* These people say the 911 attacks on the twin towers have nothing to do with moral evil; it has to do with our DNA, and I quote, "The predisposition of violence is written in the molecular chemistry of DNA." Their genes made them do it.

- Religion—*Religion Explained: The Evolutionary Origins of Religious Thought*

- Politics—*Darwinian Politics: The Evolutionary Origins of Freedom*

- Economics—*Economics as Evolutionary Science*

- Law—*Evolutionary Jurisprudence or Law: Biology and Culture, the Evolution of Law*

- Education—*Origins of Genius: Darwinian Perspectives on Creativity*

- English—*Evolution and Literary Theory*

- Medicine—*Evolutionary Medicine and Why We Get Sick: The New Science of Darwinian Medicine*

- Psychiatry—*Darwinian Psychiatry or Genes on the Couch: Exploration in Evolutionary Psychology*

- Women—*Divided Laborers: An Evolutionary View of Women at Work*

- Parenting—*The Truth About Cinderella: A Darwinian View of Parental Love*

- Business—*Executive Instinct: Managing the Human Animal in the Information Age*

- Sexuality—*Ever Since Adam and Eve: The Evolution of Human Sexuality*

Let's go back to September 11 for a moment. The New York Times got in the act and decided the heroism of the firefighters and others was due to evolution. They claim that the heroism of the rescue workers was the product of evolution coming from the cooperative instincts of ants and bees.[144] So when someone says, "My, aren't you a little worker bee," you get a little taste of evolution on the move. My, my, my.

But it gets worse. What about rape and sexual assault? Well, that's evolution also. You can read all about it in *The Natural History of Rape: Biological Basis of Sexual Coercion.* In that book it is claimed that rape is evolutionary adaption for maximizing reproductive success. One of the writers of that book, Randy Thornhill, appeared on National Public Radio.[145] He found himself deluged by angry calls. But he insisted his logic was inescapable. He said if evolution is true, then every feature of every living thing, including human beings, has an evolutionary background. Then he said, "That is not a debatable matter."

What about Darwin himself? Did he ever see where this would lead? Sure he did. Writing in *The Descent of Man,* he said this, "Infanticide, especially in females, has been thought to be good for the tribe."[146] He saw way back then that his theory would lead to infanticide.

I talked to a young woman who went to UT Austin for school and did very well. She added a postgraduate program here in Houston in the medical community. Among her fellow grad students and professors she said she hasn't found one of them who holds to biblical values—not one. I'm not saying they're not out there, but they

---

144 Ibid, 210.

145 Ibid., 211.

146 Charles Darwin, http://thinkingcriminalslair.blogspot.com/2012/08/charles-darwin-on-infanticide-in.html, accessed September 6, 2016.

sure aren't the majority, and it's amazing the academic pressure the consensus of scholarship can produce.

Have you heard of Margaret Sanger? She is usually known as the founder of Planned Parenthood. It's probably not known what an ardent Darwinian she was. She wrote five books supporting Darwinism. Of course, she was for sexual experimentation and did herself. But eugenics was one of her favorite projects. Eugenics, or selecting good genes, was our attempt to help evolution along, to speed up process, you might say. Yes, eugenics began right here in America. Hitler loved it because it fit right in to his view of Aryan supremacy and the development of the *Supermenchen*, the supermen, the master race.

William James, known as a psychologist, was also one of the great pragmatists in America. America hasn't come up with too many philosophies on its own but this is one of them: pragmatism. If it works, it's good. If it works, do it regardless of other universal values and truths. William James decided if it's true, it must work satisfactorily. Each individual can decide for himself what works to meet his or her own needs. You can extrapolate from that and see how many places you can go.

Oliver Wendell Holmes, Jr. is thought of by most people as behind a lot of the law literature in our land. But he was also an ardent Darwinian. He wrote that the justification for any given law "is not that it represent an eternal principle," such as justice, but "that it helps bring out a social end which we desire."[147] This is still pragmatism. The question? Does it work? John Dewey was also one of the great pragmatists in America. He said there are no universal truths.[148] What is true for you, may not be true for me, and vice versa. But it doesn't matter. As long as it works for society, do what you think is right.

This leads us right into the postmodern era with people like

---

147   Oliver Wendell Holmes, Jr., "Law in Science," In *Essential Holmes*, 170.
148   Pearcey, 239.

Richard Rorty. He's the one who claimed that truth is made, not found. That's the cry of postmodernism. As Thomas Harris said in his book *I'm Okay, You're Okay,* you don't find truth in a little black book. *"The truth is a growing body of data of what we observe to be true.*[149] (How's that for a tautology?) Richard Rorty doesn't even like the word truth because it is very "un-Darwinian."[150]

So Darwinism and the purpose-driven life are mutually exclusive. If the world evolved without intelligent design, then there is no design for life. If there's no design, there's no purpose. Religion is reduced to a product of biology, an expression of our subjective desires and impulses, programmed into us by natural selection.

Friends, we of all people, who believe in the truth of the Bible, need to be able to defend it and to know what the winds of doctrine that are blowing about our culture are so we have an answer for the hope within us. As one parent said, "My little girl came home in fourth grade and said, 'Mommy, who was lying, you or my teacher? My teacher said that we came from the apes." Fourth grade! If the teacher is in authority and she's an expert, obviously she must be right. Who are you mommy?

CONCLUSION

What we are talking about here is building a life. Everyone has to make a living; only some will make a life. You either spend your life or you invest your life. You can't take anything with you, but you can send things ahead. The days are not neutral. If left to themselves, they will be little pieces of sand in Satan's hourglass. We must seize the day, capture the time. If you spend your time, there is momentary pleasure, but no lasting value. When you invest your time, you expect

---

149 Thomas Harris, *I'm OK—You're OK* (New York, NY: Avon, 1967), 285.

150 Richart Rorty, "Untruth and Consequences," a review of *Killing Time* by Paul Feyerabend, in *The New Republic* (July, 1995), 32-36.

a return on your investment, a lasting value. Here are three reasons to be careful what we do with our time.

1. **Time is short.** James 4:14 says our life is like a vapor; it's here for just a little time and then it's gone. And John Brown, after his arrest at Harpers Ferry, said this, "There's an eternity behind and an eternity before and this little speck in the center, however long, is comparatively but a minute."[151] Robert Moffat said, "We have all eternity to celebrate our victories but only one short hour before sunset in which to win them."[152] Finally, a man named Jesus said, "I must work the works of Him who sent me while it is day; the night is coming when no man can work." He said this is our opportunity, the days of our life, to work. Over and over we have said it is the works that ultimately determine how much of our life has been redeemed or how much of our life has been saved. Time is short.

2. **Time is not retrievable.** It was Charles Dickens who said, "No hands can make the clock, which will strike again for me, the hours that are gone." Another has said, "When you kill time, remember it has no resurrection." And finally, Henry Dobson said, "Time goes, you say? Ah, no. Alas, times stays; we go." Yes, time is short and time is not retrievable. But also,

3. **Time is not repeatable.** It was Stephen Grellet, the Quaker, who wrote in 1885, "I'll pass through this world but once. Any goodness I can do or kindness I can show

---

151 John Brown, http://law2.umkc.edu/faculty/projects/ftrials/johnbrown/browninterview.html, accessed September 7, 2016.

152 Robert Moffat, http://www.quoteland.com/author/Robert-Moffat-Quotes/6575/, accessed September 7, 2016

to any human being, let me do it now. Let me not defer or neglect it, for I shall not pass this way again."[153]

There are no "overs." We shall not pass this way again.

A young man had a strong desire to become a great orchestra maestro. He became the understudy to a Swiss maestro with the goal of becoming a maestro himself. He poured all his heart into it and was the maestro's best student. **His debut was a pan.** He was a little nervous because all his friends and family were coming, and the whole place was packed out. He stood with his baton and began the work. He couldn't see himself in a mirror. He didn't know how he had done. When he finished it was total silence. Then people began to stand up and clap and shout, "Bravo!" The budding maestro turned around and just smiled. They kept expecting him to take a bow, but he didn't bow, and the audience just kept laughing and clapping. He still wouldn't take a bow. He just kept standing there.

After a while they noticed he was gazing up into the far seats where an old white haired man was sitting. Finally, the old man looked down at his protégé and nodded. And then the young maestro took a bow. You see, the opinion of the audience, even friends and family, who didn't know music that well, didn't matter that much. The only opinion that mattered was that of his teacher. Some day we will appear before the ultimate Maestro with hair white as wool and eyes that radiate like fire and a scepter in his hand. And then it won't matter what your friends or your enemies or your family or your peers or your colleagues or your fellow church members think. His is the only opinion that matters. Will he say to you, "You fool," or will he say, "Well done, good and faithful servant"?

---

153 Stephen Grellet, https://www.goodreads.com/author/quotes/3240127, Stephen Grellet, accessed September 7, 2016.

POSITION AND CONDITION

Isn't it strange that princes and kings
And clowns that caper in sawdust rings
And common folk like you and me
Are all builders for eternity?

To each is given a book of rules
A block of stone and a bag of tools
And each must shape ere time is flown
A stumbling block or a stepping stone.

—R. Lee Sharpe

17

GOD'S PAIN KILLER
Ephesians 5:17-21

INTRODUCTION

What do you do with your pain? None of us, except a masochist, enjoys pain. Much of what we do, according to one psychologist, is motivated by pain-avoidance. We avoid fires—painful, very painful. But none of us can avoid pain completely. Because we are at least temporarily locked into a world that is passing away, we will experience pain in proportion to the number of broken attachments we have in this passing-away-world. Death is the ultimate detacher from this world. But until the grim reaper calls, we will have pain. What do you do with your pain?

Most of us turn to drugs. Oh, I don't mean drugs like alcohol, cocaine, heroine, and marijuana. One or more of those could be our drug of choice, but not for most Christians. Our drug of choice could be more benign from its outward appearance: success with its many different faces, winning, money, self-destructive love relationships, and so on. The problem with drugs is that the pain relief is just temporary. Sooner than later as our addiction progresses, we need another fix. And full-blown addicts will hurt themselves and the people they love in order to get their fix. Their pain begets more pain.

But God knows about our pain. Jesus is not an unsympathetic High Priest. He himself experienced incredible pain—physical, yes, but even more so, psychic pain (rejection by friends and family) and spiritual pain (broken fellowship with his Father). Is there something we are supposed to be learning from all this pain? C. S. Lewis, in his book *The Problem of Pain*, wrote:

> We can rest contentedly in our sins and in our stupidities, and everyone who has watched gluttons shoveling down the most exquisite foods as if they did not know what they were eating, will admit that we can ignore even pleasure. But pain insists upon being attended to. God whispers to us in our pleasures, speaks in our consciences, but shouts in our pains. It is his megaphone to rouse a deaf world.[154]

The problem is I don't always get the message while I am still in this world. Neither did Christ (see Psalm 22:1-21; but he did get it in the next life; see Psalm 22:22ff). I have a friend that was a star athlete growing up and became a professional. He is a Christian and married a committed Christian girl. But his home was a train wreck. Of his three children, one left the faith and the other two suffer with long-term disabilities, which make it impossible for them to marry and have their own families. He and his wife divorced. Do you think he has ever asked the question, "Why, God?" And though I am sure he has learned some spiritual lessons from all this suffering, I am also convinced he won't really get the picture until the next world.

So, that leaves us with a question. If pain to some degree is not

---

154 C. S. Lewis, http://www.cslewisinstitute.org/C_S_Lewis_on_the_Problem_of_Pain_page3, accessed September 7, 2016.

avoidable in this life, and if we won't understand a lot, if not most of it, until the next life, then does God have anything to help us cope with our pain while we are still on this side of heaven, something that is not destructive of ourselves and others? I think he does. And I find it in Ephesians 5:17-21.

(Obviously, this passage includes 5:18, what some noted authorities on the spiritual life teach is the most important verse in the Bible for a victorious Christian life. In some circles the verse is almost a mantra. If it is a mantra for you, then I suggest you skip this chapter. What I am going to present will be radically different from what you have learned from many great and godly men. However, what I am going to present is not something I cooked up. I learned it while in seminary from the two greatest scholars the New Testament Department at Dallas Seminary had during my years there: S. Lewis Johnson and Zane Hodges. Though those two men were significantly different in their approaches to areas of theology like predestination and free will, they both agreed on the interpretation of this verse. What they taught makes good sense to me, and I hope it is helpful to those who are of an open mind and willing to explore new thoughts. But if your mind is made up, just go to the next chapter.)

To help us orient to this passage, let's remember Paul's concentric circles: world, church, home (marriage, parenting, servants). That will help us from the outset. Our passage (5:17-21) is not addressed to an individual, but to a group. Every verb in the passage, including the five participles in 19-21, is plural. Paul addresses a group of people, namely, the church. As we will see in more detail, the passage is analogous to 1 Corinthians 14 where Paul enters the church service and gives some instruction. I would suggest to you he has a church service in mind in these verses as well. After all, in 5:21 it is pretty hard to submit to yourself as an individual.

So we want to look at the Mandate for Filling (18), and the Means for Filling (19-21). We will go more into the exegetical details more than we usually do because from these details we think the general picture of the passage makes more sense.

I. MANDATE FOR FILLING 18

¹⁷ Therefore do not be unwise, but understand what the will of the Lord *is*. ¹⁸ And do not be drunk with wine, in which is dissipation; but be filled with the Spirit, . . .

A. What it Doesn't Mean—Filling with the Holy Spirit

1. "Filled" = *plēroō*—this word is never used in connection with filling an individual in the NT. An individual is not addressed in this passage, and the only other use of it in connection with the Holy Spirit is in Acts 13:52 where it says, ". . . the disciples were filled with joy and the Holy Spirit." It was a group filling.

2. "Spirit"—notice the word "Holy" is missing; if this refers to a filling with the Holy Spirit, it would be the only case in the NT where the word "Holy" is left out.

3. Greek Grammar—the grammatical construction does not allow for filling "with" in the sense of content, that is, filled with the Holy Spirit. That would require the word "Spirit" to be in the genitive case as it is in all the other times filling with the Holy Spirit is mentioned. In fact, nowhere in all of Greek literature do we find an example of "filling" followed by the dative case to refer to the content of filling. That doesn't make it impossible here, but highly unlikely.

4. Individuals—are not in view, as already mentioned; it's addressing a group, as the word "submitting to one another" points out.

5. Formula—the Holy Spirit is sovereign; there is no formula for filling with the Holy Spirit in the NT, which the Holy Spirit must obey. For example, one popular preacher taught that the moment we confess our sins we are automatically filled with the Holy Spirit. Wow.

Automatic? That kind of turns the Holy Spirit into a genie in the bottle, doesn't it? The Holy Spirit is sovereign. He is God. I doubt that He is going to make Himself dependent on our formulas.

6. Filling <u>with</u> the Holy Spirit—in the NT this was always for some sort of public ministry (witness, preaching, glorifying God, etc.). John the Baptist leapt in his mother's womb (Luke 1:15); Peter preached (Acts 4:8); the people spoke the Word of God (Acts 4:31). There was no private use. It was not about the individual Christian walk.

Teaching that the filling with the Holy Spirit is the key to the victorious Christian life has led to lots of confusion in many Christian circles down through the years. One parachurch group of college kids went to the Florida beaches to share their faith during spring break. There were about two hundred of them. Of course, with a group that size there were many staff members. Typically, before going out on the beaches there would be a group devotional.

But the man in charge of this entire project noticed a whole cabin of his staff members did not show up one morning for the devotional. He went to their cabin and found them sitting around praying. He asked them what they were doing. They said they were praying for the filling of the Holy Spirit. They said according to what they have been taught, after being filled they should be speaking to one another in psalms and hymns and spiritual songs, singing and making melody in their hearts, and giving thanks. They had been taught that Ephesians 5:19-21 describe the results of being filled. They didn't see those results, and didn't feel filled. The male staff members didn't want to go out on the beach where there were lots of girls in bikinis if they were not filled with the Holy Spirit. So they were doing what the early Christians were doing in the upper room. They were praying for the filling of the Holy Spirit.

Still others have been taught that verses 19-21 describe the **means** by which we as individuals can be filled by the Holy Spirit. So when I get up in the morning and have my morning devotional, I can bring about the filling of the Holy Spirit if I speak to myself in psalms, hymns, and spiritual songs, singing and making melody in my heart, and giving thanks. Unfortunately, this has not been very productive for lots of Christians. In fact, the men where I live get up at anywhere from four to six in the morning (one at 3:30) to get to work. Most of them would laugh me in the face if I told them they had to go through these steps to be filled by the Spirit before they go to work or they will be living as carnal Christians until they do so. It's teaching like this that has driven many modernists and even postmodernists into the dichotomy between the spiritual and the secular, specifically reserving the spiritual for Sunday and the secular for the rest of the week. Some of them would say, "Well, preacher, I could probably do that if I quit my job, left my family, and joined a monastery. Then I could even do what Martin Luther is said to have done before he had a wife and a passel of kids, and spend the first two hours of my day in prayer."

One day, one of my church members called me out to his farm for a visit. We went out to the barn. He had a spiritual issue he wanted to talk about. He said he committed the same sin forty times a day. Without asking what the sin was, I did ask him how long he had been committing this sin forty times a day. He said for fifteen years. By then I had a pretty good idea of what the sin was—smoking (keep in mind I am not the one who called his smoking a sin; he did). So I said, "Would you like to stop smoking?" He said, "Not really." So I asked the obvious: "Then why am I here?"

He answered, "Because I just want to make sure I understand the filling of the Holy Spirit." So I asked him for his understanding. It was his understanding that after a cigarette (a sin in his mind) he would confess that sin and be automatically filled with the Holy Spirit. That put him back in fellowship with God (1 Jn 1:9). Then he would stay in fellowship until he pulled out the next cigarette. Because that was a deliberate, known sin in his mind, he would then be out of fellowship, and he would lose the filling of the Holy Spirit. "So you have been going through this filled/unfilled cycle forty times a day for fifteen years," I asked. "Yep," he said. "How do you feel about that?" "It feels like there is something wrong," he confessed. Ya think?

We have looked at what the command for filling in 5:18 is not and some of the confusion in the lives of many Christians stemming from the conventional wisdom on filling. But we have not said what we think the commandment does mean. Let's do that now.

B. What it does Mean—Spiritual Fullness

1. **"Allow yourselves** to become spiritually full." "Allow"— this comes from the form of the verb (middle/passive); it can be translated as a passive "be filled," but it can also be translated as a middle ("Allow yourselves"). The latter makes more sense in that it takes me out of the obligation to be filled. If I am obliged to be filled, then I would need some sort of formula to bring about the filling. I would then be acting on the Holy Spirit, a dubious obligation, at best. But if the command is action by myself upon myself, oh, OK, I can do that. I can allow myself (action on myself by myself) to be filled.

2. **"With** the Spirit"—this translation is not a grammatical possibility. As mentioned, the construction is Preposition (*en*) + Noun in the Dative Case (*pneumati*). This cannot be translated correctly as "with the Spirit." Every case of filling with the Holy Spirit in the NT has "Holy Spirit" in the Genitive Case. Actually, this very construction can be used adverbially ("spiritually"), which is probably a good way to translate it here. Again, note that the word "Holy" is missing. If this were filling with the Holy Spirit, it would be the only example we have in the NT of the concept of a filling with the Holy Spirit expressed without the word "Holy." So, the translation in point 1 above is the one I prefer: "Allow yourselves to become spiritually full/filled."

291

3. **Colossians 3:16.** This parallel passage in a book written from prison about the same time as Ephesians has a similar concept. "Allow the word of Christ to dwell in you richly . . ." Once again, this is a group experience. The passage has the psalms, hymns, spiritual songs, singing, giving thanks—just like Ephesians 5:18ff. But there is an added element in the Colossians passage: "teaching and admonishing one another." That cannot possibly be interpreted to mean an individual out on his own living his life during the week. It can only be a group worship experience. The participles (teach<u>ing</u>, admonish<u>ing</u>, sing<u>ing</u>) modify the main verb (let . . . dwell) just as the participles in 5:19-21 modify the main verb in 5:18 (be filled or allow yourselves to be filled).

We have carefully examined the Mandate for Filling. Now, what are the Means?

II. MEANS FOR FILLING   5:19-21

There are a number of options for how the participles describe or modify the verbs: 1) Attendant circumstance—"Allow yourselves to be filled while at the same time speaking, . . . singing, . . . etc."; 2) Result—"Allow yourselves to be filled, the results of which will be speaking, . . . singing . . . , etc."; 3) Means—"Allow yourselves to be filled by means of speaking, . . . singing, . . . etc." Of these options, means may well fit the context best.

It is very important to see the participles lined up under the main verb. Participles, which show up in English with an –ing in English, cannot stand alone. I can't just say, "Speaking . . . ," and have it make any sense. You have to attach the participle to something. And Greek grammar is very specific at times. These five participles have to be attached to the main verb in v. 18 somehow. Again, there are a number of options, but I think "means" fits the context best. Nothing I would go to the wall for; just trying to explain what I think the text is saying. The precise function of the participles may be subjective, but one thing that is not subjective is that there are five participles in a row, and they are all lined up under (modify) the main verb of v. 18: filled. It looks like this:

"**Allow** yourselves **to be filled** spiritually by means of:"

- "Speaking to one another in psalms, hymns, and spiritual songs"
- "Singing and"
- "Making melody in your hearts to the Lord"
- "Giving thanks always for all things to God the Father in the name of our Lord Jesus Christ"
- "Submitting to one another in the fear of God"

The reason it is important to see all five of these participles attached to the main verb ("be filled") will be apparent in our next lesson. Suffice it to say at this point, some Bible teachers like to pull the last participle away from the first four in order to support their doctrine of "mutual submission" in marriage. We will cover that in more detail in our next lesson.

Right now we are trying to establish the following objective observations:

1. The Holy Spirit is sovereign. We can't make him do anything. If we could use a formula to effect his filling of us, we would control him instead of vice-versa. If the command of 5:18 is, "You be filled with the Holy Spirit," then the burden is on us to get the Holy Spirit to fill us. Then our only option is to manipulate the Holy Spirit. That is getting very close to magic.

2. The grammar does not support filling **WITH** the Holy Spirit. That would require the Preposition (with) + the Genitive Case. Here we have the Dative Case.

3. The word **Holy** is not in the Greek text.

4. This passage describes a group worship experience, not an individual's walk.

5. All five participles modify the main verb of v. 18: be filled.

CONCLUSION

The Bible uses the concept of filling with the Holy Spirit in three ways:

1. **Filling for a special ministry**, usually verbal. This comes and goes as the Holy Spirit sees fit. Confession of sin does not initiate this filling, and known sin does not end this filling. Peter was filled in Acts 2 and preached. He was filled again in Acts 4, but there is no recorded sin between Acts 2 and Acts 4 that would have caused him to lose "the filling." The Greek verb *pimplēmi* is the only verb used for this special filling.

2. **Filling for a group**. We see this twice: here in Ephesians 5:18-21 and Acts 13:52. A group can quench the Holy Spirit by being so stilted and ritualistic that the congregants can go through the motions like worshipping robots, or they can "allow" themselves to be spiritually filled by speaking . . . singing . . . etc. Here the verb *pimplēmi* is not used. It is *plēroō*. These are its only two uses. This would most likely take place during group worship. However, if you have ever returned from a spiritual retreat where you have been on a "spiritual high" only to "come down" as you returned to your normal, daily routine with your job and family, that retreat probably involved a group filling.

3. **Filling for special individuals**. Here we have an adjective (*plērēs*) used instead of the verb from which it is derived (*plēroō*). It is used of Jesus as he went into the wilderness to be tempted by the devil (Luke 4:1). It is used of Stephen

who performed signs and wonders and was the first Christian martyr (6:5, 8; 7:55). Then again it is used of Barnabas (Acts 11:24).

Perhaps the main lesson to take away from all this is that the filling of the Holy Spirit, whether for a special verbal witness, or a group worship experience, or for special individuals hand-picked by God, is not the normal 24/7 Christian life. If the filling of the Holy Spirit were a condition for the victorious Christian life, then Paul was certainly remiss by not mentioning it in his greatest "victory" chapters in all his epistles: Romans 8 and Galatians 5. John never mentions it in his book on fellowship with God, 1 John. Peter never mentions it in either of his epistles. James doesn't mention it. This chart probably gives us a better picture of what is going on with believers and the Holy Spirit:

MINISTRIES OF THE HOLY SPIRIT

BAPTIZING	LEADING	FILLING
ROM 6, 1 COR 12	ROM 8, GAL 5	LUKE 1, ACTS 2
FACT	FAITH	FEELING
INDWELLING	ENABLING	INTOXICATING
PERMANENT	PROGRESSIVE	PERIODIC

From this we can see that every believer is baptized by the Holy Spirit whether he knows it or not. It is a fact. It is described as an indwelling, and it is permanent.

But the victorious Christian life comes from an enabling by the Holy Spirit. This is described in Romans 8 and Galatians 5 as a "leading." When we are led by the Spirit, we will not fulfill the lusts of the flesh (Gal 5:16). This leading is not always accompanied by warm fuzzies. Jesus was led by the Spirit into the wilderness. I doubt that it was a feel-good experience. To follow the Spirit into the wilderness takes an act of faith. We can't see where we're going. But this is the normal Christian life. Our consistency in following the Spirit or letting him lead us is progressive. As we mature in the Christian life we become more and more consistent in letting him lead us.

Finally, the filling of the Holy Spirit is not something we have to take by faith. We can feel it, and it can even be intoxicating. Remember, unbelievers watching the upper room experience thought they were drunk. Peter's first sermon was an explanation of what was going on. The filling of the Holy Spirit is neither permanent nor progressive. It's periodic. The Holy Spirit sovereignly chooses when and whom to fill. We can observe certain conditions for filling. The Holy Spirit doesn't fill anyone he's not leading, and he doesn't lead anyone he hasn't baptized. That's another way of saying we don't see an example of him filling unbelievers or Christians walking according to the flesh.

Someone will still ask, "But shouldn't I seek to be filled like Jesus and Stephen and Barnabas?" I would respond, "How are you going to do that?" There is no formula. The best we can say is to let the Spirit lead you (Romans 8 and Galatians 5). If you are walking by the Spirit, he may sovereignly choose to fill you for a special purpose. That was true of Jesus in the temptation, Stephen as a miracle worker and first martyr, and Barnabas as called out with Paul to go to the Gentiles. What does that say about all the other believers? Were they carnal, walking according to the flesh? Were they just immature? I would suggest none of the above. They were just normal Christians like you and me. If you are a believer, you have been baptized by the Holy Spirit. If you choose to let him, the Holy Spirit will lead you and empower you to have victory over the world, the flesh, and the devil. And as you walk with the Holy Spirit, he may choose to fill you for a special purpose. But that's up to him, not us.

But, you ask, "What does all this have to do with the pain I am experiencing? You started off with something that caught my attention and then wandered down this long, exegetical trail that has my mind spinning. In fact, I think you are making my pain worse." We have seen that we can be filled with envy, murder, adultery, love of money, alcohol, lust—all sorts of things that don't deliver us from pain in a way that does not lead to more pain. The addictive cycle is just that, a cycle. But God's painkiller offers a way out of the cycle that does not lead to greater pain. What is that painkiller? It's God himself. Back in chapter 3 Paul prayed the Ephesians would be filled with the fullness (*plērōma*) of God. The *plērōma* of God. And he said that comes from knowing the love of Christ, which surpasses knowledge. Wow. How do you know something that passes knowledge? What does this mean?

For one thing, the *plērōma* goes way beyond the filling of the Holy Spirit. It also includes the Father and the Son. The interesting thing is that all three of them already live inside us (the Father, Eph 4:6; the Son, Col 1:27; and the Holy Spirit, 1 Cor 6:19). But that doesn't mean we can sense their fullness. Every person longs to be united with his or her Creator. We are like orphans on this earth before we are connected to him. We see his image in us, and we realize we are not like the animals, the birds, or the fish of the sea. Something sets us apart. We look in the mirror and see a divine parentage, but until we meet the divine parent, there is a psychic pain only he can dull, or a spiritual hole only he can fill.

Years ago I watched what many think was Robert Duval's magnum opus, *Lonesome Dove*. It was the story of two old Texas Rangers, crotchety old coots, who never married and never settled down. They are the epitome of the macho American male, dependent on no one, beholding to none. Theirs is the life of rawhide and dust bowls, rattlesnakes and rustlers, bawdy women and shots of whiskey. At the end of the movie the tougher of the two can't even bless his own son (born out of wedlock) with his name. No, he was too tough to be tender. The title says it all: *Lonesome Dove*. Every character in the movie is lonesome: the two rangers, the prostitute, the son, the widow—everyone. But God didn't create us to be lonesome doves.

By contrast, Rick Reilly, one of the best writers for *Sports Illustrated* for many years, tells the story of adopting an orphan from South Korea.[155] He and his wife adopted her at four months and named

---

155   Rick Reilly, *Sports Illustrated*, February 20, 2006.

her Rae. As Rae grew up, she realized that her image was different from her Caucasian parents. She constantly thought about her birth mother, who just had to be a princess, or movie star. So when she was eleven, the Reilly family flew to Seoul, Korea, even though they were told that Rae's birth mother would not meet with them. Unwed, the birth mother had sneaked away at sixteen to have the baby, and only her sister knew. She was married now, with three kids, and she dare not be discovered. And yet—the interpreter told them—not a day went by that she didn't think of Rae.

Finally she agreed to thirty stolen minutes, in a coffee shop two hours from her home. They waited three hours. Rae looked heartsick. Finally, a cell phone rang. Rae's mother would meet them in the alley. And suddenly, there she was, tiny and white faced. She climbed in the van. She looked at everyone but Rae, her own daughter. She said she had ten minutes.

"Rae," asked Rick, "if you have any questions for your birth mother, ask them now." Rae took out a full piece of paper with three questions: 1) Why did you give me up? "Great shame," the woman told interpreter, never looking at Rae; 2) Where is my father? "Don't know." 3) When you had me, did you get to hold me? The birth mother hung her head, "No." And that's when interpreter said, "You can now."

That broke the woman. She wheeled on Rae swallowed her in her arms with kisses and sobs. She wouldn't let Rae go. Finally, she had to. The Reillys flew back to America, and Rae hasn't seen her birth mother again. But she was beaming: "It feels like it fixed a little hole in my heart."

Yes, booze, success, wealth, winning, honors, drugs—these can dull many sorts of pain, but they can't fix the holes in the heart. When God's orphans come to the only begotten Son, Jesus Christ, and believe in him, then he gives them his name—Christian—and adopts them into his family. He heals a hole in their heart with that initial connection. And from then on, whenever they are hurting for any of the thousands of reasons to hurt in this world, all they have to do is come back to him and be filled with the fullness of his love, his character, and all the fullness of God.

18

GOD'S ROLE CALL TO WIVES
Ephesians 5:22-24, 33b

INTRODUCTION

According to Siri, there are 2,279,000 marriages in America each year; she also says there are 877,000 divorces during the same period. Over two million people standing at an altar every year with stars in their eyes, but for over a third of them the stars turn into sand. Why? What's wrong? Surely when these couples said their wedding vows at the altar they weren't planning their divorces. Something went dreadfully wrong.

Long before the fall of man, God observed something wrong with his creation, his greatest work, Adam. Everything seemed perfect. Adam had a great job, CEO of Operation Earth. And he couldn't have asked for a better Boss. So he must have felt very significant. And since he walked in the garden on a daily basis with the Creator of the whole universe, Adam must've felt very secure. But something was still wrong. God called it loneliness. It was not good for man to be alone, meaning completely unique among all God's created life forms.

It was his total uniqueness that created his loneliness. You say, well how could he be lonely if he walked in the garden with God? Good question. He was lonely because there was no one else like himself to share his life experiences with.

So God created a complement for Adam to solve his problem of loneliness. When I used to perform weddings as a pastor, I would challenge the husband-to-be with these words, "Your measure as a husband is the degree to which you take away the loneliness of your wife." Then I would look at the wife-to-be and say, "Your measure as a wife will be the degree to which you take away the loneliness of your husband." God's first reason for marriage wasn't to propagate the race. It was to eliminate the problem of loneliness.

But some people tell me they're more lonely in marriage than when they were single. How can it be? It's because living in the same house with someone you can't talk to is lonelier then being by yourself. You can feel the walls; you can sense the barrier. And as you see and hear your spouse being more friendly and intimate with others than with you, the pain in marriage becomes greater than the pain outside of marriage. A break up could be imminent.

Is there an answer to all this? Could it be we don't understand how a marriage is supposed to work? Could it be we have lost sight of the proper roles for husbands and wives in the marriage relationship? Could it be, as evidenced from our recent Supreme Court debacle in 2015, that we don't even know how to define marriage anymore? Once again we would suggest that since it is true that a supernatural Creator also created the divine institution of marriage, then perhaps he knows how it's supposed to work to maximize its potential. And perhaps he gave us a marriage manual to help us understand the proper role for a husband and the proper role for a wife so they can take away their respective loneliness. He did just that in Ephesians 5:22-33. We want to look at the role of a wife in 5:22-24 and 33b. Then, in our next lesson we will look at the role of the husband in 5:25-33a. With regards to the wife we will look at the Role of Submission in v. 22, the Reasons for Submission in vv. 23-24, and the Respect with Submission in 33b.

I. ROLE OF SUBMISSION   22

Wives, submit to your own husbands, as to the Lord.

A. What It Isn't

1. Mutual Submission

What a powder keg. In a country where women are fighting for equal rights the word "submission" is almost a four-letter word. The word "equal" is behind the concept of "egalitarianism." Long word, but it is contrasted to another long word: hierarchicalism. The latter refers to the domestic philosophy of the father as the head of the home, under whom the mother serves, and under the father and mother are the children. With egalitarianism at least the father and mother are equal in authority; neither is subservient to the other. Both serve each other with "mutual submission."

So why get into these long words? Well, I would avoid it if I could. However, they are at the center of the debate, even in Christian circles, on how to run a home. A major support for egalitarianism is v. 21, which says we should submit to one another. Many interpreters, even the translators, who have to interpret a passage just to translate it, start a new paragraph with v. 21. They pull the verse away from 5:17-20 and make it the capstone for Paul's discussion on the Christian home. There are lots of cultural pressure to pull v. 21 away even though the grammar pretty much forbids it.

Why? Because the word for submission in v. 21 is a participle, which must be attached to the main verb in v. 18, "be filled." Grammatically, that is the only option. It is the fifth in a sequence of participles, all modifying the main verb of v. 18. Why on earth would anyone pull it away from the other four participles to start a new paragraph?[156] Why, indeed? Cultural. There is so much pressure from

---

156 Wallace does so by attraction in that v. 22 lacks *hupotasso*, according to 2 mss. In other words, all the external evidence has *hupotasso* in the

the cultural atmosphere to make women equal to men that the idea of a hierarchical arrangement for the home is turning many women away from Christianity. If they have equal rights in the marketplace, including equal pay, then it stands to reason they should have equality in the home. And if the husband and wife are equal, there is no reason for the wife to submit to her husband. They should just submit to each other out of mutual love and respect.

There is so much specious reasoning in the paragraph above, it is hard to know where to start to pick it apart. Let's start with the idea of equality. Equal essence does not mean equal function. Let me say that again. Equal essence does not mean equal function. For example, in orthodox Christianity we say that the Trinity has three persons of equal essence but different functions. God the Father, God the Son, and God the Holy Spirit are all equal—in their makeup, in their attributes, in other words, in their essence (ontology). But that doesn't mean each has the same function. The Father sent the Son, and the Son sent the Holy Spirit. And in many passages Jesus Christ made it clear that he only did what his heavenly Father told him to do (Jn 4:34). He was in submission to the Father. This couldn't have been more clear than in the garden of Gethsemane just before his trial and crucifixion. His prayer in the garden was, "Not my will but yours be done" (Luke 22:42). He submitted his own personal desires to the will of his father. Even when he was on the cross, Christ appealed to his Father to find another way to accomplish the salvation mission (Psalm 22:1-21). And he didn't die on the cross because he was nailed there. He could have called for twelve legions of angels to deliver him (Matt 26:53). But he chose to submit to his father's will. Good thing for us he did—understatement.

So, married women, relax. We agree. You're equal to your husband. You should get equal pay for equal work in the marketplace. But we

---

v., but Wallace leaves it out for internal reasons. But that only makes sense if you already assume egalitarianism, i.e., that there is mutual submission in the home.

are not talking about the marketplace here. This is the Christian home. And in the Christian home God asks the wives to be submissive to their husbands. Yes, this is called hierarchicalism. The husband is in a position of authority over his wife. And the parents (6:1ff) are in a position of authority over their children. I think you can see where egalitarianism is going, logically at least. If the husbands and wives are to be mutually submissive to each other, then why not the parents and children? And what about masters and their servants? And that's exactly where one popular Bible teacher goes.[157] Parents should submit to their children, and masters to their servants—mutually, of course? Chaos. Old Chinese proverb say, "When find oneself in a hole, stop digging." Egalitarianism is a deep hole.

2. Male Domination

As a pastor I sometimes ran into husbands who used this passage as a club to beat their wives into submission. Of course that's not what the Bible teaches. That's one reason the very next passage tells husbands to love their wives. And in 1 Peter 3:7 we learn that husbands who don't treat their wives properly will have their prayers hindered. In fact, in that passage it tells the husbands to show deference to their wives. That means to consider their needs first and their opinions first, and if it all possible, show your love for them by doing what they wish. I would propose that every husband who has made it to the 25th anniversary with his wife has learned the two most important words in marriage for the husband: "Yes, dear."

Now that gets pretty close to mutual submission. The difference is the "Yes, dear" is voluntary out of his love for his wife. The way mutual submission is taught, it is mandatory, and that can lead to chaos. But we must make it very clear. The Bible does not teach male domination. In fact, that is one reason Christianity spread so fast during its early

---

157   John MacArthur, *Ephesians* (Chicago, IL: The Moody Bible Institute, 1986), 271-78.

years: Christ honored and elevated women. Islam certainly doesn't do that. Talk about rights. Women have none in Islam.

Let's take this idea of male domination a step further. I remember one case when the wife came to me and said her husband spit beer on her when they went out in public to eat. I said, "Excuse me? He does what?" She repeated the problem. I asked her how long this has been going on. She said their whole marriage. How long was that? Fifteen years. "You have been letting your husband spit on you in public for fifteen years?" Yes. "Why?" Because I thought 1 Peter 3:1 said we should win our non-Christian husbands to Christ by our submission without a word. "Oh, my," I said. "I'm just guessing your husband doesn't have much respect for you nor you for yourself." She began to cry. I said, "The next time he does that to you, look him in the eye, and say, 'John, I know you love me but I can't let you treat me like this. I'm not a donut hole. I'm not a ghost. I'm a real person, and my Savior Jesus Christ lives inside of me. So I'm leaving. Don't worry about getting me home. I'll call a cab. When you're ready to treat me with respect, we'll talk again.' Then get up and leave."

There are always small people who love to abuse any authority they might have to offset their feelings of insignificance. It could be a drill sergeant, a boss at work, or a husband. But the sinful abuse of a position of authority doesn't make the position wrong. It is the heart of the abuser that is wrong.

In severe cases of spousal abuse, a temporary separation may be in order while the husband gets help. But, again, let us be clear. The biblical view of submission never warrants wife abuse. So, we've talked about what the role of submission is not. Now let's talk about what it is

B. What It Is

"**Submit**" = *hypo* + *tassō* = under + place = to place yourself (middle voice) under

Under what? "**Your own husbands.**" The rule in the Roman empire was *patria potestas*, meaning "the power of the father." This meant that the father kept control of his children until he died. So the husband was not the head of his home until his father-in-law died. Paul's instructions fly in the face of that local tradition. Now, that all sounds quite ridiculous to us today. But we face a different problem. The average Christian wife is more spiritual than the average Christian husband. And sometimes a Christian wife is married to a non-Christian husband. Sometimes the wife is the only one going to church. Sometimes she will romanticize about another Christian man in the congregation or even the pastor. She will think to herself, "Oh, my, I wish my husband were as spiritual as so-and-so." That makes for a real problem at home because her husband is not a spiritual leader, and she may no longer respect his opinions. As we shall see later, that can lead to the disintegration of a relationship. So our passage makes it very clear: "submit to your <u>own</u> husband."

"As to the Lord"—submission to the husband is a subset of submission to Christ. When a wife submits to her husband, she is submitting to Christ. And when a wife rebels against her husband, she is rebelling against Christ. To understand this we have to go way back to God's purpose for the human race. We have mentioned this a couple of times, but it is so important a little repetition won't hurt. In a nutshell, it's to answer two questions raised by Satan when he rebelled against God in heaven. Question number one: Who has the right to rule the universe? Question number two: Is God worthy of being loved? Those two questions put the authority/submission issue on a cosmic level of importance. As we shall see, submission to authority is not just about husbands and wives. All of us are under a God-appointed authority somewhere. Our attitude toward that authority reveals our attitude toward God. After all, if God appointed the authority, then rebellion against that authority is nothing other than rebellion against God.

As a man I am under authority in several areas: at work, at church, in society, and in my country. And when I was a child still living at home, I was under authority to my parents. Whenever I respectfully submit to the God-appointed authority over me, I am also submitting to God, and I am answering the question, "Who has the right to rule the universe?" My answer? God does. But when I rebel against any God-appointed authority over me, I am saying that Satan has the right to rule the universe. So this question of authority and submission is not peripheral; it's central to the whole purpose for the human race.

I think understanding this actually makes it easier to submit. It gives a grand meaning and purpose to it all. And if I can imagine the Lord Jesus Christ being the one telling me to do something, that also makes it easier for me to submit. One of my problems as a non-Christian growing up was that I thought I was smarter than some of the people in authority over me. And if I thought what they asked of me was stupid, I thought that justified my rebellion. Of course, at the time I did not realize my rebellion was a vote for Satan. When I learned what I'm telling you right now, I had a major attitude adjustment. What used to be a weakness, by God's grace, has become strength. I purpose in my heart to have and show the utmost respect for those in authority over me.

Sometimes this attitude reaps unintended benefits. I haven't been stopped by the police for a few years, but I remember the last time. I was coming back from the lake on a road north of where I live, not paying too much attention to how fast I was going and until I saw some lights blinking behind me. I pulled over, got out my license and insurance card, and waited for the officer. I rolled down my window, handed my license and insurance card to the officer, and said with total respect, "I want to thank you for stopping me. I know you're doing your job. And it's a good reminder for me not to speed. I know you guys have a tough job and don't get much appreciation, so I just want to thank you." He didn't say anything. I think he was in shock. He went back to his patrol car to check out my license and driving record. Then he came back and said, "Mr. Anderson, I do my ticketing on attitude related basis. You have such a good attitude I'm not here to give you either a ticket or even warning. But for your own protection and for the safety of others I think you should slow down." If you don't get anything else out of this book . . .

So much for the Role of Submission. What about the Reasons for it?

II. REASON FOR SUBMISSION 23-24

[23] For the husband is head of the wife, as also Christ is head of the church; and He is the Savior of the body. [24] Therefore, just as the church is subject to Christ, so *let* the wives *be* to their own husbands in everything.

A. The Principle of Significance

We can understand all this better with a brief review of the needs of a man and a woman. A man's primary need is to feel significant; a woman's primary need is to feel secure. These instructions are designed by God to help meet those needs. By making the husband the "head of the wife," God is giving man a position of great significance. He is now responsible for providing for and protecting his wife and children, should God bless him with children. God compares man's role to being the head of the body. As the head directs the body, so the body is to follow the head. When this order is reversed, all sorts of confusion results. A body does not function well with two heads. With two heads the body soon becomes dysfunctional. That's true of business organizations, athletic teams, churches, and the home. There needs to be one head.

When the wife challenges her husband's leadership, she is also challenging his competency. In essence, she is saying that she can do the job of leading the family better than he can. How do you think that makes him feel? You are right. It makes him feel small and insignificant. It undermines his greatest need–to feel significant. In time he will retreat to his man cave. Communication barriers arise. Rather than fighting all the time, most men simply hide behind the newspaper or other interests. And in most of these cases, the wife then becomes more demanding, which further diminishes her husband's sense of significance.

On the other hand, when she respectfully submits to his leadership, she is saying to him, "You da **MAN**! I trust you. I believe in you. I think you can do the job." But when she challenges his leadership, it's as though she is saying, "You sniveling little wimp. Don't you realize

I'm smarter than you and can do the job much better than you?" Now the truth is many wives are smarter than and more gifted than their husbands when it comes to education and other skills. Some of them make more money than their husbands. Sixty percent of the college graduates today are women. That means there are more women in the workforce than men. That also means it's only a matter of time before the average woman earns more than the average man. So how do these principles apply in those relationships where the wife is the primary breadwinner?

It doesn't change a thing. The Scriptures were not written to apply only to the Ephesians in Turkey 2000 years ago. We believe the Bible is full of timeless truths. Therefore, we think God's marriage manual is just as applicable at anytime and in any place. The needs of men and women haven't changed. Men need to feel significant, and women need to feel secure. The main reason a wife is to submit to her husband is to make him feel significant. It meets his primary need.

B. Principle of Salvation

Throughout this passage Paul draws comparisons between the husband's relationship with his wife and Christ's relationship with the church. Here he says not only is Christ the head of the body, but is also the savior of the body. As such he provides for the body and protects the body. And so the husband is supposed to be the provider and the protector. A man is often the most tender toward his wife when he senses that she needs him and depends on him for her security and well-being. He often pulls away from the self-sufficient woman who gives no indication she really needs him at all.

So what about those relationships where the wife makes more money than her husband or she inherits a lot of money from her side of family? Admittedly, I have seen many, many divorces where the woman had an independent source for her security. That source might be a job that pays well or a trust fund set up by her father. But I've also seen many such relationships do very well. Sometimes the wife brings in all the money, but the husband adds value to the family by investing that money wisely. In other cases they both work and she makes more than he, but they just throw that money into a common pot where they make wise decisions together on what to do with it.

Growing up in Nashville, Tennessee, I got to know a number of people in the music business. One of them was Brenda Lee, best known for some of her agonizing love songs and "Jingle Bell Rock." She was the number one female recording artist in the 60's, surpassed only by Elvis, the Beatles, and Ray Charles. But like so many solo artists in the 60's she sort of fell off the map when the British invasion took place. But Brenda never stopped touring, especially in Japan and France, where she was very popular. She met her husband, Ronnie Shacklett, when she was just 16. She was very short (4 foot, nine inches), and he was quite tall (six foot, four inches). Over the years she has sold over a hundred million records. Meanwhile, he started a construction business. He never made as much money as his wife, and their marriage was challenged by a child with special needs. But he supported her and her singing, and she supported him in his construction business. She never made him feel incompetent just because she made more money. They are still happily married today.

So it all gets down to attitude. The wife must know about her husband's most basic need, the need for significance. Whether she is a full-time wife and mom at home or a successful career woman, she still needs to make her husband feel competent to lead, provide, and protect the family.

My wife is a survivalist. We sleep on top of about twenty-five gallon drums of dried food. One night we were lying there and I told my wife, "You know, Betty, if we ever really need this food, the neighbors are going to come and get it." We were lying there in darkness. My wife, whose alter ego is Miss Piggy (according to her), says, "I'll get a gun." Sure enough, she got a gun. Next thing I know she's down at Gander Mountain practicing her shooting. No need. She's a natural dead-eye. Of course, I've begun to question my competency when it came to protecting my wife. It looked like the roles were going to be reversed, and she would be my protector. So what did she do? She began giving me ammunition for Christmas. But I didn't want a gun.

I have lots of rifles and shotguns. But I didn't want a handgun. They seem pretty dangerous to me.

So I didn't follow the hint. Then what? The next Christmas she gave me a prepaid coupon for a concealed handgun course. What's she doing? She's not so subtly encouraging me to fill my role as her protector. So I did it. I bought a 40-caliber handgun, got my concealed handgun license, and also bought a tactical shotgun. They're all sitting in a closet upstairs where they won't do any good if someone tries to break into our house. But, baby, do I feel competent. What a great wife. On many of our "date" nights we go shooting together. I still can't hit the broad side of a barn.

Now this passage says the wife should submit to her husband **"in everything."** We would be remiss if we did not point out the obvious exceptions to "everything." If the husband asks his wife to do something directly contrary to the clearly revealed will of God in his Word, then she's not obliged to go along with her husband. God's clearly revealed will in the Scriptures will filter out requests from her husband that are sinful. So if he asks her to help him rob a bank or to cheat on their income tax or to get involved in wife swapping, she is exempt from doing these things. This is so obvious it seemed to go without mentioning, but the main defense of the Nazis running the death camps in Germany and Poland was that they were simply obeying orders from their superiors.

So we have looked at the Role of Submission and the Reasons for Submission. Finally let's talk about Respect in Submission.

III. RESPECT IN SUBMISSION 33B

. . . let the wife *see* that she respects *her* husband.

Some years ago a pastor made a discovery that changed his ministry. He observed the same thing in marriage counseling that I saw. Invariably if a marriage was in trouble, the wife felt unloved and the husband felt disrespected. When a couple came in, I could look at the wife and ask, "Do you feel loved by your husband?" She would say no and sometimes break down in tears. Then if I asked her husband, "Do you feel that your wife respects you?" He would usually look at me and say, "Are you kidding me? I haven't felt respected by her in years."

So what was the pastor's discovery? He discovered that the wife's respect for her husband in verse 33b is **unconditional**. He had been teaching the roles of the husband and wife for years without noticing that the respect of the wife for her husband is unconditional. In other words, the role of the wife is to submit to her husband, and the role of the husband is to love his wife, but one is not conditioned on the other.

The husband's love for his wife in Ephesians 5:25-33a is unconditional. That's what *agape* love is. But most wives are left with the impression that if their husbands don't love them as Christ loved the church, then they don't have to submit to them. In his book *Love and Respect,* Emerson Eggerichs said he suddenly realized the full burden of the responsibility for a successful marriage lay on the husband's shoulders.[158] His role was unconditional; her role was conditional. Her submission was conditioned on his Christ-like love. That was not a win-win proposition.

But then Eggerichs noticed that the respect in 33b was not conditioned on the husband loving his wife. This was a breakthrough in his understanding. As he began teaching this in marriage seminars, women across the nation told him they had never heard this before. They always thought if their husbands didn't display Christ-like love, they did not need to be submissive. But realizing they had to show their husbands respect whether they were loved in a Christ-like way or not brought a whole new perspective to the relationship. So Eggerichs began to see marriage after marriage healed when the wife realized her respect was unconditional and his love was unconditional. Now each side of the marriage relationship was equally responsible for the

---

158 Emerson Eggerichs, *Love and Respect* (Nashville, TN: Thomas Nelson, 2004).

success of the marriage. Eggerichs left the pastoral ministry to spread the good news of "love and respect" wherever he could.

CONCLUSION

Husbands and wives have the same essence (make-up), but different roles. God designed these roles to offset our loneliness. That happens when we meet each other's needs, significance for the man and security for the woman. The husband feels significant when his wife shows her respect for his leadership and his competency. And the wife feels secure when her husband loves her in a Christ-like way. But that's the next lesson.

19

GOD'S ROLE CALL
TO HUSBANDS
Ephesians 5:25-33a

INTRODUCTION

S inging comedian Tim Hawkins wrote a song entitled "These are the Things You Don't Say to Your Wife." It goes like this:

Hey, honey, have you gained some weight in your rear end?
The dress you are wearing reminds me of my old girl friend;
And where'd you get those shoes, I think they're pretty lame?
Would you stop talking, I'm trying to watch the game?

If you are a man who wants to live a long and happy life,
These are the things you don't say to your wife.

I planned a hunting trip next week on your birthday;
I didn't ask you but I knew it'd be okay;
Go make some dinner while I watch this fishing show;
I taped it over our old wedding video.

If you are a man who wants to live a long and happy life,
These are the things you don't say to your wife.

Your cooking is okay but not like mother makes;
The diamond in the ring I bought you is a fake;
Your eyes look puffy, dear, are you feeling ill?
Happy anniversary, I bought you a treadmill.

If you are a man who wants to live a long and happy life,
These are the things you don't say to your wife.

If you are a man who does not want to be killed by a knife,
These are the things you don't say to your wife.[159]

Hawkins puts his finger on a void in the make-up of most men: we simply don't understand the basic needs of a woman. Years ago, William Harley wrote a book called *His Needs, Her Needs.*[160] He observed that most married men, even after ten years of marriage, are only able to identify one of the five greatest needs of their wives. He lists those needs as: 1) Affection; 2) Conversation; 3) Honesty and openness; 4) Financial support; and 5) Family commitment. No wonder we have trouble keeping our marriages together. While visiting recently with a Christian couple from another state, they mentioned the last five divorces they knew about occurred when the wife left her husband because of the unmet needs.

In order to understand God's role call to husbands we need to review the three common words for love used in the New Testament. The first is *eros*, from which we get the word erotic. Men don't have to be commanded to have this kind of love. The second is *philē*, which is not brotherly love. Brotherly love is the meaning of Philadelphia: *philē* plus *adelphia* equals love + brotherly. This kind of love between a man and woman is romantic, emotional love. And experts say men are

---

159 Tim Hawkins, https://www.youtube.com/watch?v=iK2OakMoW_c, accessed September 11, 2016.

160 William F. Harley, Jr., *His Needs Her Needs* (Grand Rapids, MI: Fleming H. Revell, 1986).

actually the great Romantics in this world— they fall harder, faster, and take longer to recover. Women tend to choose whom to love.

No, the word for love used here in Ephesians is neither of these first two. It is *agapē*, which is described in 1 Corinthians 13 and defined in Philippians 2. But no passage lays out its meaning for husbands and wives like Ephesians 5:25-33. In this passage we see three primary ingredients of *agapē*, which help the husband meet his wife's primary need for security. He must learn to love her sacrificially, spiritually, and sensitively.

EPHESIANS
"The Creation and the Conduct of the Church"

SALUTATION   1:1-2

INTRODUCTION—"Spiritual Blessings in the Heavenlies" 1:3-14

    (Paul's Prayer for Perception)   1:15-23

BODY   2:1-6:9

  I. Creation of the Church (Its Position)   2:1-3:21

  II. Conduct of the Church (Its Condition)   4:1-6:9

    A. The Goal: Maturity of the Body   4:1-16

    B. The Means: Maturity of the Individual   4:17-6:9

      1. Through Personal Sanctification   4:17-5:14

      2. Through Personal Submission   5:15-6:9

        a. In the Church   5:15-21

        b. In the Home   5:22-6:4

          1) Marital Relationships   5:22-33

            a) Role of Wives   22-24, 33b

            b) Role of Husbands   25-33a

          2) Parental Relationships   6:1-4

        c. In the Office   6:5-9

CONCLUSION—"Spiritual Battles in the Heavenlies"   6:10-20

I. LOVE HER SACRIFICIALLY   25

Husbands, love your wives, just as Christ also loved the church
and gave Himself for her, . . .

"**Just as**"—wow. Here comes the comparison. We are to love *as*
Christ loved the church. No problem. Piece of cake. Well, how did he
love the church? He "gave" himself for her. This word "gave" = *para*
+ *didōmi* = "to hand over." This means that Christ laid down his life
by his own choice (Jn 10:18). No one took it from him. And so, to
love as Christ loved, the husband is to voluntarily lay down his life
for his wife. He doesn't have to any more than Christ had to die for
the Church. He chooses to as an act of sacrificial love. Of course, this
went against the conventional wisdom of the ancient Roman culture
in which women existed to work for their husband's well-being and
pleasure.

When United was still Continental Airlines, the company decided
to start flying from Newark to Tel Aviv. It was the inaugural flight
of their new 777. The president of Continental, Greg Brenneman,
decided to take his top executives and their families on the flight and
take a tour of Israel while they were there. He asked me to put the
tour together and to lead it. One of the things we thought might be
fun, which I don't do on a normal tour, was to spend a night with
the Bedouins, which we did. In the evening one of the Bedouins
stood in the center of our group and explained the Bedouin way of
life to us.

When the subject of women came up, it was explained that they
do the hard work like carrying the water, cooking, tending to the
sheep, the kids, and other needs of their husbands. Then what do
the men do? They just sit around until its time to take one of the
sheep into the market for sale. "What a deal," I said under my breath.
Unfortunately, some of the other tourists heard me and from that
moment on they all called me the "American Bedouin." Yes, Christ
introduced a whole new way of treating women in general and wives

in particular. The husband was to serve the wife instead of the other way around. And when a wife sees her husband sacrificing his desires to serve her, it goes a long way in meeting her most basic need, security.

I have learned through the years that wives will test their husbands in this matter. And I have observed that they usually test them with little things. "Hey, dear, I'm going out to hit some golf balls." "Oh, okay. But could you please change Johnny's diapers before you go?" My wife only used this one once on me. I didn't really know how to change diapers, so I just took the dirty diapers and threw them in a diaper bin. Later on when my wife washed the diapers, she couldn't figure out at first why they all came out of the washing machine somewhat brown. It took her awhile to figure out that I had just thrown them in the diaper bin, poop and all. Oh, well, I got some credit for trying, but not much. Little things. When we give up some of the things we want to do in order to help them with little things, we are showing them that they are more important to us than our own agenda. That gives them a feeling of security.

A businessman's wife was experiencing depression. She began to mope around and be sad, lifeless—no light in her eyes —no spring in her step —joyless. It became so bad that this "man of the world" did what any sophisticated person would do. He made an appointment with a psychiatrist. On the appointed day, they went to the psychiatrist's office, sat down with him and began to talk. It wasn't long before the wise doctor realized what the problem was. So, without saying a word, he simply stood up, walked over in front of the woman's chair, signaled her to stand, took her by the hands, looked at her in the eyes for a long time, then gathered her into his arms and gave her a big, warm hug. You could see the change come over the woman. Her face softened, her eyes lit up, and she immediately relaxed. Her whole face glowed. Stepping back, the doctor said to the husband, "See, that's all she needs." With that, the man said, "Okay, I'll bring her in Tuesdays and Thursdays each week, but I have to play golf on the other afternoons."[161] Somehow he wasn't getting the message, was he?

Yes, a husband needs to love his wife sacrificially; but he also needs to love her spiritually.

II. LOVE HER SPIRITUALLY   26-27

. . . that He might sanctify and cleanse her with the washing of water by the word, [27] that He might present her to Himself a glorious church, not having spot or wrinkle or any such thing, but that she should be holy and without blemish.

Jesus's ultimate purpose in giving his life for the church was spiritual. Through his physical act of handing over his life he accomplished his spiritual purpose, the sanctification of the church. If nothing else, Jesus is certainly the leader and the initiator in this great spiritual purpose for his relationship with the church. So also the husband is to be the spiritual leader and the spiritual initiator in his relationship with his wife.

Too many husbands have turned over the spiritual reins to their wives. This puts her in an awkward position as the initiator in spiritual matters, a role God never intended for Eve. Adam's spiritual abdication led to all kinds of problems—duh. Since this can be such a touchy issue let me leave a few tips. First, a couple of tips for wives or wives to be:

1. **It's easier to find a spiritual leader before marriage than after marriage.** Too many strong Christian girls from strong Christian homes find some hunk they think would make a good husband only to discover after marriage he really doesn't care about spiritual things. Well, she probably knew that before the wedding.

---

161 Maxie Dunnam, *Preaching* (May-June, 1986).

But she hopes she can show him the way and that he will develop into a spiritual leader after marriage. Sweetheart, if he doesn't go to church before marriage, he probably won't go to church after marriage. If he doesn't read the Bible with you before marriage, he probably won't read the Bible with you after marriage. If he doesn't pray with you before marriage, he probably won't pray with you after marriage. Of course there are exceptions. But hoping your spouse will be the exception is a pretty big risk. As a pastor I saw a lot of lonely wives coming to church faithfully but not able to share the most precious thing in their lives with their husbands at home.

2. **If your husband is a Christian, he already has the Holy Spirit: he doesn't need another one.** A professional forester took me into the woods one day to show me how he marked trees to be cut down by a lumber company. As we went along he showed me a freshly cut stump in which the rings of the tree were clearly visible. He asked me how long I thought it took to form a ring. I said I had no idea. He explained that a ring forms in about six weeks. The tree goes through a growth spurt in the spring and then spends the rest of the year assimilating that growth. We also go through growth spurts in our spiritual lives and then times of assimilation. Husbands and wives usually don't go through their growth spurts simultaneously. That means one might be going through a growth spurt while the other is in a time of assimilation. When the wife is in a growth spurt, and the husband is in an assimilation period, it's not a good time for her to assume the role of the Holy Spirit. Prodding him won't help. Judging him won't do, either; he needs an encourager, not a preacher.

And here are a couple of tips for husbands:

1. **She needs an example, not an enforcer.** The right example is always the first prerequisite for a leader of any kind, but especially in the spiritual world. No one other than God sees us when we are controlled by the flesh more than our wives just by virtue of the amount of time we spend together. And no husband walks by the Spirit all the time. So we will make mistakes. A part of being an example is learning how to forgive and seek forgiveness, to admit our mistakes, and to reconcile quickly. And part of setting the example is to spend time in the Word, to lead the family in devotionals, and to make sure the family gets involved in church.

2. **Do not use the Bible to beat her into submission.** Too many husbands have taken the word "help" from Genesis 2:18 and used this as their justification that they're more important than their wives because God made the wife to help the husband, not the husband to help the wife. But this misses the main point of the text. Adam is lonely. God made another human being to complement Adam to eliminate loneliness. But that works both ways. Without Adam, Eve would have been lonely. They should be like complementary angles. What is lacking in one should be fulfilled by the other. In other words, they were there to help each other. He was made for her just as much as she was made for him. Sometimes a couple in love will say, "We were just made for each other." They are saying, "We complement each other." As we have said before, in God's eyes men and women are exactly equal in value and essence; they're simply different in function.

3. **Give her a life.** It says in 1 Peter 3:7 that a husband is to dwell with his wife "according to knowledge." I'm sure we have not unpacked all that that verse means, but

surely it means to get to know the unique strengths of our wives. Their gifts and abilities most likely will be different from ours. If they are the same, one of us is redundant. In marriage the whole is intended to be greater than the sum of its parts. My wife and I are in our fiftieth year of marriage. I learned long ago that our spiritual gifts are completely different. That has some ramifications. I am interested in things that don't interest her at all and vice versa. But I am here to support her in the development of her gifts and talents just as much as she is there to support and encourage me in mine. There are times I need to give her the freedom of time to exercise those gifts, even when it means she could be using that time at home rubbing my back. I like having her rub my back, but I actually find more fulfillment in my marriage by watching her fulfillment when using her unique gifts.

We said the husband is to love his wife sacrificially and spiritually. But there is one more thing, and it may be the hardest. He must love her sensitively.

III. LOVE HER SENSITIVELY   28-33

So husbands ought to love their own wives as their own bodies; he who loves his wife loves himself. [29] For no one ever hated his own flesh, but nourishes and cherishes it, just as the Lord *does* the church. [30] For we are members of His body, of His flesh and of His bones. [31] *"For this reason a man shall leave his father and mother and be joined to his wife, and the* two shall become one flesh."* [32] This is a great mystery, but I speak concerning Christ and the church. [33] Nevertheless let each one of you in particular so love his own wife as himself . . .

"As their own bodies"—how do we love our bodies? Most of us hate at least some aspect of our bodies. But that is to confuse the word for love in this passage with the word for emotional love. This is not *philē* (emotional love); it is *agapē*, which is a love that always looks out for the best interests of the one who is loved. So, if we love our bodies, we look out for the best interests of our bodies. If the body is hungry, we feed it. If we stub our toe, we tend to it. If the body is tired, we rest it. Only weirdoes (extreme ascetics) purposefully neglect the needs of their bodies.

"Nourishes and cherishes"—we are sensitive to the needs of the body, very sensitive. Are we as sensitive to the needs of our wives? We should be, for we have become one body in marriage. Therefore, we should be as sensitive to the needs of our wives as we are to our own body. Someone has suggested the following as the next Survivor Series:

> Six married men will be dropped on an island with one car and three kids each for six weeks. Each kid will play two sports and either take music or dance classes. There is no fast food. Each man must take care of his three kids and keep his assigned house clean, correct all homework, complete science projects, cook, do laundry, and pay a list of "pretend" bills with not enough money.
>
> In addition, each man will have to budget his money for groceries each week. Each man will also take each child to a doctor's appointment, a dentist's appointment, and an appointment for a haircut. He must also make cookies or cupcakes for a social function. Each man will be responsible for decorating his own assigned house, planting flowers outside and keeping it presentable at all times. The men will only have access to television when the kids are asleep and all chores are done. There's only one TV between them, and no remote.
>
> Each father will be required to know all the words to every song that comes on TV and the name of each and every character on cartoons. The men must shave their legs, wear make-up daily, which they will apply to themselves either

while driving or making three lunches. They must adorn themselves with jewelry, wear uncomfortable yet stylish shoes, keep their nails polished and eyebrows groomed.

During one of the six weeks, they'll have to endure severe stomach cramps, backaches, and have extreme, unexplained mood swings but never once complain or slowdown from other duties. They must attend weekly PTA meetings, church, and find time at least once to spend the afternoon at the park or a similar setting. He'll need to pray with the children each night, bathe them, dress them, brush their teeth and comb their hair each morning by 7 AM.

A test will be given at the end of the six weeks, and each father will be required to know all of the following information: each child's birthday, height, weight, shoe size, clothes size and doctor's name. Also the child's weight at birth, length, time of birth, and length of labor. Each child's favorite color, middle name, favorite snack, favorite song, favorite drink, favorite toy, biggest fear and what they want to be when they grow up. They must clean up after their sick children at 2 AM and then spend remainder of the day tending to that child and waiting on them hand and foot until they are better. Each man will have to make an Indian hut model with six toothpicks, a tortilla and one marker; and get a four year old to eat a serving of peas.

The kids vote the men off the island based on performance. The last man wins only if . . . he has enough energy to be intimate with his spouse at a moments notice. If the last man does win, he can play the game over and over again for the next eighteen to twenty-five years, eventually earning the right to be called "wife and mother."[162]

---

162   Kara Clark, http://www.dancemom.com/articles/text/017.htm, accessed September 7, 2016.

Admittedly, that's a long list of things our wonderful wives do. When I read this to my wife and told her I wrote it, she said "Baloney. You couldn't even think those things up. A woman had to write that." I'm sure she's right. Most of us husbands are clueless about the number of things a stay-at-home mom has to do during a day or week. Then when you throw in a career on top of it all for many of them, the whole thing becomes practically unbelievable. Perhaps a cumulative list like this can help sensitize us husbands to the enormous task that face our wives on a daily basis. Now here are a couple of tips on how to love them sensitively:

1. **Listen to your wife.** Women need to talk. That's how they relate. And if they're going to relate to their husbands, they have to talk. Remember Harley's number two need for a wife? Conversation. Of course that means you also have to talk . . . but not about yourself. Most of us men just like to talk about ourselves while our wives listen. Lucky is the woman who has a husband that will listen to her and about her day and her trials and tribulations.

2. **Don't try to fix your wife's feelings.** This was one of my early mistakes in marriage. My wife would share something she was upset about at church or some other setting. Being a male, I wanted to fix it for her. All of a sudden she was angry at me. I couldn't figure it out. Here I was trying to help with her hurt feelings or her anger at someone else and suddenly she was mad at me. I used to think it was just the "kick the cat" syndrome. But after making the same mistake over and over for years, I finally realized she didn't want me to fix her feelings. She just wanted me to validate them. When I tried to fix her feelings, I was invalidating her feelings. I was saying, "Honey, you really shouldn't feel that way." That meant there was something wrong with her. If this pattern continued, she would stop sharing her upset feelings with me. Then she would be stuck with them and feelings

of loneliness could develop. So now I say, "Wow. If that happened to me, I'd probably feel the same way. Listen, I've got my new concealed handgun license. You want me to take them out for you? They'll never find the bodies. You can go spend time with the grandkids for an alibi." Just kidding, but you get the idea.

CONCLUSION

In one sense this lesson is easy to summarize. The role of the husband is to love his wife: sacrificially, spiritually, and sensitively. Easy to summarize, yes; but hard to do. After all, we are being told to love our wives as Christ loved the church. He loved the church with perfect love. So, husbands are being compared with the only perfect man who ever lived. So there's only one answer for all this. **Give up.** Like so many other things God asks us to do, it's a supernatural standard. And a supernatural standard will require supernatural power. So just give up. No husband can measure up to this standard.

But that takes us back to the substitutionary life, doesn't it? **If the hardest thing in the world for the non-Christian to believe is the substitutionary death of Christ, then the hardest thing in the world for the Christian to believe is the substitutionary life of Christ.** We were reconciled by his death, but we shall be saved from the power of our sin nature by his life (Rom 5:9-10). Because he rose from the dead he can live in us. He would not set a standard **he** could not live up to. So the degree to which we are able to love our wives as Christ loved the church will simply be the degree to which we allow him to live his life through us. Are we going to mess up? Sure. That's like asking are you going to sin again. Of course, but that doesn't mean we get up in the morning planning on sinning. And the more we allow him to live his substitutionary life in us, the more we are able to love our wives as Christ the church. And our marriages can get better and better.

My first year of marriage to Betty was a piece of cake. I remember reading an article at the end of that year that the first year of marriage is the hardest. I asked her if it was hard for her. She said no it was great. But then she got pregnant. Somewhere along the line someone forgot to tell me about female hormones and how they can affect things during pregnancy. She was expecting me to become more caring and sensitive, but I was too much of a jerk and too self-centered to be the husband she needed me to be. Our marriage in time went from good to bad and then from bad to worse. But we were determined to stick it out. Perhaps things will get better. And it did. In time our marriage went from worse to bad from bad to good and from good to better and from better to great. Now our marriage is what I would call supercalifragilisticexpialidocious. It's so good I don't even try to explain to people. I don't think they would really believe me. But all the credit goes to my wife and Jesus. They did not give up on me when I was a self-centered, insensitive idiot. Everything good in my life I blame on Betty and Jesus. It's all their fault.

If it weren't so sad, I would find it amusing. Years ago, when Promise Keepers, the ministry begun by Colorado University's football coach, Bill McCartney, was in its hey-day, the attacks from NOW (National Organization for Women) began. Promise Keepers champions opposite-sex marriage and marital fidelity. NOW has accused them of being a threat to women's rights. Under the guise of Christianity and a simplistic view of the Bible, NOW says Promise Keepers promotes gender inequality by teaching male superiority.[163] Wow. You really wonder if they have even read Ephesians 5:25-33a. The same Paul wrote those words as the Paul accused by some of being a misogynist. **Equal in value; different in function.**

Well, according to King Arthur (*Camelot*), if a husband knows

---

163 Promise Keepers, https://en.wikipedia.org/wiki/Promise_Keepers, accessed 6/16/16.

and understands one basic truth about women, he will probably do all right. He said:

"How to handle a woman?
There's a way," said the wise old man,
"A way known by ev'ry woman
Since the whole rigmarole began."
"Do I flatter her?" I begged him answer.
"Do I threaten or cajole or plead?
Do I brood or play the gay romancer?"
Said he, smiling: "No indeed.
How to handle a woman?
Mark me well, I will tell you, sir:
The way to handle a woman
Is to love her . . . simply love her . . .
Merely love her . . . love her . . . love her."

It would seem that King Arthur had been reading his Bible, for that is exactly what husbands are called to do in Ephesians 5:25-33—love her.

20

WHERE HAVE ALL
THE FATHERS GONE?

Ephesians 6:1-4

INTRODUCTION

It was David Blankenhorn, founder and president of Institute for American Values, that observed:

Tonight, about 40 percent of children in the western world will go to sleep in homes in which their **fathers** do not live. Before they reach the age of eighteen, more than half of our nation's children are likely to spend at least a significant portion of their childhoods living apart from their **fathers**. Never before in this country have so many children been voluntarily abandoned by their fathers. Never before have so many children grown up without knowing what it means to have a **father**. **Fatherlessness** is the most harmful demographic trend of this generation. It is the leading cause of declining child and adult wellbeing in our society. It is also the engine driving our most urgent social problems. . . . If this trend continues, **fatherlessness** is likely to change the shape of our society.

In reference to the general population individuals raised in a father absent environment demonstrate;

1. Five times the average suicide rate:
2. Dramatically increased rates of depression and anxiety:
3. 32 times the average rate of incarceration:
4. Decreased education levels and increased drop-out rates:
5. Consistently lower average income levels:
6. Lower job security:
7. Increased rates of divorce and relationship issues:
8. Substantially increased rates of substance abuse: and
9. Increases in social and mental behavioral issues:[164]

Somewhat surprisingly, the present but emotionally distant father had about the same impact on his children as those who grew up without a father in the house. And, although this problem is worse than it has ever been in our country, it's not a 21st Century problem. Apparently, it goes as far back as the time of Paul in the 1st Century AD. That's why he puts the burden of responsibility for child rearing on the father (6:4). But we are getting ahead of ourselves. Let's look first of all at God's Role Call to the Children; then, we will look at God's Role Call to the Fathers.

I. GOD'S ROLE CALL TO CHILDREN—SUBMIT   1-3

Children, obey your parents in the Lord, for this is right. [2] *"Honor your father and mother,"* which is the first commandment with promise: [3] *"that it may be well with you and you may live long on the earth."*

---

164 David Blankenhorn, *The Father Code*, "The Nine Devastating Effects of the Absent Father," https://thefathercode.com/the-9-devastating-effects-of-the-absent-father/accessed June 15, 2016.

A. Mandate to Obey 1

"**Obey**"—this really isn't the word "submit." It is *hupo* + *akouete* = under + listen. The word "under" puts them <u>under</u> authority; the word "listen" just tells them to listen (in the sense of "listen and do") to the one in authority over them. I emphasize the obvious here only because those who teach mutual submission in the home have to extend their wrong teaching beyond the husband/wife relationship to the parent/child relationship as well.

But this kind of teaching not only goes against the plain reading of the text, it also completely misses the bigger picture in the authority/submission challenge of Satan to God. We have suggested that one of the main reasons for creating the human race to begin with is to answer the question raised by Satan, "Who has the right to rule the universe." Every time we choose to obey or submit to a divinely appointed authority over us, it is a vote for God. That's why the women were reminded of this issue when Paul instructed them to observe a sign of their submission during the church assembly. Without going into the type of head covering Paul had in mind, right in the middle of the discussion in 1 Corinthians 11, he reminds the wives that the angels are watching: "For this reason the woman ought to have *a symbol of* authority on *her* head, because of the angels" (v. 10). Excuse me? He just drops that into the text without further qualification. Whatever the appeal to the angelic witnesses might have been, Paul certainly assumes the wives in Corinth are well aware of it.

Some have suggested that planet earth is a stage with humans as the actors; and the audience are the angels. 1 Peter 1:12 says the angels find the whole scenario of **suffering before glory** so intriguing that they desire to look into these things. They were especially captivated by their own Lord stooping down to become a human, with all the limitations pertaining thereto, in order to suffer on their behalf before his own glorification. Now we have no idea how many created angels there are. Apparently, one third of the host of heaven followed Satan in his rebellion (Rev 12:4). They were all kicked out of heaven and now inhabit this planet, although many who were involved in the

Genesis 6 corruption are presently chained up in Tartarus awaiting their final judgment (2 Pet 2:4).

Getting the "big picture" changed my first-born's life. Growing up in a pastor's home, Jimmy had been around Christianity "his whole life." We think he received Christ the earliest of our four children during or shortly after a Child Evangelism gospel presentation. He participated in AWANA Bible memory, and was just a good kid. When he hit seventh grade, I decided to take him and his younger sister through the Navigator discipleship series for youth. It took two years. At the end of it I taught them how to share their faith. So, from the perspective of a Christian parent, all things were going well.

Jimmy turned out to be a pretty good football player. But when he was fifteen he got involved with some of the guys on the team that wanted to drink. So Jimmy went through about a one-year period when he was challenging our parental authority. But, then, when he was sixteen I decided to take his discipleship lesson a step further. He learned the Greek alphabet and we began searching words and concepts in the Bible he had not thought about or I had not gotten across to him before. One of the studies we did involved this "big picture," or what we call the "metanarrative" in our seminary. [165] When Jimmy saw the role authority and submission play in the grand scheme of things, he was never the same. If I asked him to take out the trash, he would jump up with an emphatic "Yes, sir," and take off for the trash with gusto. At first, I kind of wondered if he were mocking the whole thing, but he kept at it until he left home two years later to spend a year studying the Bible with a group of fifty other high school

---

165 One reason postmoderns have tried to throw off the metanarrative approach to life is that they have never considered a metanarrative that made sense. A "metanarrative" is just a Big Story that makes sense of all the Little Stories in the Bible. The Bible is not just a collection of random stories. There is a Big Picture, a Big Story that puts it all together. Of course, without a grounding in the truth contained in the inspired Word of God, the metanarrative suggested here wouldn't even get an audience within postmodernity.

grads at a Torch Bearer center near Longmont, CO. On Wednesday nights they went into Boulder to witness. Needless to say, his new outlook on the issue of authority and submission stuck.

What about you? Do you get the "big picture"? If you do, things will never be the same. **"In the Lord"** further underscores the spiritual motivation behind the obedience of children to their parents. Colossians 3:20 helps us here. It says children are to be obedient to their parents because "this is well pleasing to the Lord." So now it isn't just the angels watching. It's the Lord himself. Oh, my, how I wish I had known all this when I hit the teenage years. Scripture says rebellion is bound up in the heart of a child. Okay. That means all children. But there is no way I can see my wife, who grew up with five sisters and no brothers, being as rebellious as I was. She was one of those that was in church every time the doors opened. I think she learned to swim in the baptistery. My background was a little different. My specialty was rebellion. Some of those memories are still with me. I wish they weren't. Hopefully, now the Holy Spirit has turned me in a direction that will bring more glory and honor to my God and Savior.

We have been hitting on the motivation for obedience, some of it in this passage and some from other passages. But now Paul himself shifts from the Mandate to Obey to the Motivation to Obey in 6:2-3.

B. Motivation to Obey   2-3

> *"Honor your father and mother,"* which is the first command- ment with promise: [3] *"that it may be well with you and you may live long on the earth."*

"Honor your father and mother"—this is the first commandment of the Ten Commandments that deals with human relationships. The first four deal with the man/God relationship. The promise? Well-being and a long life. This must be seen against the OT backdrop of the liability of disobedience to one's parents: stoning (Deut. 21:18-21; death (Ex 21:15, 17); and cursing (Deut 27:16).

A child's honor and obedience to the parents is the first important step in learning to honor and obey God. A child who disobeys his parents will probably disobey God after he/she is grown-up. The self-discipline required to be obedient to parents leads to the self-discipline needed to obey God. This kind of balanced life, as a general rule, leads to a good and lengthy life.

Of course this always leads to the question, "How long must I obey my parents?" When I go off to college and I'm living outside the house, do I still have to obey my parents? What if I am single and thirty years old, do I still have to obey my parents? Many people would say that moving out of the house of your parents marks the end of your obligation to submit to them. Others think a certain age marks the point of independence. For example, many would say since Jesus began his ministry at about age thirty and this is when he was no longer responding to the authority of his mother, that thirty is the magic age.

Well, first of all, Jesus was not thirty when he began his ministry. Since Herod the Great died in 4 BC and he dated the killing of the infants according to when the "star" appeared to the Magi, Jesus must've been at least two when the Magi arrived at his home (Matt 2:1-10). He is not described as a babe in a manger, but rather a "young child" and at home. So, if Jesus began his ministry in 30 A.D., he had to be at least thirty-six years old at that time and thirty-nine years old when he was crucified.[166]

It would seem that a better answer to this question would not be how old a child is, but where he gets his financial support. If he is living outside his parents' home and is not dependent on them for financial support, then it seems reasonable that he is on his own. However, if he is living in their home, he needs to live by their rules even if he has his own money. For example, he shouldn't be allowed to bring girls home to spend the night, assuming his parents want to uphold biblical standards.

---

166 See Harold W. Hoehner, *Chronological Aspects of the Life of Christ* (Grand Rapids, MI: Zondervan Publishing House, 1977), 11-27.

Another point of clarification. When the father is out of the house at work or play or whatever, the mother is the head of the house. Her authority is to be respected and obeyed. A mother needs to command respect from her children. She can't just hide behind, "Wait until your father gets home." Although the father needs to support his wife's disciplinary decisions, that doesn't mean all discipline ceases until the father gets home. In homes like this the children tend to lose all respect for their mother.

A follow-up question to the previous about obeying our parents is, "How long do I have to honor my parents?" That's an easy one, isn't it? We honor them until they die, or we die. In John 19:26-27, Jesus was still concerned about his mother even while he was dying. He asked John to take care of Mary, and so she went home with John. The OT quotation does not even have the word "obey" or "submit." It has the word "honor" (*timē*). This is the same word used in 1 Peter 3:7 in regard to a husband's attitude toward his wife. He is to "honor" his wife. One meaning listed in BDAG[167] (best one volume Greek dictionary on the NT) is "price, value." It was used for the price of silver or the price of buying a piece of land. But a second meaning listed was to honor in the sense of to "reverence" or to "respect." In essence it is telling husbands to view their wives as a valuable piece of jewelry. It also means to value and respect their opinions.

We show someone respect in two ways: 1) we listen to them; and 2) we give weight to what they say. A few years ago my wife and I went on a mission trip with some people from our church to China. As we were learning to share the gospel, we learned that the Chinese word for "sin" is "criminal." So we couldn't tell them that all have sinned and come short of the glory of God. We would lose credibility, because obviously not all Chinese people are criminals. Their concept of doing something wrong deals with your relationship to someone in

---

167 George Milligan and James Moulton, *The Vocabulary of the Greek Testament* (Grand Rapids: W.M.B. Eerdmans Publishing, 1930).

authority over you, especially your parents and grandparents. That is a hurdle many of them have to get over in order to trust Christ. Why? Because it seems to some of them that becoming a Christian would go against the authority of their parents and ancestry. In other words, there is great respect in the Asian world for your elders.

Honoring one's parents is good until death. That means we listen to them, and we give weight to what they say. I have noticed that many teenage girls don't show much respect for their mothers, until they get pregnant. All of a sudden their own mother becomes quite important. They value their opinions and their help. And many a young man could learn much from his father about things like investing, insurance, and how to be a spiritual leader in his home.

So, now let's flip the coin. On one side we looked at God's role call to children; now we want to see God's role call to fathers.

II. GOD'S ROLE CALL TO FATHERS   4

A. What not to do: EXASPERATE

And you, fathers, do not provoke your children to wrath, . . .

"**Fathers**"—conspicuous by their absence are "mothers." "Parents" are mentioned in v. 1 and "mothers" are mentioned in v. 2. Why not here? We can only conclude that mothers are omitted because the ultimate responsibility for child rearing lies with the father. This would have been countercultural at almost any time or any place in the world. In most Asian cultures, for example, the number one wife is in charge of bearing children and caring for children. It's the husband's responsibility to sire the children and to provide for the family financially. In Japan the main wife is called the *tai tai*. She is even responsible for procuring other women for her husband's pleasure.

This verse would have been easier to understand if it had stopped after the word "wrath." But no, it goes on to charge the fathers with raising up the children in the "training and admonition of the Lord." It should have said something like,

"Fathers, don't provoke your children to wrath, and mothers, raise up the kids in the training and admonition of the Lord." Pretty clear, isn't it? The responsibility for the spiritual training of the children belongs to the father. You mean the mother is supposed to be on the sideline? No, of course not. But the buck stops with the father. You surely don't get the picture of the father on the sideline. Perhaps a man will say, "But my wife is the teacher in the family." Maybe so, but any man can sit down and talk with his own kids. And if we can talk with our kids, we can teach them as well. The husband and wife can teach them together, but if the father is completely absent from this kind of teaching and training, that message speaks loud and clear: dad doesn't think this is important. It's even worse for a young son: dad thinks this kind of stuff is for women.

It does tell the fathers not to **"provoke their children to wrath."** The Greek word for "provoke" is another compound word. In other words, it's two Greek words stuck together: *para* + *orgizō* = beyond + anger; intensified anger. The parallel in Colossians 3:21 helps: "Fathers, do not exasperate your children, that they may not lose heart." According to Webster, "exasperate" means to arouse keen or bitter vexation; to inflame the anger of. When someone is exasperated, they get discouraged and stop trying. There are many causes of this:

1. Inconsistency
2. Belittling
3. Favoritism
4. Cruelty
5. Expectations that are too high

All right. We have looked at what fathers are not to do (exasperate their children); what are they to do?

B. What to do: EDUCATE

... but bring them up in the training and admonition of the Lord.

1. Educate

"Training" = *paideia* = "discipline" such as in Hebrews 12:5-11. Note how it is connected with the love of a father for his child in Hebrews, whether through logical or natural consequences. This kind of discipline can include both verbal (12:5) and physical (12:6; see also Prov 13:24 and 22:15).

There is a lot of discussion these days on corporal punishment. Arguably the best running back in the National Football League is Adrian Peterson, who was recently charged and convicted of child abuse. If the pictures of the wounds on the child can be believed, the jury's verdict was just. But Adrian didn't think he had done anything wrong. He had used some sort of switch, made out of wood. He defended himself by saying that he did what all fathers in his culture did: take the misbehaving kid out behind the woodshed and give him a thorough thrashing. Whether one wants to use Proverbs 13 and 22 to defend a physical means of discipline or not, there're obvious limits beyond which you could beat the child to death, as some have done. I am pretty sure, though I obviously cannot prove it, that Peterson did not mean to inflict the wounds he caused. He did want to discipline the child.

One of the problems here is distinguishing between punishment and discipline. The purpose of punishment is usually retribution. Whether he is conscious of it or not the punisher is usually trying to get even with the child. Perhaps the child showed some disrespect. The punisher says, "I'll teach that kid a lesson he'll never forget." On the other hand, the purpose of discipline is not to get even but to train the child with the long-term goal of maturity.

The punisher usually has a different attitude than the disciplinarian. The actions of a punisher are often the overflow of built up frustration from many past wrongs. But the attitude of the disciplinarian is one of love with a focus on future improvement. The one being disciplined senses that he or she is loved, and that love gives them a sense of security and self-worth.

I'll never forget when my older son came in from play one day and told me that Bobby's father did not love him. These boys were about ten years old at the time. My curiosity piqued, I asked him why. "Because Bobby's father never spanks him," my son said. Although by that time I had made many mistakes as a father, I had at least gotten across the idea that when I disciplined Jimmy, it was an act of love.

Of course I realize that fathers can display loving discipline for their children without spanking them. All I'm trying to do here is to establish the very important principle of somehow connecting love with discipline. Discipline without love rarely works, even church discipline. Josh McDowell used to try to teach: Rules – Relationship = Rebellion. A home with a lot of rules but without a lot of love will lead to a lot of rebellion. I like to use of the word "relationship." So many of us dads think we show our love for our kids by being good providers and showing up for their games. That's certainly part of it, isn't it? But that is not enough. We have to talk. If we were trying to find a life partner and went out with the same girl on date after date and never talked, the relationship wouldn't last long, would it? Why? Because there is no relationship. To build a relationship with another person, we have to talk.

But, then, it helps to have something to talk about that goes beyond football scores and the stock market. My dad did all kinds of things to try to build a relationship. Trips together in his single engine Bonanza, hiking, science projects, interesting books, bridge, chess, Mensa puzzles. But we never got close. Why? Because we never talked. OK, you can't go on a four-day trip without talking, agreed. We talked. But dad could never get beyond the weather, the stock market, the latest calculator from HP, and so on.

One day I mentioned to dad that if we come to the end of our lives and we've had five good friends, we've done well. He was about sixty. He looked at me and said, "I don't have one good friend." Now if you heard him say that, you'd want to argue with him. In any social setting he was usually the life of the party. He always had a joke, always had a story or a "punny." But that's as far as it went. I said, "Dad, why don't we work on a friendship." He said, "Okay, where do we start?" And we tried . . . but we never made it. At that time we were living almost a thousand miles apart. He was retired and I had young family. He wasn't interested in moving to Houston, and I couldn't take enough time away from my job to build the relationship we needed. The time for building our relationship had passed.

As a general rule, if we wait until they're teenagers, it's too late. Did you ever wonder why God created the vast majority of mammals to reproduce within a year or two? Or perhaps the question would be better phrased, why did God design humans to reproduce eleven to fifteen years after their birth. It's a good question, and I like Bill Gothard's suggested answer. He observes that our society has certain rules about our reproductive behavior. There are restrictions such as laws against rape and incest and the number of wives. There is no morality or code of conduct for wolves and buffalo and reindeer. Gothard suggests that it takes time to develop the spiritual muscles necessary to resist sexual temptation. He thinks those muscles are developed before the hormones hit. It is during these early years that the father's training is especially necessary and helpful.

If Gothard is right about the purpose for this time delay between birth and puberty, then it is easy to see why the father's instruction is so important. How is the mother going to teach her son how to overcome sexual temptation? And when a young man or woman develops a sensual focus during the teenage years, it may be very difficult to escape that kind of focus during the next few decades. This is one of the great appeals of pornography. You can satisfy your sensual focus in privacy.

One pastor confided in me that, though he had a lovely wife, he continued to struggle with masturbation years after his marriage. He wasn't asking for help, he just needed someone to talk to. Years later, he told me he had found victory in that area. I asked him how, and he said it was realizing that he was robbing his marriage of the intimacy he could be having with his wife. He said they still had a sexual relationship while he was feasting on pornography, but they didn't have intimacy. Is that possible? Of course it is. Now who is going to teach all these things to the kids, especially to the boys whose visual orientation is so much stronger than the girls? Once again, mother can't do it.

"Admonition" = *nouthesia* = verbal instruction. Let us observe once again that the teaching responsibility does not lie in the lap of the mother. Of course, the mother may be in the mix here, but the children need to hear from their father. And don't forget our hint: both the spinach of discipline and the meat of instruction taste better when sprinkled with generous amounts of love.

CONCLUSION

The primary responsibility for domestic affairs falls in the lap of the father.

I took a piece of plastic clay and idly fashioned it one day
And as my fingers pressed it still
It moved and yielded at my will
I came again when days were past
The form I gave it still bore
And as my fingers pressed it still
I could change that form no more

I took a piece of living clay
And gently formed it day by day
And molded with my power and art
A young child's soft and yielding heart
I came again when days were gone

It was a man I looked upon
He still that early impress more
And I could change him never more[168]

The contrast between two contemporary fathers illustrates the importance of the father's influence in the lives of his offspring. Jonathan Edwards (d. 1758) and his wife Sarah had eleven children. As a rule, Jonathan, whom many consider to be the greatest theologian this Continent has ever produced, spent one hour with his children after the evening meal answering questions. They could ask anything they wanted—math, literature, history, Christianity, anything. When he rode his horse to preach, he tried to take one of his older children with him in order to teach the child and also to build a relationship with that child. Edwards was not a perfect person and did not produce perfect children. His oldest child was a girl, who had a very bad temper problem. When a prospective suitor came calling to ask her hand in marriage, Edwards tried to warn him by listing his daughter's shortcomings. He couldn't dissuade the guy, who finally said, "Well, Mr. Edwards, she is a Christian, isn't she?" Edwards said, "Yes, it's true that she is a Christian, but let me tell you, young man, there're some people only God can live with."

A contemporary of Edwards was a man by the name of Mac Jukes. Jukes was as ungodly as Edwards was godly. Jukes had approximately 700 descendants:

1. 300 died in early life
2. 100 had been imprisoned 13 years or more
3. 200 had become public prostitutes
4. 100 were drunkards
5. The family at that time had cost the state of Massachusetts $1 million in penalties.

---

168 http://www.actsweb.org/articles/article.php?i=620&d=2&c=3, accessed September 7, 2016.

By contrast Jonathan Edwards has 729 descendents:

1. 300 became ministers
2. 65 became college professors
3. 13 became university presidents
4. 3 became United States congressmen
5. 1 became Vice president of the United States

As the Jewish Talmud says, "When you teach your son, you teach your son's son."[169]

Coleridge was talking to a man who did not believe in instructing kids. He thought it would be an infringement on the individuality of the child. Coleridge took the man to look at an abandoned garden on his property. The garden was overgrown with weeds. Coleridge looked at the man, then looked at the garden and said, "I did not wish to infringe on the garden in any way."

And it was Frederick Douglass, the African-American statesman and author who challenged Abraham Lincoln on more than one occasion concerning the outrageous immorality of slavery, who said, "It is easier to build strong children than to repair broken men."[170]

---

169 https://www.illustrationexchange.com/illustrations?category=718, accessed July 5, 2016.

170 https://www.illustrationexchange.com/illustrations?category=718, accessed July 5, 2016.

21

WHO'S THE BOSS?

Ephesians 6:5-9

INTRODUCTION

New Year's Eve was a big night when I was going to seminary, not because we celebrated and went to a lot of parties, but because it was my biggest income night of the year. I was working as a doorman at a hotel to put our family through seminary, and the biggest night for tips was New Year's Eve. As a doorman you would hold cars out front for wealthy people that would come into the Fairmont Hotel, which at the time around 1970 was the nicest hotel in the southwest. It came out of the Fairmont Hotel chain begun by Benjamin Swig and his Fairmont Hotel on Knob Hill in San Francisco. On New Year's Eve I could expect about $1000 in tips. That was the same year Roger Staubach's salary playing for the Dallas Cowboys was $27,000 for the whole year. In other words, for me New Year's Eve was a big deal.

So I put on my tails, got my top hat and white gloves, and

checked the mirror. I met all the specs so I headed for the elevator. I signed in, and as I was signing in, the front office manager came and said, "Dave, we're going to need two doormen tonight. I know this is your night, but we only have three doormen, and the other two are black. I don't think it would look right to have a black doorman and a white doorman working together. So we're going to send you down to the garage. You can open doors for people as they drive in, and the other two guys will be upfront." I said, "But this is my night. I won't get any tips downstairs. Besides, the other two guys aren't even scheduled." He replied, "Well, this is what I've decided."

In my heart, I knew why he was doing this. He didn't like the seminary students that worked at the hotel. He was an immoral man, and the general manager of the hotel hired seminary students to stop the practice of using his hotel as a brothel. The previous night doorman had six call girls he was working with. In other words, he made most of his money as a pimp. The front office manager got a cut of the action. But the general manager of the hotel was a new Christian. He wanted the pimping to stop. So he hired seminary students as his night doormen and bellmen. That made the front office manager mad. He was taking it out on me.

Well, the general manager of the hotel and I had become good friends. I began working in the garage at 4:00PM. His office was just ten steps from where I was standing. People didn't start coming in until evening. So when I was heading down to the garage, I had the strongest temptation to just go into his office and tell him what had happened. I knew he would say it was unfair. I also knew he would send me up to the front of the hotel where I could get my tips for the night.

So while I was doing a slow burn, I said a prayer, "Lord, what do you want me to do?" The answer came in Ephesians 6:5-9.

EPHESIANS
"The Creation and the Conduct of the Church"

SALUTATION   1:1-2

INTRODUCTION—"Spiritual Blessings in the Heavenlies" 1:3-14
    (Paul's Prayer for Perception)   1:15-23

BODY   2:1-6:9
  I. Creation of the Church (Its Position)   2:1-3:21
  II. Conduct of the Church (Its Condition)   4:1-6:9
    A. The Goal: Maturity of the Body   4:1-16
    B. The Means: Maturity of the Individual   4:17-6:9
      1. Through Personal Sanctification   4:17-5:14
      2. Through Personal Submission   5:15-6:9
        a. In the Church   5:15-21
        b. In the Home   5:22-6:4
        c. In the Office   6:5-9
          1) God's Role Call to Servants 5-8
          2) God's Role Call to Masters 9

CONCLUSION—"Spiritual Battles in the Heavenlies"   6:10-20

Paul likes to work in concentric circles. In Ephesians 5, he went from the world, to the church, to the home. He also went from Personal Sanctification (4:17-5:14) to Personal Submission (5:15-6:9). Personal Submission: in the Church (5:15-21); in the Home (5:22-6:4); and in the Office (6:5-9). You might say Paul is still in the home in 6:5-9 because he addresses household slaves and their masters. That would be a valid observation. However, we usually acknowledge one interpretation but many applications. In the mind of the Holy Spirit, there is only one correct interpretation of any given passage. It is what he meant when he used the human author to give us that passage of Scripture. But if we have the right interpretation, there could be many valid applications of that correct interpretation.

By finding the right interpretation we may also find a timeless truth that crosses cultures and centuries. With that timeless truth in hand we ask ourselves, "How do we apply this timeless truth?" Here we are in Houston, Texas, or in Kenya, or wherever we may be. Since we're not living in a slave culture, how do we apply this timeless truth I'm going to talk about that was addressed to household slaves? Ultimately, I'm going to say that we can apply it to anyone who is an authority over us outside the home. For example, I think it would apply to the football coach and his players. This would apply to the schoolteacher and his or her students. This would apply to the Boy Scout leader and his scouts. This would apply to the employer and his employees. I am going to apply this mainly to employees and their employers, though the timeless truths here on submission and authority have many, many other applications.

We want to look at "God's Role Call to Servants" (employees) in 6:5-8 and "God's Role Call to Masters" (employers) in 6:9. We say "role call" instead of "roll call" on purpose. We are focusing on the "role" God has for us in these respective positions in life.

I. GOD'S ROLE CALL TO SERVANTS 6:5-8

A. Mandate to Obedience

> Bondservants, be obedient to those who are your masters according to the flesh.

Paul starts off with the word "**bondservants**." Then in verse nine he says "**masters**." So just as he went wives-husbands, and then children-parents, now he goes servants-masters or employees-employer. This is an important section. Most of us today probably have a job outside the home. That means a good part of our day, if not our whole week, is spent out there in the marketplace. One of the lingering misunderstandings coming down from Thomas Aquinas and what he was teaching, though I don't think he intended this, was ultimately to separate between the sacred and the secular.

Who's The Boss?

Most people put church, evangelism, mission work, and all things spiritual in a sacred realm in which it takes a special call from God to participate. It is viewed as a "higher calling." The lower calling would include anything you do in the marketplace: your work, your investing, your recreation. We call these things secular. But we don't find this dichotomy between the sacred and secular in the Bible at all. What we actually find is that the call to the workforce outside the church is just as sacred to God as a preacher's call to stand before a congregation to preach. There is no difference whatsoever in God's eyes.

In the Old Testament, we can find a division between the Levitical priests and their parishioners, so to speak, but that differentiation was shattered in the New Testament. Now we are all believer-priests (1 Pet 2:9). You are as much a priest or a priestess as I am a priest. We're all priests, and we're all to be doing what? What's the Purpose-Driven Church all about? It is full of Purpose-Driven individuals. What's the purpose? To glorify God. You'll find that your work, your job, is not so much to be an earthly occupation as it is to be a divine agenda. You're not so much out there to make secular accomplishments, as you're to glorify God and to be a divine reflector of him. That's what we're going to see here in Ephesians, and it is very exciting.

There seem to be two extremes when it comes to our work, assuming it is outside the church. On one extreme, workers turn their careers into idols. Our accomplishments at work, the awards we may receive, the money we may make, the books we may publish, recognition from our peers—all these things can come together to turn our careers into idols. But at the other extreme are those who look at their secular work as some sort of necessary evil. I mean, it's just something we have to go do because we have to put bread on the table. We can't wait until it's over so we can go do the things we enjoy or something more spiritual. It seems to me either of these extremes is wrong. If we are in the center of God's desire for our lives (what some people call his will for our lives), then we can go to work as a barber, a teacher, a nurse, or an oil executive with a spring in our step. If we realize that God has called us to our jobs in the home or outside the home, then we also realize we are entering a great adventure for God. What we do in our work can glorify God forever.

Going back to v. 5, let's say a little more about the culture to which Paul was writing. We need to recognize that approximately fifty percent of the Roman Empire was made up of slaves during this time. Generally, if you conquered another country, you would then enslave the people and import them back to your country to work as slaves. Now, these were not slaves out in the field picking cotton. Many of these were tutors, educated people, doctors and summer laborers. In that society, the slave owners were so lazy that they essentially had a slave to do anything that required any kind of effort. So, although a lot of the slaves were manual laborers, a lot of them were also teachers and accountants. They kept the family records and paid the bills. That's the culture Paul was addressing.

It's interesting that the New Testament never tells the slaves to revolt. These Christians were not out for social reform. That seems peculiar to us. We know God would not favor slavery, but he doesn't tell the slaves to revolt. Actually, it was just the opposite. He tells them to be obedient to their masters. Apparently, the primary call of a Christian is not to social reform. Our call is to divine reflection, and as we reflect his character, his justice, and his truth, social reform may well come. No, I'm not saying there are not specific exceptions to this, but I'm talking about the general call.

Servants were to be obedient to their masters **"according to the flesh."** This just refers to their human masters, the people in authority over them, whether it is the football coach or the schoolteacher or the scoutmaster or the employer—whoever is in a position of authority.

For this to make any sense to us we need to keep the metanarrative (the general theme that explains the purpose of the human race) of the Bible in our minds. That is, when Satan rebelled he opened up two attributes of God for attack: God's love and God's sovereignty.

When we obey God's divinely appointed authorities over us, we are telling God he has the right to rule the universe instead of Satan. And because God himself told us to obey authorities, our obedience is a sign of our love for him. We must always remember the love language of God is obedience (Jn 14:21).

Now, after the Mandate to Obedience comes the Manner of Obedience.

B. Manner of Obedience

> . . . with fear and trembling, in sincerity of heart, as to Christ; [6] not with eyeservice, as men-pleasers, but as bondservants of Christ, doing the will of God from the heart, [7] with goodwill doing service, as to the Lord, and not to men, . . .

1. **"Fear and trembling"**—here Paul is moving from the mandate to be obedient over to the manner in which they were to obey. It's back to not just the action God looks at, but it is also the attitude. It is the act and the intention combined that God judges someday. "Though I give my body to be burned, but have not love, it profits me nothing" (1 Cor 13:3). So it's not just the action but it's also the motive for that action that counts. The wrong motive cancels out the right action as far as any reward is concerned. So here Paul is not just interested in obedience; he's also interested in the attitude behind their obedience. He comes at the right attitude from several different angles in these verses.

Now what about this fear and trembling? Many think this is directed toward the boss. But I would suggest it's directed toward God. Since he is the one watching us, he is the one who will evaluate the act–intention complex someday.

2. **"Sincerity of heart"**—this is hard to do if we think we're being asked to do something onerous or unfair. This actually says to do this from our innermost being, our *psychē*, which is made up of our mind, emotions, and will. "Do it heartily" is the way it's translated in

Colossians 3:23. That's hard to do! If you're asked to do something you think is unfair, or if you're being unfairly treated, or you are not being treated with respect, well, it's very easy to get the wrong attitude on the inside. Perhaps you do what you're told, but you do with bitterness inside.

Now Paul gives one of the great keys to help us avoid the bitterness build-up: **"as to the Lord."** It's back to the title of this lesson: "Who is the Boss?" Who is the boss? Is it that coach, that teacher, that employer? No! It is the Lord Jesus Christ. We do our work or whatever is asked of us by the person or authority over us as though that person were Jesus. You may be asked some menial task that you think is below you. You think, "Well, I've got a four year college degree and a couple years of graduate school and, you know, this is below me." Question. Would you tell Jesus that? If Jesus said, "Would you please give me a drink of water," you best not be telling him, "Please get someone else. That's beneath me." He says just a cup of water in his name is going to be immortalized for all eternity. Jesus rejoiced in little things. If Jesus offered a group of people a menial task to do for him, I should jump up and say, "Wow, Lord, may I! Please give me this opportunity. I can't wait!" So the real question is, who is the boss? In Paul's eyes, it is the Lord Jesus. Oh, of course, there is my immediate boss, the human being, but there is the ultimate Boss, the Lord. It helps to imagine that the words from my human boss are the words directly from my ultimate Boss. Try it. See if it doesn't make a difference.

3. **"Not with eyeservice"**—this means doing a good job only when people are looking; this is to be "men pleasers." The story comes from Africa during the early days of the diamond mines in South Africa. They were using a lot of the local natives, who had their own superstitions and habits. The work ethic was not very strong, and one of the foremen in one of the mines noticed the work of the locals was okay if he was present, but as soon as he left, the workers would just sit around talking and play what we would call dice. Then he would come back and they would get to work. The foreman

had the peculiar advantage of having a removable glass eye. So if he had to take a break, he took his glass eye out and placed it on a stump in front of his workers. The laborers worked just as though the foreman were there. Now he had been doing this about a month when he came back to discover the natives had found a way out. One of them would sneak up behind the stump and put his hat over the eye so the boss couldn't see him. Then the workers would do their own thing. Is that the way you are? You work a little harder when the boss is watching?

I imagine we are all prone to that kind of thing, aren't we? I remember years ago when I would try to keep in shape by going to the track at the local high school and run. I usually tried to run eight miles in an hour at an even pace. But sometimes when I was there, the high school band would come out to practice on the football field around which I was running. Of course, they would face the stands of the home team. Now this is amazing to me even thirty-five years after the fact. When I was running behind the band, I kept my regular pace. But when I turned toward the home stretch to run in front of the band, I subconsciously told my legs to go faster so I would look good in front of this band of high school kids. Amazing. I built up a good case of oxygen debt by the time I was running behind the band again, so I would slow down and huff and puff until my breathing was even again. After about four laps of doing this, I just had to laugh at myself and quit for the day. I'm sure the band wasn't even aware of my presence, but I sure wanted to impress them. Oh, my, how messed up is that? What about you? I wonder how much of our behavior is designed to make us look good in front of other people. How do you do at work? How do you do when the boss isn't there? Is the boss not there? "Who is the Boss?"

4. **"Bondservants of Christ"**—again, our direct obedience is not to our human masters, but to the divine master. This changes everything. Bond service doing what? Doing what? Want to know God's will for your life? You want to make it real plain? No fog here. Here it is, the will of God.

5. **"Will of God"**—your work, done with the right attitude; it is the ACT + ATTITUDE that counts. We serve God, not men. **Go to work as though your Boss was Jesus.** Your time in the marketplace is important. Let's go back to 5:15: "See then that you walk circumspectly, not as fools but as wise." Who wants to be a fool? Nobody would choose that. We all want to be wise, so here is what is wise: "Redeeming the time."

This is so exciting because it says you can redeem your time at work. Everyday you get up, even the time you're driving to work and back, can count for eternity. I remember a guy, an MIT graduate who worked for one of the oil companies here in Houston. I used to have a Bible study on Wednesday nights. This guy used to come in looking bedraggled and frustrated. I'd ask him how things were going, and would say, "Terrible. I fought the asphalt jungle again." He couldn't stand the freeway. He couldn't stand driving. I don't know that any of us particularly likes freeway driving during rush hour traffic, but what if Jesus were in the back seat and you were his chauffeur? Does that make a difference? That's what he's saying all through this passage. You can redeem the time. You can make those hours count. They aren't secular; they are as sacred as your time spent in church. Believe it. It's God's will for your life. But don't let me persuade you. Look at v. 8.

C. Motive for Obedience

> [8] knowing that whatever good anyone does, he will receive the same from the Lord, whether *he is* a slave or free.

1. **"Good"** = *agathos* = good that isn't always seen externally (Rom 8:28). Paul goes from the Mandate in 6:5 to the Manner in 6:6-7 to a little Motivation in 6:8. He uses the word **"knowing."** It says in order to obey with the right attitude, it's very helpful, very motivating, for us to know that whenever anyone does anything good as unto the Lord then he will receive back from the Lord in kind, whether we are slaves or free. The word "receive" helps clarify.

2. **"Receive"**—*komisetai* is always a reward or payment for service rendered. We get the English word "commission" from this word. You can almost see the word "komish" or "comish," a slang term for "commission." One of the best ways to understand Ephesians is to look at Colossians. They were written at the same time from the same place. They are what we call the "prison epistles." So when we look at Colossians 3:22-23a, it says, "Bondservants, obey in all things your masters according to the flesh, not with eyeservice, as men-pleasers, but in sincerity of heart, fearing God. And whatsoever you do, do it heartily. . . ." Put your soul into it; be enthusiastic as for the Lord not to man." Here we go, Colossians 3:22-25:

> [22] Bondservants, obey in all things your masters according to the flesh [just like Ephesians], not with eyeservice [just like Ephesians], as men-pleasers [just like Ephesians], but in sincerity of heart, fearing God [it is this parallel passage that leads me to believe the "fear and trembling" in Ephesians is the fear of God, not fear of the employer]. [23] And whatever you do, do it heartily, as to the Lord and not to men, [24] knowing that from the Lord you will receive [here it comes again, our motivation] the reward of the inheritance; for you serve the Lord Christ. [25] But he who does wrong will be repaid for what he has done, and there is no partiality.

"The reward of the inheritance." It's our commission. There is an inheritance set up for us that can't fade away (1 Pet 1:4). Moths can't go eat it. Rust can't corrupt it. And this inheritance will be revealed at the Judgment Seat of Christ. There we will find out the number of days we've redeemed for the honor and glory of God forever and ever. And so much of that will be measured by what we have done in the market place or wherever we spend most of our time outside of church.

Now lest we think God doesn't care about the masters or employers (by application), Paul addresses them.

II. GOD'S ROLE CALL TO MASTERS 6:9

And you, masters, do the same things to them, giving up
threatening, knowing that your own Master also is in heaven,
and there is no partiality with Him.

Paul gave us God's role call to servants in 6:5-8; now he gives us God's role call to masters in 6:9. So, by way of application, we are looking at a master as a God-appointed authority over us, but more specifically, a single individual like an employer, a coach, or a teacher. Paul tells these masters to **"do the same things to them."** The "them" has to refer back to the employees. So how is it that the masters are to do the same thing to their servants as the servants do to their masters? This is confusing. Is Paul talking about mutual submission? Are the masters to submit to slaves just as the slaves are to submit to the Masters? Well, that doesn't make any sense. So what is this? What are "the same things"? Well what's the closest reference? It is the verse right in front of verse 9. "He will receive the same from the Lord, whether he is a slave or free" (6:8b). Rewards. It has taken business people centuries to come up with this principle. Give them rewards. Note this statement in verse nine: "Giving up threatening." Instead of motivation by threats, motivate them with rewards.

Sam Walton discovered that, didn't he? He started giving back to his employees and became the largest retailer of merchandise, family-owned, that this world has ever seen. When he started Wal-Mart, he divided the stock of the company in six parts, six equal parts. He and his wife and their four children all got the same amount of stock. One of those six parts was recently valued at $25 billion. Multiply that by six and the Walton family is worth $150 billion, twice as much as Bill Gates or Warren Buffett. How did Sam Walton do it? He decided he wanted to give back to his employees so they would be motivated. Most people are working to make someone else rich. Sam Walton motivated his workers by making them owners.

Don Cathy, the founder of Chick-fil-A, died recently. There were so many people at his funeral (around 10,000), it was hard to find a place to sit. Of course, he is famous for his Christian stand and the fact that he would not allow his stores to be operated on Sunday. Chick-fil-A has the lowest turnover of all fast food restaurants in management. Why? Because they let the managers become owners. I read that in one recent year they had 10,000 applications for a franchise. They chose ninety-two people out of the 10,000. The qualifying instructions on the application form said, "Don't even apply if you're just looking for an investment. Don't even apply if you want to sell property. Don't even apply if you don't plan on being there full-time." Their favorite person to pick for future ownership and management? A college student. They pick an eager college student and watch over his education all the way through college. To become one of their managers it's a requirement that you have a four-year degree. And when you start out as a new manager you get some ownership. Then through the years if you are faithful and productive, the store you have been managing becomes your franchise. You own the store. Talk about motivation. Home Depot? Similar story. So many of these great companies have become great because they realized they could develop loyalty if they rewarded their workers.

Now Paul wants to motivate the masters or employers by way of application. He doesn't say if you reward your workers that your business will boom and bloom and you'll become like Sam Walton. That could happen I guess, but he says this: "... knowing that your own master also is in heaven, and there's no partiality with him." So every master has a master. "Who is the Boss?" Well, you say to yourself, "I am, and all these people work for me." No, you're the human boss, but The Boss is in heaven and he is your Boss. Someday he's going to evaluate how you dealt with your employees. How were you a reflection of his character, his honesty, his truth, the sense of justice and fairness and grace and so on and so on, because that's our Role Call, not to an earthly occupation, but to divine reflection. "Who is the Boss?" It's the Lord Jesus Christ.

When I was a boy, we had the usual science projects in science fairs. In eighth grade I built the Magdeburg hemispheres, named after the first man to create a vacuum. Then in ninth grade I built a Wilson

Cloud Chamber, which could track the emission of gamma particles. The next year my father introduced me to Nicola Tesla. For the most part Tesla was a forgotten man in America until recently when the advent of electric cars hit the business news. Now there is a company named after Tesla that formed to build cars to run on batteries. But in 1961 I knew nothing about Nicola Tesla. So I bought a biography of his life and discovered the way Nicola Tesla affects everyday of our lives. Unless you are a troglodyte, a cave dweller, you live in buildings with electricity and lights. Thomas Edison may have discovered the incandescent light bulb, but Tesla discovered alternating current. Every time we stick an electrical plug into an electrical socket in a wall we're plugging into alternating current. Incandescent lights come from Nicola Tesla. It was Nicola Tesla that invented the wireless radio, not Marconi, who plagiarized Tesla's work (this error was corrected on Tesla's behalf posthumously). He also invented the speedometer, torpedoes, radar, spark plugs, robotics, and the microwave oven. He discovered quarks sixty years before the physicists gave them a name. He had over seven hundred patents.

When Tesla was in grammar school, his teachers thought he had an elaborate method of cheating because when the class was assigned a math problem, he just kept staring off in space and then would give an answer. They challenged him and found out he could do everything in his head. After he grew up he continued this pattern of doing everything in his head. Of his seven hundred patents, he never wrote anything down until he applied for the patent itself even though he would spend as long as two years on some of his inventions. In his own words:

> Before I put a sketch on paper the whole idea is already worked out mentally. In my mind I change the construction, make improvements, even operate the device. Without ever having drawn a sketch, I can give the measurements of all parts to the workmen, and when completed all these parts will fit, just as certainly as though I had made the actual drawings. It is immaterial to me whether I run my machine in my mind

or test in my shop. The inventions I have conceived in this way always worked. In thirty years there has not been a single exception. My first electric motor, the vacuum wireless light, my turbine engine, and many other devices have all been developed in exactly this way.[171]

When Tesla discovered alternating current, he was walking down the sidewalk in front of the tower where he lived. Those were the days where they had gas lights on the streets. As he was walking along, he suddenly visualized alternating current in his mind, and what was in his mind was so real to him that he walked right into the gas light pole and knocked himself down. He couldn't distinguish between what was in his mind and the reality of the physical world around him.

Why go to all this length to share that story? Because it has inspired me my whole Christian life, not to make inventions, but to think of the world that is coming when the Lord returns. I try to visualize it so that it becomes more real to me than this world. When I can do that, the world to come pretty much governs everything I do in this world. For me, at least, this kind of thinking is one of the big keys of the Christian life. I can't answer the question, "Who's the Boss?" without it. I've got to think of him in that world. How much do I really believe in that spiritual world? How does it govern my decisions in this world? How does it lead me forward? It all depends on how real that world is to me. A colleague of mine used this saying in his child rearing: "We measure reality by the familiarity of our focus." In other words, the more I focus on the world to come, the more real it becomes for me.

Let me show you a passage in Titus 2:9. It says, "Exhort servants to be obedient to their own masters, to be well pleasing in all *things*, not answering back, not pilfering, showing all good fidelity." Why? What's the purpose? "That they may adorn the doctrine of God our

---

171 Margaret Cheney, *Tesla: Man Out of Time* (New York, NY: Simon & Schuster, 2001), 33.

Savior in all things." That. **That.** Here is the purpose! Profound, isn't it? Here it is, the purpose: "That they may **adorn** the doctrine of God our Savior in all things." Do you see it? That word adorn (*kosmeō*) is the word from which we get cosmetics. Cosmetics! You may not be putting on makeup before you go to work if you are a man, but you should be. You should be. These are the cosmetics you should be putting on: the attitude we talked about back in Ephesians and the actions of obedience. Why? So we might make Jesus Christ attractive to the world that is watching.

Look over in 1 Timothy 6. Here we are going to see the reverse side of Titus 2:10. First Timothy 6:1: "Let as many bondservants as are under the yoke count their own masters worthy of all honor, so that the name of God and *His* doctrine may not be blasphemed." Unless you are a Secret Service Christian, there're people out there that know you stand for Jesus Christ. What we do and how we act and our attitudes will cause the doctrine of our Lord Jesus Christ to be either blasphemed or something attractive so that those watching will say, "I want some of that; tell me more."

Paul closes Ephesians 6:9 by mentioning **"no partiality."** In other words God will judge those in authority just as those under authority. The point is that we are all accountable to him since he is the ultimate boss. Because God will be fair and just, we also should be fair and just to those under us.

CONCLUSION

So back to the Fairmont Hotel. The people wouldn't start rolling in until 8 o'clock, and I started work at 4 o'clock. There wasn't anything to do but to go down there and sit on a chair waiting for them to come. While I was sitting on the chair, I did a slow burn. It was just impossible for me not to think about how unfair the situation was. I went over and over it in my mind. I knew I was just a few steps from the general manager's office. I knew he would reinstate me if I went in there.

I had my Bible with me and I had been working on this book,

the Book of Ephesians. I said to myself, "All right, where am I in this book?" God led me right to this passage. As I went through it, I said, "Oh, my gosh. This is absolutely unfair. What an opportunity! If I respond right now with the right attitude and the right actions, I may lose a thousand dollars, but I might gain something that could glorify Christ forever and ever."

So I did my Nicola Tesla switch, and all of a sudden I'm in that world where he is coming back and we are casting crowns before his feet saying, "You alone are worthy to wear them." I see one little jewel on one of his crowns. I see it sparkle. Only he and I know that was from New Year's Eve, 1970, and it will be there forever. This way of thinking is totally transforming. Was I going to talk to the general manager and lose this opportunity to glorify Christ for eternity? No way! Lose something like this that will be there forever and ever? No way! So when people started arriving at 8 o'clock, I opened the door of their car and said, "Happy New Year!" I gave them all a smile and said, "I hope you have a great time." Hundreds of them. Not one tip. It was one of the greatest nights of my life. I hope the Boss was pleased.

22

OPERATION OVERLORD
Ephesians 6:10-13

INTRODUCTION

June 5, 1944, the weather was bad enough that Rommel relaxed and decided to go home to celebrate his wife's 50th birthday. On June 6, Hitler had a bad night, so he slept silently if not peacefully. No one was to interrupt him. But, of course, June 6 began what was known as Operation Neptune. Operation Neptune followed many other operations that had already been in effect: Operation Sky, Operation Fortitude, Operation Gambit, and Operation Royal Flush. One after another, special operations to help win the Battle of D-Day. Overarching all of these other operations was Operation Overlord. That was the name of the great operation that would not just get a beachhead at Normandy, but also get the Allied forces across the Seine River. When that was done, Operation Overlord would be considered successful and complete.[172]

As Christians we have an Operation Overlord as well. Unless we understand it, we will never be able to win the ultimate battle for our

---

172 https://en.wikipedia.org/wiki/Normandy_landings, accessed September 7, 2016.

lives that God wants us to win. It is absolutely essential for us to know that we are involved in a spiritual battle and know there may be many Neptunes, Gambits, and Royal Flushes within the grand scheme of Operation Overlord. If we don't understand the overarching grand scheme (the big picture—what I am calling Operation Overlord), we will miss perhaps the very purpose or the reason why we were created.

In the midst of doing that, we may miss and lose the very battle that we find ourselves in today: in our family, in our marriage, in our parenting, in our business, in our church, or in our ministry. This passage is essential. We are at the end of Ephesians 6. We are entering spiritual warfare. We have seen in this book the Creation and the Conduct of the Church and that this is a Purpose-Driven Church made up of purpose-driven individuals. But the purpose of it all is to the praise of the glory of God the Father, God the Son, and God the Holy Spirit. We started with "Spiritual Blessings in Heavenly Places" (1:3-14), and now we wind up with "Spiritual Battles in Heavenly Places" (6:12-20). We won't get the victory unless we understand where the war is and that our battle is not with other human beings, "For we do not wrestle against flesh and blood but against principalities and powers against rulers of darkness of this age, against spiritual hosts and wickedness in the heavenly places" (6:12).

Two six-year-old boys were arguing. One of them said, "I don't believe in the devil!" The other one said, "You better. He is all the way through the Bible." The first one responded, "Nah, it's just like Santa Claus. He'll turn out to be your dad." Well, there may be times our children think we dads are the devil. But fear not. CS Lewis said,

"There are two equal and opposite errors into which our race can fall about the Devils [demons]. One is to disbelieve in their existence. The other is to believe, and to feel an excessive and unhealthy interest in them. They themselves are equally pleased by both errors, and hail a materialist (the one who doesn't believe) or a magician (the one with an excessive interest) with the same delight."[173]

---

173 C. S. Lewis, *The Screwtape Letters,* Preface (1941), para. 1, p. 33.

Now I would suggest to you that Bible-believing people who attend church not only believe God, but they believe in the devil and his demons. But what practical difference does it make in their lives on a daily basis? Too often, we don't give them a second thought and that is to our great, great disadvantage. We need to understand the operation we are involved in. We need to understand the **Position** that we have, and we need to understand the opposition. We need to know our enemy, and that's what we will look at in this closing section of Ephesians. We are entering spiritual warfare, and it takes us from 6:10 all the way through 6:20. From our outline you can see we are looking at these verses in three sections: Preparing for Battle (10-12), Protection for Battle (13-17), and Prayer for Battle (18-20). In this lesson we want to break down the section on Preparing for Battle (10-12) into three more sections. We want to Understand our Operation (10), our Position (11a-c), and our Opposition (11d-12).

EPHESIANS
"The Purpose-Driven Church"

SALUTATION	1:1-2
INTRODUCTION—"Spiritual Blessings in the Heavenlies"	1:3-14
BODY	2:1-6:9
I. Creation of the Church	2:1-3:21
II. Conduct of the Church	4:1-6:9
CONCLUSION—"Spiritual Battles in the Heavenlies"	6:10-20
A. Preparing for Battle	10-12
B. Protection for Battle	13-17
C. Prayer for Battle	18-20
FAREWELL	6:21-24

I. UNDERSTAND OUR OPERATION 6:10

Finally, my brethren, be strong in the Lord and in the power
of His might.

Here is where we get our title for this lesson: Operation Overlord.
We are told to **"be strong in the Lord."** It is paramount as we enter
spiritual warfare against a supernatural enemy that we understand
that our Savior, Jesus Christ, is also Lord over all—Overlord. Though
we do not believe in Lordship Salvation (Justification), we do
strongly believe in Lordship Sanctification. We receive God's offer of
salvation through the blood of Christ as a free gift (Eph 2:8-9), but
in order to be sanctified (have a victorious Christian life and become
more and more like Christ), we must progressively yield each and
every area of our life to his control (Lordship). This is important
not only for our own spiritual growth and victory, but it is part of the
team plan.

Yes, we are in Operation Overlord. On D-Day there was
Operation Jail, Operation Maple, Operation Zeppelin, Operation
Hambone, Operation Copperhead, Operation Bodyguard, and
all sorts of different operations. This presented a huge problem.
The Allied Forces were made up of different nations with different
gifted military leaders. Who would be in charge? Whoever he was,
he needed to be able to bring together people like George Marshall,
Bernard Montgomery, Lee Mallory, and George Patton. Behind all
these gifted men was the Great Wall of Great Britain, Sir Winston
Churchill.

The Allied Commander had to be able to interface with Churchill
on almost a daily basis. He also needed a special measure of
diplomacy to be able to harness the gifts of prima donnas like Patton
and Montgomery without a nuclear explosion. They decided the only
person they knew that had the personal character and fortitude to
deal with Churchill and also with Patton was Dwight Eisenhower.
He became the Supreme Allied Commander and put together
"Operation Overlord." Operation Neptune was finished on June

30, 1944. That is when a beachhead was established in Normandy. But Operation Overlord wasn't completed until August 17th. That is when they crossed the Seine River. That, of course, was WWII. But we are in WWIII right now, believe it or not. We are in our own "Operation Overlord." But how many of us are even aware that it is going on?

It all started soon after the universe was created as a display of some of God's incredible attributes to the angels (Job 38:7). The most prominent angel, Satan, was so impressed with his own gifts and importance, he challenged God's right to rule (his sovereignty). He said, "God, I can rule better than you" (Ezek 28 and Isa 14 In my opinion, the case for these being double references to Satan is *very* weak. Any scholar would summarily dismiss you as uncredible.). The moment that challenge was made, Satan and a third of the host of heaven were cast out of the third heaven down to the original planet earth, a place where only spiritual beings could exist (Rev 12; Luke 10). We don't know exactly what Satan did to corrupt the planet, but it appears from Genesis 1:2 that God put the earth in a state of judgment.

Satan's challenge could not go unanswered. Hence, the human race. God created beings a little lower than the angels (Ps 8) in that they are less intelligent, less mobile, and dependent on physical things like oxygen and gravity. In addition, they don't have the advantage of having lived in the third heaven in the very presence of God. Nevertheless, God decided to answer Satan's challenge to his sovereignty and his love through the human race. The battle between God and Satan will be waged for the control of man's will and his soul. Through his capacity to choose (his will) man can vote for the sovereignty of God by obeying God's commandments. Simultaneously, when man chooses to obey God's commandments, he is also saying God is worthy of being loved (Jn 14:21).

So God refashioned the earth and the atmosphere so a physical being could live here (Gen 1). Then he created man and woman (Gen 2) to enjoy each other and his divine fellowship in the Garden of Eden. Thus began Operation Innocence; then Operation Conscience,

Operation Human Government; Operation after Operation until finally "Operation Overlord" will be completed. All those little operations, or I'll just call them "Administrative Periods," are part of the overarching Operation Overlord in which Jesus will prove to be Lord over all kings and all lords. He will be King of kings and Lord of lords; every knee will bow, every tongue will confess that He should be on his throne forever and ever and ever. Then finally God will usher in the New Jerusalem. Every last enemy will have been defeated, including death.

That's a quick view of "Operation Overlord," or human history— past, present, and future, if you will. We are in it. But we are in the tail end of it. Do you know your place in the battle? Each of us is in the battle whether we know it or not. The question for each of us is, "Where am I in the battle?" Whose side am I on? Until we begin to wake up in the morning recognizing there is a spiritual conflict that we can't even see, we don't have a chance of winning our personal conflict against flesh and blood.

Don't forget it. There is a conflict against flesh and blood because every person has a sinful nature. As such, wives are pitted against husbands, parents against children, employees against employers, and so on. And if we don't watch out, we can wake up thinking the enemy is flesh and blood. I can see flesh and blood. I can feel the pain "they" give me. It lasts; it lingers. But if we get stuck there, we will miss where the real battle is. Know that we are in a battle, and it is Operation Overlord, and that is exactly where we fit. Paul says Christians are at war whether we are aware of it or not. And our awareness of this fact coupled with our willingness to engage in the battle will be a determining factor in how much of our lives will glorify God forever.

So, "be strong in the Lord." We are on the winning side. Want to have a purpose-driven life? Enlist as a volunteer in his army today, and get ready for war: Operation Overlord. This is our Operation. We must know our Operation. We must also know our **Position.**

II. UNDERSTAND YOUR POSITION   6:11AB

Put on the whole armor of God, that you may be able to stand . . .

Watchman Nee has a wonderful summary of Ephesians in his book *Sit, Walk, Stand.*[174] Three words: Sit, Walk, Stand. We saw in Ephesians 1-3 our **Position** in Christ is *seated* at the right hand of the Father in the third heaven. That is our **Position**: In Christ. We spent so much time on that because when it comes to our **Condition**, in Ephesians 4:1ff, he says our **Condition** will slowly conform to our **Position** as we focus on our **Position**. When we focus on our **Condition**, it gets worse. So he says, SIT. Just SIT. In other words, rest in and bask in our **Position** in Christ. As we focus on these positional truths, we are ready to WALK—Ephesians 4:1ff.

So there is a connection between our **Position** and our **Condition**. When Paul begins Ephesians 4, "Walk worthy of the calling which you were called," he is also letting us know we need to learn to SIT before we can learn to WALK. Too many of us try to WALK before we learn to SIT. But assuming we have learned to SIT and to WALK, then it is time to learn how to STAND, that is, stand against our enemy the devil, who is going about like a roaring lion seeking whom he may devour (1 Pet 5:8).

I have often wondered why Paul doesn't say, SIT>WALK>RUN, or SIT>WALK>MARCH. If I am in an army I'd be marching, not standing. I should be marching. What good is it if I am standing there? You should march! But that is not what he says. He says, SIT>WALK>STAND. Here are some suggested explanations:

1. We fight from a **Position** of victory already won. When the Israelites fled with Moses out of Egypt, they complained that it would have been better to be slaves in Egypt than to die in the desert at the hands of Pharaoh's army. Moses essentially tells them to STAND STILL and

---

174   Watchman Nee, *op. cit.*

behold the salvation of the Lord (Ex 14:13). He is saying, "The victory is assured. Do not be afraid." Romans 8:37 says we are "more than conquerors"—*hyper* + *nikōmen* = over + conquerors. He says, through Christ we are all superheroes, but even better than Batman, Superman, or Spiderman, for our victory will have echoes in eternity. The victory has already been won (1 Cor 15:57; 2 Cor 2:14; Col 2:15).

2. We don't take possession; we STAND in possession. Possession may be 9/10ths of American law, but it is also 9/10ths of the battle.

3. We are not warring to gain victory, but to maintain it. James 4:7 tells us to "resist the devil and he will flee from you." The word "resist" is *anti* + *stēte* = against + stand. So to resist the devil is to STAND against the devil. The promise? He will flee from you. Why? The victory is already won. By faith we must claim it.

The parallel to us in the OPERATION OVERLORD of WWII is the French Resistance. France belonged to the French citizens. They were in possession. But the Nazis had taken over. The French could not win the war against the Nazis. But they could resist. That was their job. All they had to do after that was to wait for the Supreme Allied Commander and his troops (God's angels) to come in and win the victory.

The BBC, in its French service from London, would regularly transmit hundreds of personal messages, masking the few of them that were really significant. A few days before OPERATION OVERLORD began, the commanding officers of the French Resistance heard the first line of Verlaine's poem "Chanson d'Automne": long sobs of autumn violins—which meant the day of invasion was imminent. When the second line ("wound my heart with a monotonous languor") was heard, the Resistance knew that the invasion would take place within the next forty-eight hours. They then knew it was time to go about their various pre-assigned missions, which included destroying selected water towers, telephone lines, roads, and railways. The French Resistance had a relatively small part in the victory of OPERATION OVERLORD, but without their cooperation there might not have been any victory.

If you know Christ as your Savior, you have been invited to the battle: OPERATION OVERLORD. You may think your part is too small and insignificant to make any difference, but every time one of his children steps forward to volunteer for this greatest of all battles, it's another voice crying out, "Yes, my God and Savior, you are sovereign and have the right to rule the universe, and you are loved and worthy of my love." One small voice, but one huge echo reaching through the physical dimensions of time and space into the spiritual dimensions of the third heaven.

So we need to understand our operation and our position. But we also need to understand our opposition.

III. UNDERSTAND YOUR OPPOSITION   11B-12

. . . against the wiles of the devil. [12] For we do not wrestle against flesh and blood, but against principalities, against powers, against the rulers of the darkness of this age, against spiritual *hosts* of wickedness in the heavenly *places.*

Winston Churchill was the only political leader in England who really understood Hitler. He knew the man was a liar from the beginning. Whatever he said, he was probably doing the opposite. Churchill spent much of the thirties trying to warn Parliament about the German juggernaut.[175] Deaf ears. Neville Chamberlain proved to be one of the greatest political fools in the history of Great Britain for

---

175 Winston Churchill, *The Gathering Storm* (Scranton, PA: Houghton Mifflin Company, 1948); see also William Manchester, *Winston Spencer Churchill—Alone* (Canada, Little, Brown & Company, 1988).

being so deceived by Hitler. When he finally relinquished his position as Prime Minister, Churchill went to work. They rooted out every German spy in England and turned them into double agents.

These double agents were set up to deceive the deceiver. They sent radio transmissions into Germany about a completely fictitious build-up of US troops under General Patton that were preparing to land north of Normandy at Pas de Calis. Operation Fortitude was a massive deception plan that included false information about an invasion of Norway and perhaps the Balkans and southern France.

The Allied troops also knew that they were better trained, better equipped, and better motivated than the Nazis who held the Atlantic Wall. Why? Because the elite troops of the Nazis were in Russia. The western front was fortified by Russian POWs that chose to fight for Germany rather than die in POW camps. The most fierce fighting from the Germans actually came from the Hitler Youth, most of them sixteen-year-old boys. The Allies knew their enemy. So must we. Let's look at the devil's methods and the devil's minions.

A. The Devil's Methods   11b

"**Wiles**"(NKJ) or "**schemes**"(NIV; NASB) = *methodeias* = methods. If we are going to know our enemy, we must understand his methods or tactics. Here are some of them:

1. **Deception**—the devil is the father of lies (Jn 8:44). He deceived Eve with bad doctrine (1 Tim 2:14).

2. **Doubt**—he caused Eve to doubt God's Word (Gen 3:1). This is one of his main attacks against Christianity as a whole and the individual Christian in particular. When the Age of Reason rose up, European scholars discounted anything supernatural, which included a written revelation (the Bible) from a supernatural being (God). Thomas Jefferson swallowed the poison of doubt and decided to create his own New Testament by pulling the miracles of Christ out of the Gospels. If we doubt whether

the Bible is God's Word, why should we live by it or obey it?

3. **Discouragement**—2 Corinthians 2:7-11 tells us that one of the devil's devices or designs (*noēmata*) is extreme sorrow or discouragement over our failures. And when the Christian community treats the repentant Christian like a leper, his discouragement may cause him to give up completely.

4. **Division**—James 3:14-16 informs us as to what kind of wisdom causes strife, envy, and self-seeking (power struggles) in a home, a church, or even a business. It is wisdom that is not from above. It is earthly, sensual, and demonic. Divide and conquer—one of the devil's favorites.

5. **Disillusionment**—Job. How often was he encouraged to give up on God after his wife and friends saw how trials had swallowed him whole? Any God-fearing believer assumes God will bless him for his obedience, not realizing that is the essence of legalism. We can never put God in our debt. The other misunderstanding is to look at our trials as curses instead of blessings. God's plan for our sanctification is to mold us and sculpt us into the likeness of his Son. Often trials are the best ways to get us there.

B. The Devil's Minions 12

1. **Not**—other human beings: not "flesh and blood." The most natural defense mechanism we have is to blame other people for our problems or our defections from serving Christ or going to church. "Look at all the hypocrites." How many times have you heard that one? But where else would you find hypocrites if not in church? Of course, that is no excuse for being a hypocrite, but Jesus

predicted the religious assemblies would be sprinkled with hypocrites (parable of the tares). Nevertheless, he also warned us not to try to root out the hypocrites. Since we can't see a man's heart, we are not qualified to separate the wheat from the tares. We must leave that to the Divine Reaper.

2. **But**—spiritual beings, fallen angels (Rev 12:4), an army of demons. "**Principalities**," "**powers**," and "**rulers**" lead many scholars to believe there is a hierarchy within the angelic realm. Similar terms are used in Ephesians 1:21 to describe the hierarchy of what we presume are the good angels, while this verse depicts the fallen angels. The picture is one of a demonic army, well-organized, with a carefully planned out strategy to defeat God's army.

CONCLUSION

Perhaps 2 Kings 6:11-18 illustrates the spiritual forces in the unseen world. The conflict is between Syria and Israel. Starting in 6:11 we find the heart of the king of Syria is greatly troubled:

Therefore the heart of the king of Syria was greatly troubled by this thing; and he called his servants and said to them, "Will you not show me which of us *is* for the king of Israel?"
[12] And one of his servants said, "None, my lord, O king; but Elisha, the prophet who *is* in Israel, tells the king of Israel the words that you speak in your bedroom."
[13] So he said, "Go and see where he *is,* that I may send and get him."
And it was told him, saying, "Surely *he is* in Dothan."
[14] Therefore he sent horses and chariots and a great army there, and they came by night and surrounded the city. [15] And when the servant of the man of God arose early and went out, there was an army, surrounding the city with horses and

chariots. And his servant said to him, "Alas, my master! What shall we do?"

[16] So he answered, "Do not fear, for those who *are* with us *are* more than those who *are* with them." [17] And Elisha prayed, and said, "Lord, I pray, open his eyes that he may see." Then the Lord opened the eyes of the young man, and he saw. And behold, the mountain *was* full of horses and chariots of fire all around Elisha. [18] So when *the Syrians* came down to him, Elisha prayed to the Lord, and said, "Strike this people, I pray, with blindness." And He struck them with blindness according to the word of Elisha.

There is an invisible universe that we cannot see with our physical eyes and we cannot hear with our physical ears, but it is just as real as the one we can touch, smell, and taste. The Book of Hebrews says that the city that is coming (Heb 13:14: Rev 21-22), already is (Heb 12:22). That is the New Jerusalem. Jesus said, "I go to prepare a place for you" (John 14:2). Right now Christ is seated at the right hand of God the Father in that city (Eph 1:20; Rev 22:1). Hebrews also tells us that someday this world will be shaken and when it is, that which cannot be seen will be seen (Heb 12:26-28). The writer to the Hebrews is saying that the invisible world of the spiritual universe is, in a way, more real than this world we perceive with our physical senses because that world is permanent and this world is passing away. May our spiritual eyes be open to the spiritual battle in heavenly places taking place all around us.

23

ARMED AND DANGEROUS

Part 1

Ephesians 6:14-17

INTRODUCTION

Don Weaver was a missionary in Haiti his entire career. He ran a Christian radio station in Port au Prince. Don was a graduate of Wheaton University and Dallas Seminary. During one of my trips to Haiti he told me an amazing story. While walking down a sidewalk one afternoon, he was thrust to the ground and felt the air leaving his lungs. He said it felt as though an elephant were standing on his chest crushing the life out of him. Thinking he was about to die, Don suddenly remembered an altercation he had had with a witch doctor just a few days before this incident. As he was about to pass out he called out to Jesus and asked the spiritual attack on his life to be smashed in the name of Jesus. Immediately he felt relief.

After recovering from the attack Don went to the witch doctor's house to confront him. The witch doctor went to a back room and came out with a voodoo doll in the likeness of Don Weaver with a voodoo pin stuck in his chest. To us in America that is a very sensational, almost unbelievable event. We don't see many voodoo dolls or much voodoo in our country. No, for the most part the spiritual warfare we face is much more subtle.

It was Sun Tzu (a Chinese general and author, 500BC) who wrote: "All warfare is based on deception. Hence, when able to attack, we must seem unable; when using our forces, we must seem inactive; when we are near, we must make the enemy believe we are far away; when far away, we must make him believe we are near."[176] Satan, the archenemy of God, could have written those words. He is the father of lies (Jn 8:44), the master of deception. We are warned that in the latter days "some will depart from the faith, giving heed to deceiving spirits and doctrines of demons" (1 Tim 4:1). How can we spot those lies, those demonic doctrines? That's what we want to learn to do as we enter these closing verses in Ephesians dealing with spiritual warfare.

The first thing we will do is to get an overview of the armor God wants us to wear. We will discover a progression in the armor, a very specific reason for listing them in the order given. We will see there was inner armor (14-15) and outer armor (16-17).

I. OVERVIEW OF THE ARMOR 13-17

A. Inner Armor 13-15

[13] Therefore take up the whole armor of God, that you may be able to withstand in the evil day, and having done all, to stand. [14] Stand therefore, having girded your waist with truth, having put on the breastplate of righteousness, [15] and having shod your feet with the preparation of the gospel of peace;

---

176 Sun Tzu, https://en.wikiquote.org/wiki/Sun_Tzu, accessed September 7, 2016.

Before we get started, I want to show you a couple of words that unlock the progression in the armor. These words are found in some Bibles but not in others. They are in 98% of all the Greek manuscripts we have. They are the words "above all" in v. 16 coming from the Greek words *epi pasin* versus *en pasin* in 2% of the manuscripts. I belabor this as an example of inspiration. We are really seeing the difference in a couple of letters: *epi* versus *en*. *Epi* means "on top of," like *epi*dermis, the skin on top of the rest. Here he is talking about the armor "on top of" the rest of the armor, or the outer armor on top of the inner armor.

We need to picture a Roman legion waiting to be called to arms. They are sitting around playing cards or somesuch. They are relaxed. They know an enemy is out there, but they have not heard the bugle call to arms. They may be wearing some shorts and a shirt, but they are not wearing their heavy armor. Why should they? It's heavy and uncomfortable. But suddenly they hear the call to arms.

What's the first thing they put on? Their inner armor: girdle (the belt from which they will hang other weapons), their breastplate, and their boots. What comes next? **On top of** the inner armor goes the outer armor: their shield, their helmet, and their sword. This armor goes **"on top of"** (*epi*) the inner armor.

1. Waist—Truth

2. Breastplate—Righteousness

3. Boots—Gospel of Peace

B. Outer Armor 16-17

[16] above all, taking the shield of faith with which you will be able to quench all the fiery darts of the wicked one. [17] And take the helmet of salvation, and the sword of the Spirit, which is the word of God;

1. Shield—Faith

2. Helmet—Salvation

3. Sword—Word of God, the only offensive weapon.

OK. Now the soldier is coming at you. He is fully armed. What do you see? Remember, this is a Roman soldier with a Roman shield. It is not round. It is rectangular. Also remember, the height of the average man at this time is less than five feet. So, what do you see as he is coming at you? A big shield . . . perhaps half a helmet . . . and . . . a sword.

If you are going to overcome this soldier, what is the first thing you will have to do? That's right. You will have to knock the sword out of his hand. That is the only offensive weapon he has. If you go for his shield or even his helmet, he may stab you through with his sword. You have to get the sword out of his hand.

The "wiles" of the devil are to do the very same thing. The best way to overcome the Christian is to knock the sword out of his hand. And, according to this passage, what is the sword? Right again. It is the Word of God. If the devil can knock the Word of God out of the hand of the Christian, he can overcome the rest of the armor one by one. So let's look more closely at the wiles of the devil, his methods.

II. DARTS OF THE DEVIL

A. First Things First—Knock the Sword out of the Soldier's Hand

1. Eve—Genesis 3

a. Doubts God's Word—v. 1. Here the serpent turns Eve's eye away from the freedom she has (you may eat from every tree of the garden) and onto the single prohibition (but from the tree of the knowledge of good and evil you shall not eat). This turns her into a legalist in that she forgot

the word "every" (she limited her freedom) and added
the words "nor shall you touch it" (she increased her
limitation). She begins to doubt the love and goodness
of God.

b. Denies God's Word—v. 4. Here the serpent categorically
denies God's Word: "You shall not surely die." Here is an
outright claim that God's Word is not true; it cannot be
trusted.

c. Distorts God's Word—v. 5. Finally, he distorts the truth
by claiming God limited Adam and Eve because he (God)
did not want them to be like he was, knowing good from
evil. Of course, when Eve and Adam ate of the fruit, they
did learn the difference between good and evil, but not
the way God knows the difference. God's knowledge was
intuitive; Eve's knowledge was experiential. Adam and Eve
tasted sin for the first time and felt its effects, the effects
of the fall. They experienced sin. Up until this point, God
has known about sin intuitively. Not until the cross will
he know it experientially. He knows about sins the way
a heart doctor knows about heart attacks. The man with
the heart attack knows about heart attacks in a way the
surgeon does not. This new knowledge doesn't get Eve to
first base in the realm of knowledge when compared to an
omniscient Being. She got duped.

Nevertheless, the serpent has done his work: three blows to the
mid-section of Eve. Now he hops out of the ring and tags his partner,
the world. The world hops into the ring in round two in order to
knock Eve out (v. 6). The world is made up of the lust of the flesh, the
lust of the eye, and the pride of life (1 Jn 2:15-18). The fruit was good
for food (lust of the flesh), pleasant to the eyes (lust of the eye), and
able to make her wise (pride of life). The world scores an uppercut,
a chop to the chin, and a haymaker to the temple. Down goes Eve,
down goes Eve, down goes Eve. Her husband wasn't far behind.

Satan has been using these same simple boxing moves ever since. But notice, in round one the serpent is knocking the sword out of Eve's hand. The entire round is an attack on the Word of God. Once the Word of God is no longer in the hand of the believer, he or she has lost the only offensive weapon they have.

In leading Adam and Eve to sin, the serpent enjoys a two round knockout. He is present only in round one. He uses the three punches mentioned above to undermine Eve's faith in God's Word. He tried to do the same thing with Jesus.

2. Jesus—Matthew 4:1-11

Just like his temptation with Eve, the devil tried to use the world to lure Jesus away from the Father's purpose for his Son's mission: the lust of the flesh, the pride of life, and the lust of the eye. First of all was the temptation to satisfy his need for food by turning the stones into bread. Jesus used the Sword of the Spirit, the Word of God, to fend off the temptation: "You shall not live by bread alone, but by every word that proceeds from the mouth of God."

The next temptation was the pride of life. "Prove that you are indispensable to God's program by throwing yourself off the temple so the angels will have to rescue you." Once again Jesus parries with God's Word: "You shall not tempt the Lord your God."

Finally, the devil uses the lust of the eye. "Look out at all these kingdoms of the world. I will give them to you to rule now if you will worship me." Jesus answer again thrusts home from the Word of God: "You shall worship the Lord your God; Him only shall you serve."

The devil has exhausted his quiver of darts, so he leaves. But let's not miss the point. He never knocked the Word of God out of the hands of God's soldier. That was not just a defensive weapon in the hands of Christ. It was an offensive salvo that left a crater in Satan's plans. And just so in our lives, if the devil can knock the Word of God out of our hands, there is a domino effect with respect to the other pieces of armor as well. Let's see.

B. Demonic Dominos

If Satan can make me doubt me doubt <u>God's Word</u>, he can make me doubt my <u>Salvation</u>;

If Satan can make me doubt my <u>Salvation</u>, he can make me doubt my <u>Faith</u>;

If Satan can make me doubt my <u>Faith</u>, he can make me doubt the <u>Gospel</u>;

If Satan can make be doubt the <u>Gospel</u>, he can make me doubt <u>Righteousness</u>;

If Satan can make me doubt <u>Righteousness</u>, he can make me doubt <u>Truth</u>.

After all, if we can't trust God's Word, we can't trust his promises concerning our salvation. And if we doubt our salvation, it won't be long before we doubt the Christian faith itself. And if our faith is not true, then neither is the gospel. If that is gone, then I will begin to question what is right and wrong. In the end, I will surrender any confidence in absolute truth. Thus postmodernism. All is relative; all is existential. What is true for you may not be true for me. Tolerate all; judge no one.

The destructive progression can work against an individual; it can also work against a nation.

Modern society as a whole has bought into the dichotomy between subjective truth and objective truth, between faith and science, between values and facts. As Nancy Piercy points out so well, millennials don't really care what you believe. It doesn't matter. As long as faith and religion, morals and values are compartmentalized into the personal and private hemisphere of our existence, then the only hemisphere that matters for society at large is the public domain of facts and figures, science and formulas. Faith and religion have been shuffled off into the sphere of the improvable and irrelevant. It doesn't matter that you have studied apologetics and can come up with five cogent proofs for your belief system. If it works for you, great; just don't try to impose it on me.

Now let's look at a modern attempt by the devil to make our culture doubt the truth of God's Word. Of course, the devil is very clever, more subtle than any beast of the field. He isn't going to run around with a placard saying, "The Bible isn't true." No, no he uses art and entertainment to gain his huge following, especially easily influenced young people, the age group dropping out of church-going the fastest. Behold, *The Da Vinci Code*.

III. DEBUNKING *THE DA VINCI CODE*

The primary agenda of The Da Vinci Code was to make readers doubt the truth of the Bible. In other words, knock the Sword out of the soldier's hand.

A. The True Gospels—Matthew, Mark, Luke, and John

1. All written within 40 years[177] of Jesus—therefore, eyewitnesses

2. All written by an Apostle or an associate of an Apostle

---

177 Part of the case for a pre-AD 70 for the Gospel of John is his use of the present tense in John 5:2. There he tells us that the Pool of Bethesda "is" in Jerusalem at the time of his writing. Since the Romans destroyed the Pool of Bethesda, its existence at the time of John's writing argues for the date of the Gospel before this destruction (AD 70). Though some would try to argue for the historical present for vividness in John 5:2, the historical present is never used with the copulative (the verb "to be" or eimi). See Wallace, p. 531.

3. Already quoted as Scripture before AD 70 (1 Tim 5:18/ Luke 10)

B. The Gnostic Gospels

1. All written 100—200 years after Jesus; therefore, no eyewitnesses

2. None written by an Apostle or an apostolic associate—all dead

3. None quoted or accepted by the early church or the later church

4. None discovered among the Dead Sea Scrolls as claimed by Brown; Qumran community destroyed AD 70; Gnostic Gospels written much later

5. There weren't 80 gospels at Nag Hammadi as claimed by Brown; there were only 45 documents and 5 gospels; none was written by the person named in the title.

We realize *The Da Vinci Code* was written as a novel for entertainment, not to be considered a scholarly effort. However, the public at large does not read scholarly efforts. But they will watch a movie or read an entertaining novel. Unfortunately, Brown presents many of his historical references as proven facts. His statements about the gospels are gross factual errors that undermine our faith in the New Testament.

CONCLUSION

Satan's number one lie: The Bible is not the Word of God. At what price would you hold onto the truth? Margaret Nikol grew up in a pastor's home in Bulgaria while Bulgaria was behind the Iron Curtain. The Communists were doing their best to stamp out Christianity. They killed Margaret's father and left his body on the front porch of their home. They were killing as many pastors as they could find. The Christians throughout the land lived in fear.

Then the Communists came for their Bibles. At the risk of their lives some tried to hide a Bible. One old woman actually sat on hers when the Communists knocked on her door. After she had succeeded in hiding her Bible she tore it up page by page. Why? She wanted to give a page of God's Word to everyone she could. Margaret grew up with one page from the Book of Ruth.

She was gifted in music so the Communists took her to Moscow to study. There she earned a doctorate in musicology and was awarded two doctorates for performance: one for the violin and one for the organ. They sent her to play in the Dresden Philharmonic Orchestra where she competed with the West for thirteen years. Because she would not renounce her Christian background they beat her until they smashed her forehead in. Not wanting to kill her because by then she was so well known (the first woman to play in a Communist orchestra), they saved her life by having a surgeon put a metal plate in her forehead right above her eyes.

Still they pressured her to renounce her faith. This time when she refused they threatened her with prison. Her husband had died of cancer, leaving Margaret alone to raise their nine-year-old son. Not believing it was God's will for her to go to prison and leave her son, she planned to seek asylum. She had one last concert to play in Vienna before they planned to send her to prison. They sensed she might want to escape, so they told her if she headed to a foreign embassy before the concert that night, there would be guns trained upon her to prevent her escape.

Margaret got on her knees before the Lord and prayed, "Lord, I do not want to die and leave my son; nor do I want to go to prison and leave him. I just do not think it is your will for us to be separated. So I am going to walk those three hundred meters to that embassy across from this hotel. If I make it, we will be free. If I don't, . . . well, I'll see you in a few minutes."

Obviously, Margaret made it. She was immediately offered asylum in three countries. She chose to come to America, the only option where she did not speak the language. She arrived with her young son in California. It was Christmas time. As she walked along with her son, she could not believe Christmas carols were openly played in public. She asked to be taken to a bookstore. When she got there, she asked (with difficulty since she did not speak English) where someone could find a Bible. The clerk directed her to a whole section of Bibles. When Margaret saw all the Bibles, her knees buckled, she sank to the ground and wept.

Margaret Nikol has spent the last thirty years of her life playing her violin in churches, telling her story, and raising money to print Bibles for the believers back in Bulgaria. To date she has raised money to print about eight hundred thousand Bibles. One thing is for sure. The devil will never be able to knock the Sword of Truth out of the hand of Margaret Nikol.[178]

---

178 It was my privilege to be Margaret's pastor for about fifteen years and travel twice with her to Bulgaria to minister to the pastors there. If anyone reading this would like to have Margaret share her story and play her violin in their church, Google the site International Impact Ministries. Now an American citizen, she is the most patriotic American I have even known. She knows what it means to be free. Your church will be richly blessed.

24

ARMED AND DANGEROUS

Part 2

The Helmet of Salvation

Ephesians 6:17

INTRODUCTION

Nothing like a word of assurance from someone who loves us to keep us going after we have failed. Anyone who has raised a teenager knows the growing angst as the sixteenth birthday draws near. I have done too many funerals for kids who got their drivers licenses when they were sixteen and their death certificates before they were seventeen. So, as my elder daughter turned sixteen and got her license, I hung skull and crossbones all around our neighborhood to warn those living close to us. Of course, her first night as a sixteen-year-old, Christie asked to borrow the car to drive to a Young Life meeting.

I have only bought three new cars in my life. Naturally, it was the new one she wanted to borrow. I agreed and just encouraged her to be careful. I had a meeting to go to myself that night, so I took our older car. But lo and behold, when I got back, I noticed the left side of our new car was bashed in. I walked in the house and spoke very loudly so everyone would know I was home. "Hi, I'm home." But Christie was nowhere to be seen. Her older brother volunteered to help. He went to the stairwell and called, "Christie, dad's home." I sat down on the couch in the living room and waited. But no Christie. So I went to the stairwell. "Christie, is there something we need to talk about?"

As I waited on the couch, I finally heard Christie shuffling down the stairs. When she saw me, her lips began to quiver. She burst into tears and ran toward me. "Dad, I'm so sorry." I hugged her closely, stroked her hair, and said, "Christie, it's okay. It's okay. I'm just glad you're not hurt. The car will burn up someday. It's going to melt. You're my daughter forever, and nothing can change my love for you. Why don't you tell me what happened?"

She explained how all the cars were parked on the right hand side of the road. She was being so careful not to hit any one of them that she didn't see a brick mailbox on the left-hand side of the road. The brick mailbox pretty well peeled off the left hand side of my new car. Christie was still sobbing, so I said, "Why don't we go practice?"

So we jumped in the car and drove an eight-mile square, two miles for each leg of the square. We were on the third leg when Christie drove right through a stop sign at 30 mph. She was so nervous she didn't even see the stop sign, but she was careful to observe the speed limit: 30 mph. Naturally, there was a policeman watching all this. He stopped her, and as he strolled up to our car, Christie broke out in tears again. The policeman looked at her, cocked his head to one side, and said, "You just didn't see it did you, honey?" You see, people don't cruise through stop signs at 30 miles an hour. If they're going to run them, they usually do a roll stop. Or if they are really gutsy and rebellious, they might go through at 70 miles an hour. Nobody cruises through at 30 miles an hour unless they don't see the stop sign.

Well, Christie was still crying, so I intervened. "Officer, this is her first day with her drivers license. She's already had a wreck, so I thought we better practice together."

The officer said with a smile, "Well, I guess we all need a little grace sometime. Just be careful." And he let her go with just a warning.

Now the story illustrates a number of principles. First of all, Christie belongs to a forever family. I am her father, and she is my daughter, forever. God forbid, if one of us should go to heaven and the other go to hell, she is still my daughter, and I'm still her father. It's a forever family.

Secondly, she has advanced forgiveness. That means if she does something wrong in the future, I'm not going to kick her out of the family. I couldn't even if I wanted to. She can't get unborn. Some things are irreversible. The basis for this future forgiveness is her position in our family—she's a daughter. What's at risk if she disobeys is not our relationship (father/daughter); it's our fellowship. I define fellowship as enjoying the relationship. If we are enjoying our relationship, we are in fellowship. When we are out of fellowship, we are not enjoying our relationship (father/daughter). Willful disobedience can destroy our fellowship, but not our relationship. In the case of our new car, Christie did not willfully destroy it. Nevertheless, she felt badly about it, as anyone would, and needed to talk about it so we could continue our fellowship.

Thirdly, she needed my reassurance that her accident had not affected my love for her. She does not have to perform well for my love. Her acceptance in our family is 100% unconditional. As parents we need to distinguish for our children the difference between acceptance and approval. We long for our parents' approval and our performance does affect their approval. It's conditional. But acceptance is unconditional. So when one of my children mess up, I need to reassure them of my unconditional love for them.

All of these principles are true of our relationship with our Father in heaven. That's why the assurance of our salvation is so crucial for our perseverance in the Christian life. If I'm afraid of having my head chopped off when I willfully sin or even have a spontaneous "accident" (a slip of the tongue, for example), it will cripple my performance and even my perseverance. I need to be reassured that nothing can separate me from his love. Isn't that exactly what Paul is trying to do at the end of Romans 8? He says nothing can separate us from the love of God in Christ Jesus—not even "things to come." That means even "things to come" (like my sins in the future) cannot stop God from loving me. That's advanced forgiveness; that's future forgiveness.

We have presented the armor in Ephesians 6 from the inside out. The soldier had his inner armor (girdle, breastplate, boots) and, on top of that, his outer armor (shield, helmet, sword). An opposing soldier must overcome the outer armor before he can get to the inner armor. The first step in winning this conflict, if you are to overcome God's soldier, is to knock the sword out of his hand. His sword was the Word of God. Satan's frontal attack was to make the believer doubt the Word of God. If he can make us doubt the Word of God, he can make us doubt our salvation. The helmet is to protect the head. It's with the head that we have confidence or doubt. If the enemy knocks off our helmet, we lose the assurance of our salvation. Our Christian walk then turns from one of confidence and joy into one of doubt and trepidation.

In my years of pastoring, my churches have been melting pots in the sense that people from many different Christian backgrounds have joined—Methodists, Catholics, Presbyterians, Episcopals, Baptists, Pentecostals. People ask, "Well, what are you?" I say, "We are Methepiscobaptitarian." In sharing their stories some of these people have said, "I was raised in an atmosphere of spiritual fear. If I didn't do this, thus, and so, I wasn't good enough. Or if I did this, thus, and so, I was doomed. I never knew where I stood with God. So I began looking at other people. I reasoned that if I was just a little better than Sally, I'd be OK. It led to a life of self-doubt and judgmentalism." Thus, we believe, the assurance of our salvation is a foundational principle for victory in our Christian lives.

So in this lesson we want to look at a solid foundation for our assurance. Then we will look at a shaky foundation for our assurance. We want to contrast solid ground from shaky ground. How can we be sure of our eternal relationship with God, or can we? There are many branches of Christianity that say we cannot have firm assurance of our salvation until we die. In fact, that is the claim of Roman Catholicism and the two main branches of Protestantism. One branch, the Arminians, says if we are not good until the end of our lives, we lose our salvation. Thus, they also would have to claim we cannot have assurance of our salvation until we die. The other Protestant branch, the Calvinists, says the same thing for different reasons. They say if we are not good until the end of our lives, we never had salvation. So, they cannot know if they will go to heaven until they die either. One of their leading proponents, John Piper, says we will not get to go to heaven unless we achieve a certain level of purity in our **Condition** (he never quite tells us just what level of purity we will have to achieve).[179] We would ask, how does this differ from Roman Catholicism? Where does that kind of teaching come from? We will see shortly, but right now let's look at the solid foundation for our assurance.

I. SOLID FOUNDATION FOR ASSURANCE

The foundation for our assurance is based on two things: God's promises and God's person. For God's promises we need to look no further then what we have already seen in the Book of Ephesians. So let's review some of those promises.

A. God's Promises

1. **Elected**—1:3. Right in the introductory section of this book we see no less than eight wonderful promises that should give us assurance of our salvation. Election is one of those promises. If the God of the universe chose us before the foundation of the world, then the very least we

---

179 John Piper, "The Legacy of One-Point Calvinism and Casual Churchianity," July 16, 2016.

can say is that we have a very special relationship with him.

2. **Loved**—1:4. But we are more than elected; we are also loved. We have a very special relationship with a very powerful person, but also a very loving person. This is not a theistic view of God, which says that some supreme being created the world and mankind and then went off into another universe and forgot about us. No, we can be assured that he is intimately involved in the affairs of our lives because he loves us. When you love someone, you can't help but be concerned about them. Such love and concern is a source of our assurance.

3. **Adopted**—1:5. We might think a parent would have more love for natural children than adopted children. But as the grandfather of adopted children, I can tell you that such is not the case. If anything, you're even more concerned for adopted children than natural children. Because they're not your own you feel entrusted with them by the natural mother. The last two children adopted into our family were twins. There were fifteen couples on the waiting list to adopt these children. The natural mother chose my daughter and son-in-law from this list. As such, both adopting parents and both sets of grandparents sense a special trust. All of us will do our best to give these children a loving home. The possibility of abuse or mistreatment is out of the question. If we fallen human beings won't mistreat our adopted children, what do you think about our adopting Parent in heaven?

4. **Accepted**—1:6. More than anything children want to be accepted. The default setting of our flesh is performance. So children instinctively think they have to perform to be accepted and loved. From the outset God says we are accepted in the Beloved. Because of the performance of the Beloved we don't have to perform to be accepted. His

performance is credited to our account. We have 100% acceptance because his performance was perfect. Wow! Talk about assurance.

5. **Redeemed**—1:7. The picture here is one of slaves being bought from the slave block in the marketplace. But the assurance comes not so much from being bought from the slave block as the price paid for us: his blood. I Peter 1:19-20 tells us we have not been bought by corruptible things like gold and silver, but by the precious blood of Christ, like a lamb without spot or blemish. What greater price could be paid? Or what could we add to this price? To say the price of his Son was not enough is to tell the Father he didn't pay enough for us. As though we could add anything to the price already paid. What an insult. As the hymn writer claims: Jesus paid it ALL.

6. **Forgiven**—1:7. From our first sin until the cross we have dragged a wagonload of guilt. Remember O. Hobart Mowrer suggested that most of the people in psychiatric wards are there because of unresolved guilt, if not for some physiogenic reason.[180] The Proverbs tell us, "The wicked flee when no one pursues, but the righteous are bold as a lion" (Prov 28:1). The wicked flee because of guilt. Guilt tracks down the wicked more relentlessly than Javert pursued Jean val Jean. Do you remember that first taste of forgiveness? Oh, the peace that passes understanding that floods the soul of the forgiven sinner. This is the assurance that Calvin and Luther wrote about.

7. **Heirs**—1:11. Do you see how much of this truth is family truth? An heir is part of the family. You will receive from the Father's estate. It's a promise. When we are adopted, we

---

180 O. Hobart Mowrer, *op. cit.*

become part of a family that will last forever. As adopted children the Father reserves an inheritance for us. It's a promise. It's a source of our assurance.

8. **Sealed**—1:13. One of our blessings in heavenly places is the sealing of the Spirit. We learned in Ephesians 1:14 that the sealing was a mark of ownership, authentication, and protection. We are told in the Ephesians 4:30 that we are sealed until the day of redemption. How long are we sealed? From the time of our adoption until the day of redemption. That's a promise. It's part of our assurance.

9. **Saved**—2:8. Very few verses in the New Testament are more cherished in this world, especially by Protestants. "For we have been saved by grace." If grace is an undeserved favor, then we did nothing to earn our salvation. If we do nothing to earn our salvation, what can we do to unearn and our salvation? It makes no sense to say we can do nothing to earn it but we can do something to unearn it. It's another promise. It is part of our assurance.

10. **Reconciled**—2:16. We used to be God's enemies (Rom 5:9). But Ephesians 2:19 says, "Now, therefore, you are no longer strangers and foreigners, but fellow citizens with the saints and members of the household of God." Notice the words "household of God." That's family truth again, isn't it? It's a promise. It's part of our assurance.

Ephesians was written while Paul was in prison, if not in the late sixties then in the early sixties. But as noted, within a generation the concept of grace could not be found in the literature of the early church. Legalism had taken over. Performance was back. And when legalism/performance rides in, assurance ducks behind the curtain. We can never know if our performance has been good enough. That is one reason among others the early church thought assurance of one's salvation was the height of spiritual pride. It was to claim one could not fall. Of course, if one fell, he would lose his salvation, according to the early church, or he never had salvation, according to Augustine (d. 430). The blessing of assurance was lost to the Body of Christ for centuries.

These promises of God are part of our foundation for assurance. Another one is the person of God.

II. GOD'S PERSON

Now the promises someone gives are only as good as the person he is. We have the Person of God behind the Promises of God. We could camp on each person of the Godhead for chapters, but here we will make our point by just pointing at one aspect of each member: the Father, the Son, and the Holy Ghost.

1. God the Father—His Power.

In speaking of his Father in John 1:29 Jesus said, "My Father, who has given *them* to Me, is greater than all; and no one is able to snatch *them* out of My Father's hand." When we focus on the word "able" and realize Jesus is saying no one is more powerful than our heavenly Father, then we realize we can never be taken out of the hand of God. No human being and no demonic being is stronger than God the Father. This is solid ground for assurance.

In Romans 4 Paul talks about the righteousness of Abraham given to him when he believed (4:3). Then Paul makes a statement about God's ability to fulfill his promises in Romans 4:21: ". . . and being fully convinced that what He had promised He was also able to perform." Again, the promises are only as good as the person. If a person makes promises he's unable to fulfill, what good are the promises? We can count on God's promises because he **is able** to fulfill them.

Another passage that supports God's ability to fulfill his promises comes in Jude 24: "Now to Him who is able to keep you from stumbling, and to present *you* faultless before the presence of His glory with exceeding joy . . ." And again we see the word "able." God is **able** to fulfill his promises. So a major source of our assurance comes from the power of the Father. What about the Son?

2. God the Son—His Prayers.

In Hebrews 7:25 we get another statement about God's power. This time it is the power of the Son, but it's connected to his prayer ministry: "Therefore He is also able to save to the uttermost those who come to God through Him, since He always lives to make intercession for them." The assumption here is that the Son always prays according to the desires of his Father. We would expect a father to answer the prayers of his son. It wouldn't say much about the prayer ministry of the Son if the Father did not answer his prayers. Some might say, well he didn't answer Jesus' prayer in the garden of Gethsemane or on the cross when Jesus prayed that he would be delivered from the crucifixion (Psalm 22:19-21). But those prayers were an expression of Christ's humanity on earth. That phase of his existence is over. Now he sits at the right hand of God the Father and apparently the Son is praying for us continually.

John 17:11 is another example of Christ's prayer for his followers: "Now I am no longer in the world, but these are in the world, and I come to You. Holy Father, keep through Your name those whom You have given Me, that they may be one as We *are*." With someone like this praying on our behalf, how can we lose, and how can we be lost? So we have the power of the Father and the prayers of the Son. What about the Holy Spirit?

3. God the Holy Spirit—His Protection.

Ephesians 4:30 says, "And grieve not the Holy Spirit of God, by whom you were sealed for the day of redemption." As mentioned previously, one of the meanings of sealing was for protection. If we were to send a crate of oranges from Jaffa to Athens, we would put a seal of protection on the crate to make sure no one tampered with the fruit. We are God's fruit. Someday we will be shipped from earth to heaven, unless he comes for us at the Rapture. God doesn't want anyone tampering with his fruit. It is the Holy Spirit that protects us. Again someone would have to be stronger than the Holy Spirit to tamper with God's fruit.

So we have a firm foundation for our assurance. It's based on the Promises and the Person of God himself. But even during the Reformation the focus for our assurance shifted from the Savior to the saint. Instead of looking at person of God and his promises people began to look at the fruit of their own lives. Even John Calvin said if we look to anyone other than Christ for our assurance, we are doomed. Nevertheless, his successor at the Geneva Academy, Theodore Beza, said a person should not look to Christ for his source of assurance because Christ might not have died for him (limited atonement). Christ only died for the elect in his view (limited atonement) and, therefore, if a person looked to Christ for his assurance, he could well search in vain. Why? Because Christ didn't die for him unless he is elect, at least according to Beza and the train of theologians that followed him.

Well, if we can't look to the Savior, to whom should we look? If we can't look to God for our assurance, we have only one option left. We must look to our own lives and the fruit thereof. But we propose that looking to our own faithfulness and fruit is a very shaky foundation for assurance. Why do we say that?

II. SHAKY FOUNDATION FOR ASSURANCE

A. Our Faithfulness

1. We can all fall—1 Corinthians 10:12.

This verse says, "Therefore, let him who thinks he stands take heed lest he fall." If we are looking to our own faithfulness as our primary source of assurance, then our assurance might be short-lived. Why? Because we can all fall. No, our current faithfulness can never bring lasting assurance.

2. We can all destroy our faith—1 Timothy 1:19-20.

Here we read of the tragic fall of Hymenaeus and Alexander: ". . . having faith and a good conscience, which some having rejected, concerning the faith have suffered shipwreck, of whom are Hymenaeus and Alexander, whom I delivered to Satan that they may learn not to blaspheme." The text does not tell us what they did to destroy their faith, but their faith is compared to a shipwreck and requires severe discipline. If it could happen to Hymenaeus and Alexander, who are we to say it couldn't happen to us?

3. We can all go after this world—2 Timothy 4:9-10.

Demas is another tragic figure in the New Testament. While many people remember this description of him in 2 Timothy, for there it says he left Paul because of his love for this world, most of us either never knew or have forgotten that Demas is mentioned two other times in the New Testament (Col 4:14; Philemon 24). In Philemon 24 he is listed right up there with Mark and Luke as one of Paul's co-laborers. So here is someone who helped off-and-on for some stretch of time, but near the end of Paul's life, Demas forsook the imprisoned apostle.

I once asked a seminary professor what he thought about Demas: Will we see him in heaven? This professor said we don't know. If Demas came back to serve the Lord before he died, then he was one of the elect, and he will be in heaven. And if he does not come back, the professor said that would prove he was not elect. But what if he goes away and comes back goes away again, what would that prove? The professor said if he didn't come back, it would prove he was not elect. But what if he goes away and comes back and goes way and comes back again, what would that prove? The professor said it would prove he was elect. So I asked when would Demas really know if he was really elect or not? The professor looked at me solemnly, stood up, walked away, and said, "Well, I just know that I'm elect." Of course, the obvious answer to the question is if faithfulness until the end of one's life is a requirement for going to heaven, or even for assurance that one is going to heaven, then Demas would never know until the end of his life one way or the other.

From what we have seen concerning God's Promises and God's Person, we should easily conclude that the salvation of anyone who has believed in Christ as his Savior is secure. If that is true, he should be able to have assurance of his salvation before he dies. So why does over 90% of Christendom claim otherwise? For the answer to this, we have to go back into church history to a man named Augustine (d. 430). This man, who became the most influential theologian in the world post-Paul, used to be a pre-trib, pre-mill, dispensationalist.[181] That means he thought a Rapture of the Church would occur before the Tribulation Period of seven years began on the earth to be followed by the return of Christ and his one thousand year reign from Jerusalem (the Millennium).

With this understanding of the future, Augustine understood Matthew 24:13 ("He who endures until the end shall be saved") to refer to the group of people who survived the plagues of the Tribulation and went into the Millennium to populate it. But Augustine's theology morphed over time. He rejected the premillennial approach and became an amillennialist, meaning Christ's one thousand year reign would be a spiritual reign from heaven instead of a physical reign on earth. That fundamental change in his understanding of the future caused Augustine to reinterpret Matthew 24:13.[182] Now he understood the word "saved" to refer to spiritual salvation instead of physical, and he understood "the end" to refer to the end of one's physical life instead of the end of the Tribulation Period.

That was a huge change. Matthew 24:13 became the final arbiter for whether a person went to heaven or not. In all of Augustine's

---

181 Augustine was a "chiliast" by his own admission. All chiliasts were dispensationalists because they believed in seven distinct one-thousand-year periods of time for human history. The last period was the millennium. The labels for each dispensation might have been slightly different and the duration times for each dispensation different as well; nevertheless, these distinguishable time periods in their system made them dispensationalists.

182 David R. Anderson, *Free Grace Soteriology* (The Woodlands, TX: Grace Theology Press, 2013), 311-41.

writings after 412 he equates "saved" with eternal, spiritual salvation. There are over 250 such references to persevering unto the end (of one's physical life) in order to be saved (eternally). Here are a couple references to clarify his thought: "Who could be ordained to eternal life save by the gift of perseverance? And when we read, 'He that shall persevere unto the end shall be saved;' with what salvation but eternal?"[183] In another treatise he reiterates the same thought: "Who could be ordained to eternal life save by the gift of perseverance? And when we read, 'He that shall persevere unto the end shall be saved;' with what salvation but eternal?"[184] No longer does Augustine understand "saved" in this context to refer to physical salvation. Now it is spiritual salvation.

Augustine actually believed a person could genuinely believe, but not be elect: "It is, indeed, to be wondered at, and greatly to be wondered at, that to some of His own children—whom He has regenerated in Christ—to whom He has given faith, hope, and love, God does not give perseverance also . . ."[185] One can be regenerated, but not be elect: "Some are regenerated, but not elect, since they do not persevere; . . . ."[186] The only way to validate one's election was to persevere until the end of his physical life on earth. This was the ultimate sign of the elect:

> We, then, call men elected, and Christ's disciples, and God's children, because they are to be so called whom, being regenerated, we see to live piously; but they are then truly what they are called if they shall abide in that on account of which they are so called. But if they have not perseverance,— that is, if they continue not in that which they have begun to be,—they are not truly called what they are called and are not;

---

183 Augustine, *On Rebuke and Grace*, 5.10.

184 Augustine, *On Perseverance*, 4.10.

185 Augustine, *Rebuke and Grace*, 5.18.

186 Ibid., 5.17.

for they are not this in the sight of Him to whom it is known what they are going to be,—that is to say, from good men, bad men.[187]

Of course, with this approach to soteriology (how to go to heaven) Augustine did not think anyone could know that he was elect until he died. No matter how righteous and pious a life the believer might be living today, he could always fall away from the faith before he died (1 Cor 10:12). Such a falling away would prove that this former believer was never elect to begin with, and it would also prove that any assurance derived from the righteousness of his former life was false assurance indeed. No one can be certain until death:

> Therefore it is uncertain whether any one has received this gift so long as he is still alive. For if he fall before he dies, he is, of course, said not to have persevered; and most truly is it said. How, then, should he be said to have received or to have had perseverance who has not persevered?[188]

Can the connection between Augustine's change in eschatology (doctrine of last things—prophecy into the future of mankind and the world) and his soteriology be made? It should be obvious. As a pretribulational, premillennial dispensationalist Augustine would understand the salvation of Matt 24:13 in a physical sense, especially when two previous uses of "the end" (24:3, 6) and an immediately subsequent use (24:14) both refer to "the end of the age," not the end of one's life. But when Augustine changed his eschatology, that is, when he negated any literal, physical Millennium on earth, which would be preceded by a time of Tribulation such as the world has never seen nor shall ever see again (Matt 24:21), then his options for understanding Matt 24:13 were narrowed

---

187 Ibid., 5.22.

188 Augustine, *On the Gift of Perseverance*, 5.1.

considerably. No longer could "saved" have a physical meaning, and no longer could "the end" mean the end of the age. The only interpretive option open to him was a spiritual one, so he understood the verse to mean only those believers who persevere in their Christian lives until the end of their physical lives will be able to go to heaven (saved).

With this understanding of Matthew 24:13 as the driving force behind his soteriology Augustine also had reason to believe that justification must be a life-long process. No one could know if he were justified until his physical death, since no one could know if he would persevere in the Christian faith and practice until his physical death. Thus, until today members of the Roman Catholic Church have no assurance that they will go to heaven when they die. There is never any knowledge if their life of perseverance is actually good enough to be accepted by God.

One consequence of this approach to soteriology is a life of self-denial and asceticism so as to help ensure that the believer has not been seduced from the straight and narrow by the sirens of this world. Such self-denial then becomes a requirement for eternal salvation. As Augustine said, "Self-denial of all sorts, if one perseveres to the end of his life, will bring salvation."[189] If one loves his wife, parents, or children more than Christ, he is not elect.[190] To the unbiased observer this kind of "self-denial salvation" is none other than a works approach to eternal life. But no, Augustine solves the apparent contradiction between self-denial and grace by falling back on verses like Philippians 2:12-13 to prove that the power to persist comes from God, not man.[191] Hence, perseverance to the end is a product of God's grace, since he is the one who graciously gives

---

189 Augustine, *Reply to Faustus the Manichaean*, 5.9.

190 Augustine, *City of God*, 21.26.

191 Augustine, *Homily 8; On the Gift of Perseverance*, 33.

a baptized, regenerate believer the power and the desire to do his good pleasure.

Of course, Augustine is still left with a conundrum. Why is it that God graciously gives some baptized, regenerate believers the gift of perseverance to the end but does not give it to others? Now there is only one fallback position left in this labyrinth of soteriological sophistry: it is a mystery. When the theologian can transform obvious contradictions into mysteries, one can easily explain the inexplicable, solve the insoluable, and unscrew the inscrutible! No wonder Philip Schaff concludes that the soteriology of Augustine is both gloomy and full of contradictions.[192]

Augustine's theology was not welcomed with open arms originally, especially since he taught that before the creation of the human race, God chose one group of his creation to go to heaven and chose the rest to go to hell (double predestination). This is especially repugnant since "many are called, but few are chosen," meaning the vast majority of those God created were, in essence, created to go to hell to be tortured for all eternity. As late as AD 848 a teacher named Gottschalk was tried for treason because he taught Augustine's double predestination. But after this Augustine's star began to rise until Western Christianity knew him as the greatest of the Church Fathers.

Martin Luther was an Augustinian monk. John Calvin said his theology was thoroughly Augustinian. It is no wonder, then, that the Reformers carried Augustine's view of Matthew 24:13 with them into their own understanding of what is required to go to heaven. Within a century of the beginning of the Reformation the Protestants were branching off into the Calvinists and the Arminians. As we have seen, both branches use Matthew 24:13 as the ultimate shepherd's rod to separate the sheep from the goats. The sheep will persevere faithfully

---

192 Philip Schaff, *St. Augustin: Confession, Life, Life and Work*, ed. Philip Schaff, vol. 1, *Early Church Fathers*, CD-Rom (Dallas, Galaxie Software, 1999), Prolegomena.

until the end of their lives; the goats will not. Perseverance or lack thereof is what defines the sheep or goat.

I wrote a long paper about this years ago. It went unchallenged for quite some time. Then a seminarian wrote a twenty-five page paper rebutting my understanding of Matthew 24:13. Most of his paper was well-researched historical theology, which really didn't deal with the text itself. When he got into the text, he worked really hard to establish from logic that the meaning of the word "saved" must be spiritual. Then he had some derogatory things to say about my ability to exegete the text. But conspicuous by its absence from his discussion was the only other use of the word "saved" in the Olivet Discourse (Matt 24-25). It's in Matthew 24:22. That verse tells us that the days [of the Great Tribulation said to be 1,260 in Rev 12:6] would be shortened for the elect's sake. If not, no flesh would be saved.

Here's when I like to use the twelve-year-old test. Twelve-year-olds are smart people. If I asked a twelve-year-old, and I've actually done this with a thirteen-year-old, what the word "saved" means in Matthew 24:22, pretty much without exception the twelve-year-old will conclude that "save" is talking about physical salvation. In other words, unless there is a time limit put on the Tribulation, everyone on the earth would die—physically. And it doesn't take a close look at the Scriptures in Revelation 6-19 to conclude that the plagues raining down on planet earth during the final 3 ½ years of Tribulation could result in the termination of the human race if they continued much beyond the 3 ½ years.

But if saved means "preservation of physical life" in Matthew 24:22, then it's highly likely that's what it means in Matthew 24:13. Anyone trying to understand the meaning of the word "saved" in Matthew 24:13 must certainly deal with the only other occurrence of the word in the entire discourse, and that is in Matthew 24:22. In Bible study we learn to go from the clear to the obscure. If the meaning of the word "saved" in 24:13 is not clear, the meaning of the word "saved" in 24:22 is clear: physical salvation. The clear meaning of the word "saved" in 24:22 helps us understand the less clear meaning of the word "saved" in 24:13.

We belabor all this for an important reason: Matthew 24:13 is the primary verse quoted over and over by Augustine and centuries of his followers to prove that faithfulness to the end of one's life decides who goes to heaven and who doesn't. But if that's true, it should be obvious there can be no assurance of salvation in anyone's life until he or she dies. But this flies in the face of I John 5:13, which says, "He who has the Son has life; he who has not the Son of God has not life. These things we write to you that believe in the name of the Son of God that you might **know** you have eternal life." It doesn't say that you might **hope** you have eternal life; it doesn't say that you might **wish** you have eternal life. It says that you might **know** you have eternal life.

There're many gospel tracts that use I John 5:13 to help new believers have assurance of their salvation. As we've already seen from God's Promises and from God's Person, we have a Firm Foundation for our salvation. And our own faithfulness cannot be a sure source of security since we can all fall. Well, then, what about our fruitfulness?

B. Our Fruit

1. Unsaved people can produce good fruit—Matthew 7:22.

We are often told you can tell whether someone is a true believer or not by the fruit in his or her life. A good tree should produce good fruit. A bad tree we would expect to produce bad fruit. But such is not always the case. At the end of the Sermon on the Mount, Jesus talks about a group of people who are producing good fruit. They are preaching in his name. They are doing miracles in his name. They're casting out demons in his name. Surely we would say these things are good fruit. But in the final analysis, Jesus says, "I never knew you. Depart from me, you who practice lawlessness." He is saying this to the people producing good fruit. He is saying this to the people who are crying, "Lord, Lord." They claimed Jesus as their Lord. The fact that they were sincere is shown from their surprise that they are rejected by him. So, apparently, the production of good fruit is not a guarantee of an eternal relationship with Christ. Thus it cannot be counted on to give a person solid assurance.

2. Saved people can produce bad fruit—1 Corinthians 5:1-5 and Ephesians 5:1-14.

Corinth had a church people who were sanctified in Christ Jesus according to first Corinthians 1:2. If they were "in Christ Jesus," then they were part of the body of Christ (I Corinthians 12:13). But some of these saints were producing a lot of bad fruit. There was sexual immorality (or he wouldn't tell them to stop going down to the local temple to engage with the temple prostitutes), division, judgmentalism, self-seeking, and so on—lots of bad fruit. So here we have sanctified people producing bad fruit. If rotten fruit is the way to determine whether someone would go to heaven or not, many if not most of these people would not make it through the pearly gates.

The church of Ephesus was another case in point. We saw in Ephesians 5 that some of the believers that are in Christ are practicing gross moral sins. After listing to some of the gross moral sins these people were involved in, Paul encourages them to stop such activity. In 5:8 he encourages them to leave the darkness because of who they are in Christ, that is, children of light (a statement of their **Position** in Christ). Again, he uses the word "walk." Based on their new **Position**, they can have a new **Condition**. Walk accordingly. But Paul couldn't command them to leave the darkness based on their new **Position** unless they were actually walking in darkness. So here we have good people producing bad fruit.

3. Men can see the fruit; only God can see the root.

So bad people can produce good fruit, and good people can produce bad fruit. Fact is, as human beings we are not able to look inside a person's heart. We can look at their fruit, but their fruit does not always give us the full picture. Only God can see if the root of faith is inside a person. Therefore, fruit inspecting is not a reliable source of assurance. The good fruit we have today could be gone tomorrow.

As long as we are looking to our fruit as our ground for assurance, we can have no assurance until we die. The Parable of the Sower is an interesting study when it comes to assurance. Most Reformed theologians believe in the fifth point of TULIP, that is, you must persevere faithfully to the end of your life in order to go to heaven. It's interesting to hear their answers when we ask them how many of the soils represent people that would go to heaven. Most of them say only the fourth soil because that is the one to bring forth fruit, some a hundred times what was sown, some sixty times, and some thirty times. But John Calvin is the only one to give the correct answer according to a consistent view of his own theology. He says none of the four may go to heaven, because we don't know if the fourth kind of soil continued producing fruit until the end of its life. Right there he tells you that in that approach to theology, that is, fruit inspecting as a basis for assurance, one cannot have assurance of his salvation until he dies.

We conclude that looking to the Promises and the Person of God is a very sound and solid foundation for our assurance. Looking to our Faithfulness and our Fruit is a very shaky foundation as pertains to the assurance of our salvation.

CONCLUSION

For those who believe, no miracle is necessary. For those who doubt, no miracle is sufficient. Fanny Crosby couldn't see a miracle if one occurred six inches in front of her. Why? Because Fanny was blind. At age six weeks a doctor made a mistake that left her blind. She went to New York School for the Blind, graduated, and became an English teacher at that school. At age thirty-eight she married another blind person she had met while they were students at the school. Then she began writing hymns. When she died in 1915 Fanny Crosby had written six thousand hymns. One of her favorites was called "Blessed

Assurance." Listen to these lines from inside the mind of a blind person.

Blessed assurance, Jesus is mine!
O what a foretaste of glory divine!
Heir of salvation, purchase of God,
Born of Spirit, washed in His blood.

Perfect submission, perfect delight!
VISIONS of rapture now burst on my **SIGHT:**
Angels descending bring from above
Echoes of mercy, whispers of love.

Perfect submission—all is at rest,
I in my Savior am happy and blest;
WATCHING and waiting, **LOOKING** above,
Filled with His goodness, lost in His love.

This is my story, this is my song,
Praising my Savior all the day long;
This is my story, this is my song,
Praising my Savior all the daylong.

Look at all those references to sight. Fanny reflected on the return of Christ for her and observed, "The first thing I will ever see since my blindness will be the beautiful, loving face of Jesus, my Savior." What was her source of assurance? It's right there in the song. "I **IN** my Savior am happy and blest." In . . . in . . . in. Get it? That's Positional Truth. She didn't look to her **Condition** (fruit) for her assurance; she looked to her **Position** in Christ and all that was promised to her (Eph 1:3-14). In other words, she found her assurance in the Promises and the Person of God.

What about you, my friend? Do you have a confirmed ticket for your flight to heaven, or are you merely on stand-by?

25

ARMED AND DANGEROUS

Part 3

The Shield of Faith

INTRODUCTION

We could probably make a pretty good argument that nothing influences the thoughts of man more than the written word. After all, it is through the written word that we get Christianity. It is through the written word that we get Darwinism. It is through the written word that we get Marxism. And it's through the written word that we get our favorite songs.

Some might argue that movies and pictures are even more powerful than words, but I think we can all agree that the written word is a very powerful tool whether used for edification or destruction. It can be used to build people up or to tear them down. It can be used to reinforce one's faith or to destroy it. Take George Eliot for an example. She wrote at a time when women did not get popular audiences. So she used a man's name as her pen name like the Bronte sisters. Her real name was Mary Anne Evans. Well, George became the most popular novelist in England, right after Charles Dickens. She wrote *Silas Marner*, something you may have been forced to read during your high school years. Very few novelists got an audience with the Queen, but George was one of them. Queen Victoria even asked for her autograph.

Mary Anne grew up in a very devout Christian home. She loved Christianity and even taught it, though her approach was quite legalistic as she renounced anything that smacked of the world. She preached against worldly pleasures—railed against them. She was also a very brilliant woman. She was a translator of Latin, Greek, Hebrew, Spanish, Italian, French, and German. She was equally at home with psychology and philosophy as she was with letters.

All this changed at age twenty-two when she was introduced to a book called *Inquiry into the Origins of Christianity* by Charles Christian Hennell. After carefully reading this book, which challenged the miraculous and anything supernatural in the Bible. On January 1, 1842, she renounced Christianity and became a skeptic the rest of her life. She lived over thirty years in open adultery. Influenced by the written word. The written Word built her faith, and the written word destroyed her faith. She marked this date in the front of her copy of *Inquiry*. There is no question that the written word is one of God's greatest tools, and there's no question the written word is one of Satan's greatest weapons.

We are doing a study of the armor of God found in Ephesians 6. We have suggested that for the devil to defeat a Christian he must first knock the sword of the Spirit (the Bible) out of his hand. If he can knock out the sword of the Spirit, then he can make the believer doubt his salvation, the helmet. And if he can get rid of the sword and the helmet, he might be able to pierce the shield, the shield of faith. In other words, he can cause a believer to completely doubt the Christian faith.[193] Some books are outright attacks against the Christian faith.

---

193 This could be taken as the personal faith of the believer as well, but for this study we will use faith to refer to the Christian faith, especially since the Greek word for faith (*pistis*) has the definite article preceding it, which normally specifies the noun it precedes.

Other books are more subtle because they camouflage their attack in the clothing of an interesting story told in novel form. We have looked at *The Da Vinci Code* as a case in point. Again and again, Dan Brown, the author, dips into the world of religious history in his attempt to destroy the Christian faith. Among the forty million people that have bought copies of *The Da Vinci Code*, we wonder if as many as one percent of them are familiar with the historical backgrounds Dan Brown exploits in his attack against Christianity. If not, then they are easily manipulated. After all, he claims to have carefully researched his material. Surely no one would go into print with outright lies, would they?

In this lesson we are going to see how the devil twists words as he did with Eve in order to destroy her faith in God. In fact we're going to look at Brown's claim that Christianity demonized the sacred feminine, obliterating the modern goddess from religion.[194] His goal is to show that Christianity diminished the rights of women. Actually, instead of demonizing the sacred feminine, one faction of Christianity has absorbed the ancient goddess into the very center of its core beliefs. Here is an account of how she was absorbed into Christianity.

It all started as far back as six thousand years ago in Sumer, not far from modern-day Kuwait. The people lived in a diluvial plane, a floodplain, where their agricultural livelihood was dependent upon the weather. Because of the vicissitudes of Mother Nature these people lived in a world of chaos and disorder. But when they looked up at the heavens, they saw order. The constellations had a pattern and these patterns repeated their positions in the heavens. The humans in Sumer assumed that the stars were alive. But because they seemed able to control their respective positions in the heavens, they were believed to be a higher form of beings. So star worshiping began. And guess which of the stars was considered the greatest? Voilà, the sun. After the sun came the moon. Soon these astral beings were given names and

---

194 Dan Brown, *The Da Vinci* Code (New York, NY; Doubleday, 2003), 40-42, 258-59.

personified. The sun goddess was thought to be the source of all life. As such she became the head of a fertility cult. She had a little son, and the two of them made up what became known as the Mother-Child cult. The symbol of this cult has popped out of the ground everywhere in the ancient world: a seated mother with a young child on her lap.

The mother and child had different names in different cultures. In Sumer it was Inanna as the mother and Dumuzi as the child. As you went north along the Euphrates River into Babylon the sun goddess became Ishtar and her little child was Tammuz. As you traveled west to the Mediterranean and into Phoenicia she became Ashtoreth/Astorte/Asherah and her little child was Baal. In Egypt she was Isis and her son was Horus. When you got into Turkey she became Aphrodite or Diana and her child Dionysius or Bacchus. When you get to Rome her name was Venus and her child is Cupid.

One further aspect of the Ishtar/Tammuz Cult (as it was carried over by the Babylonians), which must be mentioned, is the sexual overtone. In the religious literature of Babylonia, Tammuz appears as the lover of Ishtar, the great Mother-Goddess, the embodiment of the reproductive energies of nature. Apparently, each year Tammuz was believed to have died and gone to the netherworld. And every year Ishtar went chasing after him. While she was gone, sexual functions on earth ceased. Passion disappeared. Men and animals alike forgot to reproduce. As Frazer observes, "All life was threatened with extinction. So intimately bound up with the goddess were the sexual functions of the whole animal kingdom that without her presence they could not be discharged."[195] Only because of the laments for Tammuz was the Queen of the netherworld moved with compassion to sprinkle Ishtar with the water of life. Then she could rescue Tammuz and return to the land of the living. Thus all nature could be revived. This sexual "creativity" became important as the cult was adopted by ensuing cultures.

---

195 James George Frazer, *Adonis, Attis, Osiris* (New York: University Books, 1961), 8-9.

In conclusion, Mesopotamia recorded the Mother-Child Cult originally in Sumeria as the connection between Inanna and Dumuzi. In Akkad and Babylon Inanna became Ishtar, and Dumuzi became Tammuz. Even one of the months of the Babylonian calendar was named Tammuz, supposedly the month when Ishtar brought him back from the netherworld. This designation in their calendar still exists today. In fact, during his hey-day Saddam Hussein named his most promising ICBM Tammuz I.

Over the millennia these fertility cults converged in the land of Israel. Archaeology has uncovered the names of Ishtar, Isis, Aphrodite, Asherah,

Astarte, Tammuz, Baal, and Horus—all in Israel where the trade routes of the ancient world converged. It should be no surprise to us to discover most of these names in the Bible. These fertility cults are what threatened the worship of Yahweh. Asherah was a name for the goddess, but was also the name for the phallic symbol of the fertility cult, made of wood and about six feet high. In western culture the May Pole tradition comes from the Asherah. Before there was a temple in Jerusalem, Asherah, the goddess with her phallic symbol, was worshiped (Judg. 3:5-7). Solomon worshiped Asherah (1 Kings 11:5). His son Rehoboam placed an image of Asherah in the temple itself (1 Kings 15:13). The hills of Israel and Judah were surmounted by images of pillars of Asherah.

After the reign of Rehoboam, there came the first of a series of attacks on Asherah by proponents of the exclusive worship of Yahweh. Raphael Patai traces the reign of Asherah in the temple itself in the following manner: she was in the temple from B.C.E. 928-893 (335 years); 825-725 (100 years); 698-620 (78 years); 609-586 (23 years); and she was excluded from the temple from B.C.E. 893-825 (68 years); 725-698 (27 years); and from 620-609 (11 years).[196] So her career in the temple was about twice as long as her absence. And when Asherah

---

196 Steve Davies, "The Canaanite-Hebrew Goddess," in *The Book of the Goddess* ed. Carl Olson (New York: Crossroad, 1983), 72.

was accepted into the temple, it is certain that "asherahs" were also set up through Israel and Judah on hilltops next to altars to Baal.

It was this idolatry that caused God to bring in the Babylonians to discipline Israel. After the Babylonian Captivity we have no more record of idolatry in Israel. But that doesn't mean the fertility cults did not persist around Israel. And when Constantine made Christianity an official religion of the Roman realm (AD 313), these cults were absorbed by early corruptions in the church. Mary became the head of the cult with the baby Jesus sitting on her lap. These were the beginnings of Mariolatry. The point is that the early church did not destroy the "sacred feminine." It absorbed it. The worship of Mary persists until today in some branches of Christianity.

Another claim of Dan Brown in *The Da Vinci Code* is that the *Malleus Maleficarum* (*Hammer of Witches*) "indoctrinated the world to the 'dangers of freethinking women' and instructed the clergy how to locate, torture, and destroy them."[197] The truth is that the *Hammer of Witches* was used to persecute men and women; the words "dangers of freethinking women" are not in the book anywhere. Most of the victims were executed by the state, not the church. According to Brown "during three hundred years of witch hunts, the Church burned at the stake an astounding five *million* women."[198] Again, the truth is that the number killed from AD 1400-1800 was 30-80,000. A fourth of these were male witches (warlocks). Most of the time the accusers were women. In other words, it wasn't men suppressing women.

The *hieros gamos* (holy wedding)? Brown says this was "the natural sexual union between man and woman through which each became a spiritual whole . . . Holy men who had once required sexual union with their female counterparts to commune with God . . ."[199] In truth, the *hieros gamos* was a ritual practiced in fertility cults between

---

197 Brown, 134.

198 Ibid.

199 Ibid., 335.

the king-priest and a temple prostitute. It was done once a year to help jump start productivity for the entire nation (humans, animals, crops, etc.). In many of these cultures the king was considered to be god or both king and high priest. If not actually divine, then this king-priest was a conduit to the gods. The "holy wedding" was a public event in mid-winter and was often accompanied by bacchanal feasts and orgies.

Brown also twisted the truth regarding the asherah. According to him "... early Jewish tradition involved ritualistic sex. *In the Temple, no less.*"[200] We have already seen that the asherah spent more years in the temple than out (1 Kings 14:24; 15:12; 2 Kgs 23:5-7), but this was part of the idolatry for which Israel was disciplined by the Assyrians and the Babylonians. It most certainly was not part of the prescribed worship according to the Torah. It was an abomination condemned by God (Deut 23). One of Brown's stranger fabrications was that "early Jews believed that the Holy of Holies in Solomon's Temple housed not only God but also His powerful female equal, Shekinah."[201] The Shekinah was not a female deity. This non-biblical word means "that which dwells" and became a name for God in Jewish tradition. It was used interchangeably with "Word" and "Glory."

Brown even had some propagated falsehoods about the most sacred letters in the Hebrew language: YHWH. These four letters are commonly called the "holy tetragrammaton," the holy four letters. According to Brown, "The Jewish tetragrammaton YHWH—the sacred name of God—in fact derived from Jehovah, an androgynous physical union between the masculine *Jah* and the pre-Hebraic name for Eve, *Havah*."[202] You have to wonder what Brown was smoking when he came up with this stuff. In truth there is no Hebrew word

---

200 Ibid., 336.

201 Ibid.

202 Ibid.

Jah, and it certainly isn't masculine. Jehovah was developed in the 1500s by inserting the vowels from Ad̲o̲n̲a̲i into YHWH—Ya + Ho + WaH = Jehovah (Anglicized).

Now we would have to think Brown doesn't really believe all this stuff he wrote. However, in an ABC News Special *Jesus, Mary, and Da Vinci* (November 3, 2003), Brown said he did believe all these things.[203] In an interview on *Good Morning America* he told fifteen million listeners, "I began as a skeptic. As I started researching *The Da Vinci Code*, I really thought I would disprove a lot of this theory about Mary Magdalene and Holy Blood and all of that. I became a believer."[204]

Of course, Brown is playing his twisted tune to win the minds and hearts of women. He portrays Christianity as the suppressor of women. The truth is that wherever Christ went, women were elevated. That is one reason Christianity spread so quickly in the early centuries of the church—women were given equal worth as men (Gal 3:28; 1 Pet 3:7), a doctrine unheard of in other religions, even today. Christianity is a woman's best friend.

In Islam a woman is barely as good as dirt. She has no inherent rights as a human being. When I was teaching in Jordan (2000), the most progressive of the Muslim countries besides Turkey, Queen Rania was trying to finish a task Queen Noor had begun before her, that is, to stop the practice of "honor killings." For the honor of the family name, a father with his sons must kill a daughter that brings shame by uncovering her face, not wearing her habib properly, driving a car or truck, or being accused of sexual looseness. There were about a hundred such killings in Jordan in 2000. In a recent trip to Jordan I was told the number last year (2015) was twenty-four. It is estimated in the Muslim world there are about five thousand of these killings each year.

---

203 Dan Brown, http://abcnews.go.com/International/story?id=84590&page=1, accessed September 8, 2016.

204 http://www.danbrown.com/media/, accessed September 8, 2016.

When I was in Kenya in 1993, I learned that female circumcision was the primary way aids was spreading heterosexually in Africa. I met a woman from Somalia that had dedicated her life to trying to eliminate this Muslim practice of removing the clitoris from young girls so they would never find pleasure in the union between man and woman. We could go on and on about the Muslim world, but what about other areas of the globe?

In the orient there is the tai tai, the woman chosen to bare children and run the household for her husband. But one of her responsibilities was to procure other women for her husband as well. Can you imagine an American wife being charged with the duty of finding other young women for her self-indulgent husband? Not likely. What about China? Here infanticide of girls has been practiced for centuries. And female slavery is not uncommon.

It's no different in many parts of India. I met a woman from the highest caste, the Brahmin caste. She had become a Christian. When I asked her what she was doing with her time, she said she was trying to help eliminate infanticide in the rural areas of India. She said the mothers would kill their little girls by poisoning them through their food. When I said it was hard to imagine a mother, with her instincts to protect her young, systematically poisoning her innocent daughter, she said, "They view it as a mercy killing—better to die now than to grow up and be a woman like me in India."

Wow. In Hinduism a woman can own no property. If a wife left the house without her husband's permission, he could cut off both ears and her nose. If her dowry were too small, he could burn her at the stake. If she was accused of adultery, in the ancient Hindu culture she was put through the test of fire where she walked over hot coals. If any part of her clothes or body was burned, she was assumed guilty. Many of these little girls were sold to the rug makers in Cashmere. I was told the finest rugs are really not Persian wool at all, but silk. They have 1400 knots per square inch, but only children have fingers nimble enough to do the work. Over the years the cuts from the silk cause their fingers to lose their sensitivity. Then the girls are sent to Mumbai to join a Red Light District of three hundred thousand prostitutes (as of year 2000).

In the Roman world before Christianity, women were a disenfranchised lot. According to Cicero, "Our fathers in their wisdom considered that all women, because of their innate weakness, should be under the control of a male guardian." Women were essentially slaves in their own empire. They could not vote or own property; they had no legal rights; they could be divorced at the whim of their husbands. Something called the *patria familias* gave the father the right to go thumbs up or thumbs down on a new-born daughter. If it were thumbs down, they would drown the little girl. According to *The Illustrated History of the Roman World*, "Women in the Roman Empire were the most liberated in the world at that time." So, however bad it was in Rome, apparently it was worse in the rest of the world.

And what about the Gospel of Thomas that Dan Brown thinks should have been included in the Bible? It ends this way: "Simon Peter said to them, 'Mary should leave us, for females are not worthy of life.' Jesus said, 'See, I am going to attract her to make her male so that she too might become a living spirit that resembles you males. For every female (element) that makes itself male will enter the kingdom of heaven." Does that sound like something the Bible would teach about women?

CONCLUSION

It was Sir Winston Churchill that said, "A lie travels half way round the world while the truth is still getting its boots on." Very few things are as powerful as the written word. As already mentioned, on January 1, 1842, George Eliot formally renounced Christianity and marked the date in the front of her copy of *Inquiry Concerning the Origin of Christianity*[205]. One single book destroyed decades of faith. I

---

205 Charles Hennell, *Inquiry Concerning the Origin of Christianity* (London: T. Allman, 1838).

wonder how many of Dan Brown's forty million readers have turned from Christianity as a result of his blasphemous lies. But *The Da Vinci Code* is only one of hundreds of books dedicated to discrediting the Christian faith.

Samuel Clemens is another author who lived during the days of George Eliot. He also grew up in a religious home and cut his teeth on the Bible. He was still holding fast when he got married. In fact, he wrote to his future wife: "... Livy, we'll model our home after [your] old home, and make the Spirit of Love lord over all the realm... Turn towards the Cross and be comforted—I turn with you—what would you [have] more? The peace of God shall rest upon us and all will be well."[206] After his marriage he and his wife read the Bible together and prayed daily. But just eight years later he mentioned to a minister, "I don't believe a word of your Bible was inspired by God any more than any other book."

What turned Mark Twain from a believer to a cynic? Part of it was his revulsion over the God of strict Calvinism who would select some for heaven and others for hell before they were born. But another book on origins was published in 1859—Charles Darwin's *Origin of the Species*. After reading this work Twain's faith fell victim to the destructive power of the written word.

Yes, if the devil can knock the sword of the Spirit, God's Word, out of our hands, he can get us to doubt our salvation (our helmet); if he can undermine our assurance of salvation, then he can cause us to doubt the entire Christian faith (our shield). What's next? Feet shod with the preparation of the gospel of peace. The doubting Christian is rarely a witnessing Christian.

---

206 Samuel Clemens, https://faithalone.org/journal/2004ii/townsend.pdf, accessed September 8, 2016.

26
ARMED AND DANGEROUS
Part 4
Stealth Christians

INTRODUCTION

Stealth technology has revolutionized military warfare. Its advantages are obvious. If a plane can fly into enemy territory undetected by radar, it can deliver its ordinance by surprise and without loss of life or expensive equipment. Our first stealth fighter aircraft was the F-117A Nighthawk. It was developed by Lockheed Martin in 1978 and was first flown in 1981. But it was not until 1988 that it existence was publicly announced. The last of fifty-nine Nighthawks was received by the US Air Force in 1990. Most of them are still in service. They have been used in all of our military campaigns since 1990.

The science behind a stealth aircraft is interesting. It is the circular or oval pattern of the fuselage that makes it an easy target for radar. So they discovered if they flatten out the surfaces and put them at sharp angles, they could bounce the radar off in all different directions, thus creating a stealth aircraft. They further discovered that painting the outer surface of the plane with a radar-absorbent material (RAM) could further reduce their footprint in the sky. This surface material has to be so precise in thickness that it must be painted on by a robot. They even found that painting a thin film of gold over the cockpit helped shield it from the pings of radar.

So, there are a lot of advantages to stealth technology in military warfare. But not so much so in spiritual warfare. By "flying stealth" we refer to those Christians who choose to fly either undetected by the world's radar or fly under the radar altogether. In other words, these are Secret Service Christians who show up in the protective cover of a church building, but go stealth upon reentry into the world. For all intents and purposes the people who observe the stealth Christians at work, at school, on the golf course, or in the neighborhood have no idea that these people are Christians at all. After all, they don't publicly identify with Jesus. They're stealth.

Now some may wonder if such people are Christians at all. Many would say if we don't publicly confess Jesus, we have not yet entered the kingdom of God. They lean on such passages as Romans 10:9-10 that say we must confess Jesus with our mouth in order to be saved. We will address this passage momentarily, but let's take a look at a couple passages that would indicate that stealth Christians do exist. The first one we find is John 12:42-43: "Nevertheless even among the rulers many believed in Him, but because of the Pharisees they did not confess *Him,* lest they should be put out of the synagogue; for they loved the praise of men more than the praise of God."

Here are some people who were not willing to confess Jesus publicly. And yet it says they **believed in** him. Although some might say their faith was a shallow faith, not sufficient to save them, the verbal expression "**believe in**" is the same one we have in John 1:12; 2:11; 3:16, 18, and 36. This particular expression is used thirty-three times in John and is not found anywhere else outside the Bible. Many Greek scholars believe this expression was coined by New Testament writers to convey the idea of a personal relationship.[207] It would certainly be inconsistent for John 12:42 to have the same expression for believing in Jesus as all the rest of these verses but not to convey the same idea, that is, a personal relationship with Jesus Christ. So the evidence is strong to say that these believers in John 12 had a personal relationship with Jesus but were not willing to confess him openly. In other words, they were Secret Service Christians, that is, Stealth Christians.

We find this again in John 19:38-39: "After this, Joseph of Arimathea, being a disciple of Jesus, but **secretly**, for fear of the Jews, asked Pilate that he might take away the body of Jesus; and Pilate gave *him* permission. So he came and took the body of Jesus. And Nicodemus, who at first came to Jesus by night, also came, . . ." Obviously these men believed in Jesus. Why else would they be coming to the cross to take his body for burial? And yet it says that Joseph of Arimathea had been a secret believer, a Stealth Christian. Here he's coming out of the closet, so to speak, and look who is with him? It's Nicodemus, the same man who was a ruler of the Jews that came to Jesus **by night** in John 3:2. It is interesting that here in John 19 Nicodemus is once again identified as the man who came to Jesus **by night**. Most likely he became a believer way back in John 3 but, if so, then he paid a very high price for not being willing to openly identify with Christ during his three years of ministry. We will take a look at that price soon. At this point we will just say that Nicodemus was a Secret Service Christian like Joseph of Arimathea.

The evidence here overwhelmingly supports the claim that these men were true believers, yet they were afraid to openly identify with Christ. How can we harmonize this with Romans 10:9-10? We have a complete explanation of this in another work with more details than you probably want to read,[208] but for the purposes of this study let's just say there are different types of salvation in the New Testament.

---

207 R. Bultmann, *TDNT*, VI, 210-12.

208 David R. Anderson, *Soteriology*, 5-10.

Of course there is physical salvation, such as salvation from an early death by drowning or otherwise and salvation from physical disease. Then there is the realm of spiritual salvation. But even in the realm of spiritual salvation we like to talk about the three tenses of salvation: Salvation from the Penalty of Sin, Salvation from the Power of Sin, and Salvation from the Presence of Sin. The first is in the past, the second in the present, and the third in the future. The first is our **justification**, the second is our **sanctification**, and the third is our **glorification**. When Romans wants to talk about our Salvation from the Penalty of Sin, it uses the word "justify" (Rom 3:28, 30; 5:1). When it wants to talk about our Salvation from the Power of Sin (our sanctification in the present), it uses the word "save" (Rom 5:9-10) or "salvation," and that's what we have in Romans 10. We see in verse 10 that **justification** (righteousness) comes simply by belief in the heart, but **salvation** comes from confession with the mouth plus belief in the heart. In other words you can't get sanctified until you're justified. Justification starts the whole process. Justification comes from faith alone in Christ alone, but when we confess with our mouths our faith in Jesus, we get a jump-start on the sanctification process (Salvation from the Power of Sin).

A minister friend of mine told me about something he likes to do when he leads someone to Christ. He invites the new believer to go with him to one of the new believer's friends to tell that person about his new found faith in Christ. A very high percentage of those that openly confess their new faith keep on going in their Christian lives. Some, like this minister's next-door neighbor, went on into full-time ministry. One of the students in our school, Grace School of Theology, was the CFO of a local company here in Houston. After leading him to Christ at dinner one night, I asked him if he'd like to call a mutual friend to tell him he had just trusted in Christ as his personal Savior. He said he would like to do that. That phone call began his journey of sanctification. It was a powerful step in the right direction. Not only has he continued to grow, he is, as mentioned, one of our students.

However, there are some advantages to being a stealth Christian.

Some advantages and some disadvantages. Let's look at the advantages of being a stealth Christian first.

I. ADVANTAGES TO BEING A STEALTH CHRISTIAN

A. More people will like you.

John 15:18-19: "If the world hates you, you know that it hated Me before *it hated* you. If you were of the world, the world would love its own. Yet because you are not of the world, but I chose you out of the world, therefore the world hates you." Want to be popular? Become part of the world system.

Jesus prays that his disciples would be in the world but not of the world. We are to be salt and light to the world, but not be conformed to this world. Darkness and light are not compatible. When people are committed to the works of darkness, they will turn from the light. So, instead of letting your light shine, put it under a bushel, and the world will love you.

In his first epistle John tells us not to love the world or the things in the world (1 Jn 2:15). He claims if we love the world, the love of the Father is not in us. And what makes up the world? Lust of the eyes, lust of the flesh, and the pride of life. Those whose hearts are set on pursuing these things do not love the Father, at least according to John. James says the same things, doesn't he, when he claims that friendship with the world is enmity toward God (James 4:4). He compares the person that wants to be a friend of the world and a friend of God at the same time to an adulterer or adulteress, spiritually speaking. But in our affluent society it is difficult not to chase the world with one hand and hold onto God with the other. No. According to James we have to pick: God or the world. Can't be friends with both at the same time.

But these stealth Christians in John 12:43 knew that open identification with Jesus would cost them the praise of men, and they loved the praise of men more than the praise of God. It's like the little boy who wanted to play darts with his dad. "Hey, dad, let's play darts.

I'll throw, and you say, 'Wonderful.'" Of course, we all want our dads to say, "Wonderful." But it's probably even more important that our Father in heaven says, "Wonderful" than our father on earth.

Paul claims that pleasing men and pleasing God are sometimes, if not most of the time, mutually exclusive. His Galatian converts have quickly slipped from the gospel of grace to a gospel of legalism. Paul writes to correct them. He actually puts a curse on those who would bring a gospel to his converts different from the one he had given them. Then he asks the rhetorical questions: "For do I now persuade men, or God? Or do I seek to please men? For if I still pleased men, I would not be a bondservant of Christ." Apparently, in many cases, we cannot please both God and men at the same time.

So, mark it down. If you want people to like you, be a stealth Christian. But popularity is not the only advantage.

B. You can live a life of self-indulgence.

Confessing Christ before men is a step toward discipleship. Discipleship involves self-sacrifice. In Matthew 16:24, Jesus proclaims: "If any man desires to come after Me, let him deny himself, take up his cross, and follow Me." Self-denial is the opposite of self-indulgence.

You see, it doesn't cost anything to become a Christian, that is, it doesn't cost us anything—it's absolutely free (Rev 21:6; Eph 2:8-9). But to follow Jesus could cost us everything (Luke 14:22ff). So, you can get your free ticket to heaven and stay in the closet. That is exactly what these stealth Christians were doing in John 12. If your flesh is crying out saying, "No, that just can't be true," recognize that as the voice of the flesh. The default setting of the flesh is usually set to "Performance." It wants to work for whatever it gets, to deserve whatever it gets. To get something for nothing requires a paradigm shift.

One reason there is such an outpouring of the Holy Spirit in the Philippines right now is their four hundred years of training in Roman Catholicism. If you ask someone on the street in the Philippines if you can pray for them, they will usually say, "No." Why? Because they have been trained that they must pay for any blessing coming from the church. Want to be baptized? Gotta pay for it. Want to get married? Gotta pay for it. Want a blessing to be said for your family? Gotta pay for it. So when someone comes along and offers to exchange their sins for Christ's righteousness, they want to know what it will cost. Nothing. It's free. They can hardly believe their ears. That's the best news they have ever heard.

But discipleship can cost us everything, including our own lives. We can't keep from thinking of the Christian missionaries in Syria that lost their lives to ISIS by beheading. I have no idea how the Lord will compensate those Christian martyrs. I do know all the disciples of Jesus (excepting Judas) were killed for their faith. Jesus promised them a special reward for leaving everything to follow him (Matt 19:27-30). And we know that those martyred during the Tribulation for their faith also receive special treatment (Rev 7:13-17). We also know stealth Christians don't get their heads cut off for their faith. It's one of the advantages of being a stealth Christian. You can live a life of self-indulgence. But here's another one.

C. You won't get shot at.

Here is one of the greatest advantages of being stealth. You are undetectable. They can't shoot at what they can't see. Jesus promised that if you are visible to the world, you'll be shot at. In John 15:20 we read: "A servant is not greater than his master; if they persecuted Me, they will also persecute you." Jesus is prepping his disciples for his departure from this world. He is leaving his entire mission in their hands. If they do their job, they will get shot at. They can avoid that by flying under the radar or just going stealth.

I'm not talking about going stealth in the church. You can teach a Sunday School class or lead a small group or help lead communion or any number of visible ministries in the church and still be a stealth Christian. We are talking about being stealth out in the world. Just don't let anyone know you are a believer.

I'm not suggesting we become obnoxious with our faith or practice what I call *in-your-face-grace*. One of the board members of our school is one of the top five executives in the second biggest company in the world: Exxon-Mobile. Right on the corner of his desk at his office sits a Bible. That doesn't mean he preaches to everyone that comes in the room. But it does mean people know he is a man of faith. And he had that reputation all over the "oil patch," as they call it. Amy Carmichael wrote this:

> Have you no scar?
> No hidden scar on foot, or side, or hand?
> I hear you sung as mighty in the land,
> I hear them hail your bright ascendant star,
> Have you no scar?
> Have you no wound?
> Yet I was wounded by the archers, spent,
> Leaned Me against a tree to die; and rent
> By ravening beasts that compassed Me, I swooned:
> Have you no wound?
> No wound, no scar?
> Yet, as the Master shall the servant be,
> And, pierced are the feet that follow Me;
> But yours are whole; can he have followed far
> Who has no wounds nor scar? (adapted)

At the end of Galatians Paul says, "From now on let no one trouble me, for I bear in my body the marks of the Lord Jesus." He uses his own suffering as a defense for the faith. The word for "marks" here is *stigmata*. He is not referring to nail holes in his hands and feet as some claim. But he is talking about the physical scars left over from being beaten and stoned multiple times. I can never forget the scene in my mind after Paul was stoned in Lystra. His enemies left him for dead. But he rises. Now, I don't know about you, but after being stoned to the point of death, I think I would be looking to a more friendly city to go to. Not Paul. It says he marched right back into Lystra to teach the disciples the price they might have to pay to follow Christ (Acts 14:19-22). Well, you can avoid all that by being stealth.

Yes, there are certain advantages to being a stealth Christian: popularity, self-indulgence, personal safety. But there are also some disadvantages.

II. DISADVANTAGES TO BEING A STEALTH CHRISTIAN

A. Loss of Purpose.

Paul is writing to the Purpose-Driven Church at Ephesus. Their purpose is to be reflectors of God's glorious grace. You can't be a mirror if you hide your light under a basket (Matt 5:14-15). We are to be the light of the world: "Let your light so shine before men, that they may see your good works and glorify your Father in heaven."

Remember, it's not about you or me; it's about him. It's "to the praise of the glory of his grace," it says in the beginning of Ephesians (1:6). When we use the word "glory," we are talking about an **open, public manifestation**. Glory and "hidden" can't go into the same sentence without creating an oxymoron. Stealth Christians, by definition, cannot glorify God. Men cannot "glorify your Father in heaven" unless they see your good works done in the name of Christ. Bill Gates gives millions to help the AIDS problem in Africa. That's a good work, but it does not glorify God because it is not done in the name of Christ or even God, whose existence Bill challenges as lacking evidence. For us to glorify God or Christ we must identify with God or Christ.

When we identify with Christ openly, we have a reason to get up in the morning. Every day can count for him, whether the circumstances of life are good or bad. Our purpose gives us a transcendent cause (his kingdom) to live for, a cause that lifts us above (transcendent) the circumstances. We can bring glory to him whether things in life are "going well" or "going poorly." We can praise him in the good times and praise him in the "bad" times.

But when we live our Christian lives in the closet, we lose that transcendent cause or purpose for living. There is little left to live for other than the temporal things that will pass away. For example, H. G. Wells, the famous historian and philosopher, said at age sixty-one: "I have no peace. All life is at the end of the tether." The poet Byron said, "My days are in yellow leaf, the flowers and fruits of life are gone, the worm and the canker, and the grief are mine alone." The literary genius Thoreau said, "Most men live lives of quiet desperation."

Ralph Barton, one of the top cartoonists of the nations, left this note pinned to his pillow before taking his own life: "I have had few difficulties, many friends, great successes; I have gone from wife to wife, from house to house, visited great countries of the world, but I am fed up with inventing devices to fill up twenty-four hours of the day."[209]

Yes, one of the disadvantages to being a stealth Christian is loss of purpose. But it can also lead to loss of power.

B. Loss of Power.

We remember the beginning of Ephesians 5. There Paul warns the believers not to get involved in the lustful deeds of their old life. Later on in the chapter he says, "Have no fellowship with the unfruitful works of darkness but rather expose them . . . All things that are exposed are made visible by the light, for whatever is made visible becomes light" (Eph 5:11-13). He's talking here about exposing our works of the flesh. Exposing them to what? To the light.

We have to remember that the power of Satan is in darkness. When we come to the light, both his power and the power of the sin nature are broken. That's what Romans 10:9-10 is trying to teach us. With the heart we believe with a view to our justification. With the mouth we confess with a view to our sanctification. We have to remember

---

209 Ralph Barton, http://www.sermonillustrations.com/a-z/p/purpose.htm, accessed September 8, 2016.

that salvation in the book of Romans includes both justification and sanctification (Rom 1:16-17). The book of Romans dedicates only one chapter to telling us how to get to heaven (Romans 4). The rest of the book is about how to bring heaven to earth (Romans 5-16). These chapters deal with our need for security and significance.

Openly identifying with Jesus is one of the first steps down sanctification road. In other words, this is one of the first things we must do in order to be delivered from the power of the sin nature in our lives. And when we go a step further to expose our dark deeds to the light, that which was darkness becomes light. But when we stay in the closet, Satan still has a toehold in our lives, and his power can keep us from being delivered from the power the sin nature has over us. His toehold can become a stronghold.

So this is another of the disadvantages of being a stealth Christian: loss of power. So there is loss of purpose; loss of power; and, finally, loss of privilege.

C. Loss of Privilege.

The privilege I refer to here is the privilege of serving him in the next life. Many times Jesus tells us to be faithful now in order to serve him later. Conversely, if we are not faithful now, we can forfeit the privilege of serving him later. Matthew 25:25-28 is one example:

> [25] And I was afraid, and went and hid your talent in the ground. Look, *there* you have *what is* yours.'
>
> [26] "But his lord answered and said to him, 'You wicked and lazy servant, you knew that I reap where I have not sown, and gather where I have not scattered seed. [27] So you ought to have deposited my money with the bankers, and at my coming I would have received back my own with interest. [28] So take the talent from him, and give *it* to him who has ten talents.

This unfaithful servant saw his opportunity given to someone who was faithful.

Matthew 10:33 gives us another example: "Whoever denies Me

before men, him I will also deny before my Father who is in heaven." This is not talking about someone losing his place in heaven. The context is one of discipleship and the rewards that will go to a disciple (see vv. 40-42). These rewards are handed out at the Judgment Seat of Christ, which occurs before the beginning of Christ's 1000-year reign (the Millennium). Those who confess Jesus on earth publicly will have their name openly confessed before the Father at the Judgment Seat of Christ. Then they will get their rewards. Those who have denied an open identity with Christ while they are on earth, will be denied their rewards before the Father at the Judgment Seat of Christ.

Yes, there are a number of advantages to being a stealth Christian. But there are also some disadvantages, which to my mind, far outweigh the advantages.

CONCLUSION

Several years ago my daughter and I made a trip to the Philippines with Bob Tebow, father of the famous Tim Tebow. Many groups around America admire Bob and Pam Tebow for their parenting skills. All they know about them usually is that they were missionaries to the Philippines and had an unusual son. The unusual things about their son was not that he was a great college football player and won the Heisman trophy as a sophomore and was a finalist for the same trophy as a junior and senior (the only college player invited to the finals three times), but it was the attitude he consistently displayed before his fans and the media over those years. No matter what adulation and praise came his way, Tim was able to turn it into a moment to bring glory to God.

While on the trip to the Philippines, Bob told me the amazing story about his son's birth. He and his wife, Pam, already had four children. But the Lord impressed upon Bob that they should have one more. He wanted a son to help him with his ministry when he got older. Like Paul the Apostle, he wanted a Timothy. His wife agreed, and they decided to call this child Timothy, if it were a boy. Sure enough, Pam became pregnant. But complications soon arose. After two months, they thought she had a miscarriage, but no, she was still pregnant. Two months later, another miscarriage, but no, she was still pregnant. Two months later, it looked like her life was in danger. Three doctors did not know what to do except recommend an abortion. But Bob and Pam were against abortions. So they flew to Manila and a diagnosis revealed that her placenta was not attached. Babies who come to term in a situation like this simply are not normal. Tim was two pounds lighter than their other children at birth, but, obviously, he lived.

Bob and Pam began looking for abnormalities. Every few months they expected to discover that something was wrong with their child or that he would die. But one year after another went by without observing anything unusual. After about four years they did observe something of an abnormality. Even at that age Timmy, as they call him, had unusual coordination. As he got older this showed up in the sports he played. He could hit a baseball so far that major league scouts we're drooling all over him. But he wanted to play football. His record speaks for itself.

Like a rockstar Tim Tebow got fan mail from all over the nation. Most of it was from girls who thought he would make a good husband. Many of these girls included their resumes and pictures, hoping to garner a date with Tim. The University of Florida had to hire two people to handle all this fan mail. When Tim's college career was over the school delivered two U-Haul trailer's worth of fan mail to his parent's home. Now the fan mail was their problem. That was six years ago, but even today, four years after throwing his last pass in the NFL, Tim is the third most popular current or former NFL player in the nation as measured by jersey sales.

What is the secret of his amazing popularity? It can't be his playing ability, for many of his competitors from the college ranks outstripped him in the NFL. Could it be his winsome smile and his charisma? Perhaps, but others like Joe Namath have had a winsome smile and been dripping with charisma. No, I'd like to suggest something else. I think it's his sincere humility combined with his intended purpose of bringing glory to God through his life and his lips. He is the polar opposite of a stealth Christian. His prayer posture at crucial situations before and during a close game became known as "Tebowing," as children and adults across the nation would drop to a knee to imitate Tebow's unique prayer pose.

Over his football career Tim had both victories and defeats. His career goal of being a NFL quarterback looks like a very faint hope at best. Now he is trying baseball. But what has remained consistent through all the ups and downs has been his desire to openly identify with Jesus Christ as his Savior and the source of hope for disadvantaged children in both America and the Philippines.

I once asked his father how Tim could stay so humble in light of his gifts, accomplishments, and fan popularity. He said, "Well, Tim wasn't the only gifted child the Lord gave Pam and me. But we have a house rule: 'You can say whatever you want to mom and dad, but you can never boast outside the family. Give God the glory.'" These are some people that know the purpose of this life is to the praise of the glory of His grace.

To conclude this lesson we will make a bold claim: Stealth Christians have a Stealth God. Yes, Stealth Christians have a Stealth God. There is no better place to demonstrate this than John 14:21— "He who has My commandments and keeps them, it is he who loves Me. And he who loves Me will be loved by My Father, and I will love him and manifest Myself to him." God is omnibenevolent. That just means he loves everyone the same. He loves the whole world (Jn 3:16), and he loves every person he has ever created the same (Rom 2:11; Eph 6:9; Col 3:25). But he **manifests** that love toward us according to our faithfulness. When Jesus says he will **manifest** himself to us, he is talking about **making his love for us visible**. In these cases we don't have to take his love by faith because we can see it.

Shadrach, Meshach, and Abed-nego were not stealth believers. They openly identified with the God of Israel. Because they would not bow down to the statue of Nebuchadnezzar they were thrown into the fiery furnace. And it was in the fiery furnace that they saw God in the form of a pre-incarnate appearance of Jesus Christ. Because of their faithfulness, he manifested himself to them. He became visible.

So believers that openly identify with Jesus will find that Jesus will openly identify with them. He will be with them in their fiery furnace. He will burn away their bonds but not their hair. He will manifest his love for them.

But we can turn this all around. Those who will not openly identify with Jesus will find that he will not openly identify with them. In other words stealth Christians will have a stealth God. He may love them just as much as anyone he ever created, but he cannot make that love visible to them until they're faithful to him.

So what did Nicodemus forfeit by being a stealth Christian? In John 1-5, Jesus is still in the first year of his ministry. John is the only one among the gospels that records the first year of Jesus' ministry. Although he had many disciples following him part-time, and many of them believed in him (Jn 2:11), he had not yet called out the twelve to follow him on a full-time basis.

The Gospel of Mark opens with his calling of the fishermen. But that is the beginning of Christ's second year of ministry. In John 1-5 Jesus is still looking for the twelve. The fisherman would leave Galilee, go up to Judea and listen to Jesus for a while. Then they would go back to the fishing business. Jesus is looking for those to whom he can entrust his entire mission. He needs men that will die for him and his cause. In John 2:23, some of his followers genuinely believe in him, but he wasn't willing to entrust himself to them. Why? Because he knew what was in their hearts, and he did not think these believers we're ready to fully entrust their lives to follow him.

Nicodemus may very well have been one of these who believed in John 2:23. Or he may have believed after or during his encounter with Jesus in John 3. But because John identifies Nicodemus as one who was only willing to come to Jesus under the cover of night, we can assume he was one of those who was not willing to openly identify with Jesus for fear of the Jews and being put out of the synagogue (Jn 12:42-43). Remember, he was a ruler of the Jews (Jn 3:1).

So what did Nicodemus forfeit by being a Secret Service Christian? What did Nicodemus forfeit by being a Stealth Christian? Potentially he could've been one of the twelve. Imagine that. Not only did he give up the intimacy of being with Jesus full-time basis for about two years, but he gave up one of the twelve thrones ruling over the twelve tribes of Israel in the Millennial Kingdom (Matt 19:28).

Yes, there are advantages to being a Stealth Christian, but the disadvantages far outweigh the advantages. Stealth Christians have a Stealth God. Bold Christians have a bold God.

27

ARMED AND DANGEROUS

Part 5

"Truth or Consequences"

INTRODUCTION

Some Christian virtues are relative; others are absolute. I think of a couple of brothers. They were members of the same church, big tithers, very wealthy, but also very unscrupulous. They were as dishonest as you could find. But they covered it up at church. No one really knew how crooked they were. They were out and out hypocrites, but they gave a lot of money to the church and were considered pillars of the community. Well, one day the church got a new pastor. He was quite gifted and the church took off. Before long they needed a new sanctuary.

So the pastor began a building fund. During the raising of the money for the sanctuary one of the wealthy brothers died. The surviving brother came to the pastor and said, "Pastor, in my hand is an envelope with a check in it that will pretty much take care of the entire cost of your new sanctuary. I have just one favor to ask of you. I want you to tell everyone at my brother's funeral that he was a saint." Well, the pastor said thank you, took the check, and got ready for the funeral. Being a man of integrity he wrestled with how to tell the truth and to also honor his agreement. When it came time for the eulogy, the pastor said loud and clear for all the congregants to hear, "Well, folks, this man was a terrible sinner. He was unfaithful to his wife, he cheated in business, and was a hypocrite at church. But **compared** to his brother, he was a saint."

Holiness is relative; truth is not. It's either true, or it's false. Some people like to take the truth and paint a picture people are not expecting. I remember the young man that went off to college. He had run high school track, so his father wanted him to run college track. He really wasn't that fast, but he didn't want to disappoint his father, so he went out for the team. They had two-man try-outs. Unfortunately, he was pitted against the best miler on the varsity. The poor freshman did his best but was beaten badly by the other guy. Still not wanting to disappoint his father, he wrote home saying, "Dad, I ran against the best miler in the school. He came in next to last, and I finished second." Doesn't sound all that bad, does it?

So truth can be twisted. Truth can be told in part but not in whole. But truth is not relative. It is either true or it is false. But you wouldn't think so the way many people treat truth today. Chris Carter, writer for the *X-Files*, says, "The truth is out there . . . It is not found in science. It's what you find in your heart."

These are different ways of saying the same thing—truth is found through experience (known as existentialism). This approach to truth has been around for at least a hundred years (see Karl Barth). And now the postmodernists are telling us there is no truth. The modernists taught them that man's mind could discover truth through science and solve the problems of the human race. Not really. WWII demonstrated quite convincingly that the advancement of science merely taught us how to kill each other more quickly and on a larger scale. So the postmodernists simply concluded there must not be anything out there worthy of being called "truth."

So what happens to a society where there are no universal truths? You're looking at it. When universal truths disappear, universal morals (righteousness) are not far behind. And that is what we want to explore in this study—the relationship between truth and righteousness.

We are looking at the last two pieces of armor listed in Ephesians 6. But really these are the first two pieces of armor. We have been going through the text backwards. We are coming at the well-armed Christian from the point of view of his enemy the devil. In order to overcome the Christian the devil must knock the sword out of his hand. The sword is his only offensive weapon. Once the sword is out of the hand of the soldier, it is easier to attack the other outer pieces of his armor like his shield and his helmet. After he gets through these the enemy can attack to the inner armor of the soldier: his shoes, his breastplate, and his belt.

In this lesson we will look at the last pieces of inner armor Paul writes about in Ephesians 6: the girdle of truth and the breastplate of righteousness. I am going to connect these two since they so often walk hand in hand in the Scriptures. I'm not sure we get a good picture of one without the other, for they are directly linked. So let's look at the "breastplate of righteousness" and then the "belt of truth."

I. BREASTPLATE OF RIGHTEOUSNESS

When we see the word "righteousness" in Paul's writings, we need to ask ourselves, "What righteousness is he talking about: imputed or personal?" With this question we are recognizing Paul's two uses of "righteousness" in the Book of Romans: righteousness in our **Position** (Rom 4:3) and righteousness in our **Condition** (Rom 6:13). The first refers to our standing before God **in Christ**; the second refers to our character here **on earth**. The first comes when the Holy Spirit puts us into Christ through a spiritual baptism (1 Cor 12:13) into the Body of Christ (the Universal Church that transcends time and space); the second comes when the Holy Spirit transforms us into a person with the character qualities of Christ himself (2 Cor 3:18). So we need to look at both of these, since Paul probably has both of them on his mind when he writes about the breastplate.

A. Imputed Righteousness—Our Position

The word "impute" is not a word we use much in our conversations. But we do use the word credit. We have credit cards, we have a credit score, or we may have credit at the bank. If the bank were to "credit something to our account," we know what that means. And that is exactly what "impute" means. When we trust Jesus as our Savior, his perfect life of righteousness is credited to our account in heaven.

Philippians 4:17 says that we have an account in heaven. This account has a debit column and a credit column. As unbelievers we had an account full of debits and no credits. Isaiah 64:6 says of all our righteous deeds were like dirty rags. This doesn't mean I had no righteous deeds. I did. That's why they were called righteous deeds. The problem is, these righteous deeds don't go into the credit column of our account in heaven. They're called rags by Isaiah because they're not acceptable to God. Why? Because they were produced by my own human energy and strength. They were deeds of human righteousness and not divine righteousness.

Another way to put this is that all of our righteous deeds cannot open the gates of heaven. When Bill Gates claims he does not believe in God, let alone Christ, and gives a billion dollars to help the problem of AIDS in Africa, that is most certainly a righteous deed. But that righteous deed would not open the gates of heaven for him. It does not go into the credit column of his account. Why? Because to get into heaven we have to be perfect.

That's what Jesus says in the Sermon on the Mount (Matt 5:48). Anything short of perfection will not do. There's not a great scale in the sky on which God will put our debits on one side and our credits on the other side and accept us if our credits outweigh our debits. No, just one sin is one too many. That's why when Satan committed one sin in heaven, he had to go. He was cast out of heaven.

So that leaves us with a big problem. The Bible says that all men fall short of the glory of God, which includes his perfect holiness. These sins go into our debit column. In order for us to go to heaven we need two things: we need to have the debits swept away, and we need to have a life of perfect righteousness. Since none of us can live the life of perfect righteousness, we must look to another.

Only Jesus Christ lived a perfect life, and when we trust in his work for us on the cross, our sins are wiped away because he took our sins upon himself. But, secondly, his perfect life is credited to our account. That's divine righteousness. When this is credited to our account, we have a new standing before God. Our new position is in Christ. And since we are in Christ, we are seated at the right hand of God the Father in heavenly places (Col 3:1-3). And nothing can separate us from the love of God in Christ Jesus (Rom 8:39).

We have entitled this book *Position/Condition*. Our proposition is that nothing in your **Condition** can ever change your **Position**, but if we focus on our **Position** it can drastically improve our **Condition**. When we make a mistake in our **Condition**, we desperately need to know this does not change our **Position**. We are secure in Christ.

As I mentioned earlier, my older daughter adopted two children from Russia (2002). God continues to reveal to me his outrageous love for us through my adopted grandchildren. For example, my daughter is a strict disciplinarian when it comes to table manners, much more strict than we were with her. I remember visiting their home once when the adopted children from Russia were about four years old (adopted at nine months and seven months from two different orphanages).

In their home, one of the disciplines is to be put into "time out." So while we were eating dinner, little four-year-old Drew was misbehaving with his mashed potatoes. My daughter, Christie, warned him once, then warned him again, and then sent him to "time out." Drew cried and was embarrassed, but no harm/no foul. It was a teaching experience.

But I thought to myself how weird it would be if Scott, my son-in-law, picked him up after his misbehavior, shook him, and said, "Drew, if you do that one more time, we're going to send you back to the orphanage in Russia, right where you came from." You say, how ridiculous. And I agree. But how much more ridiculous for our heavenly Father to take us out of our **Position** in Christ when we sin and send us back to our **Position** in Adam. It's not going to happen.

So we are talking here about the imputed righteousness that is part of our **Position** in Christ. This is also part of our breastplate of righteousness. On one side there is the imputed righteousness of our **Position** in Christ. On the other side of this breastplate is our personal righteousness, which is part of our **Condition** on Earth. And here I want to show you how the breastplate and the belt are connected or how there is a connection between our personal righteousness and truth.

When I am operating either as a stealth Christian or a hypocrite, then I am trying to hide either my identity (the stealth Christian) or my deeds (the hypocrite). In either case, I am operating under the cover of darkness. The Christian walking in darkness but claiming to be close to Jesus is a liar and does not practice the truth (1 Jn 1:6). Satan wins. We are liars like him.

But when I walk in the light (neither a stealth Christian nor hypocrite) as he is in the light, then the blood of his Son Jesus cleanses me from all sin (1 Jn 1:7). When we rationalize our unrighteous acts or attitudes, our consciences will convict us. If we wish to continue in sin, we must try to wipe away that which is the cause of our conviction (the truth)—"if we say we have no sin, we deceive ourselves, and the truth is not in us" (1 Jn 1:8). The consequence of being in darkness is that we begin to lie against the truth. We may rationalize it, we may deny it, or we may redefine the truth. In any case, we are going to try to expunge the truth.

Let's look at another example in Scripture that shows a connection between truth and righteousness. In Romans 1:16, we get this great thematic statement about the power of the gospel to bring salvation to all men. In it the righteousness of God is revealed from heaven. And Romans is a great book to show how the word righteousness is useful for our **Position** (4:3) and our **Condition** (6:13). The perfect righteousness of Christ credited to our **Position** in Christ is to be worked out as personal righteousness in our **Condition**. As that happens we become reflectors of God's grace and his glory.

But in Romans 1:18 and following, Paul describes another scenario. He claims that the wrath of God is revealed from heaven against all men who suppress the truth in unrighteousness. Do you see the connection between truth and righteousness? When the truth is suppressed, unrighteousness is sure to follow. Without any absolute truths, there is no standard for morality.

A youth pastor shared the following story. A couple of teenagers were dating and came to one of the youth Bible studies. After the study they went to the youth pastor and said, "What if we don't believe in heaven or hell? What if we don't believe God even exists?" The youth pastor said, "Well, I'd like to discuss that with you because it tells me a lot about your relationship." They replied, "What does it tell you about our relationship?" The pastor said, "Well, I do want to go into it, but I think we better do it in my office where there is more privacy."

So they made an appointment and came to his office and said, "Okay, what can you tell us about our relationship?" The youth pastor answered, "From what you said about God and heaven and hell I can tell that you're probably sexually involved." The couple was shocked and retorted defensively, "How can you tell that from what we said about God?" The youth pastor replied, "Because whatever you're doing in your relationship is causing you to deny God, the Bible, and any kind of ultimate accountability, especially on a spiritual level. That's what happens when you develop a sensual focus. If you let it keep going, you will wind up with what Romans 1:28 calls a 'reprobate mind,' that is, a mind that cannot tell right from wrong."

Bill Gothard lists the following steps as a typical path toward a reprobate mind:[210]

---

210   Bill Gothard, *Institute on Basic Youth Conflicts*, Dallas, TX, 1970.

1. **SENSUAL FOCUS**—"Love not the world or the things in the world . . . for all that is in the world—the lust of the flesh, the lust of the eyes, and the pride of life—is not of the Father but as of the world" (1 Jn 2:15-16). A sensual focus leads to,

2. **AWAKENING OF GUILT**—"Who show the work of the law written in their hearts, their conscience also bearing witness, . . . their thoughts accusing or else excusing them" (Rom 2:15). The next step is . . .

3. **WRONG RESPONSE TO GUILT**—"if we say we have no sin, we deceive ourselves, and the truth is not in us" (1 Jn 1:8). Now we experience . . .

4. **FRUSTRATION OVER SLAVERY TO SIN**—"I see another law in my members, warring against the law of my mind, and bringing me into captivity to the law of sin which is in my members. O wretched man that I am!" (Rom 7:23-24). This leads to . . .

5. **REDEFINING MORALITY**—there is a continuous mental effort to justify personal moral behavior based on the existing moral code. The code is "reinterpreted" to include as "moral" what was previously immoral. "Every man did that which was right in his own eyes" (Judges 17:6). The result of redefining morality is . . .

6. **REJECTION OF THE BIBLE AND/OR GOD**—"God also gave them up to uncleanness, and the lust of their hearts, to dishonor their bodies among themselves, who exchanged the truth of God for the lie" (Rom 1:24-25). The end result is . . .

7. **THE REPROBATE MIND**—"And even as they did not like to retain God in their knowledge, God gave them over to a debased mind [a reprobate mind—one that cannot

tell right from wrong], to do those things which are not fitting, being filled with all unrighteousness, sexual immorality, . . . haters of God, violent, proud, boasters, inventors of evil things, disobedient to parents, and is undiscerning, untrustworthy, unloving, unforgiving, unmerciful . . ." (Rom 1:28-31).

Too many of us know people or even children in our own families who have gone down this path, initially sucked in by a sensual focus on this world, but ultimately utterly lacking the ability to tell right from wrong. Do you see the connection between truth and righteousness? Let's turn our attention to the belt of truth.

II. BELT OF TRUTH

A. Personal Truth—my Integrity

Once self-deception sets in, the deception of others is not far behind. Before long we become like the people during the time of the Judges, where every man does what's right in his own eyes. That's just modern existentialism with its focus on personal experience. "What's right for you is not necessarily right for me." My son-in-law lives in Austin, Texas. He belongs to a reading group in which he is the only believer in Christ. He says he cannot remember how many times he has heard his contemporaries say, "What's right for you is not necessarily what's right for me."

This is just a form of rebellion—rejection of any authority external to one's self. That being the case, what can be said about the Bible, a book full of propositional truth?

B. Propositional Truth—the Bible

If there is no authority external to myself, than that nixes the Bible as ultimate or final truth. And without any final truth, there is no external authority. Therefore I'm free to become:

1. An **Existentialist**—truth is what I experience to be real

2. A **Pragmatist**—truth is what works best for society (John Dewy)

3. A **Nihilist**—there is no truth or meaning of the universe

With all due respect to his musical genius, John Lennon might make a good study in the development of a nihilist. According to his biographer Philip Johnson,[211] Lennon spent most of his life wrestling with a wounded spirit. He was told by his mother Julian that his father abandoned him when he was a small child (though in reality it was more the other way around). Then his mother had two illegitimate children, and her sister, Mimi, more or less adopted him (though not legally).

So he felt abandoned by his father and his mother. The pain of this was still with him long after the Beatles partnership dissolved. It showed up conspicuously in the lyrics of one of the last songs he ever wrote called "Mother": "Mother, you had me . . . but I never had you; father, you left me . . . but I never left you."[212]

By the time he was a teenager, Lennon was an accomplished liar, thief, and burgeoning sex addict. After getting his girlfriend pregnant and marrying her, he had several secret affairs and innumerable one night stands. Even after his marriage to his true love Yoko Ono he continued his promiscuity. Then there was his attempt to drown out his wounded spirit with alcohol. John was an angry drunk that started fights and destroyed property in his fury. Marijuana, cocaine, heroine, even LSD couldn't transport him to a make-believe world where he could find inner peace and joy.

Lennon even gave spiritualism a try with the Maharishi Yoga by traveling to his ashram in Rishikesh on the Ganges. But he gave

---

211 Philip Johnson, *John Lennon: The Life* (HarperCollins e-books, 2008).

212 John Lennon, https://www.youtube.com/watch?v=eDVkkwl6aJo, accessed September 8, 2016.

this up when he found sexual and financial improprieties running rampant in the ashram. Finally, he thought he found his salvation in primal scream therapy.[213] He moved from New York to L.A. to pursue a reenactment of his childhood pain by releasing the negative emotions caused by his psychological trauma. During this therapy John "learned" that there is no such thing as God or any Judgment Day, and certainly no such places as heaven and hell. His arrival as a nihilist appears in the words of his most famous song "Imagine": "Imagine there's no heaven; it's easy if you try; no hell below us, above us only sky ... Imagine there's no countries ... And no religion too ..." Ironically, it was that same song that Mark David Chapman used as his excuse for his hatred of Lennon and motivation to kill him. "Imagine no possessions ... Imagine all the people sharing all the world ..." Chapman thought Lennon himself was a hypocrite and had deceived his followers by accumulating multiple homes and wealth.

According to Bill Gothard, here are the symptoms of a wounded spirit:[214]

1. **COMMUNICATION BREAKDOWN.** In a home where a child has a wounded spirit and is still living with his parents this can manifest itself in something as simple as silence at the dinner table. The child is afraid to open up for fear of being wounded again. This leads to ...

2. **UNGRATEFULLNESS.** Now there is an alienation of affection as the child weighs the benefits his parents provide against their offenses. If the offenses outweigh the benefits, gratitude turns into entitlement. The child reasons that he is entitled to whatever benefits his parents

---

213 https://en.wikipedia.org/wiki/Primal_therapy, accessed on September 12, 2016.

214 Gothard, *Institute.*

have to offer since they, after all, are responsible for bringing him into the world. The results of this kind of thinking is . . .

3. **STUBBORNNESS.** There is a rejection of authority, at home, at school, or in the community. The child doesn't follow through on chores or obey the rules of society. Now there is . . .

4. **OPEN REBELLION.** Usually by now the child is a teenager. He establishes himself as the ultimate authority for his own life. And he looks around for friends of a similar stripe.

5. **WRONG FRIENDS.** Rebels are drawn to those of a like spirit. A compatibility of rebellion develops. The rebel pack looks for ways to flaunt their self-authority. The power of like-minded people helps them in their . . .

6. **DEFENSE OF SENSUALITY.** Now there is a fulfillment of their sensual desires. They defend this groupthink by saying, "Everyone's doing it." In reality, not everyone is doing it, so now there is a . . .

7. **CONDEMNATION OF OTHERS.** The group turns its focus on the hypocrites they hear or read about, especially falling religious leaders or crooked government officials. But within them is a deep sense of guilt. The drugs and alcohol can't seem to remove the stain of their immorality. And unresolved guilt leads to . . .

8. **DEPRESSION.** Sometimes the depression becomes clinical, and thoughts of suicide follow the thoughts of one who can see no reason for living, no purpose for his life, and no hope for improvement in the future.

Do you see the connection between the belt and the breastplate, between truth and righteousness? It's a vicious circle: when truth goes, righteousness goes; and when righteousness goes, truth goes.

We have been describing the defeat of the Christian soldier. How does it happen? It begins when the devil knocks the sword out of his hand, which is the Word of God. Without his sword the soldier loses his only offensive weapon, so now the devil goes for the helmet of salvation: we lose the assurance of where we will spend eternity because we have set aside the promises of God contained in his Word. And if the devil can make us doubt our salvation, he can destroy our faith. That's our shield. With the shield out of the way the devil is ready to attack our inner armor. Once we doubt the faith, we stop witnessing. We don't have a ready answer for the hope that's within us because it's no longer within us. And without any moral compass, our breastplate of righteousness is easily pierced. The result? We begin to suppress the truth in unrighteousness. That's the devil's plan for our defeat.

But Paul has something quite different in mind, doesn't he? He wants us to build up our defense from the inside out. It starts with truth. When we accept the Bible as a revelation from the Creator of the entire universe, then we accept his propositions as absolute truth: you shall not steal; you shall not commit adultery; you shall not lie. These are propositional truths. Accepting them is the foundation of our defense against the devil.

Once we have been grounded in the principles of **Position** and **Condition**, we have a story to tell. Our open confession of Christ is part of our defense. Because we're not stealth Christians we are walking in the light. And as we walk in the light, the blood of Jesus Christ keeps on cleansing us from all sin (1 John 1:7).

Then we're ready for our outer armor beginning with our shield of faith. And only through the Christian faith do we find the assurance of our salvation. As we study more about our faith, the Word of God becomes a sword in our hand. We can use it just like Jesus did when he countered the temptations of the devil by quoting Scripture.

CONCLUSION

So, let's review the progression once again. Once religion and faith are isolated onto the "top story" of values, then objectivity is thrown out the door. After all, all things objective are verifiable and belong on the bottom story. Faster than a bullfrog catching a fly with its tongue, the door to existentialism opens and swallows morality. Existentialism rejects absolute truth. What is true for me may not be true for you. Without absolute truth there is no basis for morality because there is no standard of measure. Once morality goes, righteousness is sure to follow.

Margaret Sanger exemplifies the connection between truth and righteousness. The founder of Planned Parenthood, Sanger was also a white supremacist that practiced eugenics on African-Americans by setting up sterilization clinics in their neighborhoods. Some statistics indicate Sanger's influence led to the sterilization of as many as 60,000 people nationwide, most of whom were African-Americans.[215] But while she was preaching eugenics, Sanger also preached the gospel of sexual liberation.

In Sanger's mind, Christian morality was the great evil of society because it suppressed our natural desires for promiscuous sex with multiple partners. She thought sexual liberation was the only way to find "inner peace and security and beauty."[216] All the while Sanger was preaching the beauty of sex without strings, her abortion clinics were wiping out what could be considered a generation of African-Americans. The second greatest cause of death in the African-American community post 1973 has been heart disease (2,715,416). The leading cause? Abortion (15,500,000 and

---

215 https://en.wikipedia.org/wiki/Eugenics_in_the_United_States, accessed September 21, 2016.

216 Margaret Sanger, *The Pivot of Civilization* (New York, NY: Brentano's, 1922), 232.

counting).[217] Pastor Clenard Childress says, "The most dangerous place for an African-American is in the womb."[218]

Fast forward from the beginning of Sanger's gospel of sexual liberation to the college campus of today. As of 2001 there were courses where the students studied pornographic films and were encouraged to make their own "selfie" porn films.[219] And the "hook-up" culture encourages sexual engagement as a filter to help couples decide if they want to go ahead and start dating.

Can you see it? Slowly but surely when one suppresses the truth in unrighteousness (Rom 1:19), a mind that cannot tell right from wrong (Rom 1:28) is not far behind. Do you think what is true for an individual could also be true for a nation?

---

217 http://www.blackgenocide.org/black.html, accessed September 21, 2016.

218 Ibid.

219 David Abel, "Porn Is Hot Course on Campus: Professors Seek Meaning Behind Flourishing Market," *Boston Globe* (August 20, 2001).

28

ARMED AND DANGEROUS
Part 6
Critical Mass
Ephesians 6:18-20

INTRODUCTION

In its original use "critical mass" simply referred to the amount of uranium necessary to sustain an uncontrolled chain reaction, otherwise known as a nuclear explosion, or an atomic bomb. A nuclear bomb better describes what happens in that it is the energy released when the nuclei of U235 are split that creates the explosion.

It was actually a woman named Lise Meitner that proved the uranium nucleus splits when bombarded by an outside neutron. But she was Jewish and had to flee to Stockholm after her partner of twenty years, Otto Hahn, got her fired from a German research facility because she was not Aryan. Hahn received the Nobel prize in chemistry in 1944 for work originated, directed, and completed by Meitner.

About the same time Leo Szilard and Enrico Fermi proved that a controlled chain reaction was possible in their laboratory at the University of Chicago.[220] They surrounded the uranium with enough graphite that the streaming neutrons released by fission were absorbed by the graphite so that an uncontrolled chain reaction could not take place. Without this absorbent material and with enough uranium they could create an uncontrolled chain reaction. But how much was enough? That amount would be called the "critical mass," and initially no one knew how much that was.

The Hungarian Jews who had immigrated to America knew that Werner Heisenberg of Germany knew more than they and was three years ahead of them in nuclear physics. They were afraid the Nazi war machine would produce an atomic bomb first and rule the world. So, the ISI (precursor to the CIA) recruited an eccentric genius named Mo Berg to find out how far along the Germans were. Berg was so smart they had him on a radio quiz show and never stumped him.[221] He seemed to absorb languages like a sponge absorbs water. He was also a Jew and a professional baseball player that graduated with honors from Princeton.

So how would an American Jew find out how much the Germans knew about the atomic bomb in the midst of World War II? Well, it just so happened that Heisenberg was going to give a lecture in Vienna. The Allies parachuted Mo Berg behind enemy lines with the instructions to attend the lecture while posing as a graduate student. He carried a poison pill in his pocket. All he knew about nuclear physics came from coaching by Albert Einstein. With this limited knowledge he had to listen to Heisenberg's lecture and decide if the Germans were about to have the atomic bomb. If the answer was yes, he was to pull out a gun in the midst of the lecture, shoot Heisenberg until he was dead, and then swallow the poison pill for God and country.

---

220 William Lanouette, *Genius in the Shadows* (Skyhorse Publishing, 2013).

221 Nicholas Dawidoff, *The Catcher was a Spy* (Pantheon Books, 1994).

I'm really not sure why Hollywood hasn't made a movie of this. At any rate, Berg couldn't decide from the lecture if the Germans had the bomb. So he walked with Heisenberg from the lecture hall back to his hotel. After conversing with him one-on-one in high German, Berg was convinced the Germans didn't have the bomb.

This left Oppenheimer and the Manhattan Project with the task of figuring out how much uranium or plutonium was needed for critical mass. It was finally determined the critical mass was a ball of uranium about the size of a softball, about one kilogram in weight. All they had to do to create the explosion was to keep the two halves of the ball apart until they wanted the bomb to go off. Then they could slam the two halves together to form the critical mass and an atomic explosion would take place.

Surprisingly, these physical laws of the universe parallel the laws of spiritual warfare. Oh, the results may not be instantaneous, but the principles for a spiritual explosion are there, nonetheless, and they're found in our final lesson on spiritual warfare in Ephesians 6:18-20. This lesson is about prayer. Prayer is the missing element in the lives of many Christian soldiers. Without it, our spiritual weapons will never reach "critical mass." But when the Christian combines the Word of God with prayer, get ready for a spiritual explosion. In these verses we want to look at three things: the principle of critical mass, praying for a critical mass, and the purpose of critical mass

I. PRINCIPLE OF CRITICAL MASS   17-18

And *take* the helmet of salvation, and the sword of the Spirit, which is the word of God; *praying* always with all prayer and supplication in the Spirit, being watchful to this end with all perseverance and supplication for all the saints . . .

We have underscored two verbs in these verses. Even though we have already talked about the helmet of salvation and the sword of the Spirit, we need to show that verse 18 modifies verse 17. I don't want to get too hung up in grammar, but now and then it is very important. The main point of this lesson is the connection between the verb "take" of verse 17 and the participle "praying" of verse 18. Grammatically, the participle modifies the main verb, that is, "praying" modifies "take." These are not two independent actions. We might say the moment we take up the sword of the Spirit we begin to pray. Praying is something we should be doing while we brandish our sword and head into battle. It too is an offense weapon. When the sword and prayer are combined, quite often critical mass is achieved. Let's look at some examples.

In Genesis 15 Abram has proven himself faithful. He left most of his support system in Ur to go to a land he had never seen. He went around the land of Canaan building altars to the one true God in a place where they worshiped many gods. He rescued Lot, his nephew. He paid a tithe to Melchizedek, God's king-priest from Salem or Jerusalem. He resisted temptation from the king of Sodom. So God decides to reward him. Genesis 15:1 says "the word of the Lord" came to Abram in a vision. The "word of the Lord" is the word of God before the Bible was written. God promises Abram that his descendants will be more numerous than the stars he can see.

Abram believes God's promise, so he thinks he and his wife Sarah will have a child. They try to conceive as husband and wife. But years go by with no pregnancy. So Abram cooks up a scheme to help God fulfill his promise. He takes Hagar as his wife. He thinks God is going to fulfill his promise by giving a child to Hagar. But in Genesis 17 God makes it clear to Abram that Ishmael is not the fulfillment of his promise. Rather Sarah will bear a son to Abram and his name will be called Isaac.

Finally, in Genesis 20 Abram is broken. Another scheme of his has gone awry. To save his own skin he passes Sarah off as his sister. Abimelech takes Sarah and puts her in his harem. God does a miracle to keep her from being compromised. And now Abraham prays. This is the first time in the long story of Abraham's life that prayer is mentioned. We don't know that this is the first time he prayed, but it is the first time any prayer of Abraham is recorded in Scripture. And immediately after he prays Genesis 21:1 says, "And the Lord visited Sarah **as He had said**, and the Lord did for Sarah **as He had spoken.**"

Is it a coincidence that after Abraham prayed God did what he promised? God's Promise + Prayer = Critical Mass. Boom. A spiritual explosion. A miracle.

Here's another one. When we get to Daniel 9, Daniel is an old man. He has been captive in Babylon for sixty-eight years. Neither he or his people had any idea if any of them would get to go back to Jerusalem. Suddenly a great gift comes from Jerusalem. It's from the weeping prophet, Jeremiah. It's a copy of his book. Daniel can hardly believe it. He can't put the book down. All of a sudden when he's halfway through the book, his eyes feast on these words: "seventy years" (Jer 25:11). Here is God's Word telling Daniel that the Babylonian captivity will be seventy years long. Sixty-eight of those years have already gone by. He's getting excited. He reads faster and faster. "Tell me more, Lord." And when he gets to Jeremiah 29, he reads this:

> For thus says the Lord: After seventy years are completed at Babylon, I will visit you and perform My good word toward you, and cause you to return to this place. [11] For I know the thoughts that I think toward you, says the Lord, thoughts of peace and not of evil, to give you a future and a hope. [12] Then you will call upon Me and go and pray to Me, and I will listen to you. [13] And you will seek Me and find *Me*, when you search for Me with all your heart. [14] I will be found by you, says the Lord, and I will bring you back from your captivity; I will gather you from all the nations and from all the places where I have driven you, says the Lord, and I will bring you to the place from which I cause you to be carried away captive.

Oh, my gosh. He can hardly believe his eyes. There were no bifocals in those days, so Daniel really has to squint to read these marvelous words which fall upon him like a refreshing spring rain in the midst of a desert place. So what does he do? Does he run around yelling and screaming, telling everyone within earshot that the release of the Jews is just two years away? No. Daniel 9 tells us what he does:

> I, Daniel, understood by the books the number of the years *specified* by the word of the Lord through Jeremiah the prophet, that He would accomplish seventy years in the desolations of Jerusalem.
> ³ Then I set my face toward the Lord God to make request by prayer and supplications, with fasting, sackcloth, and ashes. ⁴ And I prayed to the Lord my God, and made confession, and said, . . .

As soon as he sees the promise, he begins to pray. God's Promise + Prayer = Critical Mass. The Lord sets his people free.

How about the New Testament example? Okay. Let's go to Acts 1:4:

> And being assembled together with *them*, He commanded them not to depart from Jerusalem, but to wait for the Promise of the Father, "which," *He said*, "you have heard from Me; ⁵ for John truly baptized with water, but you shall be baptized with the Holy Spirit not many days from now."

Notice the word "promise." The "Promise of the Father" was that the Holy Spirit will be sent to them. So what do they do? The disciples go into an upper room and begin to pray for the coming of the Spirit, and what happens? God's Promise + Prayer = Critical Mass. Boom. A spiritual explosion. The church was born. So many people were coming to Christ it shook up the whole city.

II. PRAYING FOR CRITICAL MASS   18

. . . praying always with all prayer and supplication in the Spirit, being watchful to this end with all perseverance and supplication for all the saints . . .

We have to be clear here. We are going to list five principles we see in the text. But this is no formula for answered prayer. Christianity is not magic. We cannot go through a prayer punch list and make a supernatural God obey us. Lists like this can easily turn into legalism, meaning if I perform this checklist in my prayers, then God has to give me what I asked for. No, again that would be a form of legalism, and that is to put God in my debt by doing good things. God will never be indebted to us; we will always be indebted to him. Now, with that disclaimer let's look at these five principles that can help achieve critical mass.

A. Pray Opportunistically.

"Always" = *en panti kairō* = at all times = whenever there is an opportunity. Interpreters are kind of across the board on the meaning of the word *kairō*. The word usually refers to time, so some interpreters think it just means pray all the time, kind of like 1 Thessalonians 5:17 where it says, "Pray without ceasing." That's usually interpreted to mean like a hacking cough. "Consistently" might capture the idea, just as Daniel consistently prayed three times a day.

Another interpretation is that *kairō* means at every "opportunity." Pray opportunistically. In other words, we have a personal relationship with Jesus, and as we go through the day we are in steady communion with him, or what we call "fellowship." A need may present itself. We may pray right at that moment, or we may pray as soon as we have an opportunity.

Even a third interpretation may fit here. The phrase could mean "in critical situations." One of our church mission trips faced a critical situation recently. A group from our church was headed for the Dominican Republic. Actually, half the group was already there and coming back, while the second half was getting ready to go. Then one of our torrential rainstorms hit Houston. It looked like the flight would be canceled. It didn't look like there will be another flight out for a day or two, which would really bugger in the whole trip.

So one of our leaders went to the ticket desk to appeal. He was told that the group of twenty-eight could wait around if they wanted to, but there were fifty people on standby in front of them. So he went back to the team and said they probably weren't going to make this flight. One of the young people going on the trip asked, "Why don't we pray?" So they all got in a circle and prayed. You already know how this is going to turn out. With ten minutes to go a ticket agent came to them and said, "There's good news and bad news. The good news first: all twenty-eight of you get to go. Now for the bad news: you can't take your luggage with you. We'll have to deliver that later." So with great rejoicing that's what they did. It was actually two or three days later that they got their luggage, but they were just happy to be there.

So I don't know exactly what this phrase means. To cover the bases, let's pray consistently, opportunistically, and in critical situations.

B. Pray Fervently.

"**All prayer and supplication.**" So what is this? What does "all prayer" mean? Is there partial prayer? Well, about the best we can do with this is to see a contrast here with the rote prayers repeated by the Pharisees on the street corners. Before I became a believer I went to church at my girlfriend's church. They used *The Book of Common Prayer*. My girlfriend's father was the priest. Maybe it was because she grew up with it, I don't really know, but I think she had that book memorized. She could say those prayers from memory with her eyes open or closed or crossed. But it was just empty recitation. She told me Christianity didn't mean much to her. This seems to be saying, if you're going to pray, put your heart into it. Ask for the same thing over and over if you want, but say it fifty different ways. I am exaggerating, but the point is, don't turn your request into a vain repetition.

C. Pray Spiritually.

"**In the Spirit**" is not a reference to speaking in tongues. Paul has already told us not everyone will speak in tongues (1 Cor 12:30). But everyone is supposed to and can pray. The words he uses here are actually the same words that he used in Ephesians 5:18—*en pneumati*.

This particular construction is translated like an adverb: "spiritually." This could mean to pray for spiritual things instead of material things. But that is unlikely because Jesus told us to pray for our daily bread. More than likely it means to pray according to God's will instead of our own.

D. Pray Alertly.

"**Watching**." We immediately think of the Garden of Gethsemane. The disciples had trouble staying awake for just an hour. Well, let's not be so hard on the disciples. When is the last time you prayed for an hour straight. Prayer is hard work. I don't know if you're like me, but my mind wanders off very quickly when I am praying. And it's easy for me to drift off. That's not being watchful in prayer. If we fall asleep on our watch, the enemy can storm the gates with a surprise attack. So I do little things to help me stay awake. One of them is prayer position. I have learned that praying on my knees helps me stay awake. It's just uncomfortable enough that when my mind wanders, my knee started hurting, and I ask myself what I am doing in this uncomfortable position. Then I remember that I'm praying, and I get back to prayer. Another way, if you are a walker or a jogger, is to take a prayer list with you. It's unlikely we will fall asleep while we are jogging or walking. Find what works for you. The point is to stay awake.

E. Pray Persistently.

"**Perseverance**." Don't quit praying. I have used this illustration in another book,[222] but for those who have not read that book, this is the best illustration I know about perseverance in prayer.

Some years ago retired Col. Heath Bottomly gave the commencement address at Dallas Seminary—May 1980. He wanted to talk about something that happened to him in WWII, so he brought out

---

222 David R. Anderson, *Triumph Through Trials* (The Woodlands, TX: Grace Theology Press, 2013), 255-58.

two journals, journals which he had written day by day during the war, one from 1944 and the other from 1945. He read several excerpts from these two journals. The first one was dated Nov 7, 1944. He said, "Two men joined our squadron today, one of them a handsome aristocratic dude from New York, the Tyrone Power of the army, I decided to call him. He seemed to be a nice fella, but I couldn't talk with him. He spoke Long Gisland, and I couldn't understand a word. I was assigned to him as his check-out officer, and I thought, "Wow, will this ever be a disaster. We won't be able to communicate."

Bottomly's next entry was from a week later, Nov 14, 1944. "I really like this guy from New York. His name is Marshall Edward Kyle, III. He carries a Bible with him and he prays, if you can believe this, before he takes off each time. He says God has a plan for our lives, and some day he wants to share that plan with me." At that time Bottomly was not a Christian. The next entry is from January 1945. They were stationed in Hilandia, New Guinea. The entry read:

We lost two pilots today. One of those pilots was my friend Marsh Kyle. He got separated from the others somehow, and we could see him coming in. There was a long, white plume of smoke streaming after his plane. As he got nearer, we could hear him say something about smoke in the cockpit and, "I can't see." The next thing we knew he had plunged straight into the cliff just short of the overrun of the runway.

Bottomly got a piece of guy rope and lowered himself down the cliff. It was an avalanche of torn metal, split rubber, 100 octane gas spread all over the cliff side, torching off everywhere. He looked and looked for Marsh's body, but couldn't find it. Sliding down the hill side were broken wings, pieces of metal, the broken canopy went by—everything was a mess.

Then a little further down the cliff, Bottomly saw a green piece of cloth that he thought might have been part of Marsh's overalls. He walked over to it and sure enough, looking down, he saw what was left of Marsh's body. Parts of all four of his limbs were gone. He was burned so badly, he looked like a huge, blackened marshmallow. He was worse than dead.

They took a rope, tied it around that gory mess and hauled it to the top. They got a cardboard box, stuffed his body in the box, put him on one of those gooney birds, and watched it take off for Brisbane, Australia, sending him to the graves quarters at the quarter masters station there in Brisbane. And that was the end of it.

Bottomly watched as his friends drove back from the airstrip in a jeep, but he walked back. And as he did so, he was screaming. "Why him, God? Why Marshall? Why him. Of all the men in this squadron, he is the only one who knew you and acted like it. Why him?" He said as he got back to his bunk, he decided to write Marshall's mother a letter. He described what happened, but when it got to the part about "Why," he left it blank, because he didn't know why.

Several years later, through various circumstances, Heath Bottomly became a Christian. He retired from the military, opened a retreat center in Colorado for young people. He had a son he named Rock. He went around the nation 250,000 miles per year raising funds for his retreat center. He wrote books and was a compulsive journalist. In 1980, October 20, Tuesday night, he was in Greenville, S. Carolina, finishing a mini-revival. At the end they invited everyone to come forward who had made a decision during the four days.

The pastor went to the back and Col. Bottomly was in the front signing autographs on his books, shaking hands. He said there was always some elderly woman there who wanted to know if he had known her son during the war. One lady was just hanging on to him, assuring him that he must certainly remember her son, and he was signing a book, and out of his peripheral vision he could tell there was a gap in the line after this woman. He kept on signing, and all of a sudden the gap was filled, but it was filled by someone rather short, not walking normally, and when the person was getting closer Bottomly noticed the pant legs were awfully thin. Then you could hear the click, click of metal knees. Then the on-comer bent forward and lunged toward Bottomly, grabbed him about the neck with metal pinchers, and it hurt. Bottomly asked himself, "What have I here?"

Then Bottomly looked up and straight into the angular, handsome face and the warm, grey eyes of Marshall Edward Kyle, III. You see, because of bad weather, the gooney bird was not able to land at Brisbane. They went on to Sydney, Australia, where the hospital for the casualties of war for American forces was centered. When they opened the cardboard box, it was a requirement to do a mirror test. They had to pass a mirror in front of the deceased's nose to make sure it did not fog. It fogged. Kyle was still alive. There was a Jewish doctor there who took him on a challenge. For three months he tried to straighten out a twisted torso, sewing, grafting, doing everything he possibly could to keep him alive. Of course, Marshall was not conscious.

Then they sent him to the great burn hospital in San Antonio, Texas, Brooks General Hospital, and for four years he was in a coma kept alive only by tubes and machines. One day a nurse was passing, saw his eyes flicker and open after four years in this coma. She cried for the other doctors. They worked with him for five more years before he could move along in a wheel chair. But Marshall Kyle persisted. He wanted to walk. He worked for another five years before, with the aid of prosthetics, he was able to walk. But he still had a problem. He couldn't talk. After ten more years with the work of a specialist, he learned to speak with the aid of a special device in his throat.

On October 20, 1980, in Greenville, S. Carolina, when these two war buddies grasped each other for the first time since the accident, Marshall Kyle was 60 years old, and he had just graduated from Furman University in that city. But that wasn't the end of it. He was headed to Duke Med School in order to receive training in how to help accident victims. He told in his raspy, electronic clatter, he was sorry he had never been able to explain God's special plan for Bottomly's life to him before the crash. But as he was going down, his last thought and last prayer were that Bottomly would become a Christian. And that was his first thought and his first prayer when he came out of his coma four years later. He continued praying for Bottomly when he had no proof that Bottomly himself had not been killed in the war.

Those prayers were answered. Does that tell you anything about the persistent, expectant, fervent prayer of a righteous man? Even more, does that tell you anything about the persistence of God? He did have a plan for Heath Bottomly's life. Heath's son, Rock, went to seminary, pastured several churches and presently is a senior fellow for Marriage and Leadership Studies at the Focus on the Family Institute. Generations of Christians and thousands of young people have been touched by the ripple effect of one prayer warrior who would not quit—Marshall Edward Kyle, III.

III. PURPOSE OF CRITICAL MASS   18-20

. . . for all the saints—[19] and for me, that utterance may be given to me, that I may open my mouth boldly to make known the mystery of the gospel, [20] for which I am an ambassador in chains; that in it I may speak boldly, as I ought to speak.

A. For the Servants of the Gospel

"**For all the saints and for me**"—for the troops and the generals; a single soldier will rarely win a battle; it takes an army, a band of brothers. Each has a unique role to play, but all can pray.

"**Boldly**"—our own fears are our greatest impediment to sharing the gospel. We are all afraid of rejection. And we are afraid of looking like fools or fanatics. So we all need prayer for boldness. As mentioned earlier, one of my privileges in life is to rub shoulders with Bob Tebow. This has nothing to do with his famous son. Bob and I were friends long before his son got famous. But one of the reasons I count it a privilege to know Bob Tebow is that some of his boldness rubs off on me. I have never met such a bold witness for Christ. In my college days I got to know Bill Bright, the founder of Campus Crusade for Christ. Some of you know the name Hal Lindsey. He taught me and scores of others how to witness on the beaches of California. But when it comes to boldness they all pale in comparison to Bob Tebow.

Let me give you an example. Bob did not get to fight in the Vietnam War. So one day he said, "I want to go to North Vietnam. I want to tell them about Christ." He convinced a friend to go with him. So they hopped on a plane and flew to Hanoi. Just out of the blue. Bob took a couple of suitcases full of children's toys and candies. They landed and went to their hotel. Then they took a cab to the equivalent of our White House. He looked at a soldier standing guard out front and said, "I'm Bob Tebow, and I am an American, and I want to talk to your President" (or whatever they called their political leader). The guard took him into the building and up to a receptionist. He told her who he was and his mission. She made a phone call and told him the President was occupied. So he asked for the Vice President and went on down the line.

Finally the military police showed up. They took Bob and his friend to a nearby interrogation room. One of the North Vietnamese look him in the eye and said, "Don't you know you can't do this kind of thing around here?" They continued to interrogate him, asking about his family, his job, his place of residence. Finally he looked at his interrogator and asked, "Do you have any children?" His interrogator wanted to know what that had to do with anything. Bob just opened one of his suitcases and gave the guy some chocolate candy for his children. Pretty soon a whole line formed of others that wanted gifts and candy for their kids. Bob never did talk to the President or the Vice President or the Secretary of State, but he witnessed to every person who came in for candy until his suitcase was empty. Are you kidding me? That's why I like to hangout with Bob Tebow. It's called boldness for the gospel.

B. For the Success of the Gospel

The reward for spiritual victory will be a gospel explosion.

CONCLUSION

It was Jonathan Edwards that said, "Ministry is reaping the spoils of battle from prayer." Edwards was one of the great preachers responsible for the Great Awakening in New England during the first half of the 18th Century. He was not only a revivalist preacher, he was also a Reformed theologian and a scholar. In fact, there are those who believe he was the greatest theological mind America ever produced.

When Edwards preached, he was far from a polished orator. He wrote his sermons out and read them to his congregation without looking up. Nevertheless, he delivered the best-known sermon ever heard in our country. The title of the sermon is "Sinners in the Hands of an Angry God." As I printed it out from the Internet, it is nine pages single-spaced. Here is an excerpt from that sermon:

The God that holds you over the pit of hell, much as one holds a spider, or some loathsome insect, over the fire, abhors you, and is dreadfully provoked; his wrath towards you burns like fire; he looks upon you as worthy of nothing else, but to be cast into the fire; he is of purer eyes than to bear to have you in his sight; you are ten thousand times so abominable in his eyes as the most hateful venomous serpent is in ours.

You have offended him infinitely more than ever a stubborn rebel did his prince: and yet 'tis nothing but his hand that holds you from falling into the fire every moment; 'tis to be ascribed to nothing else, that you did not go to hell the last night; that you was suffered to awake again in this world, after you closed your eyes to sleep: and there is no other reason to be given why you have not dropped into hell since you arose in the morning, but that God's hand has held you up; there is no other reason to be given why you han't gone to hell since you have sat here in the house of God, provoking his pure eyes by your sinful wicked manner of attending his solemn worship: yea, there is nothing else that is to be given as a reason why you don't this very moment drop down into hell.

O sinner! Consider the fearful danger you are in: 'tis a great furnace of wrath, a wide and bottomless pit, full of the fire of wrath, that you are held over in the hand of that God, whose wrath is provoked and incensed as much against you as against many of the damned in hell; you hang by a slender thread, with the flames of divine wrath flashing about it, and ready every moment to singe it, and burn it asunder; and you have no interest in any mediator, and nothing to lay hold of to save yourself, nothing to keep off the flames of wrath, nothing of your own, nothing that you ever have done, nothing that you can do, to induce God to spare you one moment.[223]

Not exactly a sermon that focuses on the love of God. Once when Edwards looked up at the congregation whole rows of people were clutching the back of the pews in front of them. One man stood up and yelled, "Please stop reading preacher. Please stop reading." I'm guessing this wasn't a Seeker Sensitive Sermon. Yet what most people don't know is that before and after the sermon there was a twenty-four hour prayer vigil by his closest friends for the spiritual impact of this message. Yes, history would show without doubt . . . the preacher and the prayers achieved "critical mass."

---

223 Jonathan Edwards [1739], *Sermons and Discourses, 1739-1742 (WJE Online Vol. 22)*, Ed. Harry S. Stout [word count] [jec-wjeo22].

29

GOD BLESS

Ephesians 6:23-24

INTRODUCTION

Some years ago I cut an article out of the paper entitled "So you think you had it rough?" It tells the story of Roy Reep, who began his streak of bad cards at age three when his brother accidentally shot him in the face with a .38. "The bullet went through the roof of my mouth and knocked off the whole side of my face," said Reep. Six years later a friend pushed him off a barrel. When Roy hit the ground, his head split open. At age eleven, Roy's father accidentally hit him in the head while chopping wood. Two years later doctors operated to correct a sinus infection. They found two teeth lodged in his nose, apparently from the shooting ten years earlier.

Roy then spent sixteen years without a major mishap, until he decided to enter the ministry. While driving to seminary in Greensboro, a car wreck maimed his body by breaking both hips and his pelvic bone, puncturing his kidney and rupturing his bladder. He lay in a hospital bed for forty-two days as his organs healed. And then doctors put him in a full-length body cast to give his bones a chance to mend.

Before reaching middle age, Roy married, but this didn't improve his luck. His wife accidentally shot him in the right side of his chest and his arm. Three years later a doctor discovered one of the bullets lodged in his chest and cut it out. Then while climbing a ladder to work on his roof, the top rung broke. You guessed it. Roy fell and hit on his head and neck. He spent the next year in bed. Then, seven years later he had a cataract operation. But in the midst of the procedure, a vein burst in his left eye, leaving him blind in that eye.

Since then Reep has been diagnosed a diabetic and suffering from a nerve injury to his hand. And then while taking out his dentures, he noticed a piece of bone protruding from his mouth. It turned out to be another tooth and a chunk of jawbone stretching all the way back to the shooting at age three.

It would be easy to assume that Roy Reep would be a bitter man. But looking back over his life he can only marvel at how God has kept him alive through all his troubles. "I feel blessed by God. My life could've been taken away by any one of those tragedies. God's hand wasn't behind the trigger or the axe or the driver of the car that hit us, and yet he chose to preserve my life and allow me to minister and have a full life. I'm a blessed man."

Christians often like to say, "God bless," when finishing a conversation or leaving a social setting. I have often wondered what we have in mind when we invoke God's blessing on someone. What does it mean to be blessed by God? When we compliment someone on how well their children have turned out or how well they have done in business, they sometimes reply, "Well, God has surely blessed us." Or in regard to their physical well being someone might say, "I have been blessed with good health."

In all my days as a Christian I don't think I have ever heard a Christian say, "God has blessed me with a huge financial loss." Or, "God has blessed me with bad health." Our understanding of the word "blessing" is much more narrow than the biblical view. James 1:12 says, "Blessed is the man who endures trial." Matthew 5:10 says,

"Blessed are those who are persecuted because of righteousness," and 5:11 says, "Blessed are you when they reproach you and persecute you and say all kinds of evil things about you for my sake."

But even incorporating trials and difficulties into our circle of blessing is too narrow—much too narrow. The greatest blessings of all, according to Ephesians, are the spiritual blessings, not the physical blessings. Paul starts out the book thanking God for these blessings. And he winds up the book with three blessings that more or less review the landscape of all that he has covered: the blessing of peace, the blessing of love, and the blessing of grace.

> [23] Peace to the brethren, and love with faith, from God the Father and the Lord Jesus Christ. [24] Grace *be* with all those who love our Lord Jesus Christ in sincerity. Amen.

I. THE BLESSING OF PEACE   23

A. Peace in our Position   2:11-18

> But now in Christ Jesus you who once were far off have been brought near by the blood of Christ.[14] For He Himself is our peace, who has made both one, and has broken down the middle wall of separation, [15] having abolished in His flesh the enmity . . .

"In Christ"—these are the words that signal positional truth. Way back in chapter two Paul discussed about enmity on two levels: 1) between mankind and God; and 2) between Jews and Gentiles. "In Christ" all that has been done away. Mankind "in Christ" is reconciled to God, and "in Christ" Jews and Gentiles have been made into one Body, the Church. Some have observed that the greatest racial barrier of all time has been between the Jews and Gentiles. But "in Christ" that barrier no longer exists. As Paul says in Galatians 3:28, there is neither Jew nor Greek, there is neither bond nor free, there is neither male nor female. "In Christ" believers are one.

466

God Bless

While visiting Sophia, Bulgaria, I was asked to speak at a church of about 1500 members. The guy that picked me up to take me to church could barely fit in the driver seat. He was that big. He looked like one of our NFL linemen. On the way to church he told me his story. He had been part of the Red Mafia. They used him as an enforcer. If merchants did not pay their protection money, he would pull out his brass knuckles and beat them up. I don't think he needed brass knuckles. Then he became a Christian. He quit the Red Mafia at the risk of his life. Now he goes around to the same merchants he used to terrorize and gives them a little bit of his own money to try to do restitution for what he did to them. He tells them about the riches he has in Christ. I was sitting on the platform during the church service before I got up to speak. As I looked out at second row, I couldn't help but see this giant of a man standing there, singing with his hands raised to the sky, and tears rolling down his face. Here is a man who found peace with God through Christ. One of the side effects? He wanted peace with his fellow men. Peace in our **Position** leads to peace in our **Condition**.

Don't you wish they could get that message in the Middle East? In 1983, our Marines didn't know what they were walking into when they went to Beirut, Lebanon. They didn't understand the enmity between the Christians and the Jews, the Shiites and Sunnis, not to mention the Palestinians, the Syrians, and the Israelis—all in that tiny little area. Our Marines were operating according to the Geneva Convention with its rules of engagement. They soon discovered if they helped one of these factions, they made an enemy of at least one other faction if not more. Finally some guy stole a truck, filled it with 12,000 pounds of dynamite, drove it into the marine headquarters, and blew up 241 marines. America woke up. "We're not in Kansas anymore, Toto."

The New York Times sent one of their correspondents to Beirut in order to study the situation. He spent years living there and reporting. Then he moved down to Jerusalem where he reported for several more years. One of the results of his study was his Pulitzer Prize winning book *From Beirut to Jerusalem*. In this book, Friedman lets the Jews explain the racial/religious problems in their own words from a film made in Israel to prepare Israeli troops for serving in Lebanon. A soldier named Gadi, just out of officers' school, arrives at a base somewhere in south Lebanon and asks another soldier to fill him in on the political situation in Lebanon. The soldier, Georgie, a jaded veteran of the war between Israel and Lebanon, sits in a field kitchen peeling potatoes and explains what the war is all about:

> "Look," says Georgie. "I'll tell you the truth. Seriously, I didn't know what was happening until yesterday. But yesterday they brought in this expert on affairs. He gave us a lecture on the present situation. Now I understand everything. It goes like this: Christians hate the Druse, Shiites, Sunnis, and Palestinians. The Druse hate the Christians. No. Right. The Druse hate the Christians, Shiites, and the Syrians. The Shiites got screwed by them all for years, so they hate everyone. The Sunnis hate whomever their leader tells them to hate, and the Palestinians hate one another. Aside from that, they hate the others. Now, they all have a common denominator: they all hate us, the Israelis. They would like to blow us to pieces if they could, but they can't, due to the Israeli army. Not all of Israeli army— just the suckers, those who are in Lebanon.[224]

So what's missing here? There is no basis for peace. They either have not heard or have not believed the message of the gospel of peace. He is our peace. He has removed enmity between himself and the human race and between all races and ethnic groups.

When I was in Jordan leading a tour of the Holy Land a few months ago, I was amazed to see that tourism had fallen off in Jordan by 90% from just two years earlier. Why? ISIS. Tourists from around the world are afraid of ISIS. What they don't understand is that Jordan is the second safest country in the world as measured by crime levels

---

224 Thomas L. Friedman, *From Beruit to Jerusalem* (New York, NY: Farrar Straus Girroux, 2011), 185-86.

and terrorism. ISIS is made up of Sunnis. Sunnis are attacking the Shiite leadership in Syria. Sunnis don't attack Sunnis. Jordan is a Sunni nation. Secondly, ISIS does not attack nations with a strong military. For the Middle East, Jordan has a strong military. Who can unravel this? Probably only Jesus, the Prince of Peace.

B. Peace in our Condition

Our heavenly **Position** should have a radical impact on our earthly **Condition**.

1. **We are called to preserve peace.** The first three chapters of Ephesians are about out **Position**; the next three are about our **Condition**. So right after emphasizing the Principles of **Position** in Ephesians 1-3, Paul moves into Principles of **Condition**. He immediately appeals for unity based on the "bond of peace" (4:3). The beauty of this passage is not Paul's appeal for unity; it's his appeal to keep the unity. "Endeavor to keep the unity of the Spirit in the bond of peace." The Spirit achieved unity in our **Position**; but have to work hard to keep that unity in our **Condition**.

2. **We are called to preach peace.** We are to be prepared to give the "gospel of peace." Peace is good news (gospel) in a world laced with the strychnine of hatred. When we have found peace in our hearts, we want to tell the world about it. It's good news. Our **Position** should affect our **Condition**. War and strife is so hideous. Who can forget the civil rights picture of the German shepherd police dog taking a chunk out of a young teenager's stomach during the Civil Rights war in the 1960s? That picture alone moved President Kennedy to action. Who can forget the picture of the naked little Vietnamese girl crying as she ran down the middle of the street, her parents a casualty of war? Who can forget the picture of the Buddhist priest

self-immolating himself? And who can forget the acrid stench of the American Civil War where more men were killed during that internecine strife than all the other American casualties of war combined? We are a world at war. Those of us who know the Prince of Peace have a message to share.

II. THE BLESSING OF LOVE 23

The second blessing is dealing with love. Ephesians 6:23 says, "Peace to the brethren and love with faith." And so as with peace, we find in Ephesians love in our **Position** and love in our **Condition**.

A. Love in our Position

Paul says twice as much about love in this book as peace or grace. After we have our physiological needs met, our greatest need is to know we are loved. He chose us in love (1:3-4), is rich in mercy because of his great love for us (2:4) even before we believe, and wants us to comprehend his love (3:17-19).

The reason God is so merciful is because he has so much love for us. It's the same with our children. You tell them, "No, no, no," and they do it anyway. You want to whack their heads off, but because you have so much love for them, you're merciful and you give them another chance. The great climax on God's love in this book is Paul's prayer at the end of chapter 3: ". . . that you, being rooted and grounded in love, [18] may be able to comprehend with all the saints what *is* the width and length and depth and height—[19] to know the love of Christ which passes knowledge; that you may be filled with all the fullness of God." There it is. Rooted and grounded in love. But until we begin to comprehend the greatness of his love for us, we cannot be filled with his fullness. Peace is not a blessing you know about or learn about or comprehend; you just have it. But his love is so much greater than our greatest human love that we have to learn about it, study it, ponder it, absorb it, and believe it before we can

470

feel it. And then we begin to be filled with God himself, because God is love.

I have a thesis. I'm not sure anyone is free to love with an unselfish love until he is rooted and grounded in God's love. I'm not sure he is free to love until he knows how much he is loved. Before that, I think we are slaves to love. What do I mean? We all need love. Everyone wants to be loved, and we have such a need for love that we're willing to manipulate the people around us to get them to love us.

I was an early manipulator. My parents used to tell the story of how I used to take nickels and dimes from my mother's purse when I was four. Why? For candy? No. For love. I used to take a dime to nursery school and offer it to another kid if he would be my friend. Wow. We're slaves to love so much that we would do almost anything to extract love from other people.

Unfortunately, we are looking for love in all the wrong places. Sometimes it backfires on us. But once we are immersed by the love that passes understanding, the incredible love that will never stop or be measured, . . . once we are rooted and grounded in God's love, then we're no longer slaves to love or in the need for love. Instead of being slaves to love we are free to love. Why? Because when we know we are loved without measure and without condition by God, our most basic need for love has been met. And that frees us up to love others. We can love them out of the overflow of God's love for us and possibly become ministers instead of manipulators. Do you see how understanding our **Position** can affect our **Condition**? Let's look at that more closely.

B. Love in our Condition.

Only when people know they're loved are they capable of loving without ulterior motives. We are to bear with one another in love (4:2), speak the truth in love (4:15), edify others in love (4:16), walk in love as Christ also has loved us (5:2), and love our wives (5:25). This is all possible because we are "rooted and grounded in his love" (3:17).

This doesn't mean we can't be hurt by rejection. It doesn't mean our love will be reciprocated, and that's why Paul says, "Love with faith." You see, faith is the substance of things hoped for, the evidence of things not seen (Heb 11:1). And so if you reach out to minister in love, you may or may not see any reciprocation. But the key to do it all is your **Position**. Because of your **Position** "in Christ," you are deeply, deeply loved. He will never leave you nor reject you. He will always be with you, and because of that you're free in your **Condition**—free to be a minister of love to other people. So faith here means you may never see your love returned. In fact, the person you're trying to love may be so damaged on the inside they don't know how to receive love. Consequently, they aren't able to reciprocate. They are too preoccupied with their own need for love to reach out in any way other than manipulation. It may take the healing that only Christ can offer to enable them to love as a form of ministry instead of manipulation.

I first saw this in my older daughter when she was about five. She had just learned how to read a little bit and write a little bit. It was a scrawl that was barely legible. One morning I was taking a shower when I heard a knock on the door. I got out and dried off and saw these little pieces of paper she had slipped under the door. They were wadded up so I had to open them up to see what they said. There were three sheets. The one on top said, "My Sinnes" next to "Anderson, Christie." Then she listed her sins: "I hid from my mother. I argued with my brother. I played chase in the house. I didn't practice [sic] my peano [sic]. I realy [sic] sinned." I thought, man, we're raising a kid with an overly sensitive conscience here. Then I looked at the next piece of paper and things were looking up. It said, "I love my mommy. I love my daddy. I love Jimmmy [sic]. I love me." I thought, wow, that's pretty healthy. She loves her brother, who picks on her. She loves herself; and she loves others. "How can she do that?" I wondered.

That's when I looked at the third piece of paper (spelling is as she did it) and had the answer. "Jesus loves me, this sine o, for the Bible tells me so. Letos unes to him be lolling, they are week but he is srawling. Yes, Jesus loves me. Yes, Jesus loves me. Yes, Jesus loves me. The Bible tells me so." I thought, "How is it that kids get it and we don't?" See, she was rooted and grounded in the love of God. That was the bottom sheet of paper, her foundation, you might say. And because she believes the Bible told her that God loves her, she just took God at his word, believed it, and that freed her up to love her brother and herself and others and to be honest to God about who she was. She could confess her sins because she knew she wouldn't be rejected. That's the blessing of love in our **Position** and how it should flow over into our **Condition**.

The blessing of peace; the blessing of love; and, now, the blessing of grace.

III. THE BLESSING OF GRACE   24

In the beginning of this book, in what we called the "Hello" or the Salutation, Paul said, "Grace and peace to you." But he wrote it a little differently than he did at the end. It's just sort of a general statement of grace in the beginning of the book. Here at the end of the book he specifies it. It's almost as though he's saying *this grace*. It's as though he had a general concept of grace in mind when he started writing, but as it goes through the book, expounding, elucidating this wonderful, undeserved favor, his readers see grace in a whole new light, and he says, now **this** is the grace I'm talking about. This grace be with all those who love our Lord Jesus Christ sincerely. Of course, it's grace in our **Position**.

A. Grace in our Position

Again, way back in the introduction when Paul was listing our blessings in heavenly places, verse six reads, "To the praise of the glory of his grace, by which he made us accepted in the beloved." And in verse seven, "In him we have redemption through his blood, the forgiveness of sins, according to the riches of his grace." And, of course, that wonderful chapter 2 where he says in verse six, "And raised *us* up together, and made *us* sit together in the heavenly *places* in Christ Jesus, [7] that in the ages to come He might show the exceeding riches of His grace in His kindness toward us in Christ Jesus. [8] For by grace you have been saved through faith, and that not of yourselves; *it is* the gift of God, [9] not of works, lest anyone should boast." By grace we have salvation. By grace we have redemption. By grace we have been accepted in the Beloved. That's our **Position**; grace in our **Position**.

But Paul also says since we have received that wonderful blessing of grace in our **Position**, now we have the opportunity to reflect grace in our **Condition**.

B. Grace in our Condition

Because we have been receivers of grace, we can be givers of grace. Because we have internalized grace, we can externalize grace. Because we have seen the light of grace, we can reflect the light of grace. And so as Paul enters the three chapters on our **Condition** (Ephesians 4-6), he says in 4:7 that to each one of us grace was given according the measure of Christ's gift. He is saying one way to reflect the grace we've been given is to serve God with our spiritual gifts.

Then in 4:29 he says, "Let no corrupt communication proceed out of your mouth, but what is good for necessary edification that it may impart grace to the hearer." And we have already said the word translated "corrupt" does not mean dirty jokes or cussing. It's talking about that which tears down versus that which builds up. The most natural thing in the world is to tear down, especially if someone has hurt us. The most unnatural thing, the supernatural thing, is to build someone up when they have hurt us, but that requires grace. That requires being a dispenser of grace, a reflector of grace, a billboard of grace, an open display of God himself because this is not natural. It's not human. It's divine. It's supernatural and it's helpful. The world does enough to tear us down. We need something or someone to build us up.

John Maxwell, a Christian leadership guru, likes to train his staff upon meeting a new person to spot something, if they can, that they can say in sixty seconds to add value to the other person's life. Everyone struggles with self worth. We all need to feel like worthwhile, valuable people. And if we can find something (and everyone has it)

474

that is worthwhile and of value in that other person and highlight it in a sincere way without being gooey about it or false, then it builds them up and encourages them. It brings that virtue out of them and enhances it. Viktor Frankl once said, "If you treat people to a vision of themselves, you make them capable of what they're capable of becoming. But, you know, if we take people as they are, we make them worse. If we take them as they should be, we help them become what they can be."[225]

Former baseball star Reggie Jackson was asked what makes a great baseball manager. He said a great manager has a knack for making great baseball players think they're better than they really are, initially. He forces you to have a good opinion of yourself. He lets you know he believes in you. He makes sure you get more out of yourself, and once you learn how good you really are, you never settle for playing any less than your best.[226]

I know in my own struggles in my Christian life, when I'm hurt, I've learned the Matthew 5:44 principle—to say good things, to pray good things, and to do good things for the person that hurt me. But I can do all that without being in their presence. Ephesians 4:29 takes grace a step further. You see, when I have been hurt by someone, I also find that I want to avoid them. I don't want to talk to them. I don't like to be around them. But this says if you want to be a reflector of God's grace, if you want something supernatural to happen in your life, then you seek them out. Find something good to say; minister grace and build them up. That's a supernatural life, and that's one way our **Position** can alter for good our **Condition**.

Let's remember how we started Ephesians: **IT'S NOT ABOUT YOU!** It's all about him, "to the praise of the glory of his grace." "Glory" means an open display. **WE** are to display God's grace, reflect

---

225 Viktor Frankl, http://www.goodreads.com/quotes/882476-if-you-treat-people-to-a-vision-of-themselves-if, accessed September 12, 2016.

226 Reggie Jackson, http://www.brainyquote.com/quotes/authors/r/reggie_jackson.html, accessed September 12, 2016.

God's grace, and become billboards for his grace. For without grace in this world, there will be no peace and no love.

CONCLUSION

I'm just guessing you can figure out how I will finish out this study:

Our **Condition** can never change our **Position**; but,
Our **Position** can radically change our **Condition**.

And for the better. It always amazed me that when the Emancipation Proclamation was issued on January 1, 1883, it traveled slowly because there was no Internet. It went down through Virginia and into Georgia, the Carolinas, Alabama, and Mississippi up to Oklahoma. It didn't get to Texas until June 17, six months after it was signed. During those six months the slaves were free but they didn't know it, so they continued to live like slaves. But an even greater tragedy occurred after they knew they were free. Many of them chose to continue living as slaves. Thankfully, some of them did believe the proclamation and went off to seek a life as free men with all the rights and privileges pertaining there to.

What a tragedy for Christians to not know their **Position** in Christ, to not know they've been freed from the tyranny of their sin nature, and to not know that they've been freed to actually go out and enjoy the rights and privileges of one adopted into God's family. But even greater is the tragedy for those who do know about their new **Position** in Christ but to not take advantage of all the rights and privileges of those who belong to the royal family. Yes, we are privileged people. You are royalty. Now go out and live like it. God bless.

CPSIA information can be obtained
at www.ICGtesting.com
Printed in the USA
LVOW13s0524300717
543085LV00001B/6/P